Praise for THE DARK QUEENS

"A well-researched and well-told epic history. *The Dark Queens* brings these courageous, flawed, and ruthless rulers and their distant times back to life."
—MARGOT LEE SHETTERLY,
New York Times–bestselling author of *Hidden Figures*

"History owes more to Brunhild and Fredegund, two queens whose bitter rivalry left a trail of bodies in their wake, than the lies perpetuated by their enemies. So bravo to Shelley Puhak for a remarkable piece of detective work, by turns enlightening and shocking. Anyone who thought that medieval queens spent their time sewing and sighing is in for a surprise."
—AMANDA FOREMAN, *New York Times*–bestselling author of
Georgiana: Duchess of Devonshire and *The World Made by Women*

"An eye-opening medieval delight! Shelley Puhak rescues two fascinating, real-life women from the misogynistic dustbin of history, and sheds light on the origins of such strong fictional *grandes dames* as Lady Macbeth, Cersei, and every Wagnerian heroine who ever sported a Viking helmet. Impeccably researched. A delicious read."
—DENISE KIERNAN, *New York Times*-bestselling author of
The Girls of Atomic City and *We Gather Together*

"*The Dark Queens* brings the Merovingian empire to thrilling, bewildering, horrifying life. This is the story—told with a sharp eye, at heart-pounding pace—of two extraordinary women who held power in a brutal world that believed their sex couldn't rule. Many scholars 'still don't know what to do' with Brunhild and Fredegund. Shelley Puhak does."
—HELEN CASTOR, author of *She-Wolves* and *Joan of Arc*

"Bright, smart, and playful, *The Dark Queens* is a marvelous trip into the murky early Middle Ages. Shelley Puhak presents a believable and vividly drawn portrait of the Frankish world, and in doing so restores two half-forgotten and much-mythologized queens, Brunhild and Fredegund, to their proper place in medieval history."
—DAN JONES, *New York Times*-bestselling author of
The Templars and *Powers and Thrones*

"On the one hand, a story of scheming and savagery to make *Game of Thrones* look tame—on the other, a genuinely important exploration of the relationship between two powerful women, written with zest and verve. Most of us know far too little about the 'Dark Ages,' so this narrative carries the all-important sense of discovery, that feeling of 'I can't *believe* I hadn't heard any of this before!'"

—SARAH GRISTWOOD, internationally bestselling author of
Arbella and *The Tudors in Love*

"In her stirring and passionate account of the sixth-century queens Brunhild and Fredegund, Shelley Puhak breaks down the doors of history to reveal a Dark Ages we've been told to forget: when queens ruled Europe, with wisdom, piety—and poisoned daggers. . . . A brilliant reconstruction of our long-suppressed past, with all its murder and intrigue, loyalty and courage, *The Dark Queens* is unforgettable."

—NANCY MARIE BROWN, author of *The Real Valkyrie*

"These dark queens were undaunted survivors who still whisper powerful advice. Shelley Puhak has recovered forgotten biographies we must no longer neglect."

—KARA COONEY, author of *When Women Ruled the World*

"*The Dark Queens* leads the reader on a blood-soaked journey through sixth-century Europe, casting new light on the so-called Dark Ages. Puhak's compelling narration offers a surprising and thoroughly riveting take on the under-explored lives of fascinating female figures of the past."

—EMILY MIDORIKAWA, author of *Out of the Shadows*

"This gripping saga features everything from gory murders to scandalous nuns. Brunhild and Fredegund are often flattened into early medieval Europe's great villains, but in Shelley Puhak's brilliant telling, they come to rich and nuanced life."

—EMMA SOUTHON, author of *Agrippina*

THE DARK
QUEENS

THE DARK QUEENS

THE BLOODY RIVALRY THAT FORGED
THE MEDIEVAL WORLD

SHELLEY PUHAK

BLOOMSBURY PUBLISHING
NEW YORK · LONDON · OXFORD · NEW DELHI · SYDNEY

BLOOMSBURY PUBLISHING
Bloomsbury Publishing Inc.
1385 Broadway, New York, NY 10018, USA

BLOOMSBURY, BLOOMSBURY PUBLISHING, and the Diana logo are
trademarks of Bloomsbury Publishing Plc

First published in the United States 2022

Copyright © Shelley Puhak, 2022
Maps created by Ortelius Design

Bloomsbury Publishing Plc does not have any control over, or responsibility for, any
third-party websites referred to or in this book. All internet addresses given in this
book were correct at the time of going to press. The author and publisher regret any
inconvenience caused if addresses have changed or sites have ceased to exist, but can
accept no responsibility for any such changes.

ISBN: HB: 978-1-63557-491-3; EBOOK: 978-1-63557-492-0

LIBRARY OF CONGRESS CATALOGING-IN-PUBLICATION DATA IS AVAILABLE

2 4 6 8 10 9 7 5 3 1

Typeset by Westchester Publishing Services
Printed and bound in the U.S.A.

To find out more about our authors and books visit www.bloomsbury.com and
sign up for our newsletters.

Bloomsbury books may be purchased for business or promotional use. For information
on bulk purchases please contact Macmillan Corporate and Premium Sales Department
at specialmarkets@macmillan.com.

For Nate

TABLE OF CONTENTS

Author's Note
SHADOW QUEENS

WEEKS BEFORE HALLOWEEN of 2016, I found myself pacing the aisles of a costume store, frantic. My nine-year-old was determined to be a killer robot bunny, and we had spent evenings hot-gluing wires and felt to a T-shirt, scouring Etsy for the correct demonic bunny ears. I had volunteered to help with the classroom party, though, and I still needed something to wear, a quick and easy costume that wouldn't look too last-minute next to those of the two moms in charge.

I had a witch hat at home, but I was looking for something else, something a little less generic, a little more . . . commanding. I scanned the displays of Cleopatra headdresses, pointed princess hats, and rainbow-tinted wigs, until my gaze settled on the row of horned Viking helmets with long blond braids glued on.

I didn't know then that I had just started writing this book.

. . .

No raider from the north ever wore one. The horned Viking helmet has its basis not in fact but in the fantasies of a costume designer. Carl Emil Doepler, tasked with outfitting the cast of Richard Wagner's *Der Ring des Nibelungen* for the opera cycle's 1876 production, combined Greek myth and military sensibilities. Doepler's sketches featured flowing tunics and capes, long beards and armored bodices, and lots of helmets—winged ones for the female Valkyries, and horned ones for the male warriors. It wasn't long before the opera's female lead, Brünnhilde, regularly wore a helmet, winged or horned.

Wagner's *Ring* is a four-night epic, not a work for the casual fan, but even so, Brünnhilde quickly became opera's most recognizable figure: a

Doepler's costume design for the character Brünnhilde

busty woman in braids and a horned helmet, hefting a shield and spear. And then, predictably, she became one of our culture's most lampooned figures.

The cycle features a cursed ring, a power-hungry god, and incestuous siblings, with giants, dwarves, and a dragon thrown in for good measure. But it also offers an all-too-realistic allegory for patriarchy, for the fate of females who wield political power. Brünnhilde is a Valkyrie, tasked with carrying dead warriors off to the heroes' paradise of Valhalla. When she defies her father, Wotan, the king of the gods, she is punished. He strips her of her immortality and casts her in the role of a sleeping beauty, consigned to a rock surrounded by magic fire. She is able to be awakened only by a man's attentions. Brünnhilde has a chance to be loved but loses that, too. With her lover dead, she mounts her horse and rides straight into his funeral pyre, burning the whole place down.

The poignant aria that Brünnhilde belts out just before immolating herself marks the end of the fifteen-hour opera cycle, giving rise to the expression "It ain't over till the fat lady sings." This character has become yet another way to casually ridicule women's bodies, and their stories.

But while millions around the world are familiar with the image of operatic Brünnhilde, few today recall that she shares a name with an actual Queen Brunhild, who ruled some 1,400 years ago. The Valkyrie's fictional story is an amalgam of the real lives of Brunhild and her sister-in-law and rival, Queen Fredegund, grafted onto Norse legends.

I didn't know these queens' names when I stood in that costume store aisle. But at some level, I *knew* these queens. You know them, too, even if your history books never got around to mentioning them. I've called them the Dark Queens not only because the period of their rule falls neatly into the so-called Dark Ages, but also because they have survived in the shadows, for more than a millennium.

In the ancient world, all roads led to Rome, and along the way, monuments, statues, tombstones commanded: STOP, TRAVELER, AND READ! The stones were etched with biographies and eulogies, erected so that the dead might be remembered. To be forgotten was a formal punishment for treason or tyranny—the Senate ordered statues destroyed, names struck from the public record. The face of one emperor was even scratched out from his childhood family portraits. This practice, later named *damnatio memoriae*, or "condemnation of memory," sought to erase a person from the historical record completely.

This appears to be exactly what happened to Queens Brunhild and Fredegund a few centuries later. During their lifetimes, they grabbed power and hung on to it; they convinced warriors, landowners, and farmers to support them, and enemies to back down. But like so many women before them, the inconvenient fact of their success was blotted out, and their biographies right along with it.

Among the chroniclers and historians who did make note of them, Brunhild and Fredegund were dismissed as minor queens of a minor era. And yet the empire these two queens shared encompassed modern-day France, Belgium, the Netherlands, Luxembourg, western and southern Germany, and swaths of Switzerland. And they ruled during a critical period in Western history. Janus-like, they looked back toward the rule of both the Romans and tribal barbarian warlords, while also looking forward to a new era of feudal nation-states.

The lack of attention given to these queens is stranger still if one considers, for example, the fevered interest generated by Boudica, the Icenian queen whose poorly documented revolt against Rome lasted a single year. Even had they managed to accomplish nothing else, Fredegund and Brunhild should be considered remarkable for the duration of their reigns. Both ruled longer than almost every king and Roman emperor who had preceded them. Fredegund was queen for twenty-nine years, and regent for twelve of those years, and Brunhild was queen for forty-six years, regent for seventeen of them. And these queens did much more than simply hang on to their thrones. They collaborated with foreign rulers, engaged in public works programs, and expanded their kingdoms' territories.

They did all this while shouldering the extra burdens of queenship. Both were outsiders, marrying into a dynasty that barred women from inheriting the throne. Unable to claim power in their own names, they could only rule on behalf of a male relative. These male relatives were poisoned, stabbed, and disappeared at alarmingly high rates. A queen had to dodge assassins, and employ some of her own, while also combatting the open misogyny of her own advisers and nobles—the early medieval equivalent of doing it all backwards, and in heels.

Their time on the throne is recognized—when it is recognized at all—as a rare period of dual-female rule that neither has an equivalent in the early medieval world, nor, I would argue, any true equivalent today. We have female political leaders, of course, but they are "exceptional women," outliers wielding power in a world of men, figures like Queen Victoria or Margaret Thatcher. But female political rivals? I can point to how, very briefly, the careers of UK prime minister Theresa May and German chancellor Angela Merkel intersected. Or how the United States had four serious female candidates vying for the 2020 Democratic presidential nomination. We had a glimpse of women debating one another on a national stage, at least until, one by one, they were forced to drop out of the race. While I was writing this book, one of those women, Kamala Harris, was elected the first female vice president, but during the campaign her role was that of the lone woman amid a field of men. The United States has never had an all-woman ticket, or a woman on each party's ticket, debating one another. We still lack a sense of what a prolonged era of powerful women in conversation looks like.

This book will resurrect these two queens and their relationship to sketch two scratched-out faces back into the record. In order to do so, I must also sketch a scratched-out era. The dynasty the queens belonged to, that of the Merovingians, has long been synonymous with conspiracies—either that of a hidden Messianic bloodline popularized by *The Da Vinci Code*, or that of an exiled computer program in *The Matrix* movies. This dynasty's name is associated with secrecy because very little is, or was, known about the Merovingians. They left few traces in part because they adapted so well to the existing landscape, like hermit crabs, making their homes in the shells cast aside by Rome. Much in the same way, there are few traces of the queens: the abandoned shells of their biographies have been inhabited by others. Their lived experiences have been set dressing not just for opera leads, but also for fairy-tale villains and folk-tale heroines, comic strip and anime characters, and even, most recently, for Cersei in *Game of Thrones*.

There are, admittedly, many gaps and curious silences in the stories of their lives and legacies. These lacunae do not mean the sources never existed. Some were purposefully suppressed and some just did not survive. The queens ruled during the shift from one writing medium to another. The papyrus the Merovingians primarily used deteriorated easily in the cold and humidity of Europe; the animal-skin parchment preferred by the dynasty that supplanted them did not. It is amazing that we have as much from the period as we do: letters, wills, and testaments; contracts, charters, and bills of sale; poems, witticisms, and hymns; and, of course, historical chronicles.

The loss of many primary sources cannot be the only reason for the silences around the lives of these queens, though. Many historians and scholars still don't know what to do with them. There are so few approved roles for women in power—scheming seductress, perhaps, or overbearing mother, whose meddling in the affairs of her lovers or her children brings ruin and disaster. But who were they really? Daughters and mothers, wives and lovers, warriors and diplomats, faithful and fearsome, superstitious yet savvy.

The queens live on in the things they left behind: the scraps of their letters and laws, the cities and buildings they inhabited, the landscapes they traversed and the rivers they sailed. We can know how they dressed and what objects they valued based on recent archaeological finds, but we know a great deal more about who they irritated and enraged and which mores they broke based on the accounts of the men who knew them. Their memory has been kept alive through the imaginations of the men who were their contemporaries. Whenever possible, I have incorporated these primary sources, the accounts of men like the bishop Gregory of Tours, the poet Venantius Fortunatus, the pope Gregory the Great, and assorted emperors and kings. At the same time, I have been mindful that these men all had their own ambitions, biases, and axes to grind. I have been mindful that the mystery of who Brunhild and Fredegund really were—their personalities, their motivations—is compounded by the uses others made of them.

"Who am I if not your will?" Brünnhilde asks her divine father in Wagner's opera. Chroniclers and scholars—and not gods—are the makers of what we know as history, but the question still applies. Who are these queens if not our will, what we will women to be? Strange parodies of themselves, singing a song written by and for men, their ambitions hidden underneath a fantastically horned hat. This book seeks to uncover the song they might have sung for themselves—and to give that song breath.

THE DARK
QUEENS

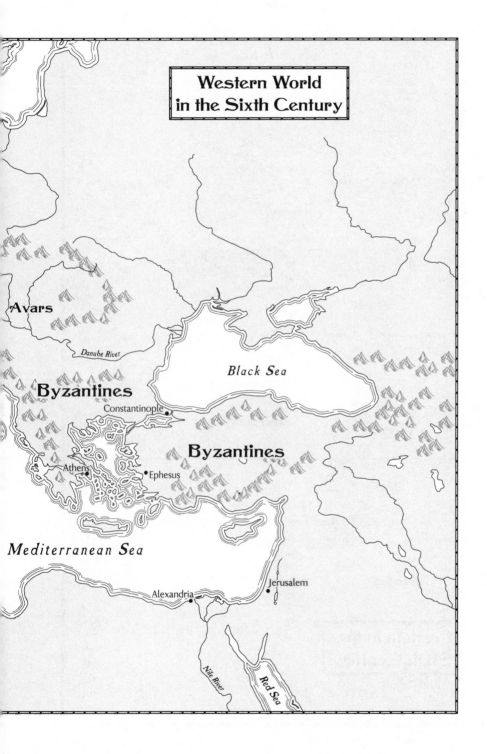

Western World in the Sixth Century

Avars

Danube River

Black Sea

Byzantines

Constantinople

Byzantines

Athens

Ephesus

Mediterranean Sea

Jerusalem

Alexandria

Nile River

Red Sea

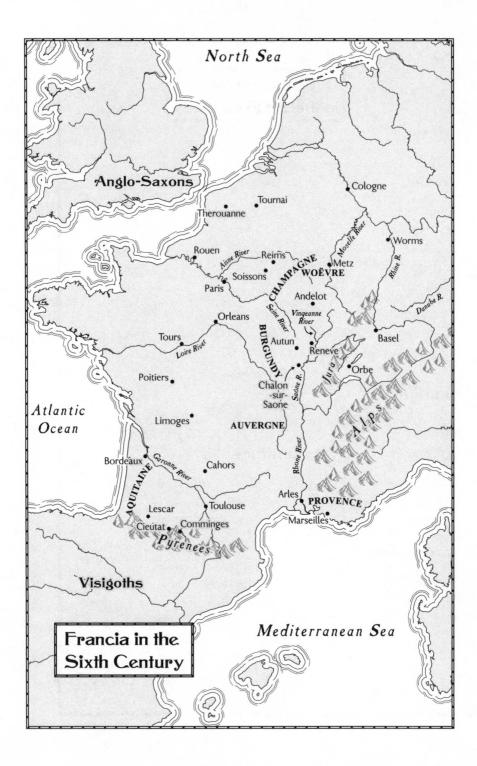

North Sea

Anglo-Saxons

Cologne

Tournai

Therouanne

Worms

Rouen   Reims
        Aisne River   Metz
              Soissons   WOËVRE
    Paris   CHAMPAGNE

                              Andelot
                    Seine River
Orleans   Vingeanne
                      River
Tours   Basel
        Loire River   Autun
              BURGUNDY   Reneve
Poitiers   Orbe

                  Chalon
Atlantic   -sur-
Ocean   Saone

        Limoges   AUVERGNE

Bordeaux   Cahors
        Garonne River   Arles
AQUITAINE   Toulouse   PROVENCE
    Lescar
  Cieutat Comminges   Marseilles
        Pyrenees

Visigoths

Mediterranean Sea

Francia in the
Sixth Century

DRAMATIS PERSONAE

In FRANCIA, the Merovingians

King Clovis
The "Famous Warrior" who unites the Frankish tribes under one crown and—after his conversion to Christianity—one religion, around the turn of the sixth century.

King Clothar
The son of Clovis who outlives his brothers to reunite Francia. His wives and children are:

> **Ingund,** and her sons **Charibert, Guntram,** and **Sigibert**
>
> **Aregund,** Ingund's sister, and mother of **Chilperic**
>
> **Radegund,** a captured Thuringian princess
>
> and the unnamed mother of **Gundovald,** his bastard

Upon his death in 561, King Clothar's lands are divided into four kingdoms: Aquitaine, Burgundy, Austrasia, and Neustria.

1) Kingdom of AQUITAINE

Charibert, the "Bright Warrior" and eldest son, who rules from Paris
Theudechild, his third wife, daughter of a shepherd
his daughters from previous marriages, **Bertha**, **Bertheflede**, and **Clotilde**

Germanus, bishop of Paris
Ragnemod, also called Rucco, his successor

2) Kingdom of BURGUNDY

Guntram, the "Battle Raven" and second son, ruling from Chalon-sur-Saône

Mummolus, his prized general, a master of strategy
Syagrius, bishop of Autun

3) Kingdom of AUSTRASIA

Sigibert, the "Magnificent Victory" and third son, ruling from Metz
Brunhild, "Battle Armor," a Visigothic princess from Spain, second
  daughter of *King Athanagild* and *Queen Goiswintha*

  their daughters **Ingund** and **Clodosinda**
  and son **Childebert** and his wife, **Faileuba**
    and their grandchildren, **Theudebert**, **Theuderic**, and **Theudelia**
    and Theuderic's four sons, including **Sigibert II**

Venantius Fortunatus, a Roman poet who gets his start in Sigibert's court
Count Gogo, King Sigibert's young right-hand man
Wolf, loyal Duke of Champagne
Dynamius, renowned poet and governor of Provence
Guntram Boso, Duke of the Auvergne, extraordinary warrior and brash
   adventurer
Ursio, deeply conservative Duke of the Woëvre
Berthefred, his loyal sidekick
Warnachar, general and palace official
Egidius, bishop of Reims
Gregory, bishop of Tours and chronicler of the era
Desiderius, bishop of Vienne

4) Kingdom of NEUSTRIA

Chilperic, the "Valiant Defender"* and youngest of the brother kings,
   ruling from Soissons

Audovera, his first wife
   their three sons **Theudebert, Merovech**, and **Clovis**
   and daughter **Basina**

Galswintha, his second wife, a Visigothic princess from Spain and
   Brunhild's older sister

Fredegund, "Peace through War," his third wife and Audovera's former
   servant
   their daughter **Rigunth**
   and their sons **Clodebert, Samson, Dagobert, Theuderic**, and
   Clothar II

Eberulf, royal chamberlain
Landeric, general and the king's trusted adviser
Rauching, sadistic and fabulously rich Duke of Soissons
Desiderius, Duke of Aquitaine
Leudast, former slave, now Count of Tours

Praetextatus, bishop of Rouen
Bertram, bishop of Bordeaux

In SPAIN, the Visigoths

King Athanagild, an aristocrat who rose in rebellion to grab the throne

Goiswintha, his politically savvy wife
and their daughters **Galswintha** and **Brunhild**

King Leovigild, Athanagild's elected successor, a widower
and his sons **Hermenegild** and **Reccared**

In BYZANTIUM, the imperial family

Emperor Justinian, known for his campaign to reclaim lost imperial
lands in the west

Emperor Justin II, Justinian's nephew and successor
Sophia, his wife and imperial regent

Tiberius, a general who becomes Sophia's co-regent

Emperor Maurice, famed general and Tiberius's successor
Constantina, his wife

In ROME, the Church

Pope Gregory, "the Great," Church reformer

Augustine, Italian Benedictine monk and very first Archbishop of
Canterbury
Columbanus, Irish missionary monk

Prologue

*W*estern Europe, Sixth Century
    Rome has fallen.

On the empire's former frontier, the old order and a new barbarian world clash. One family emerges to conquer the divide. From the Atlantic coast to the Alps, from the North Sea to the Mediterranean, they rule.

Until a terrible civil war fractures the dynasty. This war will rage for far longer than the English Wars of the Roses, engulfing more territory and killing more monarchs. This war will mark the end of antiquity and the beginning of the medieval era.

It begins with three weddings in quick succession—and one murder.

CHAPTER I

A Wedding in Metz

W hen Princess Brunhild was led into the great hall, the assembled men jockeyed for a glimpse of her, craning their necks or standing on tiptoe.

It was the spring of 567. The map of the known world, when turned on its side, looked like a pair of lungs. Just two lobes of land, and the white space between them was the Mediterranean Sea. This princess came from the very tip of the left lung, in Spain, and she had just traveled more than one thousand miles, across the snow-capped Pyrenees, through the sunny vineyards of Narbonne, and then up into the land of the Franks. Brunhild had yet to see for herself whether the stories she had heard were true: that in the forests of these Franks, the oaks were so thick that forty men could not drag a fallen one away. Or that among these trees roamed large packs of wolves, some of whom could shapeshift into men. And child-eating dragons, too—although the bishops claimed to have vanquished most of them. The clerics had not managed, though, to vanquish all of the pagans. Villagers still built altars in forest glens and hung on to their wooden idols. Some still offered sacrifice to Woden, or even Thor.

But why, as Brunhild made her way through the crowded hall, was a loud but quavering voice invoking Roman deities at her wedding—Cupid and Venus, Helios and Mars? None of those assembled Franks, nor their parents or grandparents, would have ever worshipped these gods.

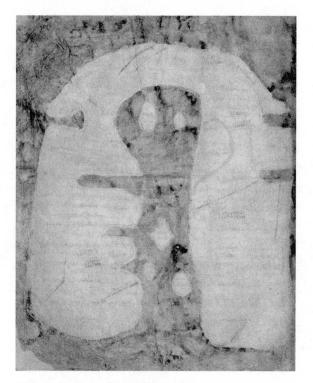

Merovingian map of the world

The nervous young man reciting these names was attempting a Roman panegyric, or formal praise poem. His name was Venantius Fortunatus, and this was his first paid commission at a royal court. Fortunatus had recently arrived from Italy, hoping to win acclaim and riches in the land of the Franks. He would have been mindful that performing well at this wedding, King Sigibert's wedding, could launch his career. In Francia, anything or, more precisely, *anyone* associated with classical Rome was all the rage—whether a zither player, a cook, or a Latin poet. Of course, another refrain would have been cycling in the back of Fortunatus's mind, too: Avoid the king's wrath. Do not slip up.

Princess Brunhild had arrived just days before, trailed by wagons piled high "with great treasures": gold and silver coins and ingots; bejeweled goblets, bowls, and scepters; furs and silks—treasures the palace slaves would have still been unloading. Now she was led into what the Franks called their "Golden Court" to meet her new subjects. It's likely that it was the king's right-hand man, the young Count Gogo, who offered to escort her. He had accompanied her all the way from Spain, and she would have been grateful for a familiar face. Taking Gogo's arm, allowing herself to be guided past those dozens of pairs of curious, eager eyes, did she wonder whether they saw her as just another lustrous treasure, too? A gleaming chalice, a prize mare?

Later, the men in the great hall would have many reasons to fear her. But if they feared anything that day, it was only that she might snicker at them, uncomfortable in their bright finery with their newly shaven cheeks scratched pink. The hall was bedecked with banners and standards; there were thick rugs on the floors and embroidered tapestries on the walls. But if the princess had peeked behind one of these tapestries, she would have noticed the fresh plaster. The ambitiously named Golden Court was still being patched together, just like the city itself. King Sigibert's palace was really just a repurposed basilica, and his brand-new capital of Metz was a former holiday town that had once served soldiers on Rome's frontier. Despite its new crowds and markets and garrisoned armies, the city was still a far cry from the glittering sophistication of Brunhild's hometown of Toledo.

Metz was, however, a logical spot for a capital, roughly in the middle of Sigibert's territories, at the confluence of two rivers and at the crossing of two old military roads. His kingdom, called Austrasia, ran the whole length of the Rhine River. At its northernmost tip were the coastal lowlands of the North Sea, and its southernmost point was Basel in the foothills of the Jura Mountains. Along its eastern border were cities like Cologne and Worms, and along its western border were the rolling hills and vineyards of the Champagne region. Sigibert also owned lands in the Auvergne and ruled over the Mediterranean ports of Nice and Fréjus, which welcomed ships, and people, from all over the known world. In his cities one could find Jews, Christian Goths, and pagan Alemanni; Greek and Egyptian doctors; even Syrian merchants.

Yet the size of Sigibert's kingdom, while respectable enough, was not what had secured this marriage. Rather, it was the magnitude of his ambitions. He had asked for the day's festivities to be billed as "Caesar's marriage." His assembled men, mostly Frankish warrior-lords, had dressed accordingly. Even though, here and there, a tribal tattoo snaked up a bare arm or leg, they were attired in long linen tunics and bright capes fastened at one shoulder with filigreed brooches. These nobles, and their king, were eager to cloak themselves not just in Roman robes, but in the fallen empire's status and legitimacy.

It was hard not to be obsessed with Rome when one lived inside its former cities' walls and among its castoffs. The former basilica was now the palace; the old gymnasium had been transformed into a church. Alongside the existing Roman buildings—some crumbling, some so deftly replastered they appeared as they did in their prime—popped up more Germanic ones with thatched roofs and timber halls. What had been the Forum was still a public square full of shops, but now it was surrounded by towering homes that kept adding stories, with no other way to expand but up.

Sigibert had only to glance around to know what was possible—if he could find the money for repairs and stop the fighting long enough to implement them. The straight Roman roads, though still well-traveled, were marred by missing paving stones and cracked concrete. The drainage ditches would clog up, and he could hardly lead a royal procession without someone's cart getting stuck in the mud. A handful of the aqueducts in other cities did still serve, piping in fresh, filtered water for palace baths or public fountains, and a few others dribbled out water for the masses. Metz's own aqueduct, a fourteen-mile feat of engineering, had once enabled public baths, latrines, and a sewage system. But repairs had stopped a century or so ago, and now the stone arcaded bridge vaulted over the countryside, useless. The city's vast bath complex, topped by dazzling golden cupolas that dominated the skyline, sat unused. King Sigibert had decided that if he was going to fashion a functioning country out of these bedraggled works, what he needed was a bride.

That year, Sigibert was coming off a series of military defeats. Yet this marriage could revive his political fortunes and replenish his coffers. He had negotiated for months for Brunhild's hand, and his subjects had to have felt hopeful, triumphant even, now that he had secured such a prestigious mate.

Beautiful (*"pulchra"*), they called her, and lovely to look at (*"venusta aspectu"*) with a good figure (*"elegans corpore"*). There is no way for us to judge for ourselves. She appears unnaturally tall and pale in illuminated manuscripts from later in the medieval period; voluptuous and glowing in Renaissance portraits; pensive and windswept in Romantic-era prints. But after her death—the statues pulled down, the mosaics obliterated, the manuscripts burned—no contemporary images of her would survive. Thanks to the efforts of kings, bishops, scribes, and soldiers, we can never be sure what she looked like as a young bride, nor even as a mature queen. Still, those present that day claimed she was beautiful, and while her enemies would later mock her mercilessly, they never once criticized her looks. There are no mentions of her being unusually short or tall, so one can assume she stood close to the average height for a woman of the period, five feet, four inches tall. And on her wedding day, Brunhild was in the full flush of youth, around eighteen years old, arrayed in the finest embroidered silks her world could muster, with her long hair loose about her shoulders and wreathed in flowers.

As the poet Fortunatus cleared his throat, he would have been relieved that the hyperbole he had composed before he had set eyes on the princess would not fall comically short. He exclaimed that she was a "glorious maiden" with a "milk-white" complexion and lips the color of roses, a jewel beyond compare. Even if she were not, as Fortunatus claimed, truly a "second Venus," King Sigibert seemed quite pleased with the match, welcoming his bride "with every appearance of joy and happiness." And although she would have been well-trained not to display any hint of disappointment, Brunhild would have been relieved, too.

Drawing of a thirteenth-century sculpture of King Sigibert

The only contemporary image of her groom that survives is that of his profile on a coin. Sculptures made many centuries later portray him as a tall and lean young man with long blond hair falling in waves to his chin. His features are well proportioned and his expression is kindly; even better, his shoulders are broad and his cheekbones are high. He appears to be a veritable medieval heartthrob.

While these are probably not close likenesses, they have some basis in fact. King Sigibert wore his hair long and it is likely that he was a blond or redhead, like many in his family. Sigibert's name meant "Magnificent Victory" and he was a renowned warrior, so he would have been fit and muscular and, at thirty-two, at the height of his physical powers. They must have made a striking couple as they stood side by side, the sumptuously attired and immaculately groomed princess, the young and strapping king.

Fortunatus continued his poem, boldly declaring: "Sigibert, in love, is consumed by passion for Brunhild." Yet everyone in the hall knew this marriage was not a love match but a carefully negotiated alliance.

What remained of Roman might was now concentrated in the East in Constantinople. Perhaps this "Caesar's marriage" would be the union that could supplant it.

. . .

Across the border, in the neighboring kingdom of Neustria, another palace overlooked the Aisne River—gentle, green, and murky. Here, the news of Sigibert and Brunhild's marriage was met with great interest and alarm. Especially by Sigibert's youngest brother, King Chilperic.

If the sculptures are to be believed, Chilperic looked very similar to Sigibert, although he had curlier hair and a fuller beard. But if they shared certain features, they did not share any brotherly affection. Sigibert and Chilperic *did* share three hundred miles of border, a border that Chilperic was constantly testing. Chilperic had spent the past few years trying to invade his older brother's kingdom and, in fact, had just launched a new attempt. And now he was furious to be outmaneuvered.

He was not surprised that Sigibert had married. Chilperic himself had started trying to beget heirs when he was still in his teens—why had his brother waited so long? But now, by choosing a foreign princess for his bride, Sigibert was openly declaring his dynastic ambitions, and Chilperic was furious.

If the king was concerned, his court was concerned. And no one more so than the slave girl. How could she not be? She tracked the king's reaction to every event, no matter how small. It seems that she was, at this point, the king's concubine, although she could have even been his official wife—the records tell us only that the king "had" her. And that he was besotted.

Chilperic was, admittedly, a king known for impulsive behavior, and when following his passions, he often took matters to the extreme. He dabbled in poetry, for example, crafting some decidedly mediocre verse, but his literary ambitions would soon have him trying to overhaul the alphabet. When he would later take up theology, he would start by writing a few hymns, before attempting to rewrite the core beliefs of Christianity. And so when he fell for the slave girl, he summarily had his queen—a perfectly suitable woman who had already given him three healthy heirs—hustled off to a convent.

As a slave, the girl's worth was less than that of a hunting dog, less than a cow. And it was a life full of hazards—open fires, undercooked and spoiled food, lice and parasites, and the groping hands of fellow slaves and overlords alike. But she had already survived much worse.

She had been born at the end of the coldest decade in the past two millennia. A volcanic eruption in Iceland had plunged the world into darkness, disrupting harvests. And while the Western world was gripped by famine, another horseman of the apocalypse had galloped in: *Yersinia pestis*, the bubonic plague, borne into Europe by rats carrying infected fleas. To this enslaved girl and the people in her childhood world, the conditions in the middle of the sixth century must have seemed like the end of days.

To be born in such times could be considered a great misfortune. But it could also be a great opportunity. The air, cold as it was, crackled with possibility for the survivors. Fortunes could be made in a month. A great family could fall, dropping dead in a matter of days. An ambitious family could move into that abandoned villa, elbowing their way into the aristocracy. Even the villa's surviving slaves had cause for hope. They could seize the opportunity to run away and melt into the crowds of refugees. They could comfort a grieving widow or widower on a neighboring estate and marry their way up. Being enslaved was not an enviable state of affairs, but it could be a temporary one.

But even in a time of such unusual social mobility, the transformation that this girl had pulled off was impressive—from kitchen slave to one of the queen's serving maids, and now the king's companion. Such a rise took iron will, careful planning, and the honing of small talents—the ability to slip in and out of a room unnoticed, to intuit which cook or lackey was likely to let slip a choice bit of information. And perhaps, as some of her contemporaries mused, such a rise required dabbling in the dark arts, too.

Temperatures had since stabilized and the initial waves of the plague receded. But it remained an age that favored the bold. She would later prove herself its equal, capable of quick and decisive action. For now, though, as the king fumed over his brother's foreign bride, the slave girl, Fredegund, was content to watch and wait.

CHAPTER 2

Meeting the Franks

Brunhild's marriage had introduced her to the world of the Franks, who had made their home within the wreckage of the Roman empire and longed for its bygone splendor. Yet for the Romans themselves, the Franks were initially the stuff of nightmares. When the Romans first encountered these barbarians in the third century, they were just one of the many Germanic tribes raiding their frontiers. But these Franks soon earned a reputation as "monsters." They were pale and enormous, and wore their hair long, like an animal's tail: "from the top of their red skulls descends their hair, knotted on the front and shaved in the nape." Another curiosity was their facial hair; instead of beards, they wore mustaches (hitherto unknown in Rome), which were described as "locks of [nose] hair arranged with the comb." These curiously coiffed barbarians would rush the disciplined formations of the Roman infantry, dressed in the skimpiest of tunics. The Romans had the advantage of superior numbers and iron chain mail, but they still found themselves unnerved by the Franks' throwing axes with their thick iron blades and short wooden handles. The Franks would use them to disable their opponents before the battle even began; they were "accustomed always to throw these axes at one signal in the first charge and thus shatter the shields of the enemy and kill the men." The Romans found the Franks so fearsome that rather than

Merovingian warrior with the distinctive Frankish mustache and throwing ax

fight them, they convinced them to become soldiers in the service of the empire. The Franks turned out to be, for the most part, amenable.

The Franks' rulers were the Merovingians, the dynasty that would eventually produce Sigibert. According to one legend, the Merovingian line began when a five-horned sea creature called the Quinotaur attacked a human woman. From their union was born Merovech, for whom the Merovingians were named. Others insisted that the tribe sprang from the remnants of once-great Troy, whose survivors had crossed the sea and then wandered west. Myths and legends aside, what we do know is that the Franks certainly didn't traverse the sea from Troy, in Anatolia; archaeological evidence shows the only body of water the Franks crossed was a river, the Rhine. But there really was a Merovech who founded the dynasty. He was a barbarian warrior who gained fame by helping Rome repel Attila the Hun.

Over time, the Franks would fix their sights on setting themselves up as heirs to classical Rome, rather than what they really were—an upstart

Germanic tribe in the right place at the right time. Despite their apparent ferocity, these "monsters" discovered they wanted to drink spring water piped in via aqueducts, to eat grain imported from North Africa, to bathe in heated pools. They began to do business and intermarry with the Romans, to adopt some of their customs, and to rise through the ranks of their army. In two generations, the Franks would go from fighting alongside Roman troops in Gaul to commanding them. But as soon as they managed this feat, there was no more Rome, at least in the west, to command. In the fifth century, the empire's territories on the Italian peninsula collapsed into ruin and barbarian overthrow, cementing the shift of Roman power toward the east to Constantinople. From their majestic capital, the Byzantine emperors would preside over the territory of modern-day Greece, northern Egypt, Turkey, Israel, Lebanon, and Syria. Back in the former province of Gaul, though, the Franks were on their own.

Undeterred, Sigibert's grandfather, King Clovis, secured the title of Consul from the Byzantines and then began dressing in purple, wearing a diadem, and insisting he be addressed as *Augustus,* as any Roman emperor would. He imitated the Romans' penchant not just for ostentation, but also for centralization. He cobbled together his own empire, one that stretched from the North Sea to the Pyrenees, uniting many Frankish tribes under one crown and one legal code, and with one capital city, Paris. Clovis was so revered for these accomplishments that twelve hundred years after his death, French monarchs would still bear the Latinized version of his name—*Louis.*

Yet Clovis made one critical error that ensured his new empire would not know peace. Upon his death, rather than designating a single heir as the Romans had often done, Clovis divided his lands among his four sons. Frankish kings were to be conquerors above all else. But now the foreign lands left to conquer were shrinking; a king could prove his masculinity and expand his kingdom only at his brothers' expense. Sigibert's father survived his brothers, slaughtered his nephews, and reunited the Frankish lands under one crown again.

But before his death in 561, Sigibert's father made the same mistake Clovis had: He divided this empire between his own four sons, dooming them to the same lifelong ruthless competition he himself endured. Four kingdoms, four boys brought up to scrap. Each brother hoped to outmaneuver the others, setting himself up as the rightful successor to Rome. Within this context, Sigibert calling his wedding "Caesar's marriage" was akin to a declaration of war.

In time, Brunhild would prove herself to have a taste for combat, so she may well have thrilled to her new husband's posturing and the opportunity for conquest it portended. Or perhaps, when Brunhild learned the story of Sigibert and his three brothers, did the teenage bride not wonder what she had gotten herself into?

These were Sigibert's brothers:

Charibert—the eldest, entitled, fearing little that his position might slip.
Guntram—the second born, the crafty one, the plotter.
And, of course, Chilperic: the youngest, the runt, the brother with whom Sigibert most often battled.

Their father's body was not yet cold when the four began brawling. Before the funeral was even held, Chilperic—nervy, hostile Chilperic—surprised his older brothers by seizing the royal treasury, bribing influential nobles with its gold, and moving his armies into Paris. He was trying to seize the empire as his own. It took the combined forces of his brothers' armies to drive him out and convince him to follow their father's will and partition the empire into separate kingdoms.

Charibert, the oldest, got the choicest bits, commandeering the capital their grandfather had established in Paris. Charibert's kingdom ran along the Atlantic, encompassing what is today called Normandy and all of the Aquitaine in the southwest. Guntram, the next eldest, ruled over Burgundy in the southeast. The younger two split the northern territories. Sigibert commanded the eastern-most portion of the Frankish Empire, what is now northeast France, Belgium, the Netherlands, and Germany, and his kingdom was named accordingly: Austrasia, from *ostar* or *aust*, for "east." Chilperic, after his antics, got the short end of the stick, the smallest share, comprising what is now north-central France, the *neust* or "west lands," Neustria.

The intervening six years had seen a fragile peace. But now, Sigibert's claims of his "Caesar's marriage" would rile his brothers. And so would his choice of bride.

Sigibert's brothers tended to be omnivorous in their romantic entanglements. Gregory, a priest who frequented Sigibert's court, acidly noted that Charibert, Guntram, and Chilperic were mostly in the habit of "taking wives who were completely unworthy of them and were so far degrading themselves as to even marry their own servants."

Gregory was, it should be noted, an unabashed snob who claimed to be able to trace his roots back four hundred years, so his sniping may reflect some bias against newcomers and upstarts. Still, he was right that Sigibert's brothers had extraordinarily messy love lives. Charibert, after divorcing his first wife to marry one of her servants, had now moved on to his third wife, a commoner. Guntram was newly single after a public feud between his wife and his concubine turned deadly, ending when one woman poisoned the other's son. This was salacious enough, but Gregory was pointedly referring to Chilperic's domestic situation, and his passion for the palace slave Fredegund.

The kings' complicated personal lives may have been less a matter of unbridled lust, though, and more of shrewd policy. Any acknowledged

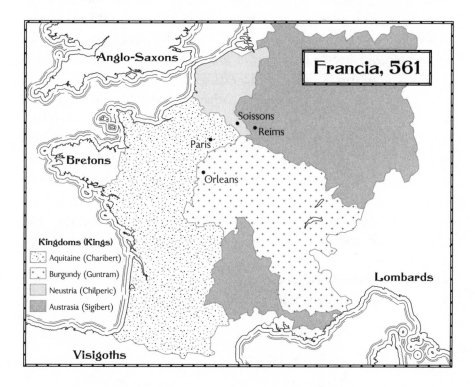

son of a Frankish king was an heir, whether he was a bastard or a legitimate son, whether his mother was a princess or a slave. A king without sons risked the stability of his kingdom, yet too many sons could be a problem, as the generations of squabbling between brothers demonstrated. Mating with a lowborn woman made a lot of sense; she might not bring a rich dowry or a political alliance into the union, but because she did not have a powerful family to contend with, she and her offspring could be easily repudiated if needed.

Brunhild would have recognized that Sigibert, in selecting her, was publicly rejecting his brothers' strategy. In contrast to them, Sigibert was styling himself as a temperate, self-possessed Roman statesman. If he had any entanglements prior to his marriage to Brunhild, he had been extraordinarily discreet—discreet enough, in fact, to spur rumors that perhaps he was not that fond of women at all. But now Sigibert's head-scratching chastity may have paid off. In choosing Brunhild for his bride, Sigibert was claiming himself superior to his brothers.

Brunhild had been raised to be more than a brood mare. Her father, the Visigoth King Athanagild, had no sons, and so she and her older sister had been trained and educated accordingly. King Athanagild had not entertained proposals for his older daughter's hand—he planned to match her with a powerful aristocratic family to solidify his power in Spain. He had been willing to part with his younger daughter in exchange for a foreign alliance, but not to just any suitor. Athanagild and his wife had been swayed by Sigibert's proposal because of the sort of marriage the Frankish king was offering—a political partnership, like the sort they themselves enjoyed. Queen Goiswintha served as Athanagild's trusted adviser and strategist, and she expected that her daughter would be a similar asset to her new husband.

Now, in ecclesiastic and international political circles, Sigibert was receiving wide acclaim for his choice of bride. His brothers' spies would have been reporting back alarming gossip—that it was declared that Sigibert and Brunhild's future sons, with royal blood on both sides, would be the true heirs to the whole Frankish Empire.

CHAPTER 3

The Fall of Charibert

In the months after her wedding, Brunhild tried to settle in at court. Metz was no Toledo, but the city was prosperous enough, thanks to the salt mines on its outskirts. And it was not an unattractive city: barges and boats dotted its rivers, and the surrounding countryside was "bright with flourishing fields" and cultivated roses. Some things would even have reminded Brunhild of home, especially the palace set up on a hill overlooking the river that wound around the city like a moat.

From the upper windows of the Golden Court, Brunhild saw not just the River Moselle and the bridge spanning it. She could also see straight down into a small amphitheater inside the city walls. Gladiator games had long been outlawed, but exotic animal hunts and bear baiting were still held here. These, sadly, seemed to be the main entertainment. The new queen quickly discovered that even what luxuries the Merovingian courts offered left something to be desired. There were mimes and actors in residence, for instance—predecessors of the minstrels and jesters later found in medieval courts—but mostly, these performers recited long-winded national epics.

Although Brunhild found herself with many admirers, she was without companions who might have been able to take the place of her mother or sister and offer advice, or comfort. The common folk rushed to catch sight of her processing to church; Brunhild cut an otherworldly figure, dripping jewels and radiant in brightly dyed tunics and gowns edged in gold, and distributing charity, whether bread, warm cloaks, or handfuls of coins. When feasts and games were held, she would be surrounded by the kingdom's leading men who offered her jeweled trinkets. But Brunhild was the only royal woman at court. (Sigibert's sister had recently died, and his mother had passed away when he was a child.) Worse, there were few Franks with whom she could converse informally. Brunhild had studied grammar, rhetoric, and poetry; her Latin was impeccable. The nobles at Sigibert's court would have spoken it, too, but theirs was often "a very deformed kind of Latin." Other nobles, and many of the servants, would have been more likely to speak Frankish than the Gothic spoken back in Spain.

For companionship and entertainment Brunhild did have the poet Fortunatus. The wandering bard had stayed on at court after her wedding while he cast about for more commissions. Fortunatus's classical education matched, if not surpassed, her own, and it is likely he regaled her as he did others—with tales of his adventures traveling across the Alps, in the dead of winter, to make his fortune in Frankish lands. He even managed to win over Gregory; the up-and-coming poet and the elitist priest became unlikely friends.

Soon, though, Fortunatus was called away. He had landed another commission. Sigibert's eldest brother, Charibert, had decided he must have a classical poem of his own.

Charibert was on the cusp of fifty—his hair was starting to gray, his back had begun to pain him, and while he had three daughters, he did not yet have an heir. All three of his brothers, younger by a full decade or two, had plenty of time to secure their kingdoms' lines of succession. But did he?

Before Brunhild's wedding, Charibert was on his third wife, Theudechild, the teenaged daughter of a shepherd. When she became pregnant, Charibert was relieved and overjoyed. Theudechild *did* give birth to a longed-for son. Her triumph, however, was short-lived, as the baby boy was "no sooner born than buried." Theudechild had come closer to giving Charibert an heir than any of his other wives. But if she expected that the king would want her back in his bed to try again, she was mistaken.

Charibert plunged into yet another marriage. And not only was his fourth wife the sister of his second wife, she was also a nun.

In the eyes of the Church, marrying a former spouse's sibling was incestuous, and the marrying of nuns was also forbidden. Now Charibert's bishops were scandalized, and his nobles were nervously discussing the line of succession. Could the king even produce an heir? And so Charibert decided a ceremony welcoming him to Paris as a conquering hero, complete with a poem by Fortunatus, would rehabilitate his image and send a message to the whole Frankish Empire about which brother was the top of the heap.

Fortunatus was a newcomer to political theater, but even a cub poet like him would have realized that staging such an elaborate ceremony in Charibert's capital would be difficult. The entire population of Paris at that time wouldn't fill Fenway Park today. The once sprawling Roman city had compressed itself onto just the Île de la Cité, the spit of land in the middle of the Seine, with one bridge onto the island and one bridge off. On the day of the ceremony, the procession into the city was likely quite short: Charibert rode north up the only major thoroughfare, what is now the Rue Saint-Jacques, crossed the bridge over the Seine, entered the city gates, and then proceeded down to the cathedral of Saint-Étienne, built on the same site Notre Dame occupies today. As King Charibert dismounted in front of his assembled subjects, clothed in his gold-embroidered robes, Fortunatus proclaimed that here was "a man who wins acclaim from the setting to the rising sun for dignity, character, good sense, and his exercise of justice."

"Romans applaud him," Fortunatus claimed. Sigibert might have dared to call himself Caesar at his wedding, but Charibert, in a show of one-upmanship, compared himself to a specific Caesar, "the famous emperor Trajan." Trajan was renowned for conquering the most territory, and this was likely a pointed reminder of exactly who ruled the largest Frankish kingdom. The clergy in the audience were told that Charibert was not just pious, but in possession of "a disciplined mind [that] conducts itself with maturity."

But if Charibert thought this performance had cowed his bishops into if not admiration at least silence, he had sorely misjudged the clergy's mood. In the Frankish world, the Church was still a relatively young and fragile institution. The Bible as we know it today had only just been stitched together; sixty of its books had been tossed out, declared apocryphal, and ordered burned. And the faith was still riven by a massive doctrinal schism. On one side was Nicene Christianity, or what came to be known as Catholicism, which professed a belief in the Trinity—a coequal God, Son, and Holy Spirit. (The Nicene Creed, which declares that Jesus is "of one being with the Father," is the one affirmed by most Christians today.) On the other side were the followers of Arius, an Egyptian priest who taught that Jesus was separate from, and subordinate to, a unitary Almighty God.

These Arian Christians—concentrated in Spain, North Africa, and parts of Italy—were generally content to live and let live. They made allowances for those who followed the Nicene Creed; one of their representatives declared, diplomatically, "it is no crime for one set of people to believe in one doctrine and another set of people to believe in another." By contrast, the Catholics were not nearly as tolerant, and they ranted on about heretics and "pagan abominations."

At the time of Charibert's fourth marriage, the Franks had been officially Christian and in the Catholic camp for less than sixty years. Naturally, the Frankish Church felt itself under siege—and not just from the Arians. While it was fast learning how to tyrannize, and terrify, the most devout, the Church was still facing challenges from the rest of the Frankish people, who persisted with their traditional pagan ways, and from the Frankish monarchs, too.

It was the current kings' grandfather, Clovis, who had converted to Catholicism for the sake of further unifying his empire. The Franks would have not just one king, one capital, and one law, but one religion, too. Clovis had set up an informal agreement whereby Frankish monarchs would rule in consultation with the Church. The exact nature of that relationship, though, was up for debate. Bishops assumed they should have the final say in certain state matters, but Clovis's sons and grandsons often expected the clerics to simply offer their blessings. The tension had recently escalated when Charibert annexed a piece of prime real estate that the Church thought of as its own.

At the same time, the Church was fighting other challenges to its authority and to its purse by inserting itself into the bedrooms of its devotees. Bishops had cracked down on same-sex relationships, decreeing that monks (but, curiously, not nuns) must stop sharing beds. These same bishops were finding their own sex lives under increasing scrutiny. Many had joined the Church later in life, after retiring from secular careers; they often already had wives and children. At first, this presented no problem. Married men had long been ordained as bishops and priests, and initially they were not even expected to be celibate. Instead, the Church asked that they be sexually temperate and only refrain from sex entirely on certain holy days. Yet when these bishops occasionally produced more offspring, they left their worldly goods to their children and not the Church. Eager to prevent this without also condoning divorce, the Church next ordered all bishops to live with their wives "as brother and sister." This was not, understandably, a popular directive; to enforce it, the Church was trying to find and excommunicate married bishops who were still sleeping with their wives.

This made Charibert's marriage to a nun especially problematic. The Church realized it could not be seen to be punishing its followers for much more private indiscretions while overlooking the very public sexual misdeeds of a king. The final straw was an epidemic that afflicted Paris in the fall of 567. The already affronted bishops chose to interpret the outbreak as divine punishment for the king's antics.

Nine of Charibert's bishops were planning to meet that autumn in the city of Tours, and the king—either oblivious to the rising tensions or overconfident in his ability to resolve them—gave his permission for this church council to take place as planned. It was a fiasco. When the bishops convened on November 18, 567, the king was in attendance; they desperately tried to convince Charibert to put an end to his incestuous marriage to a nun. He flatly refused. Shortly after, Charibert earned himself the distinction of being the very first European king to be excommunicated.

Conveniently, the nun Charibert had risked his eternal soul for died soon after in the epidemic—further proof, the bishops reasoned, that their decision was the correct one. Stunned, and now a pariah unable to mingle with his court, Charibert rode out from Paris to hunker down in one of his villas close to Bordeaux. He went out hunting to distract himself from his troubles and then promptly dropped dead of what likely was a heart attack.

. . .

What to do with an excommunicated king's body? There could be no funeral mass at the cathedral in Paris, nor a burial alongside his illustrious grandfather Clovis. Instead Charibert's body was carted off to an old Roman fort and buried in unconsecrated ground as a pagan would be, without any of the pomp and ceremony the king had so craved in life.

Back in Metz, though, Brunhild and Sigibert would have been less concerned with the disposal of the king's body and more concerned with the disposal of his considerable lands. Which brother would get what? Would Charibert's kingdom be divided equally among his brothers or would Chilperic yet again attempt a preemptive strike? Brunhild would have been trying to communicate with her father in Spain. Charibert's kingdom bordered Spain and her family would be anxious to know who their new neighbors might be.

In the midst of this unprecedented chaos in the Frankish Empire, Brunhild's ex-sister-in-law decided to stage a coup.

Charibert's former wife Theudechild, the young shepherdess, had been cast aside for a nun. But with the nun dead and that marriage unrecognized by the Church, Theudechild could now claim to be the king's legal widow and queen of the land. And a queen had certain privileges and powers. Though she could not summon armies or declare war, Frankish traditions gave her access to the royal purse, if not complete control over it. The king's treasury was kept close to his bedchamber, and from it, a queen could distribute small gifts to help her forge politically useful relationships—coins to a bishop to help him with a church construction project, a handful of garnets to a lord to sweeten his daughter's dowry.

Theudechild, though, had much bigger plans. She had all of Charibert's gold coins and plates and salvers and chalices scooped up from the chests where they were normally kept and loaded onto carts. She could not have hauled it all away herself during the dead of night. At the very least, she must have had some friendly palace guards willing to look the other way, and a few men able, on very short notice, to help pack up the gold and silver and drive the teams of horses. She also had access to land—a quiet place outside the walls of the Île de la Cité, perhaps a barn or other outbuilding—where she could hide this immense treasure while she figured out her next move.

Having accomplished so much so quickly, Theudechild was emboldened to see if Charibert's nobles might accept her as queen. Surprisingly, there was some support for her bid, but ultimately, the answer was no—the aristocracy may have accepted her as regent if her baby boy had survived, but without a living son, they would not.

Despite her lowly social position, Theudechild seems to have been well acquainted with the example of the Roman and Byzantine empresses, who were able to wield influence in matters of royal succession because their very bodies represented a kind of vessel for the power of their deceased husbands. When an emperor died, his successor often tried to gain control of the state through a physical union with the widow. Theudechild would have examined her situation and sensed a similar opportunity: She was a royal widow, and even better, she was young, presumably attractive, and had proved her capacity to produce sons. So she sent her messengers to the next eldest Merovingian, Guntram, proposing marriage.

King Guntram responded, "She may come to me and bring her treasure with her. I will receive her and I will give her an honorable place among my people. She will hold a higher position at my side than she ever did with my brother." This was exactly the answer Theudechild had hoped for. She rode south with her entourage and Charibert's treasury to Guntram's capital of Chalon-sur-Saône, prepared for a wedding. Guntram welcomed her, appraised the gold she had brought with her—and then seized most of it for himself. Worse, perhaps, he laughed at her, calling Theudechild "unworthy" to share his bed. And then Guntram "packed her off to a nunnery at Arles." Guntram went on to marry one of his ex-wife's former slaves, demonstrating that Theudechild's "unworthiness" derived not from her low social status, but from her ambition.

The surviving brothers didn't see eye to eye on much, but they could all agree that they did not want any of the other women in Charibert's life getting similar ideas. To tie up any loose ends, Charibert's daughters were bundled off to convents, too. For Brunhild, observing from her palace in

Metz, Guntram's deception and the brothers' concerted effort to quash a woman's ambition must have felt like it contained a lesson: Playing politics was dangerous business for Frankish queens. The men in charge were jealous guardians of their own hoarded power. When not long afterward Brunhild would find herself vying with these men in their own arena, she knew all too well what she was risking.

Of Charibert's wives and daughters, Theudechild was the only one to rebel against her gilded monastic prison. She managed to smuggle messages out to an unnamed Visigoth, a man she was clearly already familiar with, a man she suspected might be willing to risk it all to help her. She had another proposal: "if he would carry her off to Spain and marry her there, she would escape the nunnery with what wealth remained to her." This Visigoth enthusiastically agreed.

It was not so easy to escape a sixth-century convent, though. The night of her attempted jailbreak, the abbess "caught her red-handed," and then promptly "had her beaten mercilessly" and re-imprisoned in her solitary cell. It was there that Theudechild would remain "until her dying day, suffering awful anguish."

CHAPTER 4

New Alliances

S igibert gave every appearance of being delighted with his new bride. Given the unstable political situation, though, he was often away with his troops or plotting with his advisers, and not available to keep Brunhild company. After Fortunatus departed for Paris, Brunhild cast about for other companionship. There was one figure at court—educated, urbane, and artistic—who likely piqued her curiosity: Sigibert's illegitimate younger brother, Gundovald.

Gundovald had been recognized by his royal family throughout his childhood and educated as a prince, but when he hit adolescence, for some reason his father publicly repudiated him. Now, however, Gundovald was welcomed at his brothers' courts and even allowed to wear his hair in the royal style. Merovingian men wouldn't cut their hair after childhood, and they wore it parted in the center, flowing around the shoulders, a symbol of their strength and virility. For this, their dynasty earned the moniker the "long-haired kings," and Gundovald was permitted to look the part. In fact, Gundovald had spent so much time in Paris at Charibert's court that it was widely assumed Charibert had been grooming his much younger half brother to be his heir. Around the time Charibert's queen Theudechild had become pregnant, though, Sigibert had summoned Gundovald to Metz, perhaps to repeat the role of stand-in heir for his still-childless brother.

Brunhild and Gundovald had some sort of interaction at court, and she probably found him, at the very least, amusing. Gundovald had been well-educated in his youth, and during his periods of intermittent exile he had traveled widely. He was also a talented artist and was renowned as a painter of churches and chapels. And as later events would prove, Gundovald was charming and personable, able to thrive in a variety of environments. By all accounts, Brunhild was a memorable personality, too: "amiable and an easy person with whom to talk." Under different circumstances, they could have become good friends.

But at the Golden Court, if they chatted and joked with each other, beneath the banter ran a dark undercurrent. Each could only secure their position at the expense of the other. If Brunhild produced an heir, Gundovald would likely be sent away; if Brunhild proved to be infertile, her own future would be in question. While some have suggested there was a minor flirtation between the two, it's more probable that they were constantly, carefully, sizing one another up. Still, when Brunhild did become pregnant fairly quickly after the wedding, mixed with her triumph was likely some sympathy for her brother-in-law.

When word also came of King Charibert's death, it seemed that they had both been blessed with good fortune. Charibert had died so suddenly that he had not had time to designate an heir; Gundovald, who had spent so much time at his half brother's court in the past, was well-positioned to lay claim to his kingdom. Brunhild could have her heir, and Gundovald could still get his kingdom.

But Brunhild woke up one day to find her brother-in-law gone. Gundovald was spirited away almost as quickly as Theudechild had been.

The surviving brothers, not wanting Gundovald to cut into the shares they had coming to them, held a hurried meeting. Sigibert and Guntram decided that, while Gundovald should not be disposed of entirely, he needed to be knocked down a few pegs. Brunhild would hear that not only had Gundovald been sent away, he'd also suffered another more symbolic indignity. In a dynasty of long-haired kings, short hair had come to mean a disqualification from ruling. With this tradition in mind, Gundovald's royal half brothers had put him in his place by shearing off his locks. (He was fortunate that they decided to forgo their other option—scalping.)

If Gundovald had not been Brunhild's friend exactly, he was at least a companion at court, a fellow outsider. Now she was more alone than ever as her pregnancy advanced; her ankles swelled, and her belly ached. Brunhild's mother and her sister, far away in Spain, would have sent cheerful and encouraging messages. Brunhild had already proved her fertility, and if she produced, God willing, a healthy child, she would have done her job. But the fate of her sister-in-law Theudechild would have weighed on her—despite Sigibert's reassurances, it seemed that only a son, a living son, would guarantee her influence and position at court.

The baby was a girl.

. . .

In the early spring of 568, after a shorn Gundovald was bustled off to Cologne, on the outskirts of the empire, the three remaining brothers took to dividing up their older brother's lands. They couldn't decide what to do with Charibert's capital, Paris, and so they agreed it should be kept as neutral ground. None would enter or occupy it without the permission of the others, and they would share its tax revenue equally. Then they divided up the rest of his lands in the north and the Aquitaine. The map that resulted is a weird patchwork, as if drawn by a child. For the brothers, the determining factors were a city's prosperity (in other words, its tax revenue) and the prestige of its episcopate (which would give its king more clout with the clergy). Some of the divisions had to do with which lands adjoined others the kings already held.

Guntram had already helped himself to his brother's treasure by deceiving Theudechild, so he contented himself with a few port cities on the Mediterranean and the Atlantic. Chilperic, who had long had just a sliver of a kingdom, finally gained enough land to qualify as an equal to his brothers. Still, he was left feeling stymied again—and mostly by Sigibert, the rising star, who had the most bargaining power. Sigibert had claimed Tours and Poitiers, powerful cities that not only had plentiful tax revenues, but were also located right in the middle of Chilperic's new-won territory. Chilperic had hoped for a contiguous strip of land along the Atlantic coast but, instead, he was frustrated to find his inheritance was divided, with about two-thirds in the north and another third in the southwest.

Neither of the elder brothers would have forgotten how Chilperic had tried to seize the whole empire before their father's funeral. And Sigibert, especially, knew from experience that Chilperic would go to any lengths to take his land. Years earlier, a tribe called the Avars had risen up, and these extraordinary horsemen, successors to Attila the Hun's old empire, had attempted to invade Francia along its eastern border. Sigibert rode out to repel them and called on his brothers to help. But while Sigibert was saving the Frankish Empire from the invaders, not only did Chilperic fail to send the requested aid, but he also decided to attack. Chilperic laid siege to Reims and other cities belonging to Sigibert, starting a civil war. Sigibert, the "Magnificent Victory," managed to win on both fronts. He drove out the Avars in the east and retook his cities in the west. In the course of defending his holdings, he even captured one of Chilperic's sons, Prince Theudebert. Sigibert could have had his prisoner exiled, or even executed. But his nephew was still a boy, likely no older than twelve, sent out on a military campaign to start learning his trade. (Most Frankish princes began

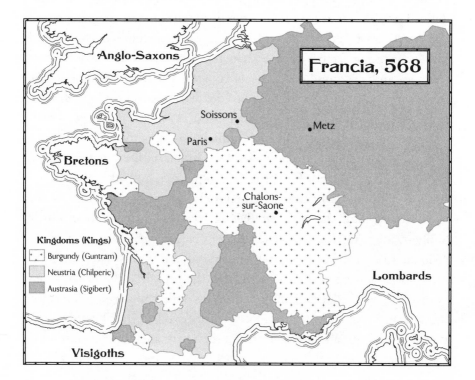

riding into battle before they hit puberty, under the tutelage of more experienced generals.) Perhaps this is why Sigibert merely made Theudebert promise not to attack again, and then sent him back home.

Now, with the Frankish Empire splayed out on the chopping block to be carved up like a side of meat, Chilperic's disappointment with his allotted portion again turned quickly into violence. Not satisfied with more than doubling his territory, Chilperic invaded Sigibert's newly inherited cities of Tours and Poitiers. Chilperic even placed his son—the very one whose life Sigibert had spared years earlier—in command of one of these campaigns, forcing his boy to break the solemn oath he had made to his uncle. But Chilperic's forces were, again, driven back.

What was the source of Chilperic's seemingly unquenchable hostility toward his brothers? One clue, perhaps, lies in their parenting: all four men shared the same father, King Clothar, but they had different mothers. Charibert, Guntram, and Sigibert had been born to a woman named Ingund, a servant of Clothar's; he also took up with Ingund's sister, who produced Chilperic. Ingund died young, and so her sister likely served as her nephews' stepmother for some time.

There is little else known about Chilperic's mother, other than what can be gleaned from her excavated tomb: she was slender and petite, just five feet tall, and she walked with a limp, a legacy from a bout with polio as a child. At some point she fell out of favor and left court. She went on to live a long life, well into her seventies, but completely out of the political spotlight. Likely, Chilperic's mother's unassuming nature held the secret to her longevity. But it also offers some hint of why Chilperic

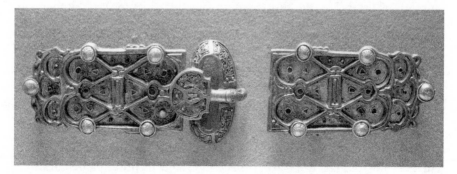

A gold and silver belt buckle with inlaid garnets from the grave of Chilperic's mother

behaved so badly. His older brothers tended to band together, and in the face of this, Chilperic would have grown up feeling like an outsider. And, crucially, he did not have a forceful mother to advocate for him with the brothers to ensure his inheritance after his father's death. And so now he constantly threatened his brothers with invasions, and constantly threatened and extorted his own subjects, as evidenced by his unusual habit of adding to the bottom of all his royal edicts, "Whoever disobeys this order shall have his eyes put out."

After his failed assault on Tours and Poitiers, Chilperic was furious to be defeated once again. He was surrounded, hemmed in not just by his brothers, but also on his southernmost border by Sigibert's new allies, Brunhild's people, the Visigoths in Spain. If Chilperic could not best his brothers in battle, perhaps there was another way to outmaneuver them—with a foreign alliance of his own. Given his new inheritance, Chilperic finally had the clout to bid for a prestigious foreign princess. No matter how much he was enjoying his palace romps with his slave Fredegund, he couldn't squander this opportunity to match, or even surpass, his brother's political standing. As Chilperic cast about for an appropriately valuable princess, one who might upstage Brunhild, he could think of no better candidate than Brunhild's own elder sister, Galswintha.

A year ago, King Athanagild would have laughed at Chilperic's proposal—why waste his first-born daughter and de facto heir on the Frankish king with the least territory and prestige?—but now Chilperic had something the Visigoths wanted: lands directly adjoining theirs. And Chilperic made a startling offer. Tradition held at the time that a bride be given a *morgengabe*, or "morning gift," after the couple consummated their marriage. The more prestigious the bride, the more extravagant the morgengabe. Sigibert, for example, seems to have given Brunhild Tribonum, a lavish estate in southern France. Chilperic, though, was willing to offer Galswintha a morgengabe that comprised the entire southern third of his kingdom.

This sort of gift was unheard of in the early medieval world, unprecedented in any kingdom or empire. Galswintha would control five wealthy cities in the Aquitaine, the entirety of Bordeaux, Limoges, Cahors, Lescar, and Cieutat. All would be hers, their cobblestones and ramparts, their citizens and soldiers, their luxurious estates and plentiful game, and their considerable tax revenues. Chilperic was taking an incalculable risk. If he and Galswintha were to divorce, or if, God forbid, he were to die, the Visigoth princess could return to Spain, bringing a third of his kingdom along with her. King Athanagild would have been a fool to turn down this opportunity.

He must have been surprised at his good fortune. Maybe he had wanted assurance he would face no incursions from the Franks to his east, or maybe he had even hoped for a grandson who would become a player in the Spanish succession. But he had not hoped for this outcome—both daughters married off in less than two years to brother-kings in neighboring kingdoms, his girls just a few days' travel from each other. Should something happen to him or his wife, their daughters would be able to offer each other support and comfort.

King Athanagild, though, had not been so dazzled by Chilperic's offer that he was willing to overlook what he saw as the king's moral failings. Warned of Chilperic's playboy reputation, Athanagild had not immediately accepted Chilperic's offer of marriage. Brunhild had converted from Arianism to Catholicism for Sigibert. Galswintha would also convert to her new husband's preferred religion, but only on the condition that Chilperic be her faithful Christian husband. The Visigoths were much more prudish in this respect; their code prohibited the keeping of concubines and mistresses. And so Athanagild demanded Chilperic swear a solemn oath, a *sacramentum*, to repudiate all other women. Everyone would have understood who, exactly, Athanagild was referring to.

This was the precondition to the marriage that Chilperic so eagerly sought: A king must swear to stay away from a slave. The fact that Chilperic was forced to make this particular promise hints that Fredegund's hold over the king had already raised some eyebrows. There seems to have been no concern that his exiled first wife might return from her cloister—even though her three legitimate sons were being groomed to be warriors in their father's armies—nor that any other of Chilperic's former mistresses would dare disrespect this new powerful queen. But Fredegund, specifically, was perceived to be a potential problem.

Chilperic agreed to this demand. He wanted this illustrious alliance more than he wanted any slave girl. He readily agreed that Fredegund would be sent away. But she would not be cast aside so easily. She kept her own counsel—and made her own plans.

CHAPTER 5

A Missive to Byzantium

If Brunhild was anxious over not having produced a son, Sigibert did not seem to mind. The birth of his daughter was widely celebrated and the baby was named Ingund after his deceased mother.

For Sigibert, 568 was proving to be a banner year. Charibert's death had enlarged his holdings and now his queen had proved she could produce healthy children; Sigibert had every expectation that sons would follow. He knew an empire needed grand buildings and public works projects, so next he undertook a building frenzy in Metz, constructing churches and official edifices, trying to create a worthy capital.

Sigibert also focused on securing all of his borders. He kept a close eye on his brothers, especially Chilperic, while also surveying the international landscape. Sigibert no longer needed to worry about the Visigoths in Spain or the Avars to his southeast. The Thuringians and Alemanni lay to the northeast, but they were tributary kingdoms now, having been conquered by his father. Further north were the Jutes and the Saxons, but they had likewise been subdued by a recent campaign. The only border that would have concerned Sigibert was his southern one, with Italy. The Byzantines, under Emperor Justinian, had long been trying to retake Italy to reunite the old Roman Empire; in fact, it was this campaign that was partly responsible for spreading the bubonic plague in the 540s, when flea-infested rats hitched a ride across the Mediterranean on Justinian's warships.

By 568, though, Italy was in the hands of the Lombards, blond, blue-eyed people from southern Scandinavia. They had just conquered the majority of the peninsula, dooming the Byzantine's plans to recapture the territory, and they were fast moving north toward Austrasia.

Justinian himself was dead, and in his place sat his ambitious nephew. Justin II had come to the throne by a suspiciously lucky accident—a single witness had happened to overhear Justinian name his nephew his heir with his dying breath. Sigibert decided his next move would be to befriend this brand-new emperor. Yet he did not want to raise the suspicions of either of his brothers, who would surely try to block him or rush to curry their own favor with the Byzantines. To do so discreetly, he decided to turn to an unlikely source for help—his father's fourth wife, Radegund, a woman who would change the course of Brunhild's life.

Like Brunhild, Radegund had been a foreign princess, and then a Frankish queen. But her path to the throne was considerably different. Radegund hailed from Thuringia, the now-subdued kingdom on Francia's northeastern border. She had been captured as a prize in battle when she was about six years old.

Up until that point, her life had been difficult enough. Radegund's mother died, and then her uncle killed her father in battle over the throne. She was being raised by that uncle when the Franks invaded Thuringia and slaughtered the rest of her relatives in front of her; it seems only a few of the royal children were spared, including Radegund and her baby brother. Radegund was carted away to be raised and educated at a country estate as one of King Clothar's future wives, presumably to strengthen his claim to Thuringia. However, once she reached marriageable age, Radegund proved to be a very unwilling consort.

Although it seems she had been born and brought up a pagan, Radegund adopted Christianity with gusto. She wielded it as a shield, even a weapon, against her captor-husband. Her incessant praying and fasting were bothersome; her refusal of the rich foods at court—and later, her strict vegetarianism—may have seemed odd. But presumably King Clothar was least thrilled with her habit of leaving the marital bed to lay on the cold floor in a hair shirt, moaning and repenting of her conjugal duties. When Clothar cajoled and chased, she subjected herself to even more extreme mortifications of the flesh—dragging iron chains, branding herself with hot iron plates.

Queen Radegund leaves the marital bed to prostrate herself on the floor in an Early Medieval manuscript

Clothar finally seemed resigned to seek more enthusiastic company elsewhere. He took up with one of his brother's widows and then fathered his bastard, Gundovald, with the wife of a mill worker. Radegund, meanwhile, kept herself unavailable with a host of charitable work, becoming increasingly involved in the Church and cultivating relationships with influential bishops. The rest of the time she avoided her husband by hiding out at the three country estates she had been given as her morgengabe.

Things might have dragged on in this way for many more years but for Clothar's political machinations in Thuringia. Radegund's baby brother had been raised in Francia and then stayed on to be close to his sister. But as he grew older, Clothar grew increasingly concerned about the boy's political aspirations. This was likely pure paranoia, and even if a genuine threat existed, Clothar had many options for dealing with the young prince, such as imprisoning him on a country estate or sending him off to a monastery. Instead, he chose to have him murdered.

That was the last straw. Radegund had been spending less and less time at court, but now she left entirely. The open joke in Francia was that Clothar had married a nun. Now the queen begged to become one. Convents were where Merovingian kings deposited inconvenient brides, and most queens fought against being relegated to such a life. (Think of the beleaguered Theudechild, whose escape plans were forever dashed.) But Radegund *embraced* the idea.

Radegund took sanctuary in a church and begged the esteemed Bishop Medard to consecrate her. The bishop refused Radegund's request. He was no idiot; some of Clothar's men had already threatened him with bodily harm if he aided Radegund, and the bishop knew others were likely to follow suit. Radegund publicly called him a coward, accusing him of "fear[ing] man more than God." Bishop Medard settled on the compromise of making the queen a deaconess, a position that allowed her to minister to the poor and participate in some church sacraments but did not annul her marriage and commit her to a life of chastity.

Radegund retreated to her country home of Saix and set up a sort of hospital and almshouse on the premises. This would have made her very popular among the public, as she offered a free daily meal and, twice a week, warm baths and fresh clothes, as well as basic medical attention. These actions helped secure her reputation as a miracle worker. Regular bathing and cleaning—as well as other interventions, like applying ointment to pus-filled wounds—helped combat disease and saved lives. Radegund also seems to have employed more skilled medical practitioners who treated patients with herbs and salves.

Radegund was content in her new life, but after several years, rumors circulated that King Clothar was planning to visit and ask her to return to court. Around this time—perhaps as a desperate last stand, perhaps the actual result of the meager diet and violent acts of penitence she was inflicting on herself—Radegund claimed to have had a series of visions through which God told her to build her own convent. Radegund then drew upon the religious connections she had carefully cultivated, getting the powerful bishops of Tours and Paris to support her. After all, if God Himself had asked for a convent, surely they should not defy Him.

Clothar was not convinced. He still begged his queen to come back. In response, Radegund increased her mortifications of the flesh, wearing the "roughest of hairshirts" and undertaking extreme fasts and all-night vigils. Clothar next tried to appeal to her sense of pity, threatening that "unless he could get her back, he scarcely wanted to go on living." But then Radegund went toe-to-toe with the king, declaring that *she* "was determined to end her life" rather than return to the king's bed. Though she was exceedingly devout, she found her husband so repulsive that she was willing to undergo eternal damnation to escape her conjugal duties.

Word of the marital standoff spread far beyond the palace. Clothar's bishops likely advised him that it was unbecoming for him to be seen forcing a pious woman, a royal woman, into sexual relations. And Clothar knew it would not help his public image for his young, popular wife to be found dead by her own hand. Finally, Clothar relented. Radegund was allowed to consecrate herself to the Lord, and Clothar grumblingly donated royal land for her new project.

The institution Radegund established in the 550s, Holy Cross Abbey in Poitiers, was one of the earliest exclusively female monastic institutions established in Francia. (It survived right up until the French Revolution over a thousand years later.) From this perch, Radegund continued to be a major political and ecclesiastical player. She was no longer queen, but she may as well have been. Barred from going out in the world, she made the world come to her: Radegund welcomed dignitaries and entertained diplomats from her base in Poitiers, including representatives from the Byzantine imperial court. And so, naturally, it was to Radegund that Sigibert and Brunhild turned for help to begin establishing their claim to the whole of Francia.

Radegund's religious ambitions would provide the perfect cover for their own earthly ones. She was anxious to validate and elevate her new convent with valued relics, the currency of the religious world. These relics were usually scraps of saints' bones or other remains; the reliquaries an institution held could draw visitors and pilgrims—and their lucrative donations. Since the Byzantine Empire physically occupied the holy sites associated with Jesus and the earliest martyrs, it could also claim to hold most of the high-status relics, including one considered the most valuable in the early medieval world: the True Cross.

Sigibert and Brunhild sent their emissaries to Radegund's convent. Fortunatus soon followed, presumably to help craft the imperial correspondence. Then, as a diplomatic overture to the Byzantines, Radegund sent messengers formally requesting a piece of the True Cross.

Along with her clerics, however, traveled a long poem, addressed to a cousin of Radegund's who was in exile at the Byzantine court. The poem has survived to this day. Titled *De excidio Thoringiae*, "On the destruction of Thuringia," it establishes Radegund as its speaker and details her childhood experience of the Frankish invasion of her homeland, offering particulars one would expect only a survivor to know: what the palace's vaulted ceiling looked like, for example, or the hair color of a slaughtered court attendant. It is one of the most remarkable political documents of its era. So, naturally, the poem's authorship is still in question, since, clearly, a woman with a spectacular education and sharp mind, a woman who regularly wrote poems, couldn't have possibly written this one. Instead, historians have long claimed that it was written by Fortunatus, even though the voice and tone are markedly different from his other work. In recent years some have reconsidered and now fully attribute the poem to Radegund, or at least acknowledge that she must have had significant input in its composition, even if Fortunatus later helped with the form and meter.

Aside from its function as a brilliant feat of statesmanship (or stateswomanship), Radegund's poem is an extraordinary work of art on its own terms. It offers an intimate glimpse of how a culture of conquests impacts individual lives, a perspective that is lost in the accounts of glorious battles in the chronicles and epics of the period. Radegund relays poignant vignettes—how the hair of one woman being dragged off as a captive is "torn," how "a wife's naked feet trod in her husband's blood," and how "a child, when snatched from his mother's embrace, kept his eyes on hers" as he was carried off to his death. But what reach to us across time through the poem, as if to grab us by the shoulder, are Radegund's descriptions of her own emotional states during and after the war that scarred her childhood. Immediately following the attack, she says, she was terrified to be separated from her older cousin, the poem's addressee, for even a moment: "I was tormented by anxiety, if we were not under the one roof; if you just went outdoors, I thought you had gone far away." Even a lifetime later, she laments that it would have been better to have died along with everyone else: "Fortune provided consolation to the men whom the enemy struck down; I alone was left surviving to weep for them all." And Radegund describes how, now, her brother's murder has opened old wounds and how she blames herself for his death. It is impossible to miss the hallmarks of a profound and lasting trauma, the hypervigilance and survivor's guilt, as palpable to this woman nearly fifteen hundred years ago as they would be to us today.

Why would Radegund send such a wrenching and intensely personal poem over hundreds of miles in an attempt to secure a religious relic? Even though the poem was addressed to her cousin, it would have been read aloud for the whole Byzantine court, as all imperial correspondence was, and Radegund would have been aware of this protocol. Was she trying to invoke pity? Was she trying to prove that she was a pious woman with no political motives, thoroughly disenchanted with the secular world and its love of war? Both are possible. Still, why detail the destruction wrought by the Franks to a cousin who had endured it firsthand—unless the poem also contained an implicit threat? Look at the atrocities the Franks are capable of, Radegund seems to say. People who had no qualms about reducing "palace courts, where art once flourished" to a pile of "sad, glowing ashes" were not people one would want as enemies. Luckily, Radegund confided, these brutes now "piously honor me as a mother." She seems to offer herself up as an intermediary. It was a masterstroke of diplomacy.

A response came not from the emperor, but from the empress. Despite his ambition, Justin II had not emerged as the dominant figure at the Byzantine court. Instead, he was overshadowed by his commanding and capable wife, Sophia, a niece of the influential Empress Theodora. If the Austrasian ambassadors and spies had done their job, Sigibert and Brunhild would have already been apprised of this fact. Possibly, Sophia had been their intended recipient all along and Radegund had crafted her poem as an appeal from one powerful woman to another.

Empress Sophia sent Radegund the prized piece of the True Cross. All of Poitiers had reason to rejoice, but the town's bishop refused to participate in the celebration. He did not appreciate being upstaged by a popular and charismatic nun who now possessed relics that surpassed those in his cathedral. He had been expected to preside over a religious ceremony that would officially install the True Cross, but instead he left town so he could not be forced to participate. With "her spirit blazing in a fighting mood," Radegund complained to Sigibert. The king immediately intervened, sending another bishop to act in his stead. Fortunatus lent his support by contributing verses for the occasion; one of these, the "Vexilla Regis," is sung in churches on Good Friday to this day. The True Cross's installation was marked with all the pomp and ceremony befitting such a grand relic.

Soon after, an additional gift arrived in Poitiers from the Byzantines: a Bible encrusted with gold and jewels, accompanied by imperial *legatarii*. Legates usually handled only serious diplomatic matters; they were not the average deliverymen for a gift from one woman to another. While the jeweled Bible was being delivered to Holy Cross Abbey, the legatarii were clearly conducting other business. Soon after, Sigibert sent an official embassy to Constantinople and the alliance between Austrasia and the Byzantine Empire was formalized, without Burgundy or Neustria being able to jettison it first.

This collaboration also offered Brunhild a chance to form an alliance of her own. Throughout this delicate process, as messengers shuttled back and forth, Radegund came to appreciate the queen's help; the abbess would later say she "loved" Brunhild "with dear affection." And Brunhild, still alone at court, was badly in need of both allies and friends.

Radegund's kindliness toward Brunhild was extended to her entire family. When Brunhild's elder sister, Galswintha, arrived in Frankish lands as Chilperic's betrothed in July of 568, trailed by even more treasure and finery than her sister had been, Radegund was the first to greet the princess upon her arrival. "With motherly love, gentle Radegund desired eagerly to see her, in case she could be of any help to her," Fortunatus recounts, and the two enjoyed "close exchanges." Undoubtedly the former queen relayed Brunhild's well wishes, as well as offering her own support.

Galswintha, though, soon left Poitiers and headed north to Rouen, where Chilperic tripped over himself to provide an even more spectacular reception than his brother had given Brunhild. He marched his army more than one hundred miles west, so they might meet his new bride "near the curved bed" of the river Seine as she disembarked from her ship. Rather than being greeted by a palace hall full of nobles, Galswintha was welcomed by Chilperic's entire army on bended knee, swearing an oath of allegiance to their new queen. Chilperic never did anything in half measure. And Galswintha was married not in the great hall of a converted basilica, but in the cathedral at Rouen.

. . .

Less than six months later, though, a third wedding would take place. No cathedral this time, just a handful of nobles quickly assembled in the great room of a royal villa.

A week before this third wedding, King Chilperic and Queen Galswintha had been fighting. As she stormed and raged, messengers were seen riding out from the palace at all hours, delivering missives and pleas to her sister and her mother. Galswintha had caught Chilperic in bed, again, with the slave girl Fredegund. The queen was furious that "he showed no respect to her at all"; she was distraught over "the insults which she had to endure." She wanted to return home. Was it truly so unendurable? Yes, to be made a fool of like that. And Chilperic had such a temper! She would return home, even if it meant leaving her enormous dowry behind.

One morning, soon thereafter, the palace woke to a horrible scene. Galswintha had been found dead in her bed, strangled in her sleep.

Three days later, arrayed in the brightly dyed linens and jewels of her predecessor, Fredegund stood at the altar, smiling up at Chilperic.

CHAPTER 6

The Slave Queen

At Frankish wedding feasts, the tables were loaded down with food we would have no trouble recognizing today: loaves of white bread, beef slathered in brown gravy, carrots and turnips sprinkled with salt and pepper, for example. The Franks' love of bacon was renowned, too, as were their sweet tooths, so much so that the kings themselves owned many of the sugar refineries of the era—the beehives. The honey was used to sweeten the cakes baked for special occasions.

Even though Fredegund's wedding was hastily organized, some kind of wedding cake was served. There was even a wedding ring. The one Chilperic slipped on the new queen's finger would have contained a garnet, transported all the way from a mine in India. The stones were all the rage and prized even above diamonds. The rest of her new jewelry had traveled just as far. The amber beads now knotted around her neck came from the Baltic, and the lapis lazuli inlaid into her earrings from Afghanistan. The jewels flowed in from the east, while the slaves, like Fredegund herself, were shipped from the north in wagon carts, their arms bound by jute rope.

Where, exactly, had she come from, this Fredegund, this strawberry-blonde slave queen?

Was she left on a doorstep? Sold to satisfy a debt? Or, most likely, captured as a child? Conquest was the mill wheel of the early medieval world. Men clamored for the chance to get off the farm and go on a grand

*In a sixteenth-century catalog of the kings of France,
Chilperic and Fredegund reign together. Fredegund
is the only queen portrayed alongside her husband.*

adventure. Nearly everyone had a friend of a friend who went off to battle
and came back with enough booty to buy a bigger farm or entice a higher-
born wife. Likewise, nearly everyone knew a story about someone who
had ended up enslaved, carried off as part of that booty.

Those captured in a raid could include both aristocrats and field hands;
regardless of their former station in life, they were shackled up and carted
down to waiting ships at Mediterranean port cities. Some, though, were
brought just to the nearest large city and pressed into service of the warlord
or king who had won them. This might explain how Fredegund ended up
in the palace in Soissons, where she managed to catch the eye of Chilperic's
first wife, Queen Audovera, who promoted her from kitchen maid to
royal servant. But it's impossible to know for sure. While the Franks loved
origin stories—as evidenced by their tales of mythical sea monsters and

Trojan warriors—the historical record is notably silent on Fredegund's exact beginnings.

Future generations have tried to provide a birthplace for Fredegund, even a title of sorts, calling her Fredegund of Cambrai, or Fredegund of Montdidier. But throughout her reign as queen, she suppressed any discussion of where she came from. It is not clear if her parents were dead or if she just wished them to be. As for her wider family, the historical record makes no mention of her ever giving an appointment to a relative, as other former slaves sometimes did when they rose to positions of influence. There is no indication she cooked up half stories about being descended from a nymph or a siren to burnish her image. But surely, if there had been rumors of a moldering Roman villa somewhere in Fredegund's family tree, she would have used this to defend against the whisper campaign now leveled at her throughout Francia—*upstart, usurper.* That she produced no such story, and that she did not have her powerful new husband manufacture one for her, speaks to the fact that enough people knew exactly the sort of family Fredegund came from: one that washed the floors, mucked the stables, and emptied the chamber pots. But now, what hold did she have over their king, and what had she made him do?

Because if Chilperic *was* grieving, he could not have done a worse job of it. He did not once address his subjects on the matter of Galswintha's untimely demise. There were no searches for her assailants or rewards offered for their capture. No one was ever questioned or punished, not even the guards who had been posted at the door of the royal bedchamber that night.

It was Fortunatus's friend Gregory who stated plainly what the whole of Francia was thinking: "Chilperic ordered Galswintha to be strangled . . . and found her dead on the bed."

Galswintha's murder has been portrayed in art numerous times throughout the centuries since, and the blame always rests on Chilperic, so much so that illuminated manuscripts and paintings portray the king of Neustria himself, wearing his crown and grinning rakishly, wrapping a cloth around the neck of his sleeping wife. In some versions, Fredegund looks on. Whether Fredegund really urged him on or not, she knew people would always assume that she had, cleverly disposing of yet another rival for the king's affections.

A Late Medieval miniature shows King Chilperic strangling his wife

An alternate version of Galswintha's murder from the same period, with Fredegund overseeing the deed

One story in circulation more than a century later claimed that she had originally caught King Chilperic's eye by outsmarting his first queen. When Audovera gave birth to her fifth child while Chilperic was off fighting the Saxons, Fredegund was said to have told her queen: "Mistress, my lord king is returning as a victor. How can he receive his daughter joyfully if she is not baptized?"

A hasty ceremony was arranged, the story goes, but there was no noble-woman available to serve as godmother. So Fredegund encouraged Audovera to stand in as godmother for her own daughter: "No equal of yours can ever be found to receive the child. Just take up the child yourself." This, however, was a trick. Church law dictated that a parent could not have a sexual rela-tionship with their offspring's godparent. When Chilperic returned from battle, Fredegund made sure to let him know what had happened: "With whom will my lord sleep tonight, since my mistress the queen as godmother of your daughter . . . is related to you spiritually?" Chilperic took events in stride, declaring, "If I can't sleep with her, I'll sleep with you."

This story cannot be true. In the 560s, the Church hierarchy was still having trouble getting people to stop sleeping with their sisters-in-law and aunts and uncles. An official ban against the practice of "spiritual incest"—that is, sleeping with godparents—was not introduced until more than a century after Fredegund died. But this tale is illuminating because it shows later chroniclers found it plausible that a slave with no formal education would be better acquainted with a technicality in church baptismal law than a queen. Fredegund not only had a reputation for being clever, but also it was assumed that she could read. It was the norm for aristocratic women during this period to be literate, since they were expected to oversee the education of their offspring. But a slave girl? And yet, there is plenty of evidence that Fredegund, who had been accustomed to communicating in Frankish, had learned to speak and read Latin too.

Such a clever woman would have known that pitching a fit on the eve of Chilperic's wedding to Galswintha was a sure way to get herself hustled off to a convent, or to kitchen duty in some remote estate even farther from the locus of political power. It made more sense to respond to the marriage announcement with a practiced cheerful indifference. She returned to her responsibilities in the palace—a very public demotion from royal mistress, but one that allowed her to make sure Chilperic caught glimpses of her in passageways and courtyards, enticing reminders of an easier and more blissful time.

Now that Chilperic had made her his queen, however, Fredegund didn't know what she was expected to give her king in return. She could provide him children, hopefully, but Chilperic already had heirs—three healthy sons, future generals, and a lovely daughter to marry off, too. What was it he wanted from Fredegund, exactly? And if she did not deliver, what would be her fate? As she slipped under the very same sheets her predecessor had occupied just days before, Fredegund, for all her bravado, must have shivered.

. . .

"Toledo has sent you two towers, Gaul," Fortunatus wrote, referring to the two Visigoth princesses. "The second lies broken," he wrote, although "the first still stands."

Barely.

Just months after Galswintha's wedding, Brunhild had received word that her father had dropped dead, presumably of a heart attack. When the next message arrived, this one from Galswintha's terrified nursemaid, it was reported that Brunhild went into shock.

In less than eighteen months, Brunhild had lost her homeland, her father, and now her only sibling. She was alone in a strange land where she could barely understand the dialect. Fortunatus, writing about this turn of events, likened the tragedy to a "fall on the brittle ice." How could Brunhild endure it? It helped to be young and lithe and supported by an important family, as she was, but of course those same things had not been enough to save Galswintha. And Brunhild would also have known that the peculiar nature of Frankish law meant its power to protect her was limited.

Sigibert's grandfather, the great King Clovis, had tried to establish one crown and one capital for all of the Franks. Neither of those had lasted, but his legal code had. His Lex Salica—which stayed in effect for centuries and upon which the legal systems of later European kingdoms were founded—assigned common crimes a corresponding fine, or wergeld. The fine for the murder of a free Frankish man was two hundred solidi (gold coins). The life of a Roman was worth half that, only one hundred solidi. The highest wergelds in the empire were for free women of child-bearing age, even higher for women who were pregnant. An ordinary Frankish woman could command a wergeld equal to that of an aristo-crat—six hundred solidi, and seven hundred if she were pregnant.

Women possessed both more value and more rights under Salic law than they had under Roman law and more than they would in most king-doms in the Middle Ages and Renaissance. Yet despite the legal code's seeming progressive bent, a woman's value was directly linked to her reproductive potential, to her ability to make more warriors or princes. For a queen at the beginning of her childbearing years, as Galswintha had been, the wergeld was incalculable. But who had the power to find her killer and make him pay up?

If Brunhild approached Sigibert directly, with pleas and a tear-stained face, he would have shared her outrage. Killing a defenseless woman while she slept—such an act contravened the laws of God and man! But a Merovingian king could not act unilaterally. He needed the backing of at least some of his court.

Brunhild had influence at court, certainly. Her dress was imitated, her hairstyles carefully duplicated. What she ate, what she wore, which musi-cians and poets she favored—all were carefully tracked. But getting a hall full of warriors to declare a sudden preference for roast duckling was not real power. What she needed was to build political alliances, to spin a hundred threads—between her and the warrior-lords who eyed her as she ate, the servants who fetched her finery, the clergy who said prayers over her, the guards who watched the door while she slept—and weave them into a net that, if she slipped, would be strong enough to catch her.

CHAPTER 7

All the King's Men

Methodically checking alliances off his to-do list, Sigibert was focused in his ambitions, even plodding. Chilperic, by contrast, was scattershot. When the novelty of his prestigious bride, Galswintha, had worn off, Chilperic had realized the folly of mortgaging off such a large chunk of his kingdom. Once the newlyweds began fighting in earnest, the idea of shipping her off to a convent would have occurred to Chilperic, but he may have been worried that she might follow in Radegund's footsteps, setting herself up as an unofficial queen on his land.

When Galswintha's father had suddenly dropped dead, though, Chilperic had seen his chance to take care of the problem without immediate repercussions. Unlike in the Frankish lands, kingship was not hereditary among the Visigoths. When a king fell, the landed aristocracy met to elect his successor. While they did so, Spain entered a formal interregnum and so would be unable to launch a foreign war for many months.

The few tears Chilperic reportedly shed shortly after Galswintha's murder may have even been genuine: He was sad that things had come to this. It was nothing personal; Galswintha was simply no longer useful to him.

But Fredegund was. Chilperic was obviously incredibly attracted to her. And his attraction also solved several problems. A low-born woman came without the complications of a powerful family; she would be happy with whatever meager morgengabe he gave her. Chilperic already had plenty of legitimate heirs, and presumably an unlimited share of potential bedfellows. What he seems to have desired was a wife who shared both his relentlessness and his nerve—a partner who could help him expand his kingdom and outwit his brothers. For this task, Fredegund's past as a slave in the royal household was not necessarily an embarrassment. It was potentially useful. She had already overheard plenty of gossip and established a network of eyes and ears throughout the kitchens and bedchambers of the Neustrian aristocracy. She knew all sorts of things—which bishop was sleeping with his serving girl, and which duke with his manservant; which noble had been overheard drunkenly threatening to slit the throat of another. She was used to being underestimated and could turn it to her advantage.

But Brunhild was a quick study, too. Of course, her upbringing had been one of privilege. She grew up playing with toy animals made from clay and dolls made from ivory. She had a nursemaid and private tutors; she was waited on by a host of servants. But Brunhild had not always been a princess. Her father had been an aristocratic general who had rebelled against the previous king. While it was Athanagild's prowess on the battlefield that deposed the previous ruler, his wife, Goiswintha, helped, if not led, the behind-the-scenes campaign to get the votes to make her husband a legitimate king. Brunhild grew up watching her mother consolidating power, learning the lay of the land, and making friends. And now Brunhild tried to follow her mother's example.

However, the political situation in Francia was almost the reverse of that in Spain—here kingship was inherited, not elected, but noble rank was, for the most part, a temporary appointment. There were just two main titles in the realm, *comes* and *dux*. A *comes*, or count, was an administrator of a given city, responsible for calculating and collecting taxes. To do so, and to defend the city from attack, he had command of armed men, what we might think of as an early police force. Of higher rank was a *dux*, or duke, a skilled warrior with sufficient charisma to command his own private army. While dukes were principally officers who conducted military campaigns, they might also be called to serve as diplomats or judges. There seem to have been about two dozen counts in the Frankish lands, and about forty dukes. Other opportunities for a title came from appointments within the royal household to positions such as royal chamberlain or royal constable (from the Latin *comes stabuli*, or "Count of the Stable").

These appointed aristocrats were usually selected from established and influential families, but this was not a given; the social hierarchy was contested and fluid. Whatever their background, none of these nobles enjoyed job security. Most averaged just a few years in power before they lost their titles, and sometimes their lives, too. While there were a few cases of counts or dukes managing to install their sons or other relatives as their successors, it would be another half century until some of these ranks became hereditary.

Despite the precariousness of their positions, these nobles were not entirely powerless. Brunhild would have been aware that Sigibert, like his brothers, needed to lean heavily on his leading men because his holdings were so spread out. In his northernmost territories, the average distance between towns was sixty-five miles, more than a twelve-hour journey by horse and cart. If raiders attacked an outpost like Cologne, it would be three days before Sigibert received the news in Metz. He needed to be able to rely on his aristocrats to fight off invaders—and challengers from within his own family.

Even if his borders and his throne were secure, a Merovingian king still needed help. He was not just a warrior; he was also an administrator, bogged down in paperwork. There were diplomats to negotiate with, court cases to decide, laws to write, taxes to collect. Given the time it took to travel and send messages, his day-to-day was riddled with inefficiencies. A dissatisfied aristocrat could exacerbate these, scuttling trade negotiations, funneling tax monies elsewhere, or even fomenting a rebellion. Several nobles banded together would present an even greater threat.

Brunhild quickly discovered the nobles of her husband's court had divided themselves into three main factions. All wanted to ensure Austrasia's survival, but each had a different idea about how to do so.

One group wanted a close alliance with the Byzantine Empire.

Another wanted better relations with Chilperic and the kingdom of Neustria.

And a third group envisioned Austrasia uniting with Guntram, squeezing Chilperic out. This was the faction, in the aftermath of Galswintha's murder, that Brunhild was eager to ally herself with.

This anti-Chilperic contingent was headed up by a man she was already familiar with, Count Gogo. The silver-tongued diplomat had been sent to Spain to negotiate for her hand and, on their month-long trip back to

Austrasia, the two had a chance to get acquainted. And after the marriage proved successful, Gogo had been rewarded with a huge promotion—at just twenty-three years old, he became one of the king's top advisers, the Mayor of the Palace, a position similar to a contemporary secretary of state—so Gogo already had additional reasons to be, if not exactly beholden, at least grateful and deferential to Brunhild.

Gogo did not come from money; he had risen in life thanks to a quick wit, a top-notch classical education, and a talent for networking. To make up for his own lack of family connections, Gogo had formed a coalition with the descendants of the old Roman aristocracy. While the conquering Franks commanded the military, men from these families generally dominated the Church and cultural life. One of these Roman cultural leaders was Dynamius, the newly appointed governor of Provence. The dashing and urbane Dynamius was not just a civic leader, but an accomplished poet and prolific writer. Even Fortunatus was dazzled by Dynamius's literary talents (and perhaps his good looks, too). Fortunatus wrote poems to his new Provencal friend that were unusually affectionate, even given the social mores of the time, addressing Dynamius as "my love" and "my source of light" and seemingly pining for him, declaring "torn from my sight, you are with me, bound to my heart." Fortunatus's attachment to Dynamius suggests why the Italian poet, too, found himself loosely affiliated with the anti-Chilperic faction at court. And along with Fortunatus came his friend Gregory, as well as other Roman allies in the Church.

These poets and bishops were joined by a more pragmatic man: Wolf was descended from an old Roman family just like Dynamius and Gregory, a family with extensive lands in the plains of the Champagne region. But instead of pursuing the usual paths for a man of his station—a career in public service or the church, or a leisurely life overseeing his country estates—Wolf had joined the army. He had hoped that this was a surefire path to advance under a Frankish king, and his gamble had paid off. Wolf had campaigned against the Danes and the Saxons in the north, and when he returned victorious King Sigibert rewarded him with the title of Duke of Champagne.

Now this faction—Gogo, the ambitious count; Dynamius, the suave governor; and Wolf, the accomplished warrior—saw an opening to gain the upper hand at court. Their queen's sister had been murdered, and

Galswintha's morgengabe, a third of Chilperic's kingdom, now hung in the balance. Could there be a more compelling reason for a campaign against Neustria—to defend their queen's honor and commandeer valuable lands? It's not clear who approached whom, but the wisdom of a partnership with Brunhild was obvious.

· · ·

Racing to block any potential retribution against Chilperic was the pro-Neustria faction at Sigibert's court. This group was headed up by Duke Wolf's archenemy, Egidius, the bishop of Reims. Both men's families had significant holdings in the Champagne region; they had long been locked in a territorial dispute. Given that these lands lay on the border between Austrasia and Neustria, a more cautious personality like Egidius was likely worried that a war between the two kingdoms might mean his lands would be invaded and sacked.

But Egidius would have preferred to portray himself as above such family rivalries and worldly concerns. He was a bishop after all. Sigibert and Chilperic had long been at each other's throats. To reconcile the two kings in the name of God would be quite an accomplishment; the holy man who managed it could expect great rewards in heaven.

Other men in Egidius's group undoubtedly saw themselves similarly, as statesmen trying to head off a protracted civil war and unify the Franks. Within their ranks, though, were traditionalist Franks, who esteemed their people's barbarian history and bore little love for adopted Roman mores. Chief among them was Duke Ursio and his loyal sidekick, Duke Berthefred. Ursio distrusted outsiders; while he loved to conquer and pillage, he did not want to lead his men in battle against other Franks. He was suspicious of foreign alliances, and especially, as events would later prove, of foreign princesses.

Right into this divide swaggered Guntram Boso. When the ladies caught sight of him at court, they batted their lashes; the men stepped aside.

Duke Guntram Boso was one of the only men we know of in Francia to have two names—presumably out of sheer necessity. Because he was so prominent, Duke Guntram's deeds were in danger of getting jumbled up with, or even eclipsing, those of another prominent Guntram, the king of Burgundy.

Guntram Boso had been born with a sort of once-in-a-generation level of raw athletic power. Today, he might have become a star quarterback or Olympian; in the sixth century, Duke Boso dazzled on the field of battle. He would thunder in on horseback, cutting down dozens of men with ease. Even a seasoned warrior like Wolf could not come close to matching Boso's talents with a sword. In a world that worshipped warriors, he enjoyed near mythical status. This adulation had, quite naturally, made Guntram Boso cocky and brash, unafraid to speak his mind. The duke enjoyed relatively free rein, as the king and other nobles wanted to keep Boso fighting for Austrasia, rather than against it.

The duke seems to have headed up a third political faction at Sigibert's court, the pro–Byzantine party. But perhaps it would be better categorized as a pro–Boso party. Guntram Boso served Austrasia in name only. Everyone knew that his own self-interest came first, even if it was often unclear—even to Boso himself—what those interests actually were. If he championed closer ties with Byzantium, it was not for any ideological reasons. Most likely, Boso was intrigued by the glamour and wealth of the Byzantine court, dreaming of greater glory than he could find in Austrasia.

As Sigibert's court debated what to do about Chilperic's latest aggression, Gogo's party would have worked behind the scenes to entice Duke Boso. Without any foreign campaigns against the Saxons or Danes planned in the near future, a war with Neustria could fill the void and provide another chance to show off his prowess and collect more booty. And when Guntram Boso signaled that he would not oppose them, despite the grumblings of the pro-Neustria faction, Gogo's faction gained Sigibert's ear.

They had a plan. Brunhild's body had always been politicized. Now her grief could be, too. Fortunatus was summoned from Poitiers, where he had taken up residence to be close to the charismatic Radegund, and was commissioned to write a formal elegy for Galswintha. Ostensibly, its purpose would be to help Brunhild mourn her sister publicly. But it was also the first salvo in a public relations campaign, one that would clear the way for Sigibert to invade Chilperic's lands and, finally, make him pay.

. . .

Fortunatus's elegy for Galswintha turned out to be one of the longest poems he ever wrote, running a full 370 lines. It portrays Galswintha and

Chilperic's marriage as doomed from the beginning, the very opposite of Sigibert and Brunhild's wedding, which was acclaimed by cupids and songbirds. Fortunatus has Galswintha shaking with fear upon finding out about her engagement to Chilperic and all of Spain mourning her imminent departure with "rivers of tears."

At the news of Galswintha's death, Spain falls into even greater lamentations, and her grieving mother "collapses in distress, her knees giving way" and faints. The enraged mother of the murdered princess was still a major player in international politics; after the death of King Athanagild, she had married his successor. Fortunatus's elegy was reminding the Franks that Chilperic's actions had left them open to a retaliatory invasion.

The poem also made much of a miracle that was reported at Galswintha's interment: a glass-encased hanging lamp fell to the flagstone but did not shatter, nor did its light go out, which was taken as a sign that her spirit had not been extinguished. Fortunatus was making it clear that Galswintha was blameless, a saint. So not only were the Franks vulnerable to the revenge of the Visigoths, but also they might be drawing down the wrath of God himself.

Fortunatus's elegy had laid the groundwork. Then in 570 a court was convened to try Chilperic for the murder of Galswintha.

This legal proceeding was spurred on by one fortunate fact: Brunhild had just given birth to a son. The boy was born on Easter, which was seen as a particularly good omen. When he was baptized on Pentecost, he was named after one of Sigibert's illustrious uncles, Childebert, a renowned warrior son of the great King Clovis (who himself was noted for his piety and had ruled for forty-five years). Brunhild and Sigibert intended this name not just to ratify their son's claim to the Frankish Empire, but also to bestow all the things royals would want for their sons: success in battle, respect from the church, and a long reign.

Childebert's birth not only secured the succession in Austrasia, but it also resolved a tension in Sigibert's budding alliance with his brother Guntram. Upon Galswintha's death, rights to the lands of her morgengabe passed to her family; there was concern that her mother and the Visigoths would seize those precious lands. Sigibert had not been able to get Guntram to agree to retaliate against Chilperic while there was still the chance that the morgengabe, if recovered, might fall outside the Merovingian royal house. But now they could argue that Brunhild should be her sister's heir. Since Brunhild had two healthy surviving children, and more expected to follow, Guntram could be assured that even if something happened to Brunhild, those lands would remain in Frankish hands.

King Guntram, now the eldest Merovingian, served as judge at the trial. He presided from a raised dais, while a jury of Austrasian and Burgundian aristocrats sat below him on benches. Forming a ring behind them were their vassals, carrying each lord's sword and shield. Sigibert stood before this court to file an official complaint on behalf of his wife, accusing Chilperic of having orchestrated the murder of Galswintha, and presenting as evidence his brother's curious behavior and hasty remarriage after the death of his queen.

Chilperic was summoned to appear before the jury. He could have come to court and taken an oath. In the absence of an eyewitnesses to a crime, Frankish law allowed a man to bring to court seventy-two of his peers, who would line up behind him, thirty-six on his left and thirty-six on his right, and take a solemn oath in support of his innocence.

Chilperic could also, of course, have acknowledged his guilt and offered to pay Sigibert a wergeld worthy of his sister-in-law, but it would be something well above the six hundred solidi required for an ordinary woman. For the crime of killing a queen, there was precedent for a wergeld as high as fifty thousand solidi, which would have drained Chilperic's coffers.

Chilperic chose a third option: He never appeared to answer the charges. Not surprisingly, he was convicted in absentia.

This conviction would be the pretext for the invasion Sigibert and Guntram already had planned. They intended to recoup the morgengabe, plus spoils and plunder to compensate their armies for their time. But although they would start with those five cities in the Aquitaine given to Galswintha, Sigibert and Guntram also hoped they could use this war as a launching pad to seize their brother's entire kingdom and divide it between themselves.

CHAPTER 8

The Siege

S igibert and Guntram's forces enjoyed many early victories. The cities of Galswintha's morgengabe, encouraged by Fortunatus's elegy, put up little resistance and were quickly captured.

Things were going so well that Guntram even began having second thoughts. Throughout his life, Guntram lacked either the courage or the will to try to seize the entire empire for himself. But he always made sure none of his brothers could pull off that feat, either. He could be trusted to help drive out an aggressor but not always trusted to follow through and vanquish him entirely. Guntram wondered, if he and Sigibert did succeed, where would that leave him? Once Sigibert commanded Neustria, would he turn his eye to Burgundy next? Guntram decided to break his alliance with Sigibert, concerned about what might happen to him if Chilperic wasn't around to temper his brother's ambitions.

Guntram was convinced to rejoin the cause, however, when Sigibert assembled an invading force on his border. In doing so, Sigibert demonstrated both his resourcefulness and his daring. These new recruits were not Frankish men; they were Germanic pagans drawn from Sigibert's vassal kingdoms to the east. Sigibert lured them into the war with the promise of immense booty to be won. Some Frankish troops were reluctant to fight other Franks; these new troops had no such compunctions. Did Guntram want this unruly force on his side or fighting against him?

Once reunited, the two brothers seemed unstoppable. They soon had Chilperic in retreat, losing more of his territory with every passing month. Chilperic was forced into ever more desperate strategies. Without the hope of conquering (and holding) cities, he began to resort to a scorched-earth policy, looting and destroying towns even in his own territories.

By 575, the fighting had spread to Chilperic's front door in Soissons. He was forced to pack up his treasury and flee. Along with him came Fredegund and their children.

Like Brunhild, Fredegund had borne a daughter shortly after her wedding, and then in 570, she also produced a son, Clodobert, his name a nod to Clovis. Fredegund's position was now slightly more secure. She was not just the king's bedfellow, but the mother of a potential heir, and the respect she was accorded increased. If she were to lose favor with the king, she might still be shipped off to a convent, but with a living son it was unlikely that she would be killed outright.

At first, Clodobert's prospects were questionable. He already had three older half brothers who were being styled as leaders of their father's armies, so his odds of inheriting substantial land holdings were slim. But as the war dragged on, even at great cost to Neustria, Fredegund would have realized that her baby son's chances in life might be better than she had initially thought.

The first to fall was Chilperic's eldest son, Theudebert, the very prince whose life Sigibert had spared after that failed campaign years earlier. This time, Chilperic left Theudebert with just a few troops to protect the route to Paris. When warrior extraordinaire Duke Guntram Boso rode in with fresh recruits, Theudebert's only choice was to fight, breaking his oath not to attack his uncle's kingdom. Duke Boso's forces quickly overwhelmed the young prince. Theudebert was killed in his saddle, leading the doomed charge.

Now there were just two other boys with whom Fredegund's son might need to share an inheritance, and both were fighting on the front. Even better, Fredegund was pregnant again. She was certain she was carrying another son, her insurance policy—an heir and a spare.

. . .

As the indomitable Duke Boso plowed northward, Sigibert and his army caught up with them. Messengers were sent back to Metz to fetch Brunhild and the children. They were to enter Paris as a family, triumphant. The royal couple's plan was coming together. They had the enthusiastic backing of their allies in Visigothic Spain to the west. With Radegund's help, they had smoothed out their relationship with Byzantium to the east. Guntram was in their corner. Although Paris had most recently been Charibert's capital, it had once been the seat of the great King Clovis; from there he had ruled all of Francia. Surely Sigibert and Brunhild, who wished for their union to start a new dynasty, understood the symbolism of seizing this city.

As news of the Austrasian army's approach reached Paris, the local bishop, Germanus, sat down to compose a letter. The city had sustained enormous damage during the civil war, and Germanus was anxious that it would be spared any further destruction. The letter was not addressed to Sigibert, however, nor to one of his dukes. Instead, Bishop Germanus wrote to Brunhild.

The most elevated title a king could aspire to in the early medieval world was that of *praecellentissimus rex*, or "most excellent king," reserved for only the most powerful of monarchs. Now Bishop Germanus crafted a similar title for Brunhild: *praecellentissima . . . regin[a]*, "most excellent queen." Fortunatus had made a comment about Brunhild on her wedding day that might have passed as mere hyperbole, but in hindsight seems prophetic: *unde magis pollens regina uocatur*, "growing more mighty, she is hailed as a queen." Now Brunhild's influence was clearly on the rise, so much so that Bishop Germanus expected *her*, more than any count or duke, to have the ear of the king. Germanus made the Austrasians an offer—he would turn over Paris in exchange for the promise not to pillage it: "Show your prudence and the vigor and perfection of your faith towards this region . . . and let the people of [this] region live in quiet."

Paris was not entirely defenseless. The Île de la Cité was surrounded by seven-foot stone ramparts and the moat of the Seine. On the west side of the island, at the site of today's Conciergerie, was a fortress that had been converted into a palace; until recently it had been the home of Charibert.

A small section of the Right Bank of the Seine was fortified and inhabited, connected to the Île de la Cité by a single bridge, the Grand Pont. A royal hunting preserve ringed the settlement to the north, an ancient oak forest thick with bears and deer. The entire Left Bank, connected to the

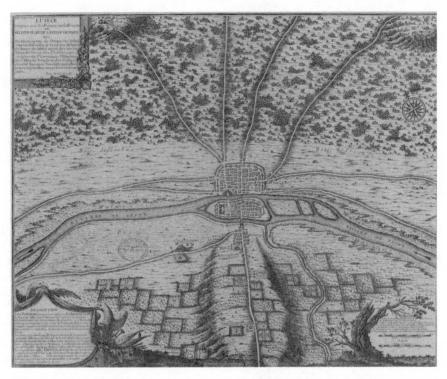

Map of sixth-century Paris

rest of the city by the Petit Pont, was unfortified and a mix of cemeteries and farmland. (Bishop Germanus would later lend his name to a neighborhood in this area of Paris: today's Saint-Germain-des-Près.) These farms, important food sources for the city, had been decimated once before during the course of this civil war. The two wooden bridges onto the island had been pulled up or burned while the Parisians waited out the invaders and watched the destruction from behind the walls of the Île de la Cité.

But this time, the bridges were left standing. With banner and standards waving, Brunhild, Sigibert, and their three children rode in triumphant and took up residence at the palace.

. . .

Bishop Germanus's entreaty to Brunhild was not the only sign of her growing influence within the Frankish Church. She had also managed to have the priest Gregory appointed Bishop of Tours.

This was an especially plum appointment. Tours was a city of great strategic importance due to its position on the River Loire, which provided access to the Atlantic Ocean and served as a north-south trade route. Tours was also the capital city of an entire ecclesiastic province. Its bishop was called a *metropolitan*, akin to a contemporary archbishop, and only the pope, far removed in Rome, was his ecclesiastical superior. And the bishop of Tours not only oversaw all of the clergy in the diocese, but he also controlled the Basilica of Saint Martin, the most important church in all of Francia. It was a towering, glittering basilica that housed the remains of the Franks' patron saint. (Their special affinity for Saint Martin likely stemmed from his service as a calvary officer in the Roman army. The soldier-turned-monk bridged the worlds of the Franks' two biggest institutions—the army and the Church.) Saint Martin's was not only an especially holy site, but it was also a politically significant one—it had been the site of King Clovis's imperial coronation.

Although Gregory had long been groomed for just such a post (there were a total of seven bishops on his mother's side of the family), his candidacy was met with some opposition. Brunhild's support, along with that of King Sigibert, had helped secure his post. Gregory was likely mortified to be seen needing a woman's help, and he conveniently omits any mention of this detail from his writings; we only find out about Brunhild's role from Fortunatus's account of the events.

Gregory of Tours had been appointed at a most unfortunate time. Before Prince Theudebert was killed in battle, he had razed the countryside on his father Chilperic's orders; one of his targets had been Gregory's new dominion. The new bishop was indignant that the prince had "burned most of the district of Tours, and would have destroyed all of it, had not the inhabitants surrendered in time." Now the bishop Brunhild had worked hard to install fell under Chilperic's jurisdiction.

There was good reason, though, to hope this turn of events would be temporary. Neustria's royal family had just fled their usual strongholds and headed north to hole up in the city of Tournai. Gregory was pleased to record an omen that seemed to indicate Chilperic's end was near: "lightning was observed to flicker across the sky, just as we saw it before [his father] Clothar's death."

. . .

While Brunhild was feted as Queen of Paris, Fredegund found herself queen of a bunker, and due to give birth again at any moment.

Tournai, a port city on the river Scheldt, could in more ordinary times have been a stopping point on a royal tour: It had been the birthplace of King Clovis, and his first capital, before he had moved his headquarters to Paris. But now Tournai's main appeal was its strong walls. Behind these walls, Fredegund and her children, her six-year-old daughter, Rigunth, and four-year-old son, Clodobert, were subjected daily to the sounds of war—sentries sounding the alarms, the whizz of arrows from the towers, the clatter of scaling ladders knocked back down, the crush of the giant rocks catapulted over the walls, the rattle of the rams against the city gates, shrieks and screams.

And the smoke. Acrid and choking, it was everywhere. There were fires for cooking and warmth throughout the stone rooms of the fortress, and also in the courtyards, not just for the soldiers, but for the merchants and country folk stuck with them behind the walls. And outside the walls, the fields, the meadows, the orchards blazed. The Austrasian army had set it all on fire, making sure there would be no place to graze the animals, no way to grow crops, nothing to forage.

Every day word came of defections, another of Chilperic's counts or dukes swearing allegiance to Sigibert. Chilperic himself had fallen into a sort of stupor, "not knowing whether he could escape alive or would be killed instead." And then Fredegund went into labor.

She survived the birth, and the baby was another boy, a cause for some small joy amid the devastation. But when Fredegund was told the news by whatever servant cleaned the infant and wrapped him in blankets, she would not take him or allow him to nurse. She did not want to see her baby, did not want to hold him.

The reason is a mystery. Gregory's is the only surviving contemporary account, and his phrasing is difficult to follow. A literal translation is that Fredegund "cast aside" the baby and "desired to kill him," although some translators have softened the expression, writing that Fredegund "wished he would die." Fredegund did so because *ob metum mortis*, because she had a fear of death.

Gregory's text does not indicate exactly whose death Fredegund feared. One reading is altruistic—Fredegund fully expected to die at the hands of the army outside the walls, either from starvation during the siege or from capture if Tournai fell, and she wished to save her baby from suffering. Or Fredegund expected to die from the birth itself, and she was delirious with some infection. Still, it is curious that Gregory relays the queen's refusal to baptize the child, as an unbaptized infant could not follow her to heaven.

A more callous reading is that Fredegund feared her baby would die, and her first priority was self-preservation—if the baby was weak or sickly she did not want to invest any time or resources into his care. A third possibility—neglected by historians, but no less plausible—is that Fredegund was suffering from postpartum depression, even psychosis. Such struggles may have been made worse by the trauma of the siege, especially if it forced her to relive the circumstances of some previous battle she had endured as a child.

Regardless of the reason, Chilperic was forced out of his stupor to intervene. He "rebuked" his queen, and Fredegund had the child baptized on his orders. The ceremony was performed by Tournai's bishop, who was stuck behind the walls with them. The baby may have received a prince's baptism, but he was given a distinctly un-Merovingian name, one that stands out in all the chronicles of the era: Samson. Naming the prince after the long-haired biblical strongman could have been a coy attempt to disguise his identity as a member of the royal family and to set him up for a life as a monk. Or possibly it was an act of defiance, to forever link the bald infant to the long-haired kings of his line. Or maybe the strange name was a premonition—this baby would never rule.

. . .

Once installed in Paris with his armies, Sigibert received a delegation from the nobles in Chilperic's northernmost territories, who offered to "abandon Chilperic and make [Sigibert] king over them." Sigibert rode out from Paris to accept their offer and to join the siege of Tournai, to finish his brother off. About forty miles outside of Tournai, Sigibert commandeered one of Chilperic's nearby royal villas. He was joined there by defecting Neustrian nobles as well as lines of troops waving white flags of surrender. Soon the fields outside the villa were blanketed with soldier's tents as thousands upon thousands gathered to celebrate a new king.

Sigibert was hoisted up on a shield, as was the custom, and carried through the admiring throngs. The soldiers beat their shields with the flats of their swords and the valley rang with their chant: "Sigibert, King of the Franks! Long live the king!"

. . .

Chilperic and the few loyal advisers he had left were up late into the night. The end was near—this was the time to make one's last confession, say prayers, write out a will and disperse one's personal property. Yet in a separate wing, Fredegund called two people into her chambers, and neither of them was a priest. They were *duo pueri*, two slave boys, and Fredegund already knew them in some capacity—whether from her own time serving in the royal household, or from her time commanding it.

She would have still been bleeding postpartum, and her breasts ached with milk. Despite whatever storm may still have been raging in the aftermath of Samson's traumatic birth, she was surprisingly clearheaded. Fredegund sat and spoke with the boys for some time. She wanted them to slip out of Tournai and ride to the gathering at Vitry-en-Artois, where the armies were celebrating Sigibert's election as king of Austrasia and Neustria. Once there, she wanted them to assassinate Sigibert.

It was a foolhardy plan, to walk into an enemy camp, during the inauguration celebration of a king. The boys couldn't be sure they would manage to get anywhere close to Sigibert, who was surrounded by tens of thousands of loyal, armed men. And even if they did, they had no hope of getting out alive. This was a suicide mission.

There was no chance of overpowering Sigibert's trained guard, so Fredegund had come up with something more innovative. It was common during the time for all men to carry a scramasax, a sort of hunting knife with a single-edged twelve-inch blade. They were more often used for cutting meat or rope and couldn't do much damage unless one was in close hand-to-hand combat. Because such knives were so ubiquitous, the boys could carry them openly on their belts and still appear unarmed. Fredegund also handed the boys a small glass vial—of poison.

While a poisoned dagger is a tired enough trope now, it was virtually unheard of at the time. The most widely available Merovingian poison was cyanide, extracted from apricots, which only worked if directly ingested. There were also a variety of toxic potions made from herbs and berries. As a result, poisoning food and drink was incredibly common. Museums showcase cups from the period that were designed with uneven bottoms as a safety measure; if their owners set their drinks down and left them unattended, the contents automatically spilled out.

Poisoned arrows were often used for hunting or war. Arrows could be tipped in substances such as dung or animal pus to make a wound likely to become infected, but those were slow killers. Much faster were concoctions made of nightshade or the sap of rhododendron. The only known poisons in the Merovingian arsenal that could kill on contact were wolfsbane and snake venom. Both had their limitations: They lost potency fairly quickly and needed to be applied right before an attack.

If this account of Sigibert's assassination is to be believed, Fredegund had access to both the medical texts of antiquity and the ability to compound dangerous herbs or extract snake venom. She was also knowledgeable enough about how these poisons worked to instruct the boys to wait until they were inside the camp before they smeared the concoction on their scramasaxes. They agreed and rode off to their certain deaths. No one knew if the plan would work.

In the morning, the boys likely managed to get into the camp by declaring themselves Neustrian defectors. They smeared their blades with the poison, hung them back on their belts, and raced to see if they could get close to King Sigibert. They were in luck. They caught up with the king on his way from one tent to another and "pretend[ed] they had something to discuss with him." Their youth and apparent lack of armor and weapons set his bodyguards at ease. As the king stopped and turned to hear what they might say, "they struck him on both sides."

It wouldn't have taken much, just the smallest wound. Confused, Sigibert gave a little cry and fell. His guard quickly killed the two boys, but it was to no avail. Within minutes, the "Magnificent Victory" was dead.

CHAPTER 9

The Witch and the Nun

W hen Chilperic summoned his wife and children, his cloak and boots would have still been coated with dust. He had ridden hard to Vitry-en-Artois to inspect the body himself, and finding it to be that of his brother, he had ordered it to be dressed in a shroud and given a Christian burial. And now, he told the children, the siege was over, thanks to their mother. They would return home to their palace, away from the shrieks and the smoke.

Sigibert's killing broke the rules of armed engagement, especially for a people who idealized confronting one's enemy face-to-face on the field in combat. One bishop disapprovingly noted that Sigibert "had already boxed [Chilperic] in" and the victor was vanquished only "through deception." Yet Chilperic seemed indifferent to the fact that others thought his brother's assassination cowardly.

This view of Sigibert's death as underhanded and shifty was only intensified by the reports of Fredegund's involvement and of her use of poison. The insinuations were contained in the words themselves—the Latin for poison, *venenum*, already overlapped with the word for witchcraft, *veneficium* (and both derived from the same root as Venus, the crafty goddess of love). Building upon this, in an account that must have been colored by his loyalty to his patron Brunhild, Gregory went so far as to describe Fredegund's actions using the Latin *malificati*, an act of witchcraft. Not

*A fourteenth-century rendition of Fredegund's
assassins stabbing King Sigibert*

only could the slave-queen read, not only could she convince a king to
cast aside a princess for her, but she could also convince her followers to
undertake a suicide mission. How could a lowly slave have such a knack
for strategy? The haughty Gregory assumed she must be a witch, and
rumors to that effect had trailed Fredegund for as long as she had been in
the public eye.

The Franks could not agree whether dragons still roamed the woods,
but there was a consensus that witches certainly did. Of course, whether
any occurrence qualified as magic or a miracle had a lot to do with whom
one's enemies happened to be. Even within the Church, an up-and-
coming cleric could be lauded for performing miracles at the same time
his political opponents denounced him as a sorcerer. But since unexplained forces swirled all around, the Franks had at their disposal a robust
vocabulary for describing those who could harness supernatural powers,
from astrologers (*astrologi*) to enchanters (*incantores*), as well as legal terms
for all sorts of witchcraft paraphernalia and crimes. There was a hefty
wergeld for casting an "evil spell" (*maleficium*). There were special terms,
too, for a man who helped carry a witch's cauldron (*strioportio*) and for the
crime of "a witch eat[ing] a man" (*granderba*).

One could not call a woman a witch casually or in jest. It was a serious
charge, one that was considerably worse than questioning her virtue. The

fine for slandering a woman as a witch was 187 ½ solidi, while it was only 45 solidi if one falsely called her a whore. The law even considered it worse to accuse a woman of witchcraft than to assault her—the wergeld was three times higher than for forcible rape. By attacking a queen in this manner, Gregory was taking a risk. He must not have seen himself as an outlier in holding this view; there was safety in numbers. If there had long been whispers among the servants about Fredegund's dark arts, now there were accusations swirling among the bishops and aristocrats.

Fredegund didn't mind. In fact, throughout her reign, neither she nor her husband ever appears to have tried to counter the charges of murder or combat the rumors of witchcraft. She preferred to be feared. When crowds gathered to watch the royal family ride back to the Neustrian capital of Soissons, Fredegund would not have bowed her head. She would have met their gaze, smiling.

. . .

Toward the end of the campaign against Chilperic, powerful Neustrians who saw which way the wind was blowing had pledged themselves to Sigibert. Now, in the uncertainty and confusion following his assassination, many who had switched sides suddenly outdid one another to prove their loyalty. They captured several of Sigibert's attendants and executed a few of them for good measure. Some opportunistic Austrasians even joined them.

The remaining Austrasians at Vitry-en-Artois, who watched their king fall at the height of his glory, were stunned. They could not know that the assassins had been extraordinarily lucky, and would have wondered how coordinated the betrayal was. Was Sigibert's young son back in Paris dead as well? They chose to make a quick retreat, to get back on Austrasian soil and regroup. On their way south, they passed by Paris, where, in the windows of the fortress overlooking the Seine, three small children and a wealthy young widow waited.

Brunhild had expected to watch Sigibert process back to Paris after his inauguration ceremony, trailed by cheering warriors. A messenger at breakneck speed would have made it to Paris within a day of Sigibert's assassination. If Brunhild had seen the lone figure galloping madly for the city gates, she wouldn't, at first, have registered the arrival with any dread. If she expected any news, it was of Chilperic's surrender or death.

The news was a double blow. She would have grieved Sigibert's loss keenly. The royal pair had shared, if not romantic love, at least mutual respect and a good working relationship. But she would also be mourning the loss of her own political position.

To ensure her own survival, one option was to try to seize the throne herself. Brunhild was in a much better position than Theudechild had been as the mother of a living son. But the royal treasury was back in Metz, and without it Brunhild did not have the financial means to guarantee the loyalty of Sigibert's nobles. Returning to Metz would take her a few days, especially traveling with three small children, but she would be unprotected in the countryside, an easy target for bandits or assassins. And marauders might be the least of her worries—like Sigibert's fleeing nobles, she had no way of knowing if Sigibert's killers had merely been lucky or if they were part of some larger plot. She decided to wait in Paris, where at least she had the protection of the city walls, while she figured out her next move.

She had to keep her son alive to have any chance of maintaining her influence. Five-year-old boys died of accidents and illnesses all the time. And the odds of such a misfortune befalling the young king would be even greater if he were to fall into the hands of his uncle, who was marching fast on the heels of the fleeing Austrasians.

Young Childebert needed to be smuggled out of Paris, and quickly. It is not clear exactly how this was accomplished—hidden in a basket of linens, a cart of vegetables? One chronicle written nearly a century later would recount how the boy was put in a bag and passed through a window. One can imagine the wooden rowboat bobbing on the murky Seine, just below the seven-foot walls around the fortress, the small splash of the burlap sack before it was hauled up, and the young mother silhouetted at the window, her hand over her mouth.

. . .

It was days later that Chilperic came face-to-face with Brunhild in the palace in Paris. This moment has long been portrayed as Chilperic bursting in on a frightened queen busy shielding her children from his wrath. But the sources closest to the event suggest that when Chilperic confronted the queen, her expression cold and imperious, he was surprised to find her alone.

There have long been questions about why Brunhild didn't bother to flee Paris with her children. Even if she could not make it all the way back to Metz, the Austrasian border was a little more than thirty miles away, not an impossible distance. Was there no country villa or noble's estate where she could hide? Was it that she was too distraught to think straight, as Gregory suggested? Or was it that she was afraid to leave her worldly treasure behind?

If she were to leave Paris, Brunhild would also have to part with what may have been her only remaining resource. She had brought some of her personal wealth to Paris, five bundles of gold, approximately 12,500 solidi. It was too much to simply abandon, nor was it easily portable, but it was not enough to guarantee her political survival, so she found the next best use for it. Borrowing a maneuver straight from the animal world, Brunhild stayed in Paris with this considerable treasure, luring Chilperic to her and giving her offspring time to escape. Not only was Childebert smuggled out of Paris, but her daughters were, too. The girls made it just over the Austrasian border to the town of Meaux.

King Chilperic seized Brunhild and her treasure, and then sent his troops to scour the countryside for her children. Young Childebert was long gone, but Brunhild's daughters were not so deep in Austrasian territory that they couldn't be scooped up. His men were able to detain his nieces in Meaux (likely with the help of his loyal chamberlain, whose family lived in this city).

Although doubtlessly annoyed that his nephew had escaped, Chilperic was in high spirits—ecstatic to be alive and to still have a kingdom. He was more magnanimous than he might have been otherwise. As his guards came to escort her away, Chilperic informed Brunhild that she was to be kept alive and treated well; however, like most royal widows, she would be warehoused in a convent. But if Brunhild was expecting to be reunited with her daughters, the king quickly disabused her of that notion.

Chilperic was not a simpleton. If Brunhild's Visigothic relatives were to consider launching a rescue mission—or if, like Theudechild, she were to get any ideas of escape—she would leave her girls at Chilperic's mercy.

Her daughters were safe for now, but the king would have made sure Brunhild understood that in her absence he might not act in their best interests.

. . .

On Christmas Day 575, a boy was installed on the Austrasian throne by a somber court. He had not yet started to lose his baby teeth and he could barely heft the scepter. For his Frankish subjects, who valued prowess in battle above all else, this was worrisome, especially as they expected an attack from Chilperic in the spring.

Who was going to lead the defense of their kingdom? Among the nobles and soldiers regrouping in Metz, anti-Neustrian sentiment was obviously high, and so was sympathy for the grieving queen now in Chilperic's clutches. The faction headed up by Brunhild's closest allies, Duke Wolf and Count Gogo, prevailed. Gogo even angled for, and received, the position of *nutritor* of the boy-king. The title translates as "one who feeds the king," and it meant that Gogo was, essentially, the boy's official regent and protector.

Brunhild, meanwhile, was brought under armed escort to the Neustrian stronghold of Rouen and placed in a convent, most likely Les Andelys in the countryside. This small convent had been established by Clovis's wife and designed for former queens. It sat high on a hill overlooking limestone cliffs and a crook in the Seine.

Many convents, including Radegund's in Poitiers and the one in Arles where Theudechild was imprisoned, followed a strict code set by the ascetic Caesarius of Arles in his *Rule for Virgins*. Caesarius dictated what foods the sisters could eat as well as the exact fabrics they could wear (white robes of "ordinary cloth or linen") and how they might be decorated (only with simple white or black crosses). Noble women, accustomed to having a throng of servants dress them and arrange their hair, found themselves barred from having even a single lady's maid. But most important, all women living under the rule of Caesarius were completely cloistered, unable to ever visit the outside world. Any exchanges with priests or tradespeople were transacted behind a veil and a wooden grille (although Radegund, true to form, managed to wriggle around this prohibition).

Even though Les Andelys likely followed a more lenient rule—we do not know for sure—Brunhild's daily routine would still have been upended.

She set aside her brightly dyed silks for simple, rough robes. She awoke in her cell in the dark at two in the morning to the bells calling her for the first of eight prayers and chants of the day. Her hours were to be spent reading religious texts, copying manuscripts, embroidering and weaving, and praying for the soul of her deceased husband. Brunhild had no wish to live her life this way, secluded and shadowed, silent. But if she did not care to remain in the convent, she needed a way out, and the fastest was a husband.

Brunhild's mother, Queen Goiswintha, had remained a player in international affairs by marrying her husband's successor. This was the map Brunhild had been handed, the practiced path to power. With a new, influential husband at her side, she could return to the Austrasian court, could even take over for Gogo as regent for her young son. But where, in the walled gardens and the vaulted corridors, was Brunhild to find herself a man?

CHAPTER 10

Back Channels

After his hair had been ignominiously hacked off, Sigibert's half brother, Gundovald, had been banished to Cologne, an outpost of the Frankish Empire. But within weeks he had escaped with the help of the Byzantines, who set him up at their court in Italy while he grew his hair out again. Despite the new alliance with Sigibert's kingdom that Radegund had helped to broker, the Byzantines had also seen the usefulness of having their own Merovingian prince, even a bastard one. Gundovald might make for a future claimant to the throne, a Byzantine puppet-king, if the rest of his brothers kept dying.

Gundovald went on to marry and have two boys; his wife seems to have died in childbirth with the youngest. Once widowed, he moved to Constantinople, joining the crowd of foreign hangers-on at the imperial court—overthrown princes, exiled nobles, and royal bastards kept in reserve. But once Sigibert fell and a five-year-old sat on the throne, the Byzantine court had the perfect job for their Merovingian prince. He was the obvious choice for a new husband for Brunhild, a carbon copy of Sigibert. The fact that he was only an illegitimate half brother of the murdered king might enable them to wiggle around the Church's incest prohibitions. Even better, Gundovald had potential claims to Charibert's former lands and, it was noted, he already had a rapport with the widowed queen.

It was an easy solution, and one that would have satisfied two of the major Austrasian factions and likely proved acceptable to Brunhild herself, but a host of complications presented themselves. The new Byzantine emperor, Justin II, had gone mad around 573, in the middle of the Merovingian brothers' civil war. The cause of his illness is now thought to have been a parathyroid tumor, but at the time his subjects assumed he was possessed. It was reported that the emperor now "barked like a dog, and bleated like a goat; and then he would mew like a cat, and then again crow like a cock," before hiding under his bed for hours on end.

His wife, Sophia, stepped in to rule in his stead. The empress had already proven herself to be an astute politician, and she did a more than competent job by herself for over an entire year. Still, at the end of 574, to win over a public wary of powerful women, she had asked Tiberius, the commander of the imperial guard, to rule with her as co-regent.

The empress had established a connection with Brunhild through the negotiations over the True Cross fragment for Radegund's abbey. But even in the best of circumstances Sophia would have found it difficult to broker a marriage between Gundovald and Brunhild while the bride was locked away in a convent in Neustrian-controlled territory. And in 575 Sophia had her hands full—she was hiring carpenters to bar the windows to keep Justin from flinging himself out. She had to continually replenish the ranks of imperial chamberlains since Justin kept attacking and savagely biting them. She could barely hear herself think: In an attempt to soothe Justin's fits and nightmares, organ music thundered night and day. In his calmer moments, one could hear the emperor shrieking over the chords as his chamberlains pushed him up and down the palace hallways in "a little wagon, with a throne upon it for him to sit upon."

Tiberius was little help. He had been in his position for only a matter of months, and didn't have the communication or transport networks in place to open marriage talks with the Austrasian court, which was still in tatters after Sigibert's assassination and the deaths and defections of so many nobles.

But another possibility soon presented himself.

. . .

It is easy to imagine them first catching sight of each other over a meal of simple stew at the long tables in the convent's great hall. Or one slipping in next to the other in a chapel pew as they knelt to chant psalms.

Chilperic's first wife, Audovera, was living in Rouen that year. Many years earlier she had been parked in a convent there, and there's little reason to believe she had since left. (It is hard to imagine Chilperic allowing his first wife to roam freely about town during his elaborate wedding to Galswintha, or to imagine that Fredegund would have allowed the same once she took the throne.) As there is no record of another convent in the Rouen area other than Les Andelys, it is very likely that Audovera and Brunhild found themselves in the exact same place.

Even if, for some reason, Audovera was not at the convent but living on some other estate in the countryside, it would have been easy enough for her to arrange a meeting. She had been in Rouen for at least a decade and had plenty of time to develop neighborly acquaintances and useful friendships that could gain her (or at the very least a trusted intermediary) access to Brunhild.

The two women had much to discuss. They shared the experience of being an ousted queen, and they also had a common pressing concern— Fredegund. She had a hand in the murder of Brunhild's sister and had arranged the assassination of Brunhild's husband. She had also taken Audovera's title, and now she was an increasing threat to Audovera's children.

To be dismissed from court by her own slave girl, ushered away with a baby in her arms, must have deeply wounded Audovera's pride. Worse still, the baby had died. But it seems Audovera tried to make the best of things, at least initially, for the sake of her children. Her other daughter might still make an important marriage, and at the time her boys had been given prominent positions in Chilperic's kingdom and stood to inherit everything upon his death. The best course of action had seemed to be to wait for her ex-husband to tire of his new plaything.

But Audovera had to be alarmed now that Fredegund had given birth to two boys. Scraps between royal women for their children's advantage often turned deadly; most recently, one of King Guntram's concubines had poisoned the son of another to benefit her own offspring. What would stop Fredegund from doing the same? Audovera would have heard the rumors circulating that Fredegund had rejoiced after Theudebert had fallen in battle. One less heir for Fredegund's boys to split the kingdom with. In fact—even though Chilperic was known to have mounted a revenge plot to hunt down Duke Boso, the party most responsible for the prince's death—it was said that Fredegund openly praised Theudebert's killer. Only the most cavalier of mothers would have dismissed the possible danger to her two surviving sons.

And so the plan took shape while Brunhild and Audovera walked back from matins or paced the gardens. But for it to work, they would need the help of their fellow nuns.

. . .

The bishop of Rouen, Praetextatus, was an old man well into his sixties. He had been appointed long before Chilperic gained his crown, but he had stayed loyal to the Neustrian king after his father's death, even throughout the civil war. It was for this very reason that first Audovera, and then Brunhild, had been sent to Rouen. It was a mark of the king's favor for a bishop to have an important royal "guest" in his city, no matter how unwilling she might be. And the bishop had been given their personal treasures to manage during their stays.

As another mark of favor, Bishop Praetextatus had been designated the godfather of Chilperic's second son by Audovera. This boy was auspiciously named Merovech after the founder of the entire Merovingian dynasty. And following the death of his older brother, Theudebert, on the battlefield, this second Merovech was now his father's most trusted general. But Merovech, like his mother, had to be aware of Fredegund's ambition. His new position as head of Neustria's army would soon draw his stepmother's attention, unless he could create alliances to keep himself safe.

Chilperic regained the territory he had lost in the civil war, and then, knowing the shambles the Austrasian court was in, he went after some of his dead brother's holdings. Chilperic had his eye on Poitiers and Tours, two important tax bases that he had already tried to snatch away from Sigibert when he was living. In the spring of 576, Merovech was sent with the Neustrian army to conquer Poitiers. But, curiously, he disobeyed his father's orders and went first to the city of Tours.

. . .

Within the walled world of the convent, women reigned. They had to rely on priests for the sacraments, but aside from that, they ruled themselves.

And while certain convents catered more to wealthy widows or exiled aristocrats than others, all communities would have had a mix of ages and social classes. Their members would have included plenty for whom the convent was a genuine refuge—women avoiding an unwanted marriage and women escaping domestic violence. The high stone walls kept them safe from rape and abduction, which were endemic at the time. For others, the convent was an opportunity for a career outside the home. The same rules that kept women segregated from the outside world also saved them from household drudgery: they were forbidden from doing sewing and cooking for anyone other than their fellow nuns, which may have been a better option than nonstop housework for one's in-laws, extended family, and children.

There were some things, though, that the women would not give up—it was said that pious Radegund hung on to her dice, games of chance being the one royal privilege she would not part with. The nuns of her abbey occasionally engaged in raucous gambling parties. And clearly, many other nuns were not willing to give up their contact with the outside world. The widowed Queen Theudechild had managed to smuggle out messages to her dear Goth, evidence that there were some pipelines to the outside.

Theudechild's plans had been stymied by the other women at the convent in Arles. Just as some had obviously helped her to smuggle messages out, someone had informed on her to the abbess. But Audovera would have had a firm handle on abbey politics, and a good idea of which sisters could be trusted to avert their eyes, or even to be of use. A door left unlocked. A wooden grille unsecured. A message slipped to a visitor—the old stonemason patching a wall, the farmwife delivering a new cow, or the family member bringing news of a birth or death. Messages could also be relayed through the religious bureaucracy, through the priests who visited to give the sacraments or the monks delivering relics that had been loaned out for particular holy celebrations.

Merovech arrived in Tours just in time for Easter week. The prince, preparing to celebrate the holiest Christian observance of the year, would have then stopped to pray in the city's grand basilica and kiss the sarcophagus of Francia's patron saint. The Basilica of Saint Martin of Tours, the site where King Clovis had been crowned Augustus, was also a fitting spot for Merovech to learn how he might gain his own crown.

It's not clear who the messenger was. The first and most obvious possibility was Bishop Gregory himself. Brunhild's ally and Merovech certainly met face-to-face; at the very least, Gregory would have, as custom dictated, welcomed the prince to the city and invited him to Easter Mass. Another potential messenger could have met with Merovech as he headed to or from Mass, as she happened to live right in the courtyard of Saint Martin's: the well-connected nun Ingritude. She had spent her youth at court and even after taking the veil, she continued to dabble in politics. Ingritude was also a friend of Radegund's (and presumably, similarly loyal to Brunhild). Inside the basilica itself was yet another prominent Austrasian: Duke Guntram Boso, the very one who had killed Merovech's older brother in battle. King Chilperic's retaliatory attempts to hunt Boso down had spurred him to seek sanctuary on holy ground, and the duke and members of his family were by this point living in hiding in the church. So while Merovech was at Saint Martin's, there were at least three separate opportunities for him to receive a communication from Audovera and Brunhild.

Merovech's holiday in Tours wasn't a quiet or sneaky detour; he had directly disobeyed his father's orders and Merovech's large army, eager to get to the fighting and looting, "did great damage to that district," which Chilperic was sure to hear complaints about. Yet Merovech stopped in Tours and prayed in the church where his great-grandfather had formalized his rule—giving himself time to send messages, to steel himself for some important decision. Because once the Easter celebrations were over, instead of proceeding south to Poitiers, Merovech marched his army north, nearly two hundred miles in the opposite direction, to visit his mother in Rouen.

· · ·

Brunhild's second wedding was less lavish, but not terribly different from the first. She had changed back into her brightly dyed linens and silks, taken off her nun's veil and let her hair loose around her shoulders, wreathed again with spring flowers. Another celebrated warrior had slipped off his armor to kneel next to her, and an influential bishop was, again, leading the exchange of vows.

This time it was Bishop Praetextatus and the groom was his godson, Merovech. Praetextatus's involvement was curious for two reasons. First, he was openly defying the king he had been loyal to for so long. And second, the union he was blessing was, technically, incestuous. Church law forbade a marriage to an uncle's widow. Just a few years before, Praetextatus had voted to excommunicate King Charibert for his escapades with two sisters, but now his standards seemed more flexible.

Perhaps Praetextatus felt his role as Merovech's godfather trumped all else. Or maybe he was interpreting the incest prohibition rather liberally and genuinely did not think it applied in these circumstances. After all, Chilperic and Sigibert had been half brothers, and Brunhild was only Merovech's aunt through marriage. Or perhaps Praetextatus had more worldly matters in mind. The groom was now the stepfather to the king of Austrasia and one of the heirs to the kingdom of Neustria. The old bishop could be more than a jailor for two deposed queens; he might become the spiritual adviser to a new king.

The cathedral of Rouen, the same cathedral that had been filled to the brim for Galswintha's marriage, was now eerily empty. One can imagine the couple sneaking a few giddy glances at each other at the altar. The groom was a few years younger than the bride, but that was of little concern. Brunhild was now in her midtwenties, still considered young, and still very beautiful. They made a good-looking couple, and they were well aware of it.

But this was not a romance. This was a rebellion.

CHAPTER 11

Uprising

The marriage between the widowed queen of Austrasia and the Neustrian prince was treasonous—incestuous, even—so what was the goal of such a risky union?

Historians' answers to this question have typically revealed their own biases. Some scholars speculate that Merovech had taken advantage of a grieving widow. Unsure of his chances of inheriting his father's throne, and understandably wary of his stepmother, the prince had decided to make a play for power in neighboring Austrasia. Brunhild, befuddled or despondent, had viewed his offer of marriage as her only option.

Yet this explanation does not fit with what we know of Brunhild as a mother and stateswoman. Having made sure her five-year-old son was safely smuggled out of Paris and then installed as king, the queen was unlikely to then conspire to unseat him. And Brunhild had been a widow for nearly half a year; no matter the depths of her grief, it's unlikely she would be immobilized by shock. She had acted strategically in the immediate aftermath of Sigibert's death and since then, she had even more time to reorient herself. It's more likely that she, with Audovera's blessing, had been the one to propose the marriage. One seventh-century scribe, while recounting the wedding, went so far as to revise the Latin grammar that casts the groom as the active subject, assigning that role to Brunhild instead: "she brought *him* [Merovech] into matrimony."

Those historians who acknowledge Brunhild as the mastermind of the marriage, however, usually cast her as exploiting Merovech for short-term gain. They claim that the young prince had met the queen prior to their marriage (perhaps, for example, Merovech had been part of his father's entourage when Chilperic confronted the widowed queen in Paris), and Brunhild had somehow bewitched him with her beauty. The queen made use of Merovech's weakness for pretty women and Audovera's concern about her children to engineer her escape from the convent.

This theory, rather conveniently, discounts the possibility of solidarity between women—between Brunhild and Audovera and between the queens and the other nuns at the convent. It also does not align with what we know of Brunhild's character. The queen had already shown her talents for forging alliances and, over the course of her life, was usually very loyal. Most important, though, such a theory also underestimates her ambition.

Brunhild wanted out of the convent, certainly, but her true aim was likely bigger than that. Her new husband was to depose his father and rule Neustria; her son would remain king of Austrasia. Female bodies transferred and consolidated power in the early medieval world; in this case, Brunhild's body would be the glue connecting the two kingdoms. And in that way, she would exercise authority, simultaneously as a queen consort and a queen mother, over two-thirds of the Frankish Empire.

. . .

As Brunhild and Merovech knelt in the cathedral, the groom's army waited outside. The whispers and scribbled messages, passed from abbess to deacon to farmer, relayed from convent novice to family relative to shepherd, had orchestrated a plot to overthrow a king.

Successful coups require soldiers, money, disaffected elites, desperate people, and impeccable timing. The new couple possessed all four of the former and prayed mightily for the latter. Merovech provided the army, and Brunhild contributed the funds. After Sigibert's death she had been trapped in Paris with her personal treasure; this treasure had followed her to Rouen and been placed under Praetextatus's care. The bishop, drawing upon those five bundles of gold and jewels, had been busy purchasing the loyalty, and the silence, of key Neustrian nobles.

Because of this, the pair had secured Rouen as their base of operations; the entire city had switched its allegiance from Chilperic and declared Merovech its king. In the Champagne region that bordered Austrasia, many great warriors from illustrious families did the same. Brunhild and Merovech had good reason to expect more support to follow. Francia had been warring for six long years, with the bulk of the hostilities between Neustria and Austrasia. Frankish warriors "burned, plundered, and slew"; this was their entire modus operandi. Whenever the fighters decimated a foreign country and returned home with fistfuls of booty, there was little complaint. Yet now the same warriors were targeting their own people, and the Franks could not endure such large-scale violence for such a long time—crops burned every year, the markets shut down, the men away on lengthy campaigns. The new couple offered merchants and farmers the chance for long-term stability in exchange for a relatively quick military action: the overthrow of Chilperic.

It's difficult to ascertain exactly how they planned to do so since there is a lacuna in the middle of the usual narratives. The two men whose accounts we tend to rely on, the poet Fortunatus and Bishop Gregory of Tours, are either completely silent or purposefully frustratingly vague. This is, of course, not unexpected, given that both men were likely tangled up in the plot or eager not to appear so. But a careful examination of the surviving evidence suggests a likely scenario. As Brunhild and Merovech said their vows, an assassin was already racing on horseback through the forests toward Chilperic. If the assassin was successful, the pair might not need to activate the rest of their plans. But if he was not, they were prepared for battle. The couple would attack Chilperic's capital of Soissons on two fronts. Merovech and his army in Rouen would move in from the west, while Duke Wolf, capitalizing on the support for Merovech in the Champagne region, would march on Soissons from the east. Brunhild and Merovech also had a man on the inside who, once Soissons was surrounded, would unlock the city gates for them.

As far as plots go, this was a sensible one that had a good chance of succeeding. Yet a month or so after the wedding, Merovech's army completely disappears from the annals. There is no mention of their surrender or their slaughter; in fact, later events indicate that many of Merovech's men dispersed and hid in the surrounding countryside. Even stranger, the next mention of the new couple has them barricaded in a glorified treehouse in Rouen while Chilperic attempts all manner of threats and persuasion to lure them out.

Why?

What happened in between the wedding and the barricade was, most likely, a siege.

The assassin was, clearly, not successful, and it seems that Chilperic received word of the marriage and subsequently marched on Rouen sooner than the couple had anticipated. Merovech and his army decided to hunker down inside the city walls of Rouen while his father's army endeavored—with the usual flaming arrows, catapulted rocks, and battering rams—to get inside. Brunhild and Merovech decided to wait for reinforcements or for Chilperic's army to run out of supplies and give up. The new couple watched the progress of the siege from the city walls and, when it either turned into a stalemate or the city started running low on provisions, they prayed for guidance in a small chapel "built of wooden planks high on the city walls."

If Chilperic were to breach Rouen's walls, they could remain inside the chapel, claiming sanctuary. The right for the king's political foes to seek sanctuary on consecrated land was a well-established tradition. (When Duke Boso, after defeating Prince Theudebert in battle, took refuge from Chilperic's wrath in the basilica of Tours, he was appealing to this same tradition.) Sanctuary was, of course, sometimes violated. Fugitives had been snatched as they walked past an open door or leaned too far out of a window. But Chilperic could not take that risk. The church the newly-weds were in, no matter how rustic, was also dedicated to Saint Martin, the patron saint of Francia; to violate any churches consecrated to him would enrage the clergy, and Chilperic needed their support to quell the rebellion.

The newlyweds also decided their best course of action was to act as if their marriage was a love match. Merovech's rebellion could be cast as personal rather than political; Merovech had been driven mad by passion, and now he was simply trying to protect himself from his father's wrath. The couple had good reason to think that the king would be sympathetic to this interpretation of events—hadn't Chilperic himself made a few questionable decisions because of his infatuation with Fredegund?

Finally, as a truce to end the hostilities, Chilperic gave his solemn oath that "insofar as it was God's will he would not try to separate them."

In response, Brunhild and Merovech emerged from the treehouse chapel. When Merovech and Brunhild agreed to this truce they would have known the second part of their plan was already underway. An army led by Duke Wolf would have begun its march on Soissons. All they needed to do was keep Chilperic occupied in Rouen for a time. Once Chilperic received word that his queen and his heirs were in danger, he was sure to leave them in Rouen to join the fight. This seems to explain how Merovech's army disappeared—the prince told his men to disperse (and likely, to reorganize themselves in the countryside, to better assist Wolf) before he and his bride went to meet his father.

We know that Chilperic then offered the couple a ritual kiss of peace and shared a meal with them. Chilperic claimed to be deeply troubled by the incestuous nature of his son's union in the eyes of the Church, yet he then acknowledged their marriage and treated Brunhild and Merovech as husband and wife. Clearly, Chilperic was willing to believe that this uprising was the unfortunate result of his son's lust for the widowed queen.

Yet within days, messengers rode into Rouen, reporting that Chilperic's capital was under attack and Queen Fredegund had been forced to evacuate the city, again, with her young children in tow. Chilperic ordered his army to pack up and leave Rouen at once. If Merovech and Brunhild had hoped that this news would draw Chilperic and his forces away from Rouen, leaving them free to plot the next stage in their rebellion, they were mistaken. The king's guards surrounded Merovech, and Chilperic informed his son that he would be coming back to Soissons. The newly-weds protested, reminding the king of his solemn oath before God and man. But Chilperic had promised to *try* not to separate them if it was God's will. And who could better know God's will than he, the king? Merovech should be eager to help defend his homeland's capital. His new wife, though, should not be brought into a war zone. Brunhild would have to stay behind.

. . .

Soissons did not fall. Duke Wolf would have been counting on battling disorganized forces, perhaps worn down from the siege of Rouen. But the men left behind in Soissons launched a valiant defense, and then Chilperic thundered in at the head of his army, overcoming Wolf's forces and driving them away. In the aftermath, many of the Austrasians who had defected to Chilperic's kingdom after the assassination now fled with the retreating army. Chilperic had wanted to believe that Sigibert's former men had willingly chosen to serve him. He had even rewarded them generously for switching sides by granting them lands and villas. And still they had betrayed him.

It stretched credulity to imagine these were all coincidences: his son's marriage to his enemy's widow and the subsequent revolt in Rouen, the Austrasian army's assault on his capital, the treachery of so many of his men. At this point, the true scope of the rebellion against him must have dawned on Chilperic. And so the king began a sweep of his court, getting rid of anyone whose loyalty might be in question. Chilperic also had Merovech stripped of his weapons and his rank and placed under guard. He bestowed Merovech's military title and command on his younger brother, Chilperic's third son, Clovis (named, of course, for his revered great-grandfather). All throughout the summer, Merovech was held in custody back at court in Soissons. With Prince Clovis in command of his forces, Chilperic continued with his expansionist agenda. Who could stop him?

It was Chilperic's brother, Guntram, who finally stepped in, honoring Sigibert's memory by honoring their old alliance. Guntram even managed to retake one of the cities of Galswintha's former morgengabe, territory that now belonged to Brunhild, and in the process left five thousand of Chilperic's men dead. Smarting from this loss, and likely urged on by Fredegund, Chilperic decreed that Merovech was officially no longer an heir to the throne.

Further steps were taken to delegitimize Merovech's marriage. After all, even though Merovech and Brunhild were physically separated, a single secret conjugal visit could forever muck up the succession. The church had recent canons against incest, dating from Charibert's trial in 567, focusing mostly on marriage to a sister- or brother-in-law. Now an addition was made to civil law. Chilperic added a peculiarly specific prohibition to the Lex Salica, barring relationships between a man and his dead uncle's wife. This made Merovech's marriage not only questionable in the eyes of the Church, but also illegal in the eyes of the state.

In the early autumn of 576, Chilperic had Merovech tonsured (given the haircut of a monk). His scalp was shaved almost bald, with only a little fringe of hair left to ring his head. As with Gundovald a few years earlier, nothing could make it clearer that Merovech, despite his name, was a long-haired Merovingian no more. Then, at the point of a sword, he was ordained as a priest. As such, while Merovech could technically stay married to Brunhild, he could not sleep with her. Any child Brunhild might bear would be a sacrilege, unable to rule.

Merovech was to be sent off to the monastery of Saint Calais in nearby Le Mans, which operated as an informal "state prison." Here, it was expected, Merovech would learn more about the new life his father was offering him. He could no longer inherit the throne, but he could become a scholar, and if Merovech behaved himself, he might even land a cushy appointment as a bishop one day. That same autumn, Chilperic gave Brunhild a choice between her new husband and her children. If she

A monk being tonsured

would abandon Merovech, Chilperic would allow her to return to Austrasia, and send back her two daughters as well.

Brunhild chose her children.

Chilperic was so eager to be rid of Brunhild that he didn't try to seize any of the money or treasure she had brought with her, commanding his men, "Let the woman have her goods back." He rushed her off, stating he was eager to avoid both "a quarrel between me and Childebert my nephew" and any future *scandalum* (scandal). The queen, though, dawdled while packing up her things, reluctant to bring her personal treasure along. Underestimating her once again, Chilperic would have assumed Brunhild was worried about being waylaid by robbers on the way back. In fact, she was more concerned with making sure Praetextatus continued to have the means to finance Merovech's rebellion. Chilperic unsuspectingly agreed to let her leave her gold and jewels with the bishop and gallantly promised her she might send servants to collect them later.

When Brunhild arrived back in Metz, she was reunited with all three of her children after a year's separation. Her six-year-old son seems to have missed her most keenly: young Childebert would hereafter cling to his mother and never again be separated from her for so long. She was also reunited with her old allies at court, Gogo and Wolf; the former was still serving as regent for little Childebert. After months of confusion in Austrasia, order had been restored, and their political faction was ascendant once again.

CHAPTER 12

The Laws of Sanctuary

The light streamed through the windows and played off the glass and gilt mosaics on the walls. The incense curled up toward the vaulted ceiling, as did the chants of the congregants: "*Kyrie eleison*" (Lord, have mercy on us.)

Bishop Gregory was presiding over the service, and at some point during the three readings but before communion, he became aware of the whinny of horses out front and the creak of the basilica's heavy wooden door. A man stepped in, his head covered, his cloak laden with mud. It was Merovech.

The prince had never made it to his monastic prison. Right before his departure, in November of 576, a deacon from the city of Tours arrived at Chilperic's court and slipped a message to Merovech. Tours was now under Neustrian control, but the city's famed basilica was still run by Brunhild's ally Bishop Gregory. And inside, under sanctuary, still resided the Austrasian Duke Boso. The message was from him, urging Merovech to join him in this basilica, where they might hide out together and plan an escape.

When Chilperic sent Merovech off to his monastery, the traveling party was lightly guarded. One of Merovech's closest friends, a man named Gailen who had been his servant since childhood, arranged an ambush. Gailen brought with him a change of clothes, including a hooded cloak, and with his bald scalp disguised, Merovech was able to ride sixty miles southwest to Tours undetected. The prince showed up with a small group of supporters at the basilica right in the middle of Mass, interrupting Bishop Gregory to demand sanctuary.

. . .

Merovech had betrayed him. Disloyal noblemen had deceived him. Seeing treachery everywhere he looked, Chilperic started to rely on his wife more and more. The queen would have encouraged his suspicions—who else could he trust? Even if it was unprecedented to allow a woman to look over battle plans and tax records, it was Fredegund who had, quite literally, saved his kingdom once before with Sigibert's assassination. She emerged during this period as not just a queen but as a political adviser with ever-increasing power.

Had Brunhild truly abandoned Merovech and his cause? Fredegund had her doubts. And she was rightfully wary of Gregory's role in the rebellion, despite the bishop's protests. Gregory would later tell King Chilperic that he granted Merovech sanctuary in his cathedral only out of fear and obligation, but Fredegund saw Gregory's fingerprints all over Merovech's escape: it was his deacon who had delivered the message to Merovech, the fugitive in his church who had proffered the invitation, and his patron, Queen Brunhild, who stood to benefit.

When two envoys—one a relative of Bishop Gregory, the other a church official—arrived at the Neustrian court on another matter, Fredegund stormed into the chamber where they were being received, shouting that they were spies: "They have come to learn what the king is doing, so they can report to Merovech!" Fredegund did not wait to relay her concerns to Chilperic, but took action on her own. She had turned to lowly servants for her first assassination plot. Now she could command nobles and palace guards, who did not hesitate to follow her orders. She had the two envoys stripped of their possessions and sent off into exile at the point of a sword.

. . .

Outside, the land was frozen hard, but the seeds of opposition had been sown. There was more grumbling as the hostilities between Neustria and

Austrasia dragged into their seventh year. In the cities that had formerly belonged to Sigibert, sympathy for Merovech's rebellion was high. Tours was one such city, and a standoff here between the king and his son appeared imminent. Bishop Gregory's church was fast emerging as a flash point in the conflict.

Saint Martin's was a grand edifice, with imposing towers, marble columns, and glass windows. It was also huge, even by today's standards: almost half a football field long. Inside, there was plenty of room for Guntram Boso, Merovech, and their respective entourages. Outside, there was a constant stream of activity. New pilgrims arrived daily; the very old and infirm were carried on litters, the rich rode on horseback, but most were on foot, trudging up from the river port. They were jostled by beggars pleading for alms and vendors hawking devotional souvenirs. The crowds made it easy for Merovech's followers, hundreds of whom were stationed in Tours, to slip in and out of the church with food, supplies, maps, and plans. But these supporters were also getting into ever more frequent scuffles with the henchmen of the Count of Tours.

In every city, the power of the Church, embodied in a bishop, could be checked by that of the secular government, which was embodied in the city's count. In Tours, Bishop Gregory's power was offset by that of his despised nemesis, Count Leudast. The two men could not have been more different. Gregory constantly bragged of his old Roman family, whereas Count Leudast was a former slave with a mutilated ear, which had been either cut off or clipped as punishment for running away. King Charibert's last queen, the ill-fated former nun, had taken pity on Leudast and made him her stablemaster. Leudast had then continued to work his way up the ranks to palace constable and then, somehow, Count of Tours. Gregory took his privilege very seriously, and nothing seemed to irritate him more than social climbers; yet Leudast had the nerve to presume to be Gregory's equal.

This count had now thrown his support behind Chilperic and decided to make life difficult for Gregory and his refugees. Count Leudast showed up wearing "his cuirass [breastplate] and mailshirt, with his quiver hanging round him, his javelin in his hand and his helmet on his head." Appearing on church property fully armed was against canon law and a clear attempt to intimidate Gregory. Merovech responded by commanding his followers to raid Leudast's properties and steal what they could. Matters continued to escalate: Leudast ambushed some of Merovech's supporters, and in return, Merovech and Boso had Chilperic's royal physician attacked and robbed. Finally, King Chilperic sent messengers to Bishop Gregory demanding he expel Merovech from Saint Martin's: "If you refuse, I will set your whole countryside alight." Gregory *did* refuse, and so Chilperic prepared to send an army to Tours in the spring.

Merovech spent the Christmas holidays in the basilica with Boso and his family, and as the new year of 577 dawned, he wrestled with what to do next. If Merovech stayed in Tours, the city and countryside would be ravaged. That was not the way to earn the support of the common people, and his father might even be enraged enough to violate the laws of sanctuary and seize him from the basilica. Did he have enough support to directly challenge his father on the battlefield? Or was it time to make a break for the Austrasian border? Merovech was seen praying beside the tomb of Saint Martin, hoping for a favorable sign from the Franks' patron saint that it was time to act.

While Chilperic prepared for war, Fredegund used her new powers to act not in concert with her husband, but behind his back. Duke Boso was still Chilperic's avowed enemy. Chilperic hated Boso for killing his eldest son in battle; he was dead set on exacting vengeance, perhaps as a way to assuage his guilt for leaving his son woefully unprotected. But Fredegund sent a message to Boso, promising that he would be richly rewarded if he could just do one simple thing: get Merovech out of the church.

The stakes were high for the queen. If Merovech were to prevail, her two sons, Clodobert and Samson, would likely be imprisoned in a monastery, or even killed. But seeking Boso's help was also a risk. He could share news of the offer with Merovech and the rest of the Austrasians; word of her deceit might even get back to her husband.

Fredegund's spy network must have told her that Boso was not famed for his loyalty. As Gregory had written of the duke: "Boso was a good enough man, but he was much too given to breaking his word." It was well known, too, that Boso had expensive tastes, and he had a reputation for acting first and thinking second. Boso was a fearsome enemy, but the combination of these traits meant he could be just as dangerous—if not more so—as an ally.

Fredegund was counting on Boso being restless after two long years holed up in Saint Martin's with his family. With Chilperic's army bearing down on Tours, he might be stuck there longer still. Winning Fredegund's favor, especially as her star was now rising, could mean safe passage back home for him and his family. And so Boso decided to accept Fredegund's offer.

It had been two months since Merovech's monastic haircut; the prince's shaved head had filled in a bit, and he could finally appear in public. Boso proposed they go hunting with hawks and hounds in the countryside: "A ride through the open fields will do us good." For Merovech, to be seen out hunting would prove he was a warrior, not a monk. The two men spent the day outside the walls of Saint Martin's enjoying the crisp air.

But something with Fredegund's plan had gone wrong. Either she never received Boso's reply, or her accomplices botched the job. In any case, no assassin managed to take Merovech down. Yet all was not lost. Fredegund believed she had discovered the chink in Merovech's armor: Duke Boso. The knowledge that Merovech's fellow asylum seeker could be bought off might come in handy later.

Merovech remained completely unaware of his new friend's duplicity, while Boso waffled over what to do next. He sought out his usual soothsayer for her advice. The woman foretold that Chilperic would die that very year and that Merovech would become the next king of Neustria. Duke Boso had a long life ahead of him, she said, first as the new king's top military commander, and then as an influential bishop. On the basis of this prediction, Boso decided not to continue to collaborate with Fredegund and instead, redoubled his efforts to help Merovech's cause. They decided that, before the spring campaign season began and Chilperic launched his attack on Tours, they would make a run for the Austrasian border together. The prince and the duke gathered five hundred of their followers and rode out during the night.

The escape itself went relatively well. The men were arrested but quickly slipped away again. They were forced to seek sanctuary in yet another church for two months. Merovech demonstrated no shortage of courage or creativity, but he was plagued by colossally bad timing. The two-month delay meant that the political situation had irrevocably changed by the time the men made it to the border.

In the spring of 577, King Guntram lost his two teenage sons to dysentery. Burgundy was without an heir, and Guntram and his third wife were old enough that it was unlikely they could have more children. At the end of April 577, Guntram made an offer to the Austrasians. He would adopt seven-year-old Childebert. The prince and a small group of nobles came to Guntram's court; Guntram sat his nephew on his throne next to him and declared Childebert his heir. Guntram also declared an alliance between Burgundy and Austrasia: "May one shield protect us and one spear defend us." But Guntram had one condition. He, too, was tired of the war, and he wanted it to end. If it did, Brunhild's son could gain two of the three crowns of Francia.

Brunhild was placed in an impossible position. Chilperic and Fredegund were her undisputed enemies; they had assassinated both her sister and husband. Her best chance of overthrowing them for good lay with Merovech. And with Merovech on the Neustrian throne, Austrasia wouldn't have to fear incursions from its western neighbor. But if she did support Merovech, she would doom the chances of her own son.

After months as refugees, Merovech and Boso reached Austrasia. Boso returned to his estates and promptly began work on a new plot—a way to extract his daughters, who were still stuck in Saint Martin's. Merovech likely enjoyed a brief reunion with his wife. But aside from Boso and his faction, Merovech found himself without many friends at the Austrasian court. Chilperic and Guntram were both leaning on their supporters to put an end to the prince's rebellion. Bishop Egidius and the pro-Neustrian faction were lobbying aggressively against him, and while the pro-Burgundy faction was more sympathetic, they did not want to openly oppose King Guntram, especially given his offer to adopt Childebert. The Austrasian nobles decided that the fugitive prince could not stay at their court. A man without a country, Merovech was on the run yet again.

CHAPTER 13

Crime and Punishment

W hen Chilperic's army arrived in Tours, Merovech and Boso were long gone. Chilperic, incensed, decided to ravage the countryside anyway. Even the Basilica of Saint Martin suffered harsh reprisals; Chilperic flouted convention and law to plunder Church goods. He also sent his men to patrol the border, even ordering dozens of small raiding parties to cross into Austrasia, in an attempt to hunt down Merovech. Although Brunhild could not openly support her husband's cause for fear of antagonizing his opponents in court, she did not entirely abandon him. Merovech hid out within Austrasia's borders, in the region of Reims on land belonging to the queen's ally Duke Wolf. The plan seems to have been for Merovech to stay out of sight until the political situation became more favorable to his cause.

As long as Merovech remained at large, Fredegund realized, an army alone would not be enough to put down the rebellion. To peel away support for Merovech and disrupt the networks Brunhild and her allies had established in Neustria, Fredegund and Chilperic also needed to locate the source of Merovech's money. Fredegund's spies soon reported back that Bishop Praetextatus was making gifts to Neustrian nobles and magnates in exchange for horses, supplies, and their oaths of loyalty to Merovech. Fredegund didn't want Praetextatus simply killed or captured; she wanted him humiliated in a public trial that might make other clergy and nobles think twice about supporting Merovech. She brought her idea to Chilperic and the king proved eager to "to ensure that the Queen has her way."

Praetextatus was arrested on charges of high treason. He was, like Gregory, a metropolitan, a bishop of the capital city of the province of Rouen, and as such he was beyond the reach of any secular court. So Chilperic, seeming to bow to the power of the Church, instead convened a clerical synod in Paris and called upon Praetextatus's fellow bishops to judge him for crimes against the faith. It was a wise decision. The royal couple had many allies within the Church. There were at least fourteen bishops who regularly helped them with diplomatic and judicial matters; the historical record tells us Fredegund had at least three more who were her devoted supporters.

The bishops gathered at Saint Peter's, outside the walls of the Île de la Cité on the Right Bank. All dressed for the occasion in their finest—white linen robes and heavy cloaks embroidered with gold thread. A white pallium was draped around the shoulders of the most distinguished bishops in attendance. They were all loyal Neustrians; Gregory was the only Austrasian to attend since Tours had recently changed hands.

Once the bishops were seated, King Chilperic charged Praetextatus not only with violating the Church's incest prohibitions by presiding over the

A bishop stands trial

marriage of his rebel son and Brunhild, but also with actively trying to overthrow him. "You actually gave gifts and urged [Merovech] to kill me!" Chilperic accused the old bishop. "You have seduced the people with money so that no one of them would keep faith with me!"

Gregory's is the only eyewitness account that survives, and he is admittedly biased. But he describes a show trial, of witnesses bribed or cowed into cooperating. And he claimed that, although Chilperic was nominally in charge, the bishops were all aware of who was actually holding the reins: "they feared the fury of the queen at whose instigation this was being done."

When Chilperic learned that Gregory was not likely to vote to convict, the king invited the bishop to dinner and mused aloud that Gregory was trying to hide his own collusion with the Austrasians. Gregory deftly sidestepped the accusation, and Chilperic threatened to orchestrate an uprising in Tours that would lead to the bishop's removal. Gregory claimed he bravely retorted: "If the people cry aloud with false cries when you attack me, it is nothing, because all know that this comes from you. And therefore it is not I but rather you that shall be disgraced in the outcries."

When Gregory returned to his lodgings after that dinner, messengers from Fredegund soon appeared at his door. If her husband's threats would not work, she was willing to try a different approach, promising Gregory "two hundred pounds of silver" to condemn Praetextatus. The messengers added that the queen had already bought the cooperation of the other bishops. Gregory could turn his nose up at the queen's money, but if he was determined to stand on principle, he would also be standing alone.

When Gregory still refused, Fredegund tried yet another tactic. She had some of the other bishops convince Praetextatus to plead guilty and throw himself at the king's mercy; this was the best way for the elderly bishop to avoid a more gruesome punishment. Perhaps Praetextatus was "tricked," as Gregory later claimed, or he simply saw that the evidence against him was mounting. Either way, the next day in open court he confessed to Chilperic: "I wished to kill you and raise your son to the throne."

Not wanting to cede their authority to the state, the bishops agreed that Praetextatus should be punished, but they would be the ones to decide the sentence and only according to church canon. And so Chilperic sent the bishops a book of canon law that had a curious addition: "a newly-copied [sixteen]-page insert" which declared "A bishop convicted of murder, adultery or perjury shall be expelled from his bishopric." Gregory stops short of calling this a forgery, but that is clearly the implication. (These canons, however, were authentic, if obscure. Gregory was either genuinely mistaken, having never seen them before, or he was trying very hard to cast King Chilperic in the worst light). On the basis of these newly copied pages Praetextatus lost his ecclesiastic title and was "grievously beaten" and sent into exile.

. . .

Merovech's support in Neustria was now seriously compromised. Praetextatus's network was demolished, and Gregory was now under close observation. In order to prevent his helping Merovech again, Chilperic posted guards outside the basilica in Tours and ordered all the doors to be closed except one so that all comings and goings could be monitored. These difficulties could have been overcome with robust outside assistance, but interest in the prince's cause was waning in Austrasia. After the failed attack on Soissons, few were willing to commit more soldiers and money; the prevailing opinion was that Austrasia needed to regroup and make sure it could defend its own borders first.

However, Merovech himself still remained at large. Brunhild and her allies kept him successfully hidden during Chilperic's incursions across the border. In the end, it would be Duke Boso who betrayed Merovech once again.

A message came from the people of Thérouanne in the northernmost reaches of Neustria, saying they backed Merovech's cause and would allow him to use their town as a base from which to launch his rebellion. This was exactly what Merovech needed, now that Rouen and Tours were no longer options for him. He did not want to stay hidden away on Duke Wolf's properties, dependent upon his wife and her allies, while every day Chilperic's position grew more secure, and his own, weaker. Without consulting Brunhild, Merovech eagerly rode out with some of his most trusted men. Duke Boso conveniently found a reason to stay behind. Not long after Merovech arrived in Thérouanne, he realized he had ridden right into a trap. He and his supporters were quickly surrounded by armed men and the prince was imprisoned in the town's inn for the night.

Waiting for his father, Merovech had time to mull over what was to come. He knew the most grievous tortures were reserved for rebellious sons. He asked his old friend Gailen, the servant who had helped engineer his escape from the monastery, for one last act of loyalty: "I beg you not to allow me to fall into the hands of my enemies. Take my sword and kill me." Before Chilperic arrived in Thérouanne, Merovech was dead.

Still, rumors of Fredegund's involvement in Merovech's death spread among the people, gossip which Gregory of Tours was eager to relay: "There were some who said that [these] last words of Merovech . . . were invented by the Queen, and that he was murdered in secret at her command." Was he merely eager to spare Merovech the reputation of a suicide? He repeated another rumor "that Bishop Egidius and Guntram Boso had been the ringleaders in this ambush" and reminded his readers of these two men's links to the Neustrian queen. Duke Boso "enjoyed the secret favor of Queen Fredegund" and Bishop Egidius had been "one of her favorites" for quite some time. Bishop Gregory could not make it any easier for his readers to connect the dots, to imagine a hurried meeting between the bishop and the duke, to see the gold changing hands, to envision Fredegund guiding the whole affair.

. . .

In the autumn of 577, although discontent still simmered in the countryside, Merovech's rebellion was stamped out.

Chilperic lost two of his heirs that year. On the heels of Merovech's death, both Fredegund and her son Samson became very ill with dysentery. Samson had survived his mother's attempts to have him killed, had survived the long siege in Tournai, but was not able to survive the fever and diarrhea. That left just Audovera's son Prince Clovis, living under the shadow of his brother's treachery, and Fredegund's son Clodobert, who was now seven.

Despite these losses, and although his brother and his nephew were now allied against him, Chilperic celebrated in the style of a Roman emperor with "bread and circuses." He moved his family into the palace in

Paris, declaring it a sort of second capital (and asserting his rights over the quarter of the kingdom his brother Charibert had governed before his death). And then he restored the Arenas of Lutetia outside of Paris' walls and repaired or built a new circus in Soissons "to offer spectacles to the citizens"—theater performances and exotic animal hunts. Soon he had even more reason to celebrate: Fredegund gave birth again, to another boy, baby Dagobert, whose name—"bright day"—represented the royal couple's hopes for a new start for Neustria.

Across the border in Austrasia, the mood was less optimistic. There had been many Austrasians in Merovech's ambushed party. One, a count, was beheaded, while others of lesser station were more "cruelly butchered." And Brunhild was a widow for the second time in just two years. Her son's elevation to heir of Burgundy had come at a high price. Yet Merovech's misfortunes did not diminish her influence at court. By 579 she somehow emerged with enough sway over Gogo and the rest of the Austrasian court to decide the matter of her eldest daughter's marriage. Twelve-year-old Ingund was yet too young to consummate a marriage, but not too young for the negotiations to begin.

Brunhild did not want her daughter to meet the same fate her sister had, finding herself without protection in a foreign court. What better solution than to marry her back into the Visigothic royal family where her grandmother could watch over her? Brunhild's mother Goiswintha had retained her power in Spain by marrying her first husband's successor, Leovigild, and acquired two stepsons in the process. The elder, fourteen-year-old Hermenegild, was expected to become king.

It was Brunhild, rather than Gogo, who conducted these negotiations, sending a bishop "on a mission to Spain to attend to [her] affairs." What more could a devoted mother hope for than this—that her son would be king of two nations and her daughter queen of another? Only this: that she herself might rule, too.

CHAPTER 14

"Wise in Counsel"

During the summer of 580, the people of Francia spoke of two things—one was the rain. The other was the rumor.

In a pattern that would continue throughout the new decade, the year had been exceedingly wet—once, it even rained for twelve days straight. Farmers could not plant their crops, and cattle were swept away and drowned.

And as for the rumor: Queen Fredegund was said to be cuckolding the king with Bertram, Bishop of Bordeaux.

Fredegund and Bishop Bertram were friendly—that was no secret. The bishop was a cousin of her husband and one of her staunchest ecclesiastical allies. At Bishop Praetextatus's trial, Bertram had functioned as Chilperic's right-hand man. The bishop and queen had worked together in preparation, perhaps had even been seen laughing and talking. But could they really be sleeping together? Was that how Fredegund had ensured the metropolitan's loyalty?

That same year in Paris, the Basilica of Saint-Denis had been left "spattered with human blood" after nobles got into a dispute over a woman's virtue. A father had gone to the tomb of Saint Denis to swear an oath that gossip about his married daughter was not true; the husband's relatives attacked him, insisting he was lying. A swordfight ensued at the altar, and by the time others intervened, the inside of the church was wrecked and its doors "were pierced with swords and javelins." Frankish law was obsessed with what a woman was called—"witch," "man-eater," "whore"—and insulting a woman's honor was the timeworn path to a blood feud like this. One man insulting another's mother, wife, or daughter would quickly escalate to physical violence. A fistfight would become a swordfight, and soon enough both families' homes would end up burned to the ground. And if gossip about a noblewoman's purity threatened her family's sense of honor, in the royal family, it threatened the entire line of succession. What of Fredegund's new baby boy? He was less than a year old, born after Praetextatus's trial, potentially even conceived during it. By August, the poisonous rumors bubbled over at the same time the rivers overflowed their banks.

The Auvergne region was especially hard-hit. The Loire, the Rhone, the Allier, the Saône, all swelled and raged beyond the measure of any previous floods. Much of Italy was underwater, too. And so the epidemic struck. Gregory relays how "dysentery seized upon nearly the whole of the Gauls."

To the Franks, dysentery was common enough. A cookbook from the era contains numerous recipes for treating it—not just boiled partridge and quinces, but barley gruel mixed with hot wine. It was understood that those with dysentery should not drink raw milk, only milk that had been boiled, and that they should stick to bland foods like cooked rice. It seems clear from this and other sources that *dysentery* was a catch-all term, used to describe all sorts of digestive upsets and degrees of food poisoning.

The illness that descended in 580, though, was on the extreme end of that spectrum: sufferers "had a high temperature, with vomiting and severe pains in the small of the back: their heads ached and so did their necks. The matter they vomited up was yellow or even green." What had caused this? Instead of imbalanced humors, the culprit was said to be "a secret poison." This explanation aligns with our contemporary understanding of dysentery—caused by a particular poison, the bacteria shigella. The flood-waters were full of fecal matter from washed-out latrines and stables as well as the bloated corpses of drowned livestock and pets. The Franks knew to drink clear, running water from mountain streams and brooks. The prac-tice of purifying questionable water by boiling had been established five centuries prior; this practice was still in use in Byzantium. But even if they did not drink the floodwater, people were wading through it; it was on their boots, their clothes, seeping through the floors of their homes.

Bishop Gregory had more to fear than catching this illness, though. The rumors about Queen Fredegund had been attributed to him, thanks to his long-time enemy, one-eared Leudast, the Count of Tours. Gregory had often insulted the count, calling him all manner of things, including "a greedy plunderer, a loudmouthed disputer and a foul adulterer." Now Leudast saw his opening and appeared before Chilperic, claiming that Bishop Gregory had been questioning Fredegund's virtue.

Gregory had, of course, accused Fredegund of many things. Despite the outraged protests that survive in his writings, it's quite likely Gregory *had* gossiped about the queen's extramarital activities, too. But while Fredegund could accept being accused of the mortal sins of sorcery or murder, she could not stand by and have her sons' paternity questioned. If her boys were not the sons of a king, they could not rule, and Audovera's son Clovis or Brunhild's son, Childebert, would be the only possible heirs to Neustria.

The rains had paused but the epidemic was in full swing when, in September, Bishop Gregory was ordered to appear before the royal court on charges of treason. Gregory was panicked enough by the upcoming trial to try to enlist all the support he could. Somehow, he managed to get the sympathy of Fredegund's own daughter. Rigunth, now eleven years old, was proving to be exceedingly headstrong. She publicly "fasted with all her household" in solidarity with Gregory, perhaps as a way to irritate her mother.

The poet Fortunatus soon received a request from his old friend Gregory. At this point, the two men had been exchanging letters, poems, and jokes for over a decade. Although Gregory was only eight years older, he acted as a parental figure to the often financially strapped poet, gifting Fortunatus practical things like sandals and grafts of apple trees, as well as many books. Gregory even gave Fortunatus a villa from his family's considerable land holdings. Now he wanted just one thing in return—Fortunatus needed to write a poem to flatter Chilperic and deliver it at Gregory's trial.

Gregory's request would finally allow Fortunatus the opportunity to travel away from Poitiers. Fortunatus had taken up residence in the city to be near Radegund; the poet and the former queen had become dear friends. They had much in common, as Radegund was known as a vora-cious reader. In contrast to her other mortifications—the severe food restrictions, hair shirts, and brandings—her obsessive reading practices seemed almost innocuous. Radegund's nuns were required to follow suit, and they spent hours every day reading manuscripts, and hours more copying them. In an abbey well known for its "unusual literary ambience," Fortunatus fit in well.

The visit, though, had not been intended to be a permanent one. During the ongoing civil war, Poitiers had fallen under Chilperic's control, which left Fortunatus cut off from his main allies and source of income—the Austrasian court. As usual, he had found a way to make the best of a bad situation, becoming a sort of court poet for the charismatic ex-queen and assisting in her efforts to broker a peace between the warring Merovingian brothers. Through this relationship, he also mixed with the officials and travelers who passed through her abbey. But with travel increasingly diffi-cult while armies roamed the countryside, Fortunatus had to set aside his life as an itinerant bard gadding about from one glittering court to the next. Instead, he regularly exchanged letters and poems with Radegund and her abbess, Agnes, and the three spent many afternoons reading aloud to one another.

He seems to have enjoyed this simpler life. The subjects of his poems changed: fewer vain rulers, more simple joys like wildflowers and fresh plums. Perhaps he found it easier, safer even, to be surrounded by Radegund and her nuns, to set aside feelings he wasn't sure what to do with. Fortunatus's personal poems expressed an increasing repulsion for female bodies and an ever-more palpable longing for certain male friends. In one poem to a church deacon he calls "lover," Fortunatus regretfully recalls leaving the man asleep without saying goodbye:

> [your] body limp-lying on the bed:
> wavering, unwilling to vex your calm with sin
> my guilt left you undisturbed.
> I crawled away, a thief in the night, no one will ever know of it

In other poems, he writes to another "lover" he calls Rucco: it was his affectionate nickname for Ragnemod, the new bishop of Paris, who would also be attending Gregory's trial. So Fortunatus may have had another reason to thrill at the opportunity to recite at the proceedings.

At the same time, he knew how much depended upon this poem. With past commissions, he had risked embarrassment, the loss of patrons and income, perhaps even the displeasure of the king or noble who had hired him. But if Fortunatus performed poorly this time, his old friend could be convicted of treason, for which the punishments ranged from defrocking and exile to dismemberment and death. If he enraged Chilperic with his poem, Fortunatus might even be arrested himself, as an accomplice.

The trial was to be held at Berny-Rivière, Chilperic's favorite villa, situated just outside the capital city of Soissons. The river Aisne cut a valley through the region, and the royal quarters were perched on one of the banks. Chilperic's most important officers and nobles had quarters there; it was the court in miniature. There, too, was kept the royal treasury, chests of gold coins and jewels well secured and guarded.

The bishops gathered again, dressed in their finest. Following a canon-law tradition, since Bishop Bertram was the wronged party he would act as prosecutor, conducting the questioning of Gregory, while Chilperic presided as judge. Standing before them, Fortunatus made sure to offer the customary plaudits: Chilperic was of noble stock. His name itself meant "valiant defender" and the king had lived up to his name with his career as a renowned warrior. Fortunatus also tried to smooth over past disagreements between Chilperic and Gregory. Gregory had called the king unjust and corrupt during Praetextatus's trial; now Fortunatus commended Chilperic's sense of fairness: "In your honest speech are held the scales of just measure and the course of justice runs straight."

Fortunatus was careful to present the king as he wished to see himself. Chilperic, who had spent so much of his life battling feelings of inferiority, especially in relation to his older brothers, emerged in Fortunatus's reframing as actually the best and brightest of Clothar's sons. He was his father's favorite, "the child he loved best." Fortunatus even took care to flatter the king's literary ambitions. Chilperic had long considered himself a poet and had even written two books of verse, but Bishop Gregory had smirked that the king's efforts were "feeble" and "observed none of the accepted rules of prosody." (Chilperic clearly did "not [understand] what he was doing," Gregory wrote, since "he put short syllables for long ones" and vice versa.) Now Fortunatus declared that Chilperic was not only the smartest in the family, but he was also a great poet. Chilperic would have been tickled to have the renowned classical poet publicly proclaim his work as "exceptional."

The second half of the poem praised Fredegund. Fortunatus included the typical compliments: in addition to being beautiful, the queen was also "a good mistress of [her] palace" and "of pleasing generosity." He called her Chilperic's "rightful consort," a slight to Audovera and the murdered Galswintha. The rumors of infidelity could not possibly be true, Fortunatus made clear, because the queen brought to the royal family only "greater honor." Praise for a queen's beauty, chastity, and household management skills are to be expected.

But Fortunatus also made a surprising number of references to Fredegund's brains and political savvy. He was also clearly aware of how the queen wished to see herself. In front of a council of the kingdom's most powerful and learned men, Fredegund is presented not as a damsel in distress, in need of their protection. She is praised as a man would be: "wise in counsel, clever, shrewd . . . [and] intelligent." She is also presented as an equal to the king, as one who "shares the rule" and "carries the oppressive weight of the cares of state" and offers her "guidance at [the king's] side."

Gregory was spared.

The jury of bishops agreed with the explanation that Gregory had offered: that his enemy and accuser, the upstart Leudast, was at the root of these rumors. The Count of Tours was excommunicated in absentia and, upon hearing the news, went on the run. Still, Fredegund never forgot Leudast's words and made sure, years later, that he paid for them. He was seized by her soldiers and after days of torture, on Fredegund's orders: "a great bar of iron was placed under his neck and they struck his throat with another." The loquacious Count Leudast died gasping for air, unable to speak.

CHAPTER 15

Fredegund's Grief

The rumors had been halted but the dysentery had not. Soon after Gregory's trial ended, the infection struck the royal family. Chilperic himself fell gravely ill, burning with fever. The king recovered, but then his youngest son, Dagobert, became sick. His parents hurried to baptize him. Then, once the baby seemed to improve for a bit, his older brother was stricken.

Fredegund panicked. Children were dying throughout the empire; it was recorded that they were the hardest hit. Her determined mind searched for a way to control what she could not see. She had always been able to bend circumstances to her iron will, but not knowing about the existence of pathogens, she could not outwit them. She settled upon another possible cause. If epidemics were God's judgement, this one must be punishment for something she had done.

The year before, with the coffers of the kingdom's treasury exhausted from the long civil war, Chilperic had levied harsh new taxes on his realm. These taxes were so severe that many of his subjects preferred to emigrate to other kingdoms. Landowners had to pay one amphora of wine for every arpent (French acre) of land, or approximately "five gallons of wine for every half-acre" they owned along with taxes on other goods and slaves. Riots broke out in response, especially in the cities once ruled by Sigibert: the last gasps of Merovech's rebellion. These were the worst in

Limoges, one of the contested cities of Galswintha's morgengabe. The people tried to kill the tax collector and burned the tax registers in protest. Chilperic, in retribution, tortured and killed any who had protested the taxes, even if they were clergy, and then levied even more taxes.

Among the Merovingians, intrafamilial violence was accepted as a hazard of the job. But if a sovereign was expected to be ruthless with his own family, he was also supposed to be compassionate with the common people, to follow Jesus's example with the poor and sick. Fredegund took the idea of the good king (*bonus rex*) to heart.

She decided that her son's illness was God's punishment for her greed. "It is the tears of the poor, the outcries of widows and the sighs of orphans that are destroying [my boys]!" she was reported to have cried. She found the tax registers for her own cities, the cities gifted to her as her morgengabe, and tossed them in the fire. And then she convinced Chilperic to do the same for every city in his realm. All tax debts were forgiven: the kingdom's entire tax policy wiped out in an afternoon.

And still, baby Dagobert died. It was to be expected; few young children had escaped the epidemic. But Prince Clodobert was nine or ten at this time. His father had recovered; surely he might, too.

In a fourteenth-century miniature, Fredegund rebukes Chilperic and convinces him to burn his tax registers

Fredegund and Chilperic had the prince placed on a stretcher and quickly carried to the tomb of Saint Medard, less than two miles outside the palace at Soissons. In the same crypt was buried Chilperic's father—as well as his murdered brother, Sigibert. But the irony of begging God for mercy mere feet away from the tomb of one of their victims was lost on the royal couple. In front of the saint's tomb, a hulking limestone sarcophagus, the king and queen prayed incessantly for their son's recovery, although by then the prince "was worn to a shadow and hardly drawing breath."

Their entreaties came too late. Just twenty days after Gregory's trial convened—a trial the whole purpose of which was to quash rumors about the paternity of Fredegund's sons—both of the boys were dead.

. . .

The death of the Neustrian heir was a national tragedy. Prince Clodobert's funeral procession was joined by hundreds of ordinary citizens, "the men weeping and the women wearing widow's weeds." It extinguished any hope of an uncontested handover of power after the king's eventual death. It could also have signified the end of Fredegund's career. The political survival of a queen without sons was in question.

The portrait emerging from this period is not that of an insecure queen, however, but a domineering one. Records of the time indicate Chilperic bent to her moods and whims, anxious to please Fredegund or, at least, not to displease her. This perception may well be colored by the biases of nobles and bishops angry over her influence or eager to display Chilperic as weak and ineffectual. But in many instances, Chilperic clearly acted against his own self-interest to cater to his queen. Chilperic had, for example, invested time and resources into his new tax policy, and had risked his immortal soul by killing and torturing clergy to defend it in the face of virulent opposition. But then he did an abrupt about-face at Fredegund's urging. Still, nowhere is Fredegund's hold over Chilperic more evident than in his treatment of his one remaining son, Prince Clovis.

In October of 580, right after Prince Clodobert's state funeral, Fredegund and Chilperic left Berny-Rivière and retreated deep into the forests of Cuise. This was prized hunting preserve (and would continue to be for all of the future kings of France) thick with majestic oaks and beeches. They wanted privacy to grieve, but they also wanted to avoid the dysentery epidemic that was still raging at the royal villa, no doubt because of its proximity to the flooded Aisne River. At the end of the month, when the outbreak still showed no signs of relenting, Fredegund suggested that the king send Prince Clovis to Berny-Rivière. We have to assume she hoped that the prince would fall victim to disease, too. Chilperic would have understood that his wife was asking him to pick her over his kingdom and his own good. And yet, Chilperic agreed, ordering his only remaining heir to his likely death. Although Clovis was probably sent to Berny-Rivière under some pretense, told he was needed to stand in for his father on official business, the prince would not have missed how cavalier his father and stepmother were about his health during a raging epidemic.

Somehow, Prince Clovis survived. If the royal couple had asked for a sign from God, here it surely was: just like his namesake, the great King Clovis, this prince was divinely favored, the chosen successor. Chilperic invited his son to join him and the queen at yet another of their country estates, the hunting villa of Chelles; he was publicly acknowledging that Clovis was his heir. The son celebrated his change in fortune: he strutted; he caroused; he flirted with servant girls. Thinking himself invincible, he even crowed, "My enemies are now in my power and I can do to them whatever I choose."

At these remarks, Fredegund was reported to be terrified—*pavore nimio terrebatur*—absolutely consumed by fear. Fredegund had banished Clovis's mother and sister to a convent; she had celebrated the death of one of his brothers and helped engineer the ambush and death of the other. If the prince were making a list of his enemies, his stepmother was certainly at the top of that list.

Fredegund was now around thirty years old, and despite giving birth at least four times she had only one living child, a daughter. No matter her hold over the king, the concern that another woman might catch Chilperic's eye would have flitted through her mind, as it would any woman who was utterly dependent upon the king's favor. Fredegund also had to worry that Chilperic, now over forty and no longer a young man, could die himself—whether in battle or through illness. What would happen to her then?

Naturally, Fredegund closely surveilled all the supporters and hangers-on surrounding the Neustrian heir. But she fixated on one girl in particular, the daughter of one of her servants, whom Prince Clovis was quite taken with. Hadn't she herself once been much like this girl, hoping to catch the eye of a royal?

Another servant, jealous, repeated a rumor to the queen that Clovis's new girlfriend and her mother were witches. The girl was quite beautiful; the prince's desire for her needed no supernatural explanation. But Fredegund had no trouble believing this potential rival would dabble in the dark arts to secure her position. Soon, she became convinced that it was this ambitious girl's witchcraft that had caused the death of her beloved boys. Hadn't she repented? Hadn't she prayed? Wasn't it a little too convenient that Audovera's son had survived this terrible epidemic while both of her sons had not? Maybe Clovis's survival hadn't been a sign of God's favor, but of something much more sinister. If his new girlfriend fervently wished to be queen, how easy to have her mother, Fredegund's own servant, slip something into the princes' food or drink.

Fredegund ordered the girl disfigured and humiliated—her glossy locks hacked off, her pretty face beaten bloody—and then had her tied to a stake where Clovis would be sure to see her. The girl's mother was tortured until, to make the pain stop, the poor woman admitted she was indeed a witch and she had helped Prince Clovis cast spells to kill Fredegund's sons. When Fredegund presented Chilperic with her servant's confession (along with a few added details of her own), the king crumpled. At Fredegund's request, he had Clovis stripped of his weapons and finery, chained, and then turned over to Fredegund for further questioning. The queen then had her stepson removed to another estate where, it was later reported, he found a knife and stabbed himself. How he managed to do this while alone in a cell with his hands bound behind his back was never explained. Prince Clovis's body was buried so quickly the king never had time to confirm the reported suicide for himself.

Fredegund dispatched her own soldiers to Rouen to deal with her predecessor Audovera. The former queen would have cursed the day she had selected a quick-witted kitchen slave to become one of her maids. Even as a cast-off ex-wife, though, Audovera's position had seemed unassailable; she was the mother of three heirs. Now she had outlived them all.

Audovera's machinations were not those of a woman scheming for her own advancement, but of a mother desperate to save her children.

Now Audovera was seized and savagely murdered. Her daughter, Basina, was sent to Radegund's convent, the family's sole survivor. Some assumed Basina was raped by Fredegund's soldiers. Whether or not that was true, the stain on her reputation was indelible. Now dishonored, Basina could not be married off; only Fredegund's daughter, the increasingly mouthy Rigunth, would be a suitable bride for a marriage alliance.

Fredegund's servant, the mother of Clovis's girlfriend, recanted her confession once she was no longer being tortured. She was not a witch; she had not killed the princes. She was dragged from her prison anyhow, tied to a stake, and "set alight while still alive."

CHAPTER 16

Brunhild in the Breach

Horses whinnied and strained; the soldiers beat their wooden shields with the flats of their swords.

When Duke Wolf set out for his estates in the Champagne, he and his men certainly were armed. But they had been prepared for bandits, not an ambush such as this. Now their passage was blocked by the armies of Bishop Egidius of Reims and his supporters. The soldiers lined up in the clearing were in full armor—breastplates, chain mail shirts, and distinctive peaked helmets—and brandishing throwing axes, spears, and swords.

When she received word of the standoff, Brunhild made up her mind. Her breath would have hitched as she hefted the heavy belt, fastened it around her waist, and gripped the hilt of the sword in its scabbard.

The suave and eloquent Gogo had managed to rein in Egidius's pro-Neustrian faction for over a decade. But now Gogo was dead, leaving the position of regent to eleven-year-old King Childebert glaringly open. The count had fallen ill so quickly that the coalition he had spent so many years building had not yet had a chance to regroup. Bishop Egidius's contingent had seen their opportunity. Now that Chilperic was without an heir, previously resistant nobles could be convinced that the Neustrian king was not a serious threat. After a few such conversations, Egidius had been able to strong-arm the court into accepting his candidate for young Childebert's regent, limiting Brunhild's access to her son and commandeering the regency.

Egidius now had the power to settle old scores, and his first target was Duke Wolf; the men's families had ongoing land disputes in the Reims region. Gogo's silver tongue could no longer broker a peace, and King Childebert was too young to have the authority to command his nobles to stop. But Brunhild could not let such a steadfast ally fall. Duke Wolf had not only openly acknowledged her authority, he had gone so far as to help with Merovech's bid for power, even hiding the unfortunate prince during his last months. Brunhild had tried to serve as a mediator, but the nobles would not listen to her—a queen might manipulate the law, but a king was the one to enforce it. The best way to be granted the deference due a king, Brunhild decided, was to dress like one. So she "armed herself like a man," *praecingens se viriliter*, ready to do battle. Then Brunhild strode out onto the field, placing herself in between Wolf and the assembled army.

There were some Frankish men who dressed, and lived, as women. One even resided in Radegund's abbey, and the offhand way his story is mentioned implies he was not the only one. In another case, a person biologically sexed as male was buried with all the trappings of an older woman. The opposite, however, does not seem to have been true; or, at least, while there were accounts of women disguising themselves as men to enter monasteries, there are no surviving accounts or archeological evidence of Frankish women dressing as warriors. And Brunhild was not only dressing like a warrior, she was acting like a king in trying to ensure peace in the realm.

It was a symbolic gesture as much as it was a practical one. A Frankish man's belt and sword were not just weapons; they were symbols of his social status. The first thing Chilperic had done to disinherit his rebellious son Merovech was to have him "deprived of his arms." By arming herself, Brunhild was asserting her right to a power exclusively reserved for royal men.

Brunhild drew her sword and, striding back and forth on the field, ordered: "Warriors, I command you to stop this wicked behavior! Stop harassing this person who has done you no harm!"

The soldiers on both sides gaped at first. The charge was halted. Finally, a man's voice rang out: "Stand back, woman! It should be enough that you held regal power when your husband was alive!"

It was Duke Ursio, Egidius's ally, voicing a fear many Austrasian nobles shared—the queen did not seem to know her place. They were worried about the influence she exercised over her son. She had already been able to get Childebert to follow her counsel, in defiance of his regent; he had vetoed one handpicked bishop and installed one of Brunhild's choosing instead. Would she stop at a bishop or two, or did she have bigger ambitions?

Brunhild called again for them to lay down their arms. "Stop fighting each other and bringing disaster upon our country, just because of this one man!"

Ursio would not be lectured to. "Now your son is on the throne, and his kingdom is under our control, not yours."

Brunhild yelled for them to turn back.

"Leave us or our horses' hooves will trample you to the earth!" Ursio menaced.

The queen would not budge.

What could the warriors on either side do? Allow Ursio to carry out his threat? Charge the field and trample the queen?

Ursio and Brunhild shouted back and forth.

Still, she did not budge. There was grumbling, but eventually, the forces dispersed. The queen had held her ground and won the day.

Wolf knew, though, that Brunhild could not protect him forever. Egidius's army soon returned to raid his home, carrying off anything of value they could find and calling for his head.

The usually optimistic Wolf was so shaken by that encounter that he fled Austrasia altogether. He had always advocated for a closer relationship between Austrasia and Burgundy, and now King Guntram rewarded him by offering his protection. Wolf, and later his friend Dynamius, decided to wait out the ascendancy of the pro-Neustrian faction from the safety of Burgundy.

. . .

After the death of Fredegund's sons, there was grave concern for the queen. She ordinarily was cool and haughty; now she had been observed crying raggedly in public.

Chilperic seemed similarly bereft and distracted himself with a flurry of new projects. The king had set aside his poetry and decided to take up theology. Soon he wrote up a decree abolishing the Trinity. When the king read aloud this decree to Gregory, the bishop was horrified. Gregory diplomatically pointed out to the king that belief in the Trinity was the very foundation of their faith; the Roman Church had long battled the Arians over this very same principle. Chilperic huffed: "I will put these matters to men who are more wise than you and they will agree with me." But they did not. The next bishop reacted even more strongly to the proposed change, saying that "if he had been able to reach the paper on which [these decrees] were written he would have torn it into shreds."

Chilperic abandoned theology and moved on to crafting hymns, but Gregory claimed that they were so poorly constructed that "it was impossible to use them." One can see why; one of these hymns survives and shows Chilperic had a poor grasp of Latin and virtually none of poetic rhythm. Undeterred, Chilperic next tried his hand at making additions to language itself. He wanted four new letters added to the alphabet. He commanded that this new script be instituted in schools and that all old textbooks "should be erased with pumice and rewritten." (While these letters never would never take hold in Francia, they would be adopted by the Angles and enter the Old English alphabet. They have since been dropped from English but live on in Scandinavian alphabets to this day.)

Chilperic was dabbling so desperately because there was concern that he could not have more children, and a king without sons needed to ensure his legacy in some other way. It is unclear why, exactly, but the Neustrian nobles thought the situation urgent enough that they made a case for Chilperic to adopt an heir. Fredegund had been remarkably fertile, bearing five children in thirteen years, and she was still quite young, in her early thirties. Less than a year had passed since the princes' deaths, and so the most logical course of action would be to wait a little longer and see if the queen became pregnant again. But those at court may have been privy to information about some injury or a particularly devastating miscarriage that did not make it into the histories or chronicles. There could also have been fear that the dysentery that had taken Chilperic's sons had compromised his virility, or that the dark forces that assassinated their two sons had not yet been vanquished.

King Guntram had adopted Brunhild's son, Childebert. Now Chilperic's advisers clamored for Chilperic to do the same; why not convince Austrasia to break its treaty with Burgundy and join with Neustria instead? The plan found support in Austrasia, too. For all his personal vendettas, Bishop Egidius was more ambitious than vindictive, seeking to leave his mark on the political landscape. Egidius had long dreamed of an Austrasian-Neustrian alliance, and he poured his energy into lobbying on its behalf.

Both queens would have been less than thrilled with this proposed arrangement. Fredegund had fought hard to exclude anyone but her own children from the line of succession, and Brunhild did not want the couple who had killed her sister and husband to symbolically adopt her son. Still, while the two queens may not have liked the idea of an alliance between Neustria and Austrasia, neither actively lobbied against the treaty that formalized it.

Brunhild and Fredegund have long been portrayed as locked in a blood feud originating with Galswintha's murder, blinded by an intense hatred for each other. Yet this alliance suggests that each queen viewed their conflict not as a series of personal vendettas and reprisals, but as a political rivalry. Merovingian politics were a blood sport, but the violence was generally not personal; kings frequently forged and broke alliances, partnering with a brother they had tried to kill only days before. Brunhild and Fredegund proved they could be just as pragmatic: for the good of their respective kingdoms, they were willing to work together.

In 581 Egidius traveled to the outskirts of Paris to meet with Chilperic at his riverside villa in Nogent-sur-Marne. There they hammered out the terms of the agreement. At the ceremony celebrating what came to be known as the Nogent Accords, Chilperic publicly designated his nephew, King Childebert, as his heir, declaring "Childebert shall inherit everything that I manage to keep under my control. All that I ask is that for the term of my natural life I may be left to enjoy these things in peace and quiet."

This is not the voice of the brash young king who usually ended his edicts with a threat to put people's eyes out, who constantly tested borders and limits. This is a humbler king—still in the throes of grief, and possibly, now in his forties, experiencing a midlife crisis, too. A similar glimpse emerges from the days just before the ceremony. Bishop Gregory tells of meeting with Chilperic at his villa. The king seems eager to have company and hurries to show Gregory the precious objects he owns, including a fifty-pound jewel-encrusted solid-gold salver. Chilperic muses that he would like to have more salvers like this made, but only "if it is granted to me to live." Here is a king surrounded by worldly treasures, but with no son to bequeath them to, he is contemplating his own mortality.

Chilperic, resigned to his fate, signed the Nogent Accords, and it was ratified by both kingdoms. History was then rewritten to accommodate this new treaty: it turned out that Sigibert had not been assassinated by Fredegund's men, but rather, by King Guntram! Chilperic boldly stated: "For if my son Childebert would seek the path of reason, he would know at once that it was by my brother's connivance that his father was killed." It was likely that Burgundy would retaliate for Austrasia's treachery in breaking its treaty; now Neustria and Austrasia had a pretext to strike first.

While the treaty was being negotiated, Chilperic had been sending Bishop Egidius money: two thousand solidi along with other regular bribes. After ratification, the king sent a message too: "The stalk which emerges from the soil will not wither until its root is severed." In other words, once Guntram had been dealt with, their next target had to be Brunhild. If they hoped to control young King Childebert, they would need to rip out "the root" of the family: his mother.

. . .

Further support for the new alliance between Neustria and Austrasia came from the Byzantines, who had their own reasons for wanting Guntram out of the way.

After Emperor Justin died in 578, raving mad, Empress Sophia had expected that Tiberius, the general she had brought on as her co-regent, would marry her and they would continue ruling together. But Tiberius had rebuffed Sophia's offers of marriage, refusing to divorce his current wife. Worse, he had told Sophia, who was just a handful of years older than he, to think of herself not as his wife, but as his mother. After Sophia plotted a palace coup, she was removed even further from the locus of power, even though she still retained her title.

Tiberius, now at the reins, was gripped by the old nostalgia for a united Roman Empire. Most of all, he was set on the idea of getting Italy back, even though it was firmly in control of the Lombards. To eject the Lombards, the Byzantines would need to attack from the north through the Alpine passes controlled by the Franks. The three best-known Alpine passes, in use for centuries by the Romans, ran through Burgundy and were controlled by King Guntram. But Guntram adamantly refused to assist the Byzantines with their dreams of reconquering Italy.

The Byzantines could wait and hope for Chilperic and Egidius to remove Guntram. But another possibility presented itself—they could finally make use of Gundovald, the long-haired bastard prince they had been keeping in reserve for many years. If the Byzantines helped Gundovald overthrow Guntram and gain his throne, in exchange Gundovald would allow the Byzantines to use Burgundy as a launching pad for their invasion into Italy.

There were a few reasons to think such a plot had a chance of succeeding. Guntram was nearly fifty, and his third wife had died in the same dysentery epidemic that took the Neustrian princes. It was unlikely Guntram would produce a new son, especially since he planned to spend his remaining years unmarried, in service to his Lord. Yet the Franks idolized virile warrior-kings far more than elder statesmen. Gundovald, in contrast, was now a widower with two sons, a younger Merovingian who could offer a stable succession.

The Byzantines tested out the idea with a whisper campaign, and were pleased to find there was support for an alternate Merovingian not just in Burgundy, but in all three kingdoms. An entire swath of the nobility was unhappy with their current options: the increasingly paranoid and despotic Chilperic or the aging and pious Guntram—both without an heir—or an untested boy-king and his overbearing mother.

Of all the current options, the latter seemed the worst of all. Accordingly, the plot to bring Gundovald back garnered the most enthusiasm in Austrasia. In the late summer or early autumn of 581, the wily Duke Boso set sail for Constantinople. His assignment was to bring back Gundovald, along with whatever money and treasure Tiberius would contribute to the plot. Boso had been selected for this errand by the Austrasian court, despite his reputation for double-dealing, because he was a persuasive speaker and because he and Gundovald had been friendly as young men.

Gundovald warmly greeted his old acquaintance. Boso presented him with letters of invitation to come rule from leading men in both Austrasia and the other kingdoms, yet Gundovald demurred. He was accustomed to his relatively luxurious life at court in Constantinople, and he was not sure he would receive as warm a welcome as Boso promised. The two men traveled to twelve holy sites in the city and Boso swore an oath at each one that no harm would come to Gundovald in Francia. For the first time, Gundovald believed that everyone was clamoring for his return.

CHAPTER 17

The Regency

In the spring of 582, less than a year after the Nogent Accords were signed, the premise for the Austrasian-Neustrian alliance crumbled. Fredegund was pregnant again, and as her pregnancy progressed, Chilperic reconsidered the wisdom of having named his nephew his heir.

The baby, a healthy boy, was born in December of 582. Chilperic's response to the news revealed his relief and a near-delirious joy. Every prisoner in Neustria was released; all fines his subjects owed were erased. Despite Paris' designation as a city to be shared between the three kingdoms, Chilperic was feeling confident enough to commandeer it and move his family into the palace, just in time to celebrate his new son's baptism. The baby, named Theuderic, was baptized on Easter morning, 583, with full honors in the cathedral of Saint-Étienne. The bishop of Paris, Ragnemod (or, as Fortunatus called him, Rucco), presided over the ceremony.

Still, the Nogent Accords meant that the Austrasians and Neustrians were out campaigning together the summer of 583, preparing to invade Guntram's lands. Egidius and his closest advisers were riding with Chilperic, planning to invade Burgundy from the west. The rest of the Austrasian forces, with thirteen-year-old Childebert symbolically leading them, would invade from the north.

Childebert's troops started to grumble on the long march south. Why were they heading off to fight in the first place? King Chilperic had a new baby son. Was he really going to keep King Childebert as his heir?

Someone was encouraging their discontent. But who? Gogo was dead, Wolf and Dynamius had both defected to Burgundy for safety, and Fortunatus was back at the abbey in Poitiers. Still, someone was quietly lobbying against Egidius, and the most likely candidate was Brunhild. She preferred to work quietly, but she would have begun reaching out to some of Gogo's old friends, and even some from Egidius's party who were growing increasingly disaffected.

The grumbling grew louder the longer the march went on. Why, the soldiers asked, were they risking their lives if their king would not benefit? What quarrel did *they* have with Burgundy? Was Chilperic planning to use the Austrasians as pincushions for Guntram's archers? The army began to march slower and slower, in no hurry to arrive at the border.

Chilperic and Egidius reached the Burgundian frontier only to find the other Austrasians were not yet in position. They were forced to fight without their expected reinforcements, against Guntram's forces of over fifteen thousand men, a huge army by Merovingian standards. A blood-bath followed outside the city of Bourges; Gregory would claim that casualties from one battle numbered at least seven thousand on both sides. Guntram then sent in even more men, finally squashing Chilperic's army. The two brothers negotiated a peace between them.

Egidius and his men, retreating northward, caught up to the Austrasian forces dragging their feet on their way south. When Egidius pitched camp with them, overnight the grumbling became open revolt. Some of the soldiers, irate to discover how their countrymen had been slaughtered for a fruitless alliance, started chanting, "Down with those who are handing [Childebert's] cities over to an enemy power! Down with those who are selling Childebert's subjects into foreign slavery!" This went on all night; come morning, they grabbed their weapons and went looking for Bishop Egidius.

Egidius fled the camp on horseback, pursued by soldiers throwing rocks. The bishop rode so hard for his stronghold in Reims that when one of his shoes fell off, he did not dare stop to retrieve it. He arrived in Reims, one-shoed and terrified, and shut himself within the city walls.

Around the same time, Brunhild emerged from the shadows, taking her place at the head of her son's council. She was, finally, the regent of Austrasia.

How had she managed this? A woman was not the obvious choice for the position, especially if other alternatives existed. But Gogo's old network, no matter how diminished, supported her, and those who had previously opposed Brunhild changed their minds for pragmatic reasons. No matter how much they feared a woman wielding political power, they feared the alternatives even more. Had Egidius been meaning to make them a mere protectorate of Neustria? They likely reasoned the queen could at least be trusted to fiercely defend her own son. And she offered a sensible alternative to civil war, positioning herself as above the fray, someone who could mediate disputes between various dukes and their factions. Other officials and nobles, knowing the plot to bring Gundovald back to Francia was already underway, bit their tongues and made themselves agreeable. There was no sense in wasting political capital challenging Brunhild's regentship when the queen might well find herself shoved aside within a year.

For his part, King Guntram would have preferred Brunhild resign herself to a convent, which was clearly the proper place for widowed queens. But while he did not particularly like Brunhild, he disliked his brother Chilperic even more. And while Brunhild was not especially fond of Guntram, she was committed to returning Austrasia to its former alliance with Burgundy and undoing Egidius's work.

Brunhild, for her part, likely planned to position her son as heir to Guntram's kingdom, and then continue to battle Chilperic until she could commandeer his kingdom by force. But Brunhild was also shrewd enough not to overlook the plans that had been put in place by her predecessors for Guntram's overthrow (and potentially her own). Duke Boso had been successful in his errand; Brunhild's old friend Gundovald, carting along a staggering treasure donated by the Byzantines, had landed in Francia in September of 582. In anticipation of Gundovald's arrival, one of King Guntram's most valued military commanders, Duke Mummolus, had defected to Austrasia.

Guntram should not have been surprised by Mummolus's actions—the duke's entire career was founded on betrayal. As a young man, Mummolus had been sent to the king with gifts to secure his father's reappointment as count of Auxerre. Instead, he had double-crossed his father and obtained the post for himself. After that, his climb was rapid—first a count, then a military leader, finally a duke. On the battlefield, as in life, Mummolus made good use of the element of surprise—trickery, traps, ambushes. He subdued the Lombards, and then the Saxons; his talents had helped beat back Chilperic's armies during the earliest phases of the brothers' civil war. Guntram had rewarded him with land, a villa, and immense wealth. But Mummolus, insatiable, wanted more, and decided to gamble on Gundovald.

After his flight, Mummolus, along with his family and followers, had hunkered down in the walled city of Avignon. Gundovald joined him to spend the winter and prepare for the military campaign in the spring. It was here that Gundovald learned that the political situation in Francia was markedly different from what he had expected.

Guntram Boso had, naturally, fudged the details a bit to entice Gundovald back. He had told the bastard prince that Chilperic was dead and without an heir so Neustria was for the taking. Gundovald could rule all of Francia, Boso said; all that stood in the way were the childless, aging Guntram and a boy-king, Brunhild's son.

And so, upon his return, Gundovald was understandably surprised to learn that King Chilperic was not only alive, but also his queen was pregnant. On top of that, the Austrasian-Neustrian alliance had crumpled; Gundovald's whole plan had been predicated on the assumption that the Austrasians would be willing to attack Guntram, too. By the time little Theuderic, heir to the Neustrian throne, was being baptized on Easter morning, 583, Gundovald had retreated to a Mediterranean island to rethink his options.

Would Gundovald launch a new invasion? Brunhild had to be on friendly terms with whoever ended up ruling Burgundy, whether that be Guntram or her old friend Gundovald. She also had territorial ambitions: she wanted to recover cities like Tours and Poitiers that had formerly belonged to Austrasia, and she had not forgotten the matter of Galswintha's morgengabe, either.

Brunhild had an additional worry on her hands in the form of her daughter, Ingund. Across the Pyrenees in Spain, Ingund's marriage was proving to be a disaster; the newlyweds had become embroiled in a rebellion with international consequences.

Ingund's husband, Hermenegild, was the older son of the Visigothic King Leovigild. While Leovigild was out campaigning in 579, he had left his two sons in charge. His younger son was to administer the northern territories, while Hermenegild was to govern the south from the city of Seville. Once installed in Seville, though, Hermenegild had risen up against his father.

At first this rebellion had been mostly bloodless, full of the sort of posturing one might expect from an adolescent boy bucking his much older father's authority. King Leovigild barely responded, and he initially seems to have been more exasperated by his son than angered. Besides, Leovigild was busy in the north fighting with the Basques. He had enough on his mind.

But now, after nearly four years, things had taken a turn for the worse. Leovigild had moved south, determined to quash the rebellion. Ingund had petitioned her mother and brother to send help. But at that time, Egidius was in control, and Brunhild did not yet have the power to override him. The Byzantines, though, had sent troops and supplies to assist the newlywed rebels.

Now Brunhild was finally in a position to help her daughter, but it looked like the situation in Spain was rapidly deteriorating. Hermenegild and Ingund were holed up in Seville under siege. Worse, Brunhild's first grandchild had been born in the middle of these circumstances. Ingund, now fifteen, had given birth to a son. She named him Athanagild, after Brunhild's deceased father.

The Byzantines said they would continue to help Hermenegild and Ingund only if Austrasia would attack the Lombards in Italy in return. Brunhild paced the halls of the palace in Metz, overlooking the lapping waters of the Moselle, weighing her options. King Childebert, approaching his fourteenth birthday, would soon be considered old enough to command an army. A successful foreign campaign could help cement his status as a warrior-king and gain respect and support from the Austrasian people. Yet so much could also go wrong on a foreign campaign—should she risk her son to save her daughter and grandson?

CHAPTER 18

Set Ablaze

Typically, rebellion is a younger brother's game. Eldest sons inherit the best bits, and younger sons resent this. Hermenegild had already been established with his pretty new wife in his own territory with little day-to-day oversight. And King Leovigild was in his sixties, and not in the best health. (Indeed, he would turn out to live only two more years.) Simply waiting would have seemed to be the prudent course for even the most ambitious prince.

What, then, could a firstborn princeling like Hermenegild wish to accomplish by rising up against his father?

Hermenegild is cast as a religious martyr today, thanks in large part to Gregory, who claimed that religious differences were at the heart of this new rebellion. Gregory, though, found religion at the heart of everything; he had no contacts in or special knowledge of Visigothic Spain. True, Hermenegild did convert from Arianism to Catholicism, but not until long after his revolt began. His reasoning seems eminently practical: Catholicism was very popular among the people in the south of Spain whose support he was trying to gain.

So Hermenegild's motives in launching his rebellion are puzzling. Yet a Visigothic source points to Brunhild's mother, Goiswintha, as the mastermind. She had clashed with her second husband, and her stepson had sided with her and her political supporters. Three generations of women—Goiswintha, Brunhild, and Ingund—were tangled up in succession politics.

The most likely explanation for Hermenegild's revolt is that he was merely a pawn in Goiswintha's game. Her support had been essential to secure Leovigild the Visigothic throne, but there is no record he ever thanked her by granting her significant lands of her own. Over the years, Leovigild had been successful at expanding the Visigothic lands through conquest—so much so that Goiswintha now felt there was room enough for her to get her due and establish her own domain in the south of Spain. Perhaps she felt drawn to the region because it had been the home base of her first husband, Brunhild's father: Athanagild had launched his claim to the throne from Seville, and it was there that Hermenegild launched his.

In Goiswintha's vision, this second Visigothic kingdom would be ruled over by her granddaughter and stepson (Ingund and Hermenegild) and allied with her daughter's kingdom in Francia. Further, now that Brunhild was regent, she should be able to secure the five cities that constituted her late sister's morgengabe. These lands, in the southwest of Francia, might even be annexed to this new Spanish kingdom.

While Leovigild was preoccupied with fighting off the Basques, Goiswintha and her allies seized the opportunity to launch the rebellion. Likely they hoped that the war with the Basques would take long enough that Leovigild, unable to sustain fighting on two fronts, would quickly aquiesce to their demands. But now Ingund and Hermenegild were stuck in Seville as the siege dragged on.

Ingund and Hermenegild slipped out of besieged Seville and made their way to the town of Córdoba, which was under Byzantine protection. This should have been a much-needed opportunity to regroup and then redouble their efforts. But sometime before early March of 584, King Leovigild offered the Byzantines in Córdoba a bribe of thirty thousand solidi to stay away while he stormed the city. The Byzantines accepted and stayed in their camp, ignoring Hermenegild's cries for help.

Hermenegild took sanctuary in a church and a standoff ensued. And back in Francia, Brunhild was having trouble finding out what had happened not just to her son-in-law, but to his teenaged wife and infant son.

. . .

Goiswintha still commanded her own faction and political networks in Spain, and Leovigild worried that she might work with Brunhild to launch a retaliatory invasion or some sort of mission to rescue Ingund and her new infant. He needed to create an international alliance to counterbalance his wife's, so he sent envoys to Paris bearing gifts for Chilperic.

Leovigild knew that Chilperic had his own worries about a retaliatory invasion, now that Guntram and Brunhild were allied against him. He had heard that the Austrasians had even levied an army, saying they intended to invade Spain. So the Visigothic king proposed a marriage between his loyal younger son Reccared, who was now seventeen or eighteen, and Chilperic's fourteen-year-old daughter, Rigunth. Chilperic had been holding Rigunth in reserve. Lacking a son, the king would have to use his daughter only for an alliance that would ensure his political fortunes. But now that his new son, Theuderic, had survived his precarious first year, Chilperic and Fredegund were willing to consider marrying their daughter off. Even better if, in the process, they could subvert their enemy Brunhild's ties to her home country and claims to the lands of Galwsintha's morgengabe.

After concluding the negotiations and formalizing plans for a wedding that summer, King Chilperic left Paris to journey to Soissons, a two- to three-day ride. Frantic messengers flew after him, telling him to turn back. The rains had been heavy, the rivers kept overrunning their banks, and the dysentery had returned again. This time it was baby Theuderic who was stricken.

. . .

Up to this point, Chilperic and Fredegund had lost three boys in seven years. Now, they lost a fourth. The word "devastated" can only begin to capture the loss they must have felt.

After the deaths of their two sons in 580, Fortunatus had written a poem for the grieving parents—indeed, a surprisingly humanizing one. In a prayerful passage invoking the royal couple's next child, Fortunatus writes: "May his father play with him, his mother feed him at her breast, and may he snuggle round his parents' necks." It is easy to imagine the Merovingians as indifferent to or reserved with their offspring, inured to the loss of a child because of the sheer frequency with which it happened. But as ruthless as they might need to be as rulers, it was still expected that Chilperic and Fredegund were, or should pretend to be, affectionate, involved parents.

Even if they were as upset about the dynastic implications of their son's death as they were about no longer having a baby to "snuggle," the king and queen were said to be "prostrate with grief." Theuderic was buried in Paris and the entire city was in mourning. Chilperic sent for the Spanish ambassador who had just departed, telling him to postpone the wedding because "I can hardly think of celebrating my daughter's wedding when I am in mourning because I have just buried my son." Chilperic was grieving, but he was also not ready to send his daughter off to a foreign country embroiled in its own civil war; he had to reconsider how to best deploy what was now his most valuable asset.

The Visigoths apparently pushed back, wanting to solidify this alliance so they had one less border to worry about. Rigunth was not his only living child. Chilperic thought of Basina, the sole surviving offspring from his first marriage, sequestered away in Radegund's Holy Cross Abbey.

While Fredegund likely had her soldiers rape Basina and forever stain the girl's honor, either the queen had kept this detail from Chilperic, or he reckoned that the Visigoths were so eager for this alliance that they would be willing to accept a second-rate princess. The king put the proposal to Basina, offering a way out of her monastic prison. A marriage to a foreign prince would offer a fresh start, a way out from under the politics that had so brutally claimed her brothers and mother. Basina might also have realized the marriage was an opportunity, too, to wield power, and perhaps to be able to exact some small revenge against her stepmother one day.

But Basina refused. Perhaps she was not willing to do her father any favors; better the devil she knew than the foreign prince she did not. Chilperic persisted, but Radegund stepped in. "It is not seemly," she lectured her stepson, "for a nun dedicated to Christ to turn back once more to the sensuous pleasures of this world." Radegund would not release Basina from her monastic vows and there was, Chilperic knew, no sense in arguing with Radegund. She was too powerful and stood ready to call in any number of bishops, even the pope, to lecture him on church law. Rigunth would eventually have to marry the Visigothic prince, or Chilperic would have to call off the alliance.

. . .

It is easy to imagine Fredegund at this point, her eyes bruised from lack of sleep, her hair hanging lank, wandering the damp hallways of the palace in Paris, seemingly pitching forward as she walked, murmuring prayers.

Her mind was churning, desperately trying to work out what had gone wrong, yet again. She did not believe in coincidences, having engineered so many of them herself. She was encouraged in this belief by someone who told her the cause of her son's death was not dysentery again, but *maleficia et incantationes*, witchcraft and incantations. Fredegund had blamed her earlier loss on her own misdeeds and tried to atone by revamping the tax code and donating money; witchcraft was a solution that did not require heaping more blame upon herself.

While the queen was contemplating this possibility, she overheard a seemingly innocuous anecdote. One of Chilperic's tax collectors was overheard giving advice to someone whose child had recently died of dysentery. He claimed he had a special remedy, "a certain herb," with special powers—"if anyone who is attacked by dysentery drinks a concoction of it, he is immediately cured, however desperately ill he might be."

And why, knowing the young prince was ill, had he not offered this very herb to his queen? Her suspicions were aroused. Besides, she reasoned, one who could make a potion to cure dysentery might also be able to make a potion to cause it. Fredegund found this idea so credible because she herself knew and employed people who claimed to do this very thing.

In Francia there was a whole class of healers and spellcasters, *incantores*, who could tell fortunes, treat illness, and cast love spells on someone you admired and bad luck charms on someone you despised. The Franks still had access to the medical texts of antiquity, as well as to pagan traditions of herbal balms, salves, and potions. The Catholic Church, of course, was eager to promote priests and saints as the only legitimate seers and healers. But early medieval entrepreneurs combined old and new. They might carry a cross, holy oils, and what they claimed were saints' relics, all while dispensing pagan folk remedies. After all, it was a fine line between saint and witch. An alliance between the Byzantine Empire and Austrasia had been brokered via a scrap of wood, and bishops and dukes carried around hair from a saint's beard or a shard of a martyr's shinbone to ward off disease and misfortune. Bishop Gregory claimed swallowing dust from Saint Martin's tomb had completely cured his own bout of dysentery. Even though they were termed *maleficia*, were the contents of an ordinary healer's bag—"roots of different herbs and . . . moles' teeth, the bones of mice, the claws and fat of bears"—so different?

Some *incantores* were employed by royal courts and nobles; among them was the soothsayer Duke Boso held in such high esteem. Fredegund herself would at times employ a fortune-teller whose services were so highly valued that she paraded around "loaded with jewelry." Common folk were treated by other *incantores*, such as one wandering healer active during the 580 dysentery epidemic whose customers were "the prostitutes and women of the lower class." And others were employed by wealthy merchants and civic officials, by people like this unfortunate prefect.

Fredegund had him arrested and questioned, but he insisted—even while "hung to a beam with his hands tied behind his back," "stretched on the wheel and beaten with triple thongs," and enduring "splinters under his finger and toe nails"—that he had nothing to do with the baby prince's death. He did admit, though, that in addition to his dysentery cure, he had received from certain women *unctiones et potiones*, ointments and potions, and he had used them to try to secure the favor of the king and queen. These sorts of charms to help one's professional life would ordinarily be considered harmless folk magic, lumped in with love spells and concoctions to ward off aging. The Church saw these practices as a nuisance, not as true threats to the faith.

Fredegund, though, thought differently. She sincerely believed that two years earlier, Prince Clovis and his girlfriend had used the dark arts to strike down two of her sons. That witch had been dispatched, but what if she had associates still at work? The source of the prefect's potions was a group of Parisian women, likely healers or midwives; Fredgund had them rounded up and arrested. Under torture, these women, of course, admitted all sorts of things—they were witches, they were responsible for several

Fredegund orders the witches of Paris to be burned alive or broken on the wheel in a Late Medieval manuscript

deaths, and so on. Under even more torture, they agreed with Fredegund's central thesis. Yes, they had practiced the dark arts to strike down baby Theuderic; in fact, they had performed a rite to exchange his life for that of the prefect. But the poor women's agony did not end with that confession: "then the Queen used severer torture on the women and caused some to be drowned and delivered others over to fire, and tied others to wheels where their bones were broken."

When she was done burning women, Fredegund began burning anything that had belonged to her baby son.

The gold buckles and trinkets, the child-size ax and spear, all were melted down in a furnace to ingots. His baptismal linens, his silks and furs, his bassinets and wooden toys, the tapestries on the walls, the furs on the floor—they "filled four carts." The carts were drawn out to the courtyard and set ablaze.

Women were known for turning their pain inward. Radegund and her severe mortifications of the flesh are but one example; she was the most famous representation of all the nuns, mothers, and daughters who grew lightheaded from lack of food, who stumbled under the weight of chains and hair shirts, who bit their lips bloody and shoved their pain down.

But here was trauma incandescent, a grief so white-hot the people could not look away.

This moment would be preserved in myth and emerge more than a thousand years later in the final scene of Richard Wagner's opera cycle, where the Valkyrie builds a gigantic funeral pyre. On horseback, she is silhouetted against the flames and smoke, watching it all burn.

However, there is one critical difference. Wagner has his warrior maiden, unable to bear her pain, riding into the fire and immolating herself. Fredegund, though, just nudged her horse, turned, and rode back inside the palace gates.

. . .

The torture and execution of the Parisian housewives, the burning of her baby boy's possessions—these have long been taken as evidence of Fredegund's bloodthirsty and vengeful nature. But given the realities of the era, they were protective, preventative measures; they were, in fact, maternal.

What chroniclers and historians have always overlooked is that Fredegund was, at the time, very pregnant. The interrogations happened after Theuderic's death in March but before Easter on April 18. During that time, Fredegund was at least eight months along, but she was keeping the pregnancy a secret.

She had fallen into a depression after giving birth to Samson during the siege of Tournai, consumed by *ob metum mortis*, a fear of death. Now the old fear was back.

And how could it not be?

Chilperic's mood was darkening. He expected an imminent attack from a newly re-allied Austrasia and Burgundy and was preparing for another siege. He moved his treasury out of Paris to the suburb of Cambrai and then "sent messengers to his dukes and counts to tell them to repair the walls of their cities, and then shut themselves up inside these fortifications." The wars dragged on, Fredegund's husband was increasingly paranoid, and her baby boys kept dying, assassinated by some dark unseen power.

The extremes she went through were not just meant to avenge baby Theuderic, but to protect the baby she was carrying, to root out the assassins before they might strike again. She may have even used the torture sessions as reconnaissance—did the witches even know she was pregnant? They did not seem to; perhaps her baby was safe, for now.

The royal couple were so terrified that, even after Fredegund was safely delivered of another baby boy in late May or very early June, they did not disclose the birth. News of another heir would have increased Chilperic's stature immediately, especially given the fact that some of his nobles were conspiring to bring back Gundovald. Still, there was no announcement and the baby remained unnamed. The boy was cared for "in the manor of Vitry, for [Chilperic] was afraid that, if he appeared in public, some harm might befall him."

Fredegund's bonfire may have been an outpouring of a violent grief, but it was also a practical precaution. There could be no hand-me-downs; they could not risk an enchanted toy or charmed bit of cloth infecting the new infant prince hidden away in their country villa. Better it all burn in the palace courtyard as spectacle. Better the people assume the queen was desperately bereaved than guess that she was hiding a secret.

CHAPTER 19

Brunichildis Regina

B runhild, too, was in great fear of harm befalling her child. She scrambled to get news about her daughter and new grandchild. Had they been injured or killed in the fighting? But word was excruciatingly slow to arrive; the usual travel time from Spain to her capital in Metz was six weeks. By the end of April, though, Brunhild was able to piece some of the story together.

The standoff between Hermenegild and his father had ended.

Hermenegild had spent a great deal of time in sanctuary. Finally, his younger brother, Reccared, entered the church and convinced Hermenegild to come out and throw himself on their father's mercy, promising that Hermenegild would likely find himself only banished for a period of time. This was either a ploy, or the younger son had genuinely underestimated their father's fury. The old king greeted his rebel son warmly, but then had him seized, chained up, and hauled away. Brunhild's son-in-law was currently in a prison, stripped of his title, but he was alive.

Even better, it appeared that Hermenegild had made his last stand alone; his wife and son had not followed him to Córdoba. They had been offered protection by the Byzantines. Brunhild's relief at hearing that her daughter and her grandson were alive and safe was quickly tempered by the news that they were being transported to Constantinople. The

Byzantines planned to hang on to them as their guests, under guard, until a satisfactory compromise might be found.

These resulting negotiations provide us with the only surviving glimpse of Brunhild's voice: five of her letters to the Byzantine court escaped destruction. These letters would have been dictated to a scribe, of course, and their words were heavily constrained by tradition, but they clearly show Brunhild styling herself as ruler. She calls herself *Brunichildis regina*, Queen Brunhild, and adopts the "royal we" favored by the kings before her.

The letters are, unfortunately, quite general. The most delicate matters were not written down, in case an envoy were to be ambushed. The messenger, once ushered into the emperor's presence, would read the letter out loud to the entire imperial court. The letter would establish the overarching topic and indicate that the messenger himself was authorized to convey the rest of the information, which he would then do in a more private setting.

In the first letter, Brunhild writes back to the new emperor of Byzantium. Tiberius had died and been replaced with his son-in-law, the general Maurice. Emperor Maurice had addressed his missive to Childebert, but Brunhild's curt response made clear his error; she was the one he ought to be corresponding with, since she was the one with the power to decide how to proceed: "The letter directed to our most distinguished son, King Childebert, from the clemency of your most serene sovereignty arrived and we have counselled peace," she writes. She acknowledges receipt of certain messages sent by imperial legates, says she is sending her own messengers with gifts, and agrees that an alliance would benefit both parties.

The alliance the Byzantines were requesting hinged upon Austrasia finally agreeing to mount a campaign against the Lombards in Italy. They had sent fifty thousand solidi to compensate the Franks for the supplies, horses, and men they might need. Agreeing to these terms, the Byzantines made clear, was the only way to ensure the safety, and possible release, of their new hostages.

There wasn't much time to think the matter over. The Alpine passes would open in May, and because the march into Italy would take at least eight weeks, an army would need to be assembled and move out fairly quickly to have enough time to accomplish its business and return before snow and ice closed the passes again.

Austrasia's new regent decided to launch her first military campaign. And for King Childebert, who was barely old enough to grow a mustache, this would be another first—riding with his armies into a foreign nation.

. . .

A Merovingian king was not just a warrior and an administrator, he was the head judge in the realm. While his bishops conducted their own trials (although at the king's command, and often with his considerable royal involvement, as in the trials of Praetextatus and Gregory of Tours), the king was responsible for overseeing all civil and criminal cases in his realm. The vast majority of these cases—cases of stolen livestock or damaged crops, disputes between landlords and tenants or between family members—were ruled on by local judges. But more serious cases like rapes, murders, and charges of treason were often adjudicated by the king himself.

As one of her first public acts as regent, Brunhild presided as judge over the royal court to hear one such case. This was a groundbreaking act and is the first recorded instance of a woman presiding over a court not just in Francia, but in all of Western Europe. Women appeared in court all of the time, but as plaintiffs, defendants, or witnesses. But now a woman was acting as the embodiment of the law, a power previously reserved exclusively for kings. And it is clear that Brunhild acted on her own authority, not alongside her son: the defendant "was summoned by Queen Brunhild and appeared before her."

The case concerned a clash between church and state in Javols, a town in the far south of Francia. The accuser was the local count, and the defendant was the town's abbot, who was alleged to have slandered the queen. Later, in his chronicle of these events, Gregory dared not even repeat what the abbot was supposed to have said. Perhaps, out of loyalty to Brunhild, he did not want to give the remarks credence, or more likely, Gregory had learned the hard way from his own trial that it did not pay to repeat insults about a queen. Whatever the alleged comments were, they must have been serious enough to warrant a charge of sedition. Presumably, they were similar to those Fredegund had faced four years earlier—rumors of past sexual infidelity that could raise questions about her son's legitimacy.

There are no details of the trial itself, except for the verdict—the abbot was acquitted and Brunhild told him to return home. On his way, he was attacked by his accuser on the banks of the Aisne River and beheaded. The Count of Javols disposed of the evidence of his crime, putting the abbot's head "in a sack weighted with stones," tying the body to a large rock, and tossing both into the river.

To the people of Javols, it seemed as if their abbot had simply vanished. Had he run off with a woman? Been waylaid by robbers? Eaten by a wild beast? Somehow, the headless body floated free of the rock anchoring it to the riverbed. When it was found floating in the Aisne, though, there was no reason to connect it with the case of the missing abbot. The shepherds who had found the unidentifiable corpse, being good Christians, prepared to bury it. It was at this point, they later claimed, that a miraculous event occurred: "there suddenly appeared an eagle, which fished [a] sack out of the bottom of the river and placed it on the bank." However the sack came to them, inside they found the abbot's head, and the mystery of the corpse's identity was solved. The alleged eagle was interpreted as a sign of divine intervention, the abbot was declared a saint, and an informal shrine was made of his tomb.

Once it was clear the abbot had not gone missing, but had been murdered, the Count of Javols was the glaringly obvious suspect. This would have appeared to be yet another case of a hot-tempered noble and a blood feud if it were not for what happened next. Once the crime was uncovered, rather than being punished, the culprit was rewarded. The Count of Javols never stood trial for the murder, and a few months later he ended up a bishop. He was a rather unlikely candidate; he wasn't even a clergyman. But when a vacancy opened up, Brunhild championed him for the job. The count was placed in Rodez, a diocese whose lands bordered those of Cahors, one of the cities incorporated into Galswintha's morgengabe. As her late sister's heir, Brunhild felt entitled to Cahors, but it was still under Neustrian control. As soon as he was installed in Rodez, the count-turned-bishop began a turf war with the bishop of Cahors, trying to gain back disputed land for his queen.

It was the responsibility of a Frankish monarch to intervene in feuds, yet here was a monarch using one to her advantage. An enemy who was disparaging Brunhild had been dispatched, and she had gained an ally who was willing to defend her interests. She had seen the virulence of the men opposed to her; three years earlier, when she made her battlefield appearance, Count Ursio would have gladly trampled her if he thought he would get away with it. It made sense to build alliances with any men who would openly acknowledge her authority, no matter how short their tempers.

. . .

When Chilperic learned that the Austrasians were headed to Italy with Childebert at their helm, he relaxed. He would not face a combined assault from Austrasia and Burgundy. He and Fredegund were not ready to publicly reveal the existence of their new baby, but they finally felt comfortable enough to send Rigunth to be married.

His daughter was to be seen off with as much pomp as possible to make up for the equivocation and delays. The royal family came back to Paris in late summer, consumed with the preparations.

Chilperic, who was already given to lavish displays, seized upon his daughter's wedding as yet another opportunity to demonstrate his power. Sixteen years ago, he had welcomed a Visigothic princess with the vanguard of an army on bended knee; now he intended to send his daughter off to the Visigoths with the same sort of spectacle.

Chilperic wanted Rigunth to have the largest possible entourage, but he ran out of royal servants to send along with her, so he then looked to the servants on his country estates and had them "carted off in wagons." Rigunth's nurse and attendants would have always expected to serve the princess after her marriage, but ordinary servants were startled to discover they were now expected to live in far-off Spain. In response, "they wept bitterly and refused to go" and Chilperic was forced to have them "guarded closely" to prevent their running off. Despite that, some were so unwilling to leave behind their families and homes that they "hanged themselves in their distress."

Once Rigunth's escort was forcibly assembled, fifty carts were piled high with "vast weight of gold and silver, and many fine clothes," so much so that Fredegund had to reassure the nobles assembled for the farewell party that she had not emptied the treasury: "Everything you see belongs to me."

Fredegund's response grants us insight into the considerable wealth she now controlled. She mentions that not only had Chilperic given her gifts, but so, too, had the nobles. In addition, she had "put aside quite a bit from my own resources, from the manors granted me, and from revenues and taxes." A slave who had started with nothing had accumulated enough personal capital to fill fifty carts with valuables. The dowry was as much a display of her own power as it was of Chilperic's, and it was so extravagant that he had to gather a force to guard not just his daughter's person but also her dowry.

The Visigoths arrived on September 1, 584, to collect their bride. The Neustrian nobility assembled and weighed down the young princess with even more gifts. When the farewell ceremony finally concluded with tears and kisses, Rigunth ascended into her carriage and started off, accompanied not only by the reluctant slaves and servants but also by three dukes, a count, several chamberlains, and four thousand soldiers. But as Rigunth passed under the city gate, an axle on her carriage broke. There were audible gasps, as many took this to be an unlucky sign.

Having been much delayed because of the farewell party and repairs, the procession did not make it far before dusk fell. They pitched camp for the night just eight miles outside the city, which turned out to be a mistake, as this was still familiar territory for many of the slaves and servants seized from the countryside. During the night, fifty men saw their chance to escape and slipped away, taking with them "a hundred of the best horses with golden bridles and two great chains." They headed for Austrasia, finding a rival Frankish kingdom preferable to life far away in Spain. Fifty men were hardly any at all given the size of the wedding entourage, but it provided an example for others. Almost every night, a few more people helped themselves to some coins or jewels from the heaping carts and vanished.

About ten days into the journey, when they had made it as far as Poitiers, some of the nobles (by prior arrangement) turned back for Paris. There is no mention of Radegund coming out of her convent in Poitiers to greet the princess or offer her blessing, which the former queen did for so many other dignitaries. Perhaps she was afraid to open her abbey to the princess's entourage. A force of close to five thousand needed to stop frequently to replenish supplies, which they simply took from the towns they encountered—grain stores, entire vines of grapes, cows, and pigs—earning them the ire of the poor and comparisons to swarms of locusts.

PICTURING THE DARK QUEENS

No contemporary likenesses of Brunhild or Fredegund survive. However, the images of other sixth-century female rulers, such as the Byzantine Empresses Ariadne and Theodora, give us an idea of how they might have been portrayed.

This is the earliest extant image we have of Fredegund. In the twelfth century, Fredegund's tomb was dug up and given a new mosaic slab. This work seems to have been commissioned by another woman, a queen (Adelaide of Maurienne) eager to link herself to a powerful predecessor.

14th century: Fredegund the Fierce

Amid the many crises of the fourteenth century, Fredegund was portrayed as a warrior king would be, leading her troops into battle and overseeing the torture of her enemies.

15th century: Victim of Ambition

Fifteenth-century illuminated manuscripts reveled in the gruesome execution that cleaves through the queens' story. Alarmed by the power wielded by the likes of Isabella, the She-Wolf of France; Yolande of Aragon; and Margaret of Anjou, chroniclers used these images as a warning to other women with political ambitions.

6 *jmpudique*

Fredegonde

Concubine, puis femme de Chilperic
Roy de France qu'elle fit mourir,
voyant qu'il auoit découuert ses
adulteres auec Landry de la Tour.

This deck of playing cards designed for a young Louis XIV showcases various queens. While some are described as *saincte* (holy) or a *bonne femme* (a good wife), Brunhild and Fredegund are cast as murderous villains, the sort of women the young king ought to avoid.

8 *cruelle*

Brunehaut

Femme de Sigisbert Roy de Mets.
Elle fit mourir plus de dix Rois
ou fils de Rois de France. entre
autres elle prit par le pied le fils
de Theodebert, et luy cassa la teste
contre vne colomne .

18th century: Foremothers of France

A century later, both queens were rehabilitated. The rise of nationalism led to an obsession with the great men of the past. Brunhild and Fredegund were transformed into the respectable wives of the kings they overshadowed in life.

FRÉDEGONDE, REINE DE FRANCE,

III.ᵉ FEMME DE CHILPERIC I;

née à Avaucourt en Picardie en 542; morte à Paris en 597.

BRUNEHAUT, REINE D'AUSTRASIE,

FEMME DE SIGEBERT, PUIS DE MEROUÉE, FILS DE CHILPERIC I;

née en 548; morte en 613, et enterrée dans l'église de Sᵗ Martin d'Autun.

19th century: Defiant Heroines

At a time when the ideal woman was submissive and self-effacing, Brunhild and Fredegund were cast as fighters. In a woodcut, Brunhild is carried by her warriors, and in an illustration, Fredegund battles with her daughter.

19th century: Opera Darlings

By the end of the nineteenth century, both queens enjoyed newfound popularity. They appeared as the subjects of poems, the protagonists of plays, and, most notably, the leads of operas.

FRÉDEGONDE ET BRUNEHAUT

— Je te dis « Maire du Palais. »
— Veux-tu te Clotaire... espèce d'historique!

Dessin de L. Métivet.

20th century:
The Catfight

Illustrators lampooned Brunhild and Fredegund's decades-long political rivalry. The two queens box one another on the back of a turn-of-the-century magazine; by mid-century they have progressed to yanking each other's hair out in a lottery advertisement.

EN 589
Frédégonde et Brunehaut
se prirent aux cheveux

AVEZ-VOUS PRIS
VOTRE BILLET?

LOTERIE NATIONALE

Plundering the countryside as it went, the large procession crawled southwest, hemorrhaging servants and treasure along the way. The caravan hoped to make it past the Pyrenees before the snow started with at least some of the dowry left.

Chilperic had not yet received word that his daughter's marriage procession was being looted in slow motion. Exhausted from the preparations, he and Fredegund retired to his villa at Chelles. It was late September, hunting season, time to chase stag and boar.

It was dusk when he returned. The other nobles in his party had already dismounted and were trudging off to their quarters. The king's horse was one of the last to trot up to the stable yard. A slave stepped forward to take the reins. The king swung one leg over the horse's back, placing his hand on the slave's shoulder to steady himself.

Another man stepped forward. It was quick—a dagger into the king's armpit, then his belly. The blood dribbled from his mouth as he tumbled from his horse.

CHAPTER 20

The King Is Dead

The king was the law, and once the law was dead, chaos reigned. Nobles fastened their cloaks, pulled on their boots, and saddled up their horses. Some grabbed gold, some grabbed documents, and some even grabbed the meat and wine in the royal cellars. Meanwhile, as they rushed back and forth, Chilperic remained where he had fallen from his horse in the stable yard. The sky turned from violet to black and the shadows of the surrounding forest fell across the crumpled king, now completely alone.

Finally, one figure crept up to the body. The bishop of Senlis had been camped out on the estate for three days, hoping to be granted an audience with the king. Now he fetched Chilperic's body and dragged it back to his tents. It was he who undressed and washed the king's body, wiped away the blood from his mouth. He sent his servants to gather finery from the king's chambers, re-dressed the king, and then spent the night keeping vigil over the body, "singing hymns."

Fredegund would not or could not do these things for her husband of fifteen years because she was in the private chambers of one of her husband's advisers, in hushed conversation. When she left, white-faced, she ordered servants to pack quickly and dispatched messengers on whatever horses remained.

The next morning, the bishop of Senlis fetched his boat, likely a flat-bottomed barge with a single sail, and loaded up Chilperic's body. He navigated down the Marne River to the point where it empties into the Seine and then past the walled Île de la Cité and over to the Left Bank, where Chilperic's body was unloaded onto a cart in the middle of the fields and meadows and taken to the small church that is now Saint-Germain-des-Prés.

Fredegund did not attend her husband's funeral. She traveled with the body only as far as the Île de la Cité; the bishop stopped to allow her to disembark, pass through the city gates, and make her way to the cathedral, where she threw open the doors and demanded sanctuary from Fortunatus's darling Rucco, the bishop of Paris.

The cathedral had an interior more opulent than that of the Paris palace: the paneled ceiling was supported with exotic black marble pillars, and the walls glittered with mosaics illuminated by the large stained-glass windows. It was a formidable church, half an acre in area, large enough to easily accommodate a queen, her infant son, and as much of the royal treasury as her servants could manage to spirit away. Soon, the city would be surrounded. Fredegund was in the exact same position her rival had been a decade earlier—newly widowed and trapped in Paris.

. . .

The assassin escaped.

A rumor circulated that, whoever he was, he had been hired by the grieving widow. One account claimed Fredegund hurriedly eliminated Chilperic after her affair with General Landeric, the Mayor of the Palace, was discovered. The discovery is painted in convincing detail:

> Fredegund was in the bedroom washing her hair with her head in the water. The king came up behind her and whacked her on the buttocks with a stick. She, thinking it was Landeric, said: "Why do you do this, Landeric?" Then she looked up behind her and saw it was the king; she was very scared. The king, indeed, was very much saddened and went off to his hunt.

According to this source, Fredegund summoned Landeric; the two assumed they were about to be arrested and tortured. While Landeric supposedly panicked and began crying, Fredegund came up with a plan and had implemented it by the time the king returned from the hunt. She sent assasins who were "drunk on her wine" to waylay the king. As he dismounted from his horse, the men "stabbed the king in the belly with two scramsaxes. Chilperic cried out and died." This account of Chilperic's murder shares obvious symmetry with that of his brother Sigibert: two assassins, fortified with liquid courage, stabbing a king with two scramsaxes.

Before they escaped the men yelled: "Ambush, ambush, this is what King Childebert of Austrasia did to our lord." They claim to be Austrasian agents; clearly, if Fredegund wanted her husband out of the way, everyone knew she was sensible enough to frame her rival for the deed.

Although this narrative is deliciously scandalous, there are compelling reasons why it may not be accurate. The first is that it was written over a century after the assassination, during the fall of the Merovingian dynasty and the dawn of the Carolingian dynasty. This tale of Fredegund's adultery was written just as Charlemagne's grandfather, himself a Mayor of the Palace, was revolting against a king named Chilperic II. A story about Chilperic II's namesake being cuckolded by his own Mayor of the Palace would have been especially resonant.

However, even if this account was exaggerated or dramatized to gain the favor of the current ruler, there was likely some bit of truth to it. General Landeric was one of Chilperic's top political advisers; Fredegund, another adviser, would have had at least a working friendship with Landeric. They would have been seen walking together to meetings and chatting at councils. It's possible, too, that Fredegund was working with Landeric, although not sleeping with him, to circumvent the sometimes contradictory decrees of her increasingly paranoid and capricious husband. Long after Chilperic's death, Landeric and Fredegund remained friendly, and Landeric prospered; there is still a village in northeastern France named after his country estate, Landreville, or "Landeric's villa."

Of course, it is possible that the slights against Fredegund's honor were more than the usual misogynistic attacks. Perhaps Fredegund *had* been unfaithful to Chilperic or, at least, had been actively working to make sure she had an escape route at the ready should she lose favor with the king or if he were to die suddenly. That would certainly be consistent with her nature; she was a survivor, first and foremost.

The eighth-century account of her adultery might have garbled some of the details but gotten the essence of the story correct. Bishop Gregory was bold enough to risk slandering Fredegund a second time in claiming that after Chilperic's murder, Fredegund had asked not Landeric but the king's chamberlain, Eberulf, the official who controlled the treasury, "to come live with her, but he had refused." Eberulf's support may have been part of the contingency plan she was desperately trying to put into motion the night of her husband's assassination; it is likely that Fredegund had left Chilperic laying in the stable yard not because she was in Landeric's chambers but because she was in Eberulf's, trying to gain his support. If he agreed to marry her, they might rule together. Eberulf rejected her offer, likely because he already had a wife, but Fredegund would not soon forget this humiliation.

. . .

The other obvious suspect was Queen Brunhild.

Her ally Bishop Gregory called Chilperic "the Nero and Herod of our time" and then listed all of the king's faults, sins, and shortcomings, making it appear that nearly everyone had cause to murder the king. Of course, if his patron had ordered the assassination, he would have good reason to gloss over that fact and spread the blame around.

An account written in Burgundy half a century later did hold Brunhild responsible, stating: "Chilperic was killed at the villa of Chelles, not far from Paris, by a man named Falco, who had been sent by Brunhild." This author was using Bishop Gregory's work as a guide, but he also had access to other royal and church archives as well as the accounts of foreign ambassadors; perhaps the supposed name of the assassin was recorded in one of these. The unadorned and offhand manner in which he offers this information suggests it was regarded in some circles as common knowledge.

Brunhild certainly had both means and motive. She had been involved in a previous attempt to assassinate Chilperic after her marriage to Merovech, and she still held the king responsible for the murders of her sister and husband as well as the death of Merovech. Brunhild's ambassadors had been at the Neustrian court just weeks prior to Chilperic's death and had the opportunity then to plant or hire an assassin.

King Chilperic is stabbed by an unknown assailant in this fourteenth-century miniature

It is highly likely that Brunhild did not know about the four-month-old baby Fredegund was hiding. If Chilperic were to die without an heir, Brunhild would have expected that her son Childebert would rule all three kingdoms.

Childebert had spent the summer campaigning in Italy and had just made it back home, unscathed. Conveniently, he and Brunhild were in Neustrian territory, just twenty miles away from Chelles, at the time of the assassination. Chilperic's treasury officials packed up the gold and jewels that had been at Chelles and "lost no time in joining King Childebert" who happily enriched his coffers. Hearing that Fredegund had already slipped past them and left Chelles, Childebert and the Austrasian forces marched on Paris to catch up with her.

Not only were Brunhild and Childebert remarkably close by and well-positioned to accept the gold brought by fleeing treasury officials, but also Brunhild had a military leader poised to take back territory she considered hers by right. An Austrasian duke swooped into Limoges, one of the contested cities of Galswintha's morgengabe, then marched north to try to take back the cities of Poitiers and Tours.

. . .

There is also a third possible scenario: that Chilperic was assassinated as the result of a conspiracy linked to his bastard brother, Gundovald.

In this version, Brunhild was still involved or at least somehow alerted in advance and thus able to position her son and dukes to best capitalize on the chaos afterward, but she was not the prime instigator of the events. Such a conspiracy would have involved nobles from all three kingdoms working together, men of disparate backgrounds and with different political aims, but it is not so far-fetched if one looks at the series of events that followed the assassination.

Gundovald had spent the summer on a Mediterranean island, likely in one of the archipelagos off the coast of Marseilles or Cannes (but possibly a more distant spot like Corsica), staying in close contact with his supporters. The news of Chilperic's death launched Gundovald's boat; as far as he knew, Chilperic had left behind only two daughters—one on her way to Spain, another locked in a nunnery. Gundovald landed in Francia for the second time in late September 584, and made his way, again, to Avignon. He believed the conditions Duke Boso had promised him back in 581 were finally in place: Neustria was for the taking, and the only Merovingian royals were the aging Guntram and the teenage Childebert.

In the meantime, Princess Rigunth had made it as far as Toulouse, a little over a week's journey from the Spanish border, and was not yet aware that her father was dead. Her escorts pressed her to stop. They needed to make repairs and freshen up. They appealed to the princess's vanity, telling her they wanted to save her from the "ridicule" of appearing before her groom "travel-stained," and the princess, wanting to look her best, consented to the delay.

While the vast caravan was idling in Toulouse, an unscheduled guest caught up with them— Desiderius, the Neustrian duke of Aquitaine. Once messengers on fast horses thundered up, confirming that Chilperic was dead, Desiderius called a meeting with the leader of the troops in the princess's escort. There is no record of what was discussed, but immediately

afterward the two generals commandeered the princess's troops and treasure in Gundovald's name.

Rigunth could have tried to reach the Spanish border on her own. But
without a dowry and trousseau, even a princess could not expect the
wedding to go ahead as planned. And with Chilperic dead and no clear
successor named, the Visigoths might no longer wish to ally themselves
with Neustria. Reeling, Princess Rigunth stayed where Desiderius left
her—in sanctuary in a church in Toulouse, waiting for someone to send
troops to escort her back home.

One of the servants in this ill-fated entourage rode as fast as he could
all the way back to Paris. He found Fredegund in her quarters at the
cathedral. Hearing the news, the queen fell into a frenzy—*furor*—enraged
beyond reason. Fredegund did not shoot the messenger, but came very
close to it. She attacked the servant, ordering the clothes to be ripped
from his back and his ceremonial belt taken away. She was always most
ferocious whenever she was most vulnerable; she would rather the world
hear of her temper than her fear. As others from the entourage stumbled
home to Paris in the upcoming weeks, "cooks and bakers" and others,
Fredegund made sure they paid dearly for witnessing her daughter's
humiliation—they were "beaten, plundered, and maimed."

Fredegund had counted on her daughter being safely ensconced on the
Visigothic throne, perhaps had even been contemplating Spain as a possible
escape route. If that avenue was no longer open to her, she needed her
personal treasure, and the loyalty it could buy, now more than ever. Duke
Desiderius had sworn his loyalty to her family, had bowed to her at
feasts—now he had seized her money and dishonored her daughter? After
such a public betrayal, other indignities and affronts were sure to follow.

The beleaguered queen even seemed to fear that her husband's grave
might be desecrated. Although she had been unable to attend Chilperic's
funeral, it appears that Fredegund ordered a very specific inscription
carved into his stone sarcophagus. The Latin epigraph was two lines long.
The second line is a posthumous plea that the king be allowed to rest in
peace: "I, Chilperic, pray that my bones will not be removed from here."
The first line is in a different voice, that of Fredegund herself: *Tempore
nullo volo hinc tolantur ossa Hilperici*, or "At no point do I want the bones of
Chilperic to be taken from here."

Fredegund knew, though, that her demand might not be obeyed. And if Chilperic was no longer venerated, were he to be erased from public memory, she would be too. Without family to shelter her or protect her holdings, Fredegund knew she needed a man to help her cling to power. Spurned by the chamberlain Eberulf, and with news that many of her husband's other nobles were fleeing or defecting, she saw no other option but to send her messengers to King Guntram. Two decades earlier, King Charibert's widow, Theudechild, had offered herself and the royal treasury to King Guntram. Fredegund could have done the same —Guntram was single and in need of an heir, and Fredegund had proved she was exceedingly fertile.

But Fredegund was careful to learn from Theudechild's error. Even if a way could be found around the Church's new incest prohibitions, Guntram resented powerful women, and he did not appear to want another wife. Instead, Fredegund offered what Guntram did not have and wanted even more. Her message read: "Let my lord come and take charge of his brother's kingdom. I have a tiny baby, whom I long to place in his arms. At the same time I shall declare myself his humble servant."

The baby was a complete surprise to Guntram. Chilperic and Fredegund had done such a good job keeping his birth a secret that he was now unacknowledged, unbaptized, even unnamed. In fact, had the baby died and another been substituted, no one would have any way of knowing. Fredegund would not have dared show up empty-handed.

Fredegund had a knack, well-honed over a childhood and adolescence of servitude, for figuring out exactly what those in power wanted to hear. Even better, she had the ability to seemingly shape-shift, making herself a blank slate for the desires of others. In crafting her invitation, Fredegund was also careful to learn from the experiences of her rival. Guntram grudgingly respected Brunhild, but neither did he like her nor approve of a widow striking out on her own. Here, he thought, was a new widow coming to him as she ought, not as an equal or as a partner, but deferential, in need of his protection.

Guntram took the bait.

He raced to Paris with a small force and ordered the gates shut to everyone else. Childebert and his Austrasians arrived shortly after, surrounding the city. Brunhild had her son, her envoys, and her allies repeat the rumors that Fredegund had killed Chilperic. Childebert and his army demanded, "Hand over the murderess, the woman who garroted my aunt, the woman who killed first my father and then my uncle!"

But Guntram refused, telling Childebert's assembled men that he was now Fredegund's protector, "She has a king as her son and she therefore cannot be surrendered."

CHAPTER 21

The Vexations of King Guntram

While Brunhild and Guntram were locked in a battle over Fredegund's fate, Gundovald and his supporters launched a new effort.

Gundovald now had at his disposal thousands of horses and troops, both those under his ally Mummolus's command in Avignon and those Desiderius had commandeered from Rigunth's wedding party. He also had the talents of the two dukes themselves, who were among the best-respected military minds of their generation.

But though Chilperic's assassination opened new avenues of opportunity for Gundovald, his position was also weaker than it had been two years earlier when he returned to Francia backed by gold from Constantinople. Now that the Byzantines held Brunhild's grandson hostage, they had leverage over the Austrasians and no longer needed to install Gundovald on the throne to get what they wanted: the land route to Italy. The Austrasians had even joined Constantinople in its campaign against the Lombards. To the Byzantines, Gundovald was just another strategic investment that hadn't matured; they had moved on.

If his original plan had been to conquer the entire Frankish Empire, Gundovald would now have to temper his ambitions. In the middle of October of 584, a month after Chilperic's assassination, he set his sights instead on carving out a kingdom in the Aquitaine in southwestern Francia. He had a decent claim to the region: Before, when Francia had been divided into four kingdoms, the Aquitaine had belonged to the eldest brother, Charibert, and it was at his court that Gundovald had been groomed as a possible heir. This claim would not infringe upon the territory of the Austrasians and would leave Guntram with some of his kingdom intact. Essentially, Gundovald's plan would return Francia to status quo antebellum, the four-way split that was in place before 567, as if all of the ensuing assassinations and land grabs, reprisals and reversals—the whole awful business of civil war—had never happened.

To formalize his ambitions, Gundovald went to the contested region of Limoges and was raised on a shield in the traditional Frankish fashion and proclaimed a king. This, in itself, was an act of war.

At the same time, numerous assassination attempts were launched against Guntram in Paris. Guntram took to always traveling with armed guards, even to church. The threat was deemed so great that he gave a public address at Mass, begging he be spared for "three years at least," so he might sort matters out for his nephews and so the Franks would have at least one "full-grown man" to protect them.

Brunhild had no immediate reason to do away with Guntram; as annoying as his obstinance over Fredegund was, Childebert was still set to inherit Guntram's kingdom. If Brunhild was worried that Fredegund's new child would cut into her own son's share, she would have been best served by focusing her efforts on kidnapping, or assassinating, the infant. Eliminating the only other adult Merovingian male, though, certainly benefitted Gundovald.

As he marched into the Aquitaine, Gundovald passed through Austrasian territory. Brunhild, curiously, did not interfere with his progress, either by prior arrangement or simply because she was too preoccupied with the events unfolding in Paris.

Childebert was still demanding that Guntram "hand over that witch Fredegund" so she might be held accountable for the death of his father, Sigibert; his uncle Chilperic; and even his cousins Merovech and Clovis. He had other demands, too. Brunhild had been hoping that important cities like Tours and Poitiers—which had belonged to Austrasia until they were conquered by Chilperic—would now be returned to her. But Guntram had sent his forces in to occupy them, claiming dominion over all of Chilperic's recent conquests. Guntram was refusing to negotiate directly with Brunhild, willing to speak to only Childebert himself, who was not yet of age.

Brunhild, in response to this slight, sent some of the Austrasian nobles to meet with Guntram in Childebert's stead. She did not send the nobles who would be most sympathetic to Guntram and likely to make the most headway during negotiations. She sent Bishop Egidius and Duke Guntram Boso, a selection that seemed designed to spark a confrontation rather than an agreement.

When the Austrasian contingent asked Guntram for Tours and Poitiers back, the king erupted in a fury. He had made Childebert his heir and all he had received in return was double-dealing. Guntram had laid his hands on Chilperic's archives and now had copies of the secret Nogent Accords, indisputable proof that the Austrasians had betrayed him three years earlier. This treaty, of course, had been engineered by Egidius before Brunhild had claimed the regency. And now it was Egidius who dared ask him for concessions?

But King Guntram's outrage over this former Neustrian-Austrasian alliance was eclipsed by his scathing anger at Boso, who had engaged in some head-spinning duplicity.

After collecting Gundovald from Byzantium in 582, Boso had sailed with him back to the city of Marseilles, a major trading port connecting Francia with the eastern Mediterranean world. It was a contested city that had passed back and forth between Burgundian and Austrasian hands; at that time, Austrasia was in control. Boso and Gundovald were greeted at the docks by the city's bishop, Theodore, who had been installed by Sigibert and was a staunch supporter of Austrasia.

Gundovald's men emptied the boats of their cargo. The immense treasure was loaded up into carts that were then hitched up to the horses Theodore provided. Unbeknownst to the prince and the bishop, Boso had helped himself to a portion of Gundovald's treasure. And then, as soon as Gundovald had ridden out of Marseilles, Boso had Theodore arrested.

The charges? Introducing a Byzantine agent into Frankish lands.

Theodore was incredulous. Hadn't Boso been on the same boat with this supposed Byzantine agent? Theodore even produced a letter signed by the leading men of Austrasia, showing he was just following orders in welcoming Gundovald.

Still, Boso brought Bishop Theodore to Guntram, informing the king of Gundovald's return and accusing Theodore of treason. Why Boso would do so is still a mystery. Had he suddenly, in a matter of hours, soured on Gundovald? Or had Boso imagined the King of Burgundy would be eternally grateful to him for the tip and reward him accordingly?

Boso proceeded on to the Austrasian court at Metz, where he announced Gundovald was, at this moment, on his way to Avignon. Boso accepted congratulations for a successful expedition; he did not, of course, mention that he had pocketed a bit of Gundovald's gold and delivered Bishop Theodore into Guntram's hands.

When Boso returned to his estate, he found strange soldiers in his home, surrounding his wife, two daughters, and young son. King Guntram himself was there. He had taken the risk of riding over the border into Austrasia to let Boso know he had uncovered his foul play: "It was your invitation which brought Gundovald to Francia! And it was to arrange this that you went to Constantinople!"

No, Boso insisted. Not him. It was Guntram's former duke Mummolus, who was one of Gundovald's biggest supporters. Gundovald was at Mummolus's estate in Avignon right now.

To clear his name, Boso offered to go capture Mummolus in Avignon and bring him back to Guntram. Boso even offered his little son to the king as a hostage until he returned. Guntram agreed to the plan and provided Boso with some troops.

Mummolus had made sure the city of Avignon, set on the banks of the Rhone, was virtually impenetrable. He also had some inkling of Boso's treachery and had taken extra precautions. Mummolus had switched out all the rowboats on the banks of the Rhone. When Boso and his men had made it halfway across, the boats fell apart. Boso and the other survivors only made it to shore by swimming or hanging on to planks of wood.

When they approached the city walls of Avignon, gasping and soaking wet, Mummolus was waiting atop the ramparts. He invited Boso and his men to enter: "There's nothing to be afraid of." All they would have to do was wade across a shallow moat. They soon discovered, though, that someone had dug deep pits into the riverbed—Boso lost even more of his companions and had to be fished out himself. Needless to say, Boso never captured Mummolus, and King Guntram lost quite a few of his men in the process.

So when Boso came face-to-face with Guntram almost two years later, during the negotiations of 584 about Fredegund's fate, Guntram sputtered in rage: "You traitor, who have never been known to keep your word!"

Most men would have panicked at being publicly accused of treason by a king. But Duke Boso didn't flinch. Instead, he demanded to know who had told Guntram this information: "Let him now step forward and speak out." No one volunteered. Boso proclaimed he would clear his name through ordeal by combat. Dueling Boso on the king's behalf would be an easy way to gain the king's favor, yet not a single noble stepped forward. They were all silent, clearly afraid.

To save face, King Guntram tried to extract a promise from all gathered that despite their differences, they could at least unite against Gundovald. Guntram railed on about Gundovald: This man was not his brother. Gundovald's father was not King Clothar but a mill worker, he claimed. And a wool worker. Both were lowly professions, usually held by women or slaves—the furthest thing from a royal pedigree.

But Guntram's insult did not have its intended effect. Likely egged on by Boso's earlier boldness, one of the envoys asked how Gundovald could have two fathers, a miller and a weaver. "It becomes you ill, King, to talk so foolishly," he chided.

The rest of the Austrasians burst out laughing.

Worse, they hinted that maybe Gundovald *would* prevail. As they packed up to leave, one envoy darkly intoned that there was an ax hanging over the king's head.

Unable to confront Boso and his fellow envoys in person, Guntram contained his wrath until the men were outside of the city gates. Then he had his soldiers catapult garbage at their retreating figures—moldy hay, mud from the town's gutters, and horse dung. Boso traveled all the way back to the Austrasian court, soaked in shit.

. . .

Guntram assembled the remaining nobles of Neustria and had them swear an oath of loyalty to Fredegund's little boy. The king had decided that the infant should be named Clothar after Guntram's father.

If Fredegund had hoped that Guntram would offer her protection while still allowing her some modicum of control, she had been mistaken. Guntram had no intention of sharing power with any woman. He now saw himself as supreme king of the land, the adoptive father of his two young nephews, ruling all of Francia in their stead.

Guntram moved Fredegund out of the cathedral and back into the palace, but he made it clear that she was not mistress of her home. Fredegund knew she had to let Guntram think he was in control for the time being, but still she chafed under his paternalism. Guntram insisted that Fredegund dine with him most nights, another subtle show of power.

One night as they ate together, she excused herself from the table. When Guntram protested that she should stay and eat more, she insisted she really needed to be excused: "I am pregnant again."

Guntram was said to be "astonished" by this news. Court gossips were likely delighted—was this evidence that Fredegund had taken up with a lover (or continued a relationship with one) since her husband's death? But Guntram was also said to be shocked because Fredegund had so recently given birth; her infant son was just four months old. It was technically possible for Chilperic to have fathered another child with Fredegund; there was a roughly two-month period between their baby's birth and his assassination, but such a timeline would have meant the royal couple were flouting church law.

It was considered sinful to become pregnant too quickly after a birth; some mothers who became pregnant shortly after having a baby attempted abortions rather than face the public shame. It was expected that mothers would nurse their babies, and the church decreed that a new mother's "husband ought not to cohabit with her till that which is brought forth be weaned." Of course, Fredegund would not have been able to breastfeed her baby boy, with him being hidden away some distance from her, so she clearly made use of a wet nurse. But even in such cases, couples were supposed to avoid sex for, at the very least, forty days after birth while the mother was still bleeding. To have conceived a child so quickly, they had likely violated that prohibition. Of course, in a desperate rush for heirs, the king and queen would not have stood on ceremony.

At her meal with Guntram, Fredegund's insistence that she couldn't choke down another bite may genuinely have been because she was in the

Fredegund excuses herself from a dinner with Guntram, declaring that she is pregnant, in a Late Medieval miniature

early stages of a pregnancy and felt nauseated. But curiously, this pregnancy then disappears from the historical record. It may be that Fredegund miscarried later, or that she was honestly mistaken about her condition; the physical symptoms she was having, after all, could just as well have been due to the immense stress and strain she was under. Or her declaration may have been a calculated ploy from the start; she may have been trying to make doubly sure Guntram wouldn't dispose of her but keep her living baby Clothar. Guntram clearly thought the best place for a widowed queen was a convent, but he wouldn't send her to one if she might be pregnant with another heir. Claiming to be pregnant would also keep Guntram at arm's length while they were in Paris together: sex with a pregnant woman was also considered sinful and unclean. While Fredegund could be certain Guntram wouldn't try to marry her given the church's incest prohibitions, she didn't know what else he might intend.

If the pregnancy bought her a little more privacy with Guntram, it did not buy her a reprieve from her other adversaries.

Another dinner guest of Guntram's was her longtime foe Bishop Praetextatus. After the bishop received word of Chilperic's death, he had returned from his exile and was welcomed enthusiastically in Rouen. Encouraged, the elderly cleric traveled to Paris for an audience with King Guntram, asking for his former conviction to be thrown out. Fredegund protested, but other bishops—including Ragnemod, who had given her sanctuary in Paris—backed Praetextatus, stating the old bishop had already done penance enough.

Guntram restored him to his position of metropolitan bishop, and worse, he ordered Fredegund away from court, so she would not involve herself in any more of his decisions. Fredegund was sent to a manor house on the outskirts of Rouen to raise her infant son. It was not a convent, but it was little better, and in many ways, it was worse—she was now, technically, under Praetextatus's dominion.

Another humiliation. Fredegund was now *valde maesta*—depressed or intensely sad—by this turn of events, seeing that "much of her power had been brought to an end." But she had a baby to protect; now was not the time to appear weak. Fredegund needed to remind the nobles of Neustria why Chilperic had allowed her a place at his table.

The first person she went after was Brunhild. Perhaps she felt Brunhild was to blame for her husband's death and her own decline, or perhaps she was just jealous of the power her rival enjoyed. She sent a cleric to Metz with instructions to get himself hired at Brunhild's court. While he succeeded in getting a job, something aroused the suspicion of Brunhild's servants. He was questioned, and during a brutal flogging, he confessed he had been sent by Fredegund to assassinate their queen.

Brunhild, notified of the plot, decided to send her rival a message. The would-be assassin was shipped straight back to Rouen, as one would do with a delivery of flawed cloth or glass. Fredegund's amateur plots were no more than an inconvenience to the queen of Austrasia. Fredegund, both enraged and mindful of the usefulness of a spectacle, punished the bumbling assassin "by having his hands and feet cut off."

Next, Fredegund went after Eberulf, the royal treasurer who had rebuffed her advances. She publicly denounced him as a traitor, as "the ringleader" of the plot that led to Chilperic's assassination.

Here was a narrative that suited Guntram's purposes. He would not wish to acknowledge the other suspects. He wanted to give no more mention to the pretender Gundovald, whose support was growing; he certainly did not want to admit publicly that a queen, a mere woman, was capable of taking out a king. But a chamberlain poisoned by his own ambition—that was a story line Guntram could work with. Fredegund was offering him a gift. Eberulf could serve as both a scapegoat for the murder and as a cautionary tale for any nobles in Guntram's own court who might be thinking of eliminating their king.

Guntram swore a public oath, "[I] will destroy not only Eberulf himself but also all his kinsmen to the ninth degree, in order that by their death the wicked custom of killing kings might be ended."

Guntram had Eberulf's title revoked, his property seized, and his lands sold off at public auctions. Soon Bishop Gregory found himself with another fugitive hiding out in Saint Martin's. Guntram sent a man to try to lure Eberulf out so he could be killed away from church property. Fredegund, though, could not allow Eberulf the time to organize a defense and disseminate a counternarrative, especially one that might denounce or embarrass her. She sought out Guntram's man and loaded him down with gifts, telling him to do whatever was necessary to eliminate Eberulf, even if that meant "cut[ting] him down in the vestibule of the church." In the holiest church in all of Francia, a bloodbath ensued, one that started with a swordfight and ended with Guntram's man run through with spears and Eberulf's "brains scattered" across the altar, while supporters of both men looted the church.

Guntram was "furious" at the desecration of such a holy site, especially as it was contrary to his explicit orders. He may have suspected Fredegund's involvement, but he did not chastise her for this or any other of her numerous small rebellions. At the time he was more preoccupied with Gundovald, who was sweeping through his territory.

CHAPTER 22

The Gundovald Affair

G undovald was rapidly gaining supporters. Defectors came from Burgundy, dissatisfied with Guntram, or from Neustria, still unaware that Chilperic had left behind an infant-king. Even Bishop Bertram of Bordeaux, Fredegund's longtime friend and supporter, abandoned the queen and went to Gundovald's side. Gundovald also had a staggering amount of money, a combination of what was left of the Byzantines' investment, Rigunth's immense dowry, and the contributions of his wealthy supporters.

What Gundovald needed next was a mantle of legitimacy. Already, two women from the Merovingian royal family were willing to vouch that he was the late King Clothar's bastard son. His supporters had contacted Radegund at her convent in Poitiers and Ingritude at her convent in the courtyard of the basilica of Tours. Both women had been at court around the time of Gundovald's birth and had firsthand knowledge of the king's extramarital dalliances. Radegund, in particular, had kept her husband under surveillance in order to avoid his sexual advances, so her testimony carried great weight. Furthermore, it was inconceivable that two holy women would lie about such a matter. With their support, Gundovald was certain the Church would not speak out against him. He needed only to solidify his support among the nobles and common people. Marriage to a powerful queen could further strengthen his claim.

When Guntram heard rumors of an imminent marriage between Gundovald and Brunhild, he was understandably alarmed.

Guntram's advisers tried to placate him. The marriage rumors were a ploy—Gundovald was trying to force the hand of the Church. He was hoping a bishop would speak out and condemn such a union as incestuous. Of course, the marriage could only be considered incestuous if the Church publicly acknowledged that Gundovald was the half brother of Brunhild's first husband, Sigibert, and thus, a son of King Clothar.

Most likely, though, Gundovald was in earnest. The incest prohibitions could be wriggled around with help from the Byzantines. Gundovald had not seen Brunhild for more than eighteen years, but she was still said to be a beauty. More important than her reputed physical charms, however, was her political acumen. By the spring of 585, Gundovald controlled one-sixth of the Frankish lands, everything south of the Dordogne river, a substantial chunk of the Aquitaine. Brunhild controlled another third of the empire. Combining their territories and their talents, they might eliminate Guntram and Fredegund and rule all of Francia together.

Such a union would give Gundovald access to even more land, troops, and resources. Brunhild, though, was hard-pressed to see how she might benefit, no matter how kindly she may have once felt toward her brother-in-law.

Still, Brunhild decided not to cut off the marriage negotiations entirely but to stall and delay. She rather enjoyed news of Guntram's discomfiture. And she knew that Austrasian nobles had been involved in the plot to fetch Gundovald from Constantinople in the first place. Men advising her in her councils and at court, feasting at her table, had plotted against her son and might be plotting against him still. She did not yet know the identities of everyone involved. By marrying the candidate these men had favored, or at least by appearing receptive to the idea, she could effectively neutralize that threat.

Gundovald, though, presented another threat. He was now a widower with two sons. Where might that leave young Childebert in the succession?

Brunhild had always fiercely defended the interests of her son. Gundovald knew enough to assuage her doubts by protecting Childebert, too. When Gundovald swept through towns that had belonged to Guntram or Chilperic, he demanded the people swear an oath of loyalty to him. But whenever Gundovald rode through a town that had once belonged to Sigibert, "he demanded an oath of allegiance to King Childebert."

Gundovald probably wanted Brunhild to envision a scenario where they ruled all of Francia together. He was not a threat to her power. His two sons could one day rule Burgundy and Neustria while Childebert would continue his rule Austrasia. She would give nothing up. And they could offer the nobles and common people a continuation of the current three kingdoms of Francia. In an age without much certainty, a promise of stability had its appeal.

Still, Brunhild had other family obligations to consider. She had a daughter and grandson being held hostage. The Byzantines had favored Gundovald, even financed him, and so supporting him might curry favor with Emperor Maurice. But if Brunhild did send her army to help Gundovald, then she could not send it on another campaign into Italy, which the Byzantines had made clear was a prerequisite for the release of Ingund and her baby. And wasn't it better to be the mother of the king than the wife of one? Her son was proving loyal and easy to influence. A new husband, no matter how handsome or cultured, might not be.

. . .

Buoyed by recent victories, Gundovald sent official envoys to Guntram to open negotiations. Guntram had them arrested, refusing to extend to them the usual expected diplomatic immunity. They could not be official envoys, Guntram argued, because they were not sent by a true king. Despite having been raised alongside Gundovald, despite his own uncles and brother having acknowledged Gundovald as a royal, Guntram was adamant that this man was not his half brother, was not King Clothar's son.

The envoys passed along Gundovald's challenge: "When we meet on the battlefield, God will make it clear whether or not I am King Clothar's son." Under torture, the envoys proved to be much less defiant. They ended up divulging some of their master's plans, sharing that Gundovald was not acting alone, and that "all the more senior people" in Austrasia were in on the plan.

Guntram realized he was not just dealing with a Byzantine-funded half brother who had caught the fancy of a handful of disenchanted dukes and a lonely widowed queen. There were potentially dozens of other nobles in Austrasia who had been scheming to supplant him and would be eager to see their queen united with Gundovald. Guntram realized that if Gundovald was earning Brunhild's favor by helping her win back land and promoting her son, he would need to do the same to outwit his challenger.

He invited Childebert and many of his nobles—but pointedly not Brunhild—to visit him at his riverfront capital of Chalon-sur-Saône, a bustling port city since Roman times. Guntram was determined to dazzle and flatter the young king. Banners hung from the ramparts and bridges. In his great hall, Guntram had installed two thrones of equal height next to each other. After a warm reception, Guntram called his fifteen-year-old nephew up to sit next to him. He hefted his ceremonial royal spear, and then, following an old barbarian custom, handed it to Childebert, announcing before the assembled court: "This is a sign that I have handed the whole of my realm over to you."

King Guntram hands his royal spear to Childebert, proclaiming the boy his heir, in a twelfth-century illustration

This, certainly, got everyone's attention. Guntram went on to declare that Childebert was now old enough to rule on his own; at fifteen he was able to be considered "a grown man." After calling him "my son" several times, he reiterated that no one else, including Fredegund's baby, had a claim to his kingdom: "I exclude all others from the succession. It is you who are my heir." To sweeten the deal, Guntram finally gifted back to Austrasia several cities, including the much-desired Tours and Poitiers, that had been conquered by Chilperic and now were under Guntram's dominion.

Would Brunhild dare throw all these gains away by marrying Gundovald? Guntram was giving her what she wanted: land and power for her son. But Guntram was also limiting her power, by knocking the regency out from under her, naming Childebert sole ruler. Guntram hoped he had made it clear that in order for Brunhild to get what she wanted, she needed to step back and take on a role more becoming a widowed mother.

And in case Brunhild still didn't get the message, Guntram took his nephew aside. He was a man now, wasn't he? Then it was time for some frank talk, man to man. Guntram warned Childebert which nobles to be cautious around, which were likely supporting Gundovald. Some of this advice was sage—he did, for example, warn him never to trust Egidius, the bishop his mother had wrested control from. But he also warned the boy about his own mother and asked him "not to give her any opportunity of writing to Gundovald or of receiving communication from him."

Guntram, assuming Childebert had taken his counsel, assembled his army and directed them to march south to catch up to Gundovald and put a stop to his insurrection once and for all.

. . .

Guntram asked Childebert to keep the details of this meeting private, which he clearly did not do, since Brunhild's ally Gregory was able to record them for posterity.

If Guntram had been hoping that, by taking Childebert into his confidence, by clapping him on the back and treating him like an adult, he had gained the young king's loyalty, he was sorely mistaken. The only thing Childebert seemed to have taken away from his uncle's assurances that he was now a man was the encouragement to start having sex. The teenage boy found himself a concubine and promptly impregnated her.

Poor Childebert. Charismatic parents often don't produce equally charismatic offspring. While Ingund was reported to possess steely determination and political savvy, Brunhild's son and younger daughter made no great impression on the chroniclers of the era. There should have been much to praise. Childebert had been well educated by the eloquent Gogo and instructed in military strategy by the greatest men of his kingdom. He had campaigned in Italy without any major debacles. He was young and fit and probably not ugly. But in poems of the era, he is cast only in the vaguest platitudes—"glorious in his eminence!"—always overshadowed by his mother.

He was a boy of no great passions or preferences, but he was a boy devoted to his mother. And Brunhild did what she could to ensure that devotion. King Guntram had been right to worry about Brunhild's influence over her son. When Childebert's tutor died, Brunhild decided not to replace him, assuming complete control over her son's education.

After Childebert's dalliance with the concubine, Brunhild decided it was time to marry him off. In court there had been talk of a grand alliance with a foreign princess, but instead Childebert was matched with a girl who seems to have had as colorless a personality as he did. Faileuba had no great wealth or political connections to commend her; her saving grace seems to be that she quickly became as devoted as her new husband was to the power behind the throne: Brunhild.

. . .

Gundovald, disappointed by Brunhild's many delays, made an overture to the only other powerful single queen in Francia. Fredegund seemed willing to at least discuss the possibility further. She dispatched one of her dukes to Toulouse to collect Rigunth and, it was rumored, to try to make contact with Gundovald. Fredegund wanted, at the very least, to offer Gundovald some support; the longer Guntram was occupied elsewhere, the better chance she had to reconsolidate her power in Neustria. She may have, cynically, seen it as the best way to get some of Rigunth's dowry back. It is possible, too, that the newly widowed queen wasn't averse to marrying another Merovingian; it would free her from Guntram's grip. The fact that Gundovald had once been Brunhild's friend would make the match all the sweeter.

Fredegund's duke arrived in Toulouse, and he was able to locate Rigunth in her hiding place in the little church of Saint Mary's, but he could not find Gundovald. He had arrived just after Guntram's army, and the fighting had been pushed farther south.

. . .

The biggest blow to Gundovald's campaign would not be the lack of a bride, but the news that Chilperic had left behind an heir. When reports of little Clothar's birth first began trickling in, they were pegged as the usual wild rumors that spread after any king's death. But when confirmation came that there was, indeed, a baby, and that he had been seen in public and was now under the protection of King Guntram, morale sagged.

Gundovald's first attempt at grabbing the throne had been aborted when Chilperic's last son had been born, and now this new son presented the same existential threat. Of course, infant mortality rates being what they were, there was no guarantee a baby would survive to see his first birthday, much less long enough to rule. But the news gave some of the Neustrian converts pause. They had rallied behind Gundovald when they thought all was lost and their kingdom would devolve into civil war. Now some, like Desiderius, the duke who had delivered Rigunth's treasure, decided to abandon Gundovald's cause.

Still, Gundovald could draw on plenty of support from the other two kingdoms as well as the insights of Duke Mummolus, Guntram's former star general, who knew how the king was likely to conduct a war and position his troops. When word came that Guntram and his enormous army were marching to meet them, Gundovald and his advisers decided to withdraw to the town now known as Saint-Bertrand-de-Comminges in the foothills of the Pyrenees and on the border with Visigothic Spain. It was a wise decision—if one has to endure a siege, Comminges might be the best possible place to do so. Set high on a peak, it looms over the valley below, and its walls are carved right into the rocks. Inside the protected walls a "great spring gush[ed] forth," so Gundovald's men had access to plenty of fresh, clean water. They had stores of corn and wine that could "last them many years," and one of Gundovald's wealthy supporters could feed the troops from his own private storehouses.

Gundovald expected reinforcements to arrive shortly from Visigothic Spain; his two sons were currently in the country, lobbying for support. The Visigothic King Leovigild had just arranged an alliance with Neustria; now with Chilperic dead, he would be looking for another Frankish king to ally himself with. Gundovald could afford to hunker down and wait.

As expected, King Guntram's troops arrived and laid siege to the town. But his soldiers couldn't climb the walls, and their battering rams couldn't be used. Anytime they tried to wheel them into position, Gundovald's men dropped "flaming barrels of pitch and fat" or "boxes of stones" over the walls, which burst open as they tumbled down the peak, killing everyone in their path. Gundovald's forces did not need to do much to defend themselves; one of his men simply strolled around the ramparts, casually tossing rocks off.

It was clear the siege had little chance of succeeding. So King Guntram tried luring Gundovald out with trickery. Earlier in the year, Guntram had intercepted a missive Gundovald was sending to Brunhild; now he forged a reply, telling Gundovald to leave his army and come to Bordeaux. Gundovald didn't budge.

Next, he tried to demoralize Gundovald. Some of Guntram's soldiers would climb five hundred feet up, to the only high point nearby, and shout "Pretender! Puppet!" They jeered at his work painting church walls; they claimed he was just a commoner. These insults had at least some discernible effect—after days of this, Gundovald climbed up to a spot on the ramparts and shouted back to defend his honor.

Eventually, though, Guntram sunk to even more dishonorable methods. A messenger was sent to Mummolus with proof that Guntram was holding the duke's wife and young children hostage. Guntram had launched a secret attack on the general's stronghold in Avignon, killing his older sons in the process.

Mummolus quietly gathered the three other most prominent of Gundovald's supporters. They had good reason to fear their own families would be next. All agreed to hand Gundovald over if their own lives would be spared. Once they received that assurance, they convinced Gundovald

A fourteenth-century portrayal of the attack of Comminges. When a siege proves unsuccessful, Mummolus is blackmailed to betray Gundovald.

that King Guntram was finally willing to negotiate. Here, at long last, might be the public acknowledgment he so desired.

Gundovald was suspicious enough of Guntram's sudden change of heart that he made Mummolus swear several oaths that it was not a trap. At one point, Gundovald was even said to have begun "sobbing" with frustration. "It was at your invitation that I came to Gaul!" he cried to his four leaders. "I am not such a fool that I cannot see through your words!" Still, Mummolus and the others gave him their solemn word and whether reassured or resigned, Gundovald descended to the fortress gates and greeted the party waiting for him on the other side. But when Gundovald stepped foot outside and his companions, instead of following, slammed the gates shut behind him, he knew he had been betrayed. Gundovald made the sign of the cross and begged God to swiftly strike down those who had deceived him. The opposing soldiers jeered and mocked him, then shoved him down one of the sides of the steep slopes; someone tried to stab him, but Gundovald's shirt of chain mail stopped the blow. Gundovald started trying to climb back up the cliff, and made it several feet, but then a rock thrown at his head knocked him off, and he fell to his death. His body was collected and dragged through the enemy camp. The long hair on his head was ripped out, and then the body was left to rot in the sun.

. . .

Gundovald's supporters, as agreed, left Comminges the following day and were escorted to the enemy camp to finish surrender negotiations. Although Guntram had been livid with Duke Boso for double-crossing him, the king had no qualms about doing the same to others. Gundovald's final prayer for vengeance was answered; his supporters soon found themselves surrounded. General Mummolus, an excellent swordsman, managed to hold off several of his assailants for a time, but he was ultimately run through by two lances, one in each side.

Despite having already surrendered, every single man in Comminges was then executed. Guntram's men made no allowances even for the clergy. A bishop was beheaded, and the priests "were murdered where they stood at the church altars." Guntram's men then burned the entire city down.

Despite the deaths of the most prominent leaders of the revolt, despite having reduced the site of Gundovald's last stand to "bare earth," Guntram spent the rest of the summer of 585 fuming. He raged at banquets, even stormed out of Mass. He tried to root out disloyalty, re-arresting Bishop Theodore of Marseilles for good measure. But the conspiracy against him was so vast, Guntram was forced, grudgingly, to pardon or overlook the more minor conspirators.

Mostly, Guntram was irritated at his fellow rulers, Brunhild and Fredegund. He had spent most of his younger years embroiled in the machinations of his series of wives. And now, even as a widower devoted to God, he found himself surrounded by defiant women. He railed against their treachery, especially after he had done so much for their children. Ingrates, the both of them.

Brunhild had not married Gundovald, though, and for that Guntram shared with Austrasia some of Gundovald's recovered treasure. Guntram also continued to acknowledge Childebert as his heir. But still he smeared Brunhild, publicly accusing her of threatening to assassinate him.

Guntram next turned on Fredegund. He had doubtlessly heard about the duke she had sent to Toulouse, looking to bring Gundovald back to her court. After Chilperic's murder, had Guntram not come to her aid, saving her from certain death? Had she been scheming against him all throughout her retirement in Rouen? He openly berated Fredegund's favorite, Bertram, the bishop of Bordeaux, for having met with Gundovald. And then he rode into Paris, ready to publicly humiliate Fredegund herself.

Guntram called the people of the city together and gave a speech. He was supposed to be the godfather of Fredegund's son, Clothar. And yet the queen did not seem very eager to hold the baptism. Three holy days had passed—Christmas, Easter, and Saint John's Day—and the ceremony had not yet been held. What possible reason could there be for such a delay? Guntram announced smugly to the assembled crowd, "I am beginning to think he is the son of one of my *leudes*." The bastard child of some vassal or other would hold no claim to any throne.

Fredegund would have been unnerved. This could not stand. She and her son could be cast out entirely. And if she were assumed to be an adulteress, she would be assumed to be a murderer, too.

Fredegund needed to answer the king's charge publicly, and quickly, before the accusation took root. There were two ways to clear one's good name under the Lex Salica—by trial or by ordeal. Fredegund was not going to challenge Guntram to a duel, but she did the next best thing. A provision in the law allowed for a certain number of men to vouch for one's reputation. The number required to clear a person of a charge was usually twelve men—the basis of our current jury system.

Landeric, the official rumored to be the queen's lover and coconspirator, knew he was as endangered by these charges as his queen was. If the queen lost her power, he lost his standing; but if she were to be found guilty, he might conceivably lose his life. He called in favors; he harangued; he cajoled. In many cases, he did not have to plead too hard. Guntram's charge that the queen was a whore sent proud Neustrians rushing to her defense. And where else would they go? Gundovald was now dead; they saw no option for keeping their kingdom together other than the toddler-king and his mother. The nobility were encouraged not only by respect or fear for their queen, but also by a growing sense of nationalism. Hadn't Guntram openly claimed all their lands, called them all his *leudes*? Did Neustria really wish to be dominated by Guntram?

When Fredegund swept into the cathedral in Paris, she was flanked not by twelve men, but dozens upon dozens: three bishops and three *hundred* nobles. All stood, solemnly, while she swore that young Clothar was indeed Chilperic's legitimate son. In the face of such overwhelming support, Guntram was forced to smile, bow his head, and graciously declare the charge dismissed.

Guntram might not have been able to malign the queen as an adulteress, but he might be able to chip away at her reputation in other ways. He began openly grieving his nephews, the princes Merovech and Clovis, bewailing that he did not know where they were buried. He offered rewards for the recovery of their bodies so they might be properly mourned. Once they were located and exhumed, Guntram arranged large funeral processions and Masses. Fredegund had dedicated countless hours to making sure her stepsons would never share in her husband's legacy, that they would be erased from the Merovingian line. But now they were laid to rest next to King Chilperic in the small church that is now Saint-Germain-des-Prés, interred with every honor, the stone church flickering "with so many candles it was not possible to count them." Upon her death, Fredegund knew, she would be buried with them, and they would molder together, a cozy foursome for centuries.

CHAPTER 23

The Diplomatic Arts

B ecause Brunhild did not send her army to support Gundovald, she had been able to call her troops for a second Italian expedition. The first campaign had not been a failure, but it wasn't the kind of success that would get Emperor Maurice to release Ingund and her baby. The Lombards had offered the Franks a bribe to leave Italy. The emperor was so irritated that he asked for his money back. He had sent the Austrasians fifty thousand gold solidi to finance the expedition; he was paying the Franks to inflict damage on the Lombards, not to let their teenage king win a handful of battles and fill his coffers.

Even though Brunhild had not secured Ingund's release, the Italian expedition had not been a complete waste. It had unified the Austrasian army in a common goal that, for once, did not involve fighting other Franks. The men had returned home in time for the fall harvest with handfuls of Lombardian gold, having seen a bit of action and made a bit of money but without losing many lives.

So during the summer of 585, Brunhild sent another army into Italy; this time Childebert, as a newly recognized king, stayed at home. But nothing more was accomplished; the Austrasian commanders argued with one another about strategy and ended up coming back home without any notable victories. Again, the Byzantines were not pleased.

Brunhild was trying to build support for a third Italian expedition when she received the news that her daughter was dead, and likely had been for some time, perhaps even before Brunhild had mustered the second army to send into Italy. On the way from Spain to Constantinople, Ingund's imperial captors had stopped in the port of Carthage, where she took sick and died rather suddenly. The most likely cause was the bubonic plague, which was resurging in the area at the time. Ingund was buried there, and her escort continued on with its single hostage, her baby boy. Brunhild had been slow to get this news, either because the raging plague slowed communications or, most likely, because the Byzantines found it most useful to withhold it until the Franks had made inroads for them in Italy.

Brunhild's next letter to the Byzantines was addressed to her baby grandson, a burbling toddler who could barely talk, much less read. But Brunhild's intended audience was the emperor, and her goal was to shame Maurice into action when the letter was read aloud in court, especially in front of his bishops, who so frequently proclaimed the sanctity of maternal love. Accordingly, she shifts back and forth between the personas of bereaved mother and outraged royal, between pleas and barbs.

She begins the letter, "Renowned Lord, and with unutterable sighing and longing, Most Dear Grandson, King Athanagild, from Queen Brunhild." With the conventionally feminine "sighing and longing," Brunhild combines a hint of steel—the reminder that the young hostage is royalty, "King Athanagild" just like his famous grandfather. But he is also her "sweetest" grandson and her chance for "great happiness." She mourns for "my sweet daughter, whom wrong-doing has stolen from me." Her grief is intertwined with a clear accusation—the Byzantines have Ingund's blood on their hands. Brunhild then begs, "I do not lose [my] daughter completely if, with the Lord helping, her progeny is preserved for me."

How deep did Brunhild's grief truly run? It is impossible, across the chasm of so many centuries, to ever know. Some historians have viewed these letters as evidence of Brunhild's fierce maternal instincts; others insist the emotion expressed in them was manufactured for politically expedient ends. It is most likely that both are true. Can any person ever completely divorce her genuine emotions from socially and politically useful ones?

Among Brunhild's children, Ingund seems to have been the most similar to her. And she was Brunhild's firstborn, the baby she had cradled while she mourned her father and her sister in a strange land. Baby Athanagild was both a point of connection to her lost daughter and a politically valuable asset. He was a potential claimant for the Visigothic throne and was also in the line of succession for the Austrasian throne, should anything happen to Childebert.

When she received no response, Brunhild sent more letters, addressed not to Emperor Maurice, but to the women in his life. She wrote to the emperor's mother-in-law, notifying her that Austrasian legates were en route to negotiate baby Athanagild's release, and asking her to make sure Maurice responded. She also wrote to the emperor's wife, Constantina. In her first letter, Brunhild hails the empress as a joint ruler ("we recognize [you] as governing the Roman state with your spouse") and shares her hope that they can work together in a "cause of common benefit."

Her second letter to Empress Constantina is Brunhild's longest surviving missive and the only one in which she refers to herself using "I," instead of the royal "we." The tone is friendly and much more personal, even though the two women had never met. Brunhild starts as a proud parent sharing good news: her son, King Childebert, has attained his majority. She then euphemistically refers to her grandson's captivity, saying the "mishap has brought it about that the infancy of my little grandson is consigned to be spent wandering in foreign parts."

Brunhild's tone shifts when she refers to the empress's own young son, Theodosius, and wishes for no misfortune to befall him. Brunhild hopes the empress "would not see your most devout Theodosius carried off and so dear a son not separated from the embrace of his mother." At the same time, she had Childebert send a letter to Theodosius, expressing his hope that the young boy will not "meet with the wretchedness of being orphaned, nor that you should pass your childhood without parents." Taken together, these messages seem just as sinister as a gangster musing "It would be a shame if anything were to happen to your son." Fortunes can quickly change, the queen seems to be warning.

Brunhild, though, quickly alters her tone again, layering on the guilt in the rest of her letter. She begs the empress, "that as I lost a daughter I may not lose the sweet pledge from her that remained to me, that as I am tortured by the death of the child, I may be comforted through you by the swift return of the captive grandchild."

And then the steel returns to her voice as Brunhild reminds the empress of her Christian duty, snidely hoping that she "may receive the mercy of glory from God who is the universal redeemer." She muses that if baby Athanagild were freed "the charity between both peoples may be multiplied by this and the term of peace extended." And if he is not returned, Brunhild ominously implied, that peace might collapse.

. . .

Peace was in danger of collapsing on another front.

Guntram had found, in the unfortunate fate of his niece Ingund, an opportunity to enrich himself. Guntram had his eye on a particular Visigothic territory called Septimania—a narrow finger of land along the Mediterranean coast, running from the Pyrenees over to the Rhone. It was the only Visigothic province outside of the Iberian peninsula, and it butted right up against Guntram's kingdom. Even though one could attribute Ingund's death simply to the bubonic plague—or, credibly, to the Byzantines, for taking her hostage and putting her in the path of the disease—Guntram blamed the Visigothic King Leovigild for her death. If Leovigild had been honorable, if Ingund and her baby had not felt themselves in danger, they would have never fled to the Byzantines in the first place. Guntram, of course, ignored the hypocrisy of condemning Leovigild for acting dishonorably when he himself was in the regular habit of holding women and children at swordpoint, as he had done with Boso's family or with Mummolus's wife and small children. Guntram loudly trumpeted his outrage and mustered an army, preparing to invade Septimania.

But Brunhild was not the only queen tangled up in the affairs of the Visigoths. Fredegund, subscribing to the adage that the enemy of her enemy was her friend, had begun corresponding with King Leovigild. One of Leovigild's responses, though, ended up in Guntram's hands:

> Quickly kill our enemies, that is, Childebert and his mother, and enter into peace with king Guntram; purchase this with many gifts. And in case you have insufficient money, we are sending some ourselves in secret, with the sole aim of enabling you to fulfil what we ask for.

Fredegund's talent for assassination was now apparently so renowned that foreign kings were trying to procure her services.

Guntram shared this intelligence with Brunhild and Childebert as an act of goodwill. Shortly after, two men dressed as beggars were arrested and found with poisoned scramsaxes in their possession.

The men confessed that they had been sent by Fredegund. Two assassins, four poisoned blades. It was an eerie replay of the strategy that had been so successful a decade ago against Sigibert. Perhaps Fredegund had a love for symmetry, and wanted the entire Austrasian royal family assassinated in the same way. Or she had simply decided to stick with what had already worked. With poisoned blades, an assassin did not need to be terribly skilled; he just needed to get close. Still, Fredegund's ability to compound dangerous herbs or procure snake venom was no small feat, and nearly as difficult and expensive a task as hiring a more skilled assassin might have been.

The men claimed that Fredegund had instructed them to gain access to the young king by pretending to be beggars: "When you have prostrated yourselves at his feet, as though you are begging for a penny, stab him in both sides." If the men found "the boy . . . so heavily guarded" that they could not get close to him, they were still to track down Brunhild and show her no mercy: "Kill her as an enemy." In fact, Brunhild seems to have been the main target of the operation. The whole point in going after her son was "so that at last Brunhild, who takes her arrogance from him, may fall as he collapses, and be subject to me." If the men died during the course of their mission, Fredegund had promised their families would be richly rewarded and elevated to the nobility. She had also given them a special potion, they claimed, to provide them with courage.

They would need it. This was the second time Brunhild had captured Fredegund's assassins. The first time, she sent the assassin back; Fredegund had cut his hands and feet off. This time, Brunhild was not so merciful, and ordered both of the men executed.

. . .

Fredegund's overtures to Leovigild were not an isolated strategy. She was chafing at her enforced retirement in Rouen, and even more so under the eye of her de facto jailer, Bishop Praetextatus.

The two quarreled. Praetextatus had no qualms about insulting Fredegund's "stupid, malicious behavior" and "boastful pride," and he expressed his concern for her eternal soul.

Fredegund might have forgiven him this, once her temper cooled. But he also reminded her of how fleeting her grasp on power might be. She threatened him that one day he might find himself exiled again. He retorted: "In exile and out of exile I have always been a bishop, but you will not always enjoy royal power."

Fredegund was incensed. The implication was that she was not a queen by blood, and that once her son was a bit older, she would be discarded. All throughout her life, she would overreact to barbs about her status. To do so, she thought, was to be as Frankish as the great King Clovis.

There is an anecdote about King Clovis that was included in almost every history textbook in France well into the 1960s. Before he had unified the Franks, when he was still a pagan marauder, he and his men pillaged a church in Soissons, making off with many valuables. The Church petitioned King Clovis for the return of one particular vase of immense beauty and worth. Clovis agreed to return the item. At the time, the Franks had the tradition of sharing the spoils of war equally—everything was held in common and distributed evenly. When Clovis claimed that particular vase as his own, a soldier challenged his authority to do so, and in the ensuing argument the soldier smashed the vase with his ax.

A year later, when Clovis's grip on power was even more secure, he saw that soldier again. This time, he smashed the man's head open with an ax, saying, "Just as you did to the vase at Soissons." The anecdote, captured by the phrase "Souviens-toi du vase de Soissons!" soon became a shorthand for a comeuppance.

This mythic tale has been used to illustrate the centralization of power under Clovis, the shift from elected warlords to absolute monarchs. Clovis understood that, to effect this change, a king could never forgive or forget a slight to his authority. Fredegund had internalized this lesson. A few weeks later, when Guntram headed south to oversee his campaign against Visigoths, Fredegund saw a door opening.

On Easter morning, the cathedral of Rouen was crowded with people eager to commemorate the Resurrection and end forty days of fasting—during Lent, the faithful had been allowed only a single vegan meal every day. Praetextatus was celebrating the Mass. He intoned the triumphant antiphon—*Christus resurgens ex mortuis, ex mortuis, jam non moritur, mors illi ultra non dominabitur*, "Christ has risen from the dead and dies no more; death will no longer have dominion over him." The elderly bishop had been up all night for the Easter Vigil, and he was exhausted; during the congregation's chanted response he rested on a bench. A man took this opportunity to run up to the front of the church, dagger drawn, and stab him in the armpit.

This stab wound should have severed his axillary artery; a victim should bleed out quickly. But Bishop Praetextatus did not slump unconscious. Instead he rose, clutching his wound, and cried out for help. The other clergy had either been forewarned or they were frozen in shock, because none rushed to assist him. The old bishop dripped blood over the altar until some of those in the congregation rushed forward to carry him to his bed in his adjoining quarters.

The bishop was propped up in his bed when Fredegund arrived, flanked by two of her dukes. The queen expressed her astonishment that she had "lived to see the day when such a crime as this should be committed, and while you were performing the office too." She added her hope that the assassin would be quickly caught and punished.

Praetextatus retorted that he was pretty certain he knew who the perpetrator was.

She ignored the accusation, offering to send her own household doctors to tend to the bishop. Praetextatus, no fool, refused. His lungs were filling up with blood; his breath was growing more labored. But while he could still talk, he accused Fredegund of this crime, as well as many others: the murder of kings, the shedding of innocent blood.

"As long as you live you will be accursed, for God will avenge my blood upon your head," he cried, imagining his curse flying ahead to the ears of the angels and saints who would soon be greeting him.

Fredegund was unruffled by the threat of eternal damnation. She coolly bid the bishop goodbye, left his quarters, and waited for word to come of his death.

Praetextatus expired later that day.

The people of Rouen were outraged—to have their holiest authority slaughtered in their holiest site on the holiest day of the year? This was the bloodiest Easter they could remember. The town leaders came immediately to Fredegund's quarters, not doubting who had sent the assassin. "You have never done anything worse than this!" one declared. They informed her they would be launching an inquiry into Bishop Praetextatus's murder.

They wisely declined the queen's invitation to dine at her table, but their leader made the mistake of accepting a traditional Frankish drink of absinthe, wine, and honey. After his first sip, he realized his mistake. Poison. He shouted for his companions to flee "lest you all perish with me!"

The man managed to mount his horse, but made it only a half mile before he fell off, dead.

If the civil authorities could do nothing, the Church was determined to intervene. The bishop of Bayeux headed the investigation. To encourage the citizens of Rouen to be more forthcoming, all the churches in the area were closed. No one could be married, buried, or baptized; the faithful worried they might die without being absolved of their sins. Under such pressure, certain people were arrested; their confessions all led to Fredegund.

The Queen, though, remained adamant. She had had nothing to do with Praetextatus's death.

Praetextatus's extended family began clamoring for justice, too. Guntram was alarmed by the queen's defiance and the threat of a blood feud breaking out, but he had his hands full.

To say Guntram's campaign in Septimania was going poorly would be an understatement. The aging monarch had not led the campaign, leaving that to his dukes. But they were unable to keep their men in line, and undisciplined troops greedy for plunder ended up looting Frankish towns and churches along the way. With their most violent impulses sated after months of raping and pillaging, when they got to Septimania, they half-heartedly laid siege to a single city and then gave up. Leovigild offered a truce, but Guntram was too stubborn to accept it. So Guntram now, daily, was receiving report after report that he was losing additional territory to the Visigoths.

Unable to head an investigation into Bishop Praetextatus's murder himself, Guntram dispatched three other bishops, telling them to report back to him directly. The bishops went to confer with the Neustrian nobles charged with guarding baby Clothar, assuming they would cooperate with the investigation and share their suspicions that the queen was behind the attack.

These nobles, though, made it clear that Neustria no longer had use for Burgundy's protection: "We are quite capable of punishing local misdemeanors ourselves."

Guntram sent orders that Fredegund was not to install a successor to Praetextatus. She ignored him and did so, reopening the churches, showing she had seized control of both the nobility and the Church.

Fredegund did produce an assassin, handing over one of her slaves to be punished however Praetextatus's family saw fit. The slave, under questioning, claimed that Fredegund had plotted the murder with the help of two clergymen, one of whom had just been named Praetextatus's replacement. The queen had promised the slave and his wife their freedom, as well as two hundred gold pieces, in exchange for stabbing the bishop. Despite this confession, the poor man was still executed for his crime.

A Late Medieval portrait of Fredegund reigning as regent for her infant son

Guntram could see the situation in Neustria was spinning out of his control. But there was little he could do. The Septimania campaign had been such a disaster that when Guntram's military commanders returned, they went into sanctuary in a church rather than have to face their king. Guntram visited the church and threatened to put an ax in their skulls, as Clovis had done. To save face with the public, Guntram blamed his military's poor performance not on the lack of strategy or leadership, but on the lack of religion in the lives of the younger generations.

Guntram had no troops in reserve to send into Rouen to subdue the Neustrians; he was spread too thin. Fredegund increased the pressure upon Guntram, sending in two separate teams of assassins after the king. One set was secreted in a Neustrian diplomatic party while the other lay in wait for Guntram in church. Neither was successful, but perhaps they didn't need to be. Fredegund only had to remind Guntram of how persistent she could be, and how close she could get.

Eventually, Guntram had to throw up his hands and concede defeat.

By the end of the summer of 586, Fredegund was regent, the undisputed ruler of Neustria.

CHAPTER 24

The Dukes' Revolt

The national uprising in Neustria was followed by the unusually warm fall and winter of 586. It was so warm that the plants bloomed again in September and the trees bore a second crop of fruit. The strange weather was clearly a portent, but of what, no one could say.

It was during this time that Brunhild welcomed her second grandchild. King Childebert's concubine gave birth to a boy. The baby was named Theudebert, a name that combined the Frankish words for *people* and *bright*—he was to embody the Frankish people's future. As a mother, Brunhild had prided herself on her children having royal blood on both sides; as a grandmother she did not appear to have the same concern. Although a bastard, Theudebert seems to have been treated as a presumed heir right from his birth.

The following year, Childebert's wife, Faileuba, gave birth to another boy, Theuderic, "the people's ruler." Before his seventeenth birthday, Childebert had already headed up a foreign campaign and produced two heirs. The Frankish people liked virile warrior-kings, and Brunhild had given them one. Perhaps now they would not think too hard about who was really running their government.

There were some nobles, however, who were unhappy. They had assumed Brunhild would be stepping back from power once her son had reached majority; they had expected to have more influence over the young king, not to have to go through his mother with their every griev-ance and project. Brunhild heard the grumbles in her councils and banquets, even if she did not yet know which men were behind them.

Fredegund also heard word of this discontent, and she tended it as she had patiently tended so many hearth fires: raking the embers, tossing in small bunches of dry kindling. There was still a pro-Neustrian faction in Austrasia, even if its ranks were diminished. It was now headed up by Ursio and Berthefred, the dukes who had once threatened to trample Brunhild on the battlefield. Bishop Egidius, after his fall from power, stayed away from court, but he could still be counted on to provide his old friends some discreet support. Fredegund renewed the old communica-tion channels between these men and her court. If she followed her husband's example, we can assume she sent not only messages but also gold.

Ursio and Berthefred, hunting for another supporter to anchor their faction, began courting Rauching, the Duke of Soissons. Soissons had long been the official capital of Neustria, even after the royal family began favoring Paris. But once Guntram had taken up residence in Paris and sent Fredegund off to Rouen, Austrasia had grabbed up Soissons. Duke Rauching had decided it wisest to switch sides, and to prove his loyalty to his new queen, he had even been the one to capture the most recent assas-sins Fredegund had sent to eliminate Childebert.

Rauching was a dandy, always immaculately groomed and draped in the finest linens and silks. He loaded his wife down with so many jewels that the common people gossiped he must be some sort of king, perhaps another bastard son of old King Clothar. Rauching was as well known for his wealth as he was for his sadistic treatment of his servants. He was said to torture servants during dinner, selecting one and then holding a lit candle to the man's bare legs. The man would be forced, with a blade to his throat, to remain silent and not move while his skin bubbled and Rauching laughed uproariously. Rauching even punished two of his slaves who eloped without his permission by burying them alive.

Brunhild was either unaware of these predilections or had turned a blind eye because she would rather have Rauching working for her than against her. He was, in addition to being fantastically rich, also a gifted general. But Fredegund, who desperately wanted Soissons back, knew that Rauching's appetite for the finer things made him susceptible to a particularly generous bribe.

Together, Rauching, Ursio, and Berthefred started plotting what came to be called the Dukes' Revolt. Their plan was to assassinate King Childebert. The real target of their ire, though, was Brunhild: "they were full of hostility" toward their queen and wished to "humiliate her." Removing her son would also remove her from power; they would then become regents for Childebert's two baby sons. Once they controlled Austrasia in the princes' names, they would undertake an alliance with Neustria and return Soissons to Fredegund.

Word of the plot, though, made its way to King Guntram. He liked certainty; he desired order. As much as Guntram wanted to see Brunhild forced out of public life, he was stinging from Fredegund's power grab in Neustria. If Childebert were assassinated, Guntram would have no choice but to name Fredegund's son his heir, and once Fredegund had a foothold in all three kingdoms, who would be able to stop her? And so Guntram sent messengers to Childebert, warning him that his dukes were on the verge of revolt.

· · ·

The warning came just in time. Duke Rauching was on his way to a private audience with Childebert, intending to carry out the assassination, when the king and his mother heard news of the plot. As Rauching was being ushered to the king's private rooms, Childebert was frantically signing orders to seize the duke's property, pressing his big signet ring into the sealing wax. Servants exited the king's chambers clutching scrolls, the wax still warm, passing the doomed duke in the corridor.

Childebert invited Rauching in. The king gave no indication that he had any suspicions or worries; he did not even have a guard in the room. Rauching must have relaxed, confident that his task was going to go more smoothly than he had expected.

Once the door was shut behind Rauching, royal guards took up position in the hall. Childebert conversed with Rauching, staying a safe distance away, and then found some reason to ask Rauching to look out into the hallway. When he opened the door to peer out, some of Childebert's guards tripped him while others fell upon him, hacking his head "until the whole of his brains were exposed." The dead duke was tossed, naked, out a window to the street below, a lesson for the citizenry.

When Rauching's wife learned of her husband's death, she was in the middle of a procession down the streets of Soisson on her way to Mass, "bedecked with fine jewels and precious gems, bedizened with flashing gold" and surrounded by servants. She promptly hopped off her horse, ducked down a side street, ripped off her finery, and hurried as fast as she could to sanctuary in a church. She knew all was lost, and she was right; at that very moment, the king's men were ransacking her home, confiscating everything of value.

But Ursio and Berthefred did not get word as quickly. They assumed the assassination had been successful; at the head of a large army, they started marching toward Metz. When they finally realized that the plot had fallen apart, they aborted their march and took refuge in a hillside church near Ursio's estate, preparing to make a last stand against the king's forces that were surely heading their way.

· · ·

Childebert had just narrowly escaped one assassination plot; surely there would be others. He now had a wife and two young princes to worry about, and Guntram was not getting any younger. Though Guntram had already declared Childebert his heir years ago, Brunhild pushed Guntram to further formalize the alliance between the two kingdoms.

Guntram was willing, but he asked for one favor first. He wanted the head of Duke Boso.

King Guntram had dealt with many treacherous nobles, but Boso had rattled and infuriated him like no other. He had never forgiven Boso for his duplicity during the Gundovald affair, and had made the duke's downfall a sort of pet project.

Brunhild did not share his enthusiasm. She had long tolerated Boso, even after his betrayal of her second husband, Merovech. Brunhild had even allowed Boso to stay at court after she became regent. The duke was exasperating, but at least everyone knew where his loyalties lay—to himself. Soon after the full extent of his machinations in the Gundovald affair had been uncovered, Brunhild had taken the precaution of seizing some of Boso's property and forcing him to move away from court. Some men might have considered themselves lucky and kept a low profile on their country estates, but not Boso; he had, not surprisingly, gotten himself tangled up in the Dukes' Revolt.

Boso had begun circulating among his old colleagues, testing his prospects for a comeback. He had been uniquely vulnerable to the persuasions of the revolt's leaders, who had likely promised him a way to regain his prestige and influence. Boso was never a key figure in the plot; he was too far removed from the locus of power. He had, though, been overheard saying some injudicious things about the queen and flattering the rebel dukes.

Guntram had no legal right to demand that Boso be punished, and Austrasia could assert its sovereignty and protect the wily duke as long as it wished. But with a valuable alliance at stake, Brunhild discovered that she also "loathed" Boso.

An order went out for Boso's arrest. He was charged with having "heap[ed] abuse and insults upon Queen Brunhild and . . . encouraged her enemies, too." Boso took sanctuary in yet another cathedral, this time in the city of Verdun, and asked its bishop to intercede on his behalf. The bishop did so, but Childebert still demanded Boso appear in person before him to answer the charges.

Boso thought this would be a formality. He appeared in court, in chains, begging for mercy from Childebert: "I have sinned before you and your mother, I have refused to obey your commands, and I have acted against your will and against the public [good]."

Childebert told him to rise, but made it clear that a deal had already been struck: "I will take whatever action King Guntram ordains."

Boso did not have to wait long to find out what action that might be. The Austrasian court would head to the Champagne region to meet up with Guntram, and Boso would be coming along.

. . .

The summer of 587 proved to be exceptionally rainy, even for a decade when this was fast becoming the norm. The floodwaters delayed the meeting between Burgundy and Austrasia. While they crept even higher, the great Radegund lay on her deathbed.

Radegund, in her late sixties, had already fought through a year of bad health. Her decline had been slow enough that Fortunatus had enough time to publish his second book, a collection of poems that honored her and the nuns at Holy Cross.

As ill as she was, she remained mindful of the tenuous political situation facing Brunhild, given Fredegund's assumption of the Neustrian regency and the Dukes' Revolt. Radegund made a statement in support of her old friend. As part of her last will and testament, she commended Holy Cross Abbey, with God as her witness, to the kings and holy churches of Francia, and to "that most serene lady, queen Brunhilda, whom she has loved with a deep affection."

Soon after, Radegund died on August 13. The bishop of Poitiers had resented Radegund's power in life, and now he refused to bury her. But even in death, Radegund maintained her power and status. Bishop Gregory stepped in, traveling to Poitiers to preside at her funeral; he even wrote her eulogy. A movement was immediately started to recognize Radegund as a saint. The nuns at Holy Cross attributed miracles to her tomb—the curing of a blind man and of a possessed woman. They even claimed that drinking water from her tomb could heal common ailments. Fortunatus contributed to the effort by undertaking to write her biography.

Even with this project to keep him busy, though, Fortunatus was unmoored without his main patron and his substitute family. Radegund and Agnes, the abbess of Holy Cross, had been his constant companions. The three had enjoyed a pleasant domestic routine; they exchanged poems, shared meals, and debated theology. Gregory, seeing how bereft his old friend was, helped him pack up his things. Fortunatus soon ended up back where he had started his career—at the palace in Metz.

. . .

The worst of the summer flooding hit Guntram's lands in Burgundy. It was November by the time the waters had receded enough in his territories for the king to safely undertake a river journey north. The royals had decided to meet at the villa of Andelot, on the banks of a tributary of the Marne. Boso was led, still in chains, onto one of the flat-bottomed barges that would make the journey.

Nearly the entire court was traveling on the other barges: Childebert, his two young sons, and his wife, Faileuba; Brunhild, as well as her younger daughter, Clodosinda; various officials, cooks, and servants; and the court also brought a bishop, Magneric of Trier, to attend to their spiritual needs.

When the Austrasians arrived at Andelot, there was a reunion of sorts. Not only were Guntram and his officials waiting for them, but also two old friends. Duke Wolf and the magnetically handsome governor of Provence, Dynamius, had both sought refuge in Burgundy years ago. Now it finally seemed safe for them to return home to Austrasia.

They were all gathered to hammer out the terms of a treaty between Austrasia and Burgundy. But first, the assembled royals met to decide the fate of Guntram Boso. Brunhild was irritated with Boso, of course, but more inclined to punish him with exile. Guntram, though, was not feeling merciful. He had demanded Boso's head, and treaty negotiations would not proceed until he had gotten it. The decision was reached that Boso had outlived his usefulness and should be executed immediately.

Boso, hearing of this verdict, couldn't find a church to hide out in, so he did the next best thing. He "ran at full speed" to the lodgings of Bishop Magneric and locked himself in, taking the old man as a hostage. With his sword drawn, Boso told the bishop that their fates were now tied together: "Either obtain my pardon or we shall die together."

Boso believed the old bishop would have some influence with both sets of monarchs. Guntram was loath to be seen crossing the Church, and Bishop Magneric had a special tie with the Austrasian royal family, having baptized Childebert's eldest boy. Magneric tried to send his abbots out to negotiate with Guntram, but the king, ever suspicious of Boso and his plots, pegged the bishop as an accomplice rather than a hostage. Guntram ordered the house they were in set on fire in an attempt to smoke both of them out. Clerics broke down the front door and carried the bishop out of the fire, unscathed. Boso tried to escape, too, bursting out of the flames with his sword drawn. But soldiers and bystanders were waiting for him.

Even as outnumbered as he was, Boso was such a renowned swordsman that no man dared get too close. Instead, they attacked him with weapons that enabled them to keep their distance. Boso was hit in the forehead with a javelin; that blow, combined with the smoke, disoriented him. He was then pelted with a barrage of spears and lances. Boso died on his feet, with so many weapons "sticking in his body and the shafts supporting him [that he] was unable to fall to the earth."

. . .

Once Boso had been disposed of, the courts of Austrasia and Burgundy set to work negotiating the terms of their continued alliance.

The documents they finally signed at Andelot on November 28, 587, are the earliest surviving medieval treaty. What makes this treaty even more extraordinary is that women were involved in its negotiation and ratification. This is made clear in the opening of the treaty itself, where Brunhild is included as an equal party: "When the most excellent lords, kings Guntram and Childebert, and the most glorious lady queen Brunhild met lovingly in Christ's name at Andelot . . . it was affectionately settled, resolved upon and agreed between them . . ." Even her title, *domna regina*, acknowledges she is a peer to a king, *domnus rex*.

The treaty reaffirmed Childebert's right to inherit Burgundy, and made it clear that if something should happen to Childebert, his young sons would become Guntram's heirs. To resolve any discord between the two kingdoms, it was determined which kingdom owned which contested city—Guntram's grant of Tours and Poitiers back to Austrasia was formalized, for example, while Burgundy would receive Étampes and Chartres. On the heels of Gundovald's campaign and the Dukes' Revolt, the treaty also sought to solidify the Merovingian dynasty's hold over the Frankish nobility: nobles were forbidden from switching sides. If a Burgundian duke were to seek refuge in Austrasia, he would be expelled, and vice versa. The nobles would, however, be placated by a provision that would allow them to petition to reclaim lands they had lost in the recent civil wars.

Guntram secured the right to remain in Paris; until his death, he would administer his and Childebert's thirds of the city. (The other third, belonging to Neustria, he had already coopted when he came to Paris at Fredegund's request.) But Brunhild also secured an important legal victory, one she had been pursuing for almost twenty years—the treaty reaffirmed her right to the lands of her sister Galswintha's morgengabe.

Neustria had gained some measure of independence under Fredegund, but Guntram had not relinquished control over this contested third of the kingdom that was composed of Bordeaux, Limoges, Cahors, Lescar, and

Cieutat. Brunhild was allowed to take possession of Cahors immediately (thanks in part, perhaps, to her long-standing campaign of harassment against the bishop of Cahors). The other four cities would be administered by Guntram "while he lives, on condition that after his death they shall pass by God's favor with every security under the control of the lady Brunhild and her heirs."

. . .

Once the treaty had been signed and the two kingdoms had sealed the deal with gifts and a lavish banquet, Brunhild and Childebert returned home to finish off the Dukes' Revolt.

Ursio and Berthefred were hunkered down at the former's estate in the Lorraine region. Abandoned by most of their soldiers, they had taken up sanctuary with their families in a small country church on a hill.

Brunhild often favored a strategy of divide and conquer. She sent word to Berthefred, whom she judged to be the weaker of the two. She offered him clemency in exchange for betraying his friend. Had Berthefred been more like Boso, he would have leaped at the chance, but instead he chose to make his last stand at his friend's side.

Brunhild and Childebert sent in troops, led by a man who happened to be the son-in-law of Duke Wolf. Ursio and Berthefred had once driven Wolf off his lands and into hiding; now Wolf's kinsman made sure to burn down and loot both dukes' estates. Then he and his troops surrounded the church and, borrowing the strategy that Guntram had used against Boso, set it on fire. Ursio came out of the flames swinging his sword; while he was no Guntram Boso, he was such a formidable swordsman that, even heavily outnumbered, he managed to kill a great number of troops before he was overcome.

Berthefred escaped during the fracas, and the duke leading the attack, following Brunhild's orders, was willing to let him go: "The main enemy of our master lies dead! Berthefred can have his life!"

But Childebert, issuing what seems to have been the only truly independent ruling of his life, overrode his mother and insisted Berthefred die, too. Soldiers tracked Berthefred down; following Boso's recent example, he, too, had fled to seek sanctuary in the cathedral of Verdun; again, the bishop refused to turn his guest over. The soldiers then tore tiles off a portion of the basilica roof and entered that way, killing Berthefred, leaving another holy site "polluted with human blood." A purge of the court followed, with some nobles demoted and loyalists installed in their place. The rebellion had been crushed.

. . .

The mood on the boat was festive. The royal tour of 588 was heading first for the Bavarian territories. As the flat-bottomed barge traveled north on the winding Moselle, the court sunned themselves on the deck while harps and flutes played.

If one squinted, one could pretend time had been suspended and it was twenty years earlier. Here was Fortunatus back at court, jotting down verses about the "smoke-wreathed roofs" of the whitewashed riverfront villas and the vineyards terraced into the cliffs. Bishop Gregory was bent in cozy conversation with Duke Wolf, as he had been in the earliest days of their alliance. And Brunhild once again sat at the side of a king. They were addressed as a "couple" and "royal pair," mother and son, ruling together.

Their lands were prosperous, shown to their best advantage in spring. The rivers overflowed with fish, the terraced vineyards bloomed with "honey-sweet clusters," and the "level tracts of fertile farmland" were newly plowed. The royal party stopped at the town of Andernach, where the Moselle meets up with the Rhine, and mother and son sat together, "enthroned in the banqueting hall," feasting on fresh salmon pulled from the river.

There is no indication of how Childebert's wife, Faileuba, felt about not being considered part of the royal pair. Even the meekest and most agreeable of wives might find the situation difficult. But if Faileuba felt any resentment, she swallowed it. She was not ambitious by nature, and she had good reason to be very grateful to her mother-in-law. In the Treaty of Andelot signed just months ago, Brunhild had pushed hard for, and won, legal protections for herself, her daughter, and her daughter-in-law.

A full third of the treaty was, surprisingly, dedicated to the affairs of Merovingian women. Knowing Guntram's predilection for shelving inconvenient women away, Brunhild made sure that neither she, her daughter, nor her daughter-in-law could end up in a convent against their will. Guntram agreed to offer them his protection if anything should happen to Childebert. But most important, the women were guaranteed financial independence. Their property would remain outside of Salic law—"cities, lands, revenues, and all rights, and every kind of property, both what they actually possess at the present time and what they are able justly to acquire in the future"—for them to administer, sell, or bequeath as they saw fit. A similar clause extended the same protections to Guntram's only surviving child, a daughter named Clothilde, and all of her "goods and men, both cities, lands, and revenues."

Brunhild had looked out for the interests of her daughter-in-law, ensuring her loyalty and binding their fortunes together. But even if Faileuba had complained to her husband, there was not much he could have done. Even if mother and son were addressed as equals, as two "most excellent lords," Brunhild was the acknowledged head of Austrasia. Forgers learned to imitate her signature, not Childebert's; nobles petitioned her directly for mercy, not the king. One of Fortunatus's formal poems, supposedly addressing Brunhild and her son as equals, in fact focuses almost entirely on her, calling her a "mother radiant in glory." Thanks to the Treaty of Andelot, peace now reigned in Burgundy and Austrasia, and Brunhild's grip on power had never been more secure.

CHAPTER 25

A Royal Engagement

With the domestic front secured, Brunhild again looked abroad to increase her power.

Brunhild's mother, Goiswintha, had regained her influence in Spain. Old King Leovigild had died in 586, and his youngest son, Reccared, had been elected to rule in his place. (Poor Hermenegild was out of the picture, beheaded the year prior by his father's orders.) Goiswintha still retained a substantial power base; to maintain the peace, Reccared had proposed an alliance with his formidable stepmother, offering "to acknowledge her as his own mother."

Before, Goiswintha had dreamed of creating a separate nation in the south of Spain, allied with her daughter's Frankish lands. Now, with influence over the new king of Spain, she wouldn't need to create a separate kingdom—she could try for an alliance between the whole of Spain and Austrasia. She still had one unmarried granddaughter—Brunhild's youngest, Clodosinda—and Reccared was single after his disastrous engagement to Princess Rigunth. Hermenegild and Ingund were supposed to have secured a Frankish-Visigothic alliance; now, though the couple was dead, the hope was not. Through their siblings, Queen Goiswintha envisioned a second chance.

The first obstacle to such an alliance was the ongoing war in Septimania. Brunhild's ally, Guntram, despite his many defeats, was still attacking

Visigothic territory. Goiswintha pushed her stepson, Reccared, to bring this war in Septimania to a close.

Envoys had already come to Guntram three times asking for peace, but he had refused. Now Reccared tried again, offering an alliance to both Austrasia and Burgundy. He assumed his new Catholic faith would make him more a more palatable neighbor to the pious Guntram. Reccared's conversion was a calculated political move necessitated by the revolt Hermenegild had unleashed. Overturning the Arian religion enabled Reccared to centralize his authority by redistributing Church lands from old-guard Arian bishops to brand-new Catholics. Maybe it would also remove one of the reasons Guntram was using to justify his designs on Septimania.

When the envoys arrived at the Burgundian court, though, King Guntram would not admit them. He did not care whether their king was Catholic; no amount of flattery or number of gifts could sway him.

King Childebert proved more amenable. With the encouragement of his mother and his grandmother, Childebert indicated he was open to negotiating. The second obstacle to an alliance, though, was the Franks' resentment of Ingund's death. In accordance with Salic law, the Visigoths returned with a wergeld of ten thousand solidi. Even though Ingund had not perished at their hands, the compensation was offered as an apology for not protecting her, and as a means to acknowledge the agony her death had caused the king and his mother.

The Austrasians now agreed to a marriage between Princess Clodosinda and King Reccared. But according to the terms of the new Treaty of Andelot, Brunhild and Childebert would need to get Guntram's approval first, and the king was reluctant to give his blessing. He claimed he was still too distraught over Ingund's death and that he could not bear the idea of her sister meeting the same fate. Likely, though, he was also concerned about how an alliance between Austrasia and Spain would affect him, too.

Brunhild cajoled. They had worked together to crush Boso, hadn't they? And Austrasia was honoring its commitments according to the Treaty of Andelot.

Brunhild sent her old ally Bishop Gregory (along with a friend of his named Felix) to try to convince the king. Guntram made a big show of going over the treaty with them, of pointing out how he had not yet been compensated for one city or another. But after the negotiations were concluded, the men's conversation turned to the gossip of the day—the relationship between the other two rulers of Francia, the two queens.

Was the rumor he had heard true? King Guntram? asked Felix. Had he somehow managed to "establish warm friendly relations" between Brunhild and Fredegund?

Gregory drily answered for his friend: "The 'friendly relations' which have bound them together for so many years are still being fostered by them both. That is to say, you may be quite sure that the hatred which they have borne each other for many a long year, far from withering away, is as strong as ever."

Reassured that the two queens had, at least, not allied themselves against him, Guntram finally agreed to allow the wedding to go ahead.

. . .

While the preparations for the wedding of Clodosinda and Reccared were underway, Rigunth sulked about the royal villa in Rouen. Was her cousin going to steal her betrothed while she was left without any prospects, practically a spinster?

First, her baby brother had died, postponing her wedding, and then her father been assassinated when she was just a few days from the Visigothic border. She should be ruling as Queen of Spain right now. Instead, she had been humiliated—robbed of her dowry and trousseau, forced to hide in a small church for weeks like a petty criminal. And this was all, Rigunth raged, her mother's fault.

"Why do you hate me so?" Fredegund moaned, genuinely puzzled.

Fredegund had always made sure her daughter was materially better off than she had been. She had emptied her personal coffers to send her daughter with an incredible dowry; she had made sure to rescue her and bring her back home safely.

Of course, it is likely that Fredegund hadn't lavished much attention on her daughter, occupied as she was with constantly birthing, then mourning, baby boys. The irony of Merovingian succession—of any patrilineal line of succession—is that baby boys were so much more fragile than baby girls. More boys were born every year but fewer of them survived; they were more susceptible to disease and death. Rigunth had been a hale and healthy firstborn; there are no recorded instances of her being seriously ill throughout her childhood. She was well educated, and we can assume, given the good looks and sexual charisma of her parents, relatively attractive. Yet her parents had invested the bulk of their time and resources in her brothers, whose constant dying plunged the kingdom into chaos.

Of course, Rigunth wouldn't have thought this, or if she did, she wouldn't have the language to process or articulate her resentment. But she seems to have suffered from a sense of purposelessness, a vague undefined ache, which she placated with one palace flirtation after another. These, her mother drily pointed out, were unlikely to help her marital prospects.

The arguments became screaming matches. Fredegund pleaded. She knew, all too well, what even the appearance of sexual impropriety could mean for a woman's political career.

Rigunth was not grateful for the advice. Her mother had no right to talk to her that way! Rigunth was the one with royal blood running through her veins. Her mother ought to go back to being a palace slave, ought to start waiting on *her*!

The screaming matches escalated to physical altercations, with palace staff witnessing "slaps and punches."

After one such argument, Fredegund took her daughter into one of the locked rooms of the treasury. The queen opened a chest of jewels and, appearing resigned, told her daughter, "You can take all your father's things which are still in my possession and do what you like with them."

Rigunth leaned over and reached in.

Fredegund grabbed the lid of the chest and slammed it down, hard, right on her daughter's neck.

Rigunth fought for air. Her neck was caught against the edge of the chest and the lid.

The servants in the room began shrieking, but Fredegund pressed down.

Rigunth's eyes bulged; she could not breathe.

One of the princess's servants ran out into the hallway, shouting for help. Attendants burst in. Some pulled the queen off of the trunk lid; others escorted her gasping daughter outside for more air.

. . .

Custom and protocol dictated that the families of the bethrothed exchange gifts before the wedding, and accordingly, Brunhild had her artisans create "a great salver [tray] of incredible size made out of gold and precious gems . . . together with a pair of wooden dishes . . . which were also decorated with gold and jewels." The envoy tasked with delivering these valuables, while passing through Paris on his way to Spain, was seized and searched—the soldiers even looking in his shoes—before he was hauled in front of King Guntram.

"You miserable wretch!" the king shouted at him.

The envoy was likely bewildered.

Guntram raged that the presents the poor man was carrying were not for his niece's impending wedding, but for Brunhild's. The king raged that Clodosinda's wedding was just a ruse to enable her mother to marry one of Gundovald's sons: "Now you are carrying presents to Gundovald's sons and no doubt inviting them back to [Francia] to cut my throat!"

During their father's bid for power, Gundovald's sons had traveled to Spain to try to secure reinforcements and remained there after his death. But there is no evidence that they had expressed any interest in returning to Francia. And the envoy, despite being threatened with immediate death, held firm that the gifts were indeed intended for the Spanish king. Eventually Guntram relented and allowed him to continue on his jouney.

It's not clear why King Guntram was suddenly convinced that Brunhild was intent on marrying one of Gundovald's boys, who were half her age and without land, title, or great wealth. Bishop Gregory said "someone reported [these rumors] to him," but it is not clear who that someone might have been. Was it one of Fredegund's agents, trying to scuttle Clodosinda's marriage arrangements?

Perhaps Guntram was right to wonder if Brunhild could be trusted. One of Gundovald's staunchest supporters had managed to escape; he promptly "fled to Queen Brunhild, and she received him graciously [and] gave him presents." He had other reasons to be suspicious. Brunhild's envoy was reported to often visit Spain—did the marriage negotiations really require so many trips? Guntram had even more reason to be concerned once his army suffered another defeat trying again to invade Septimania. Now fat, stooped, and gray, the king could no longer deny that his strength was waning. Both his body and his military were betraying him; maybe his ally was, too.

Feeling vulnerable and likely embarrassed, Guntram lashed out again at Brunhild. Despite all he had done for her and her son, the queen did not know her place. Guntram claimed that she was the real power behind the throne, ordering her son to do her bidding, which she most certainly was. And he renewed his accusations that Brunhild was intent on marrying one of Gundovald's sons. The possible ramifications of such a union would have terrified a man already suspicious of female power. With military support from Spain, would Brunhild replace him with one of Gundovald's sons, another young puppet she could manipulate just like her son? Could one woman end up with sway over all of the kingdoms of Francia?

Guntram decided to close Burgundy's borders so no other Austrasian envoys on their way to Spain could pass through, a move that would delay Clodosinda's wedding. And in a fit of pique, he ordered a church council to convene on November 1, 588, to try Queen Brunhild.

Whatever the actual charge was, Bishop Gregory was too careful to repeat it, which suggests it was perceived to be very damaging to the queen. (The bishop of Tours did not hesitate to repeat Guntram's accusations that Brunhild had violated a treaty, or even tried to assassinate him.) And the choice of a trial by ecclesiastical tribunal was a curious one, suggesting that Guntram believed that Brunhild was violating a moral law. One possible charge was that Brunhild was trying to contract an incestuous marriage—Gundovald's sons would have been the queen's nephews through marriage. (Of course, such a charge would have required that Guntram acknowledge Gundovald as having been his half brother after all, something Guntram had resisted doing while Gundovald was alive.) Another possible charge could have been some form of fornication, even though assignations between the queen and her supposed paramour would have been exceedingly difficult to arrange given the distance and logistics involved.

Whatever the charge was, it was serious enough that Brunhild thought it would jeopardize the Spain-Austrasia alliance, the very alliance her own marriage more than twenty years before was supposed to secure. Beyond exasperated, Brunhild decided to go on the offensive. While bishops were still packing up their households, preparing for the long journey to the church council, Brunhild rushed off to Guntram's court. Once there, she publicly swore an oath proclaiming her innocence, as only a man could do under Salic law, and cleared her name.

The bishops were ordered, mid-journey, to turn around and head back home; Guntram opened his borders again. The wedding finally could proceed. But while Brunhild gathered a dowry and her daughter made ready her trousseau, another complication presented itself. Her mother, Goiswintha, had managed to get herself arrested.

Goiswintha had become alarmed that her stepson was not proving to be as grateful, or as pliable, as she had hoped, and she had started looking for ways to constrain his power. She joined forces with the bishop of Toledo, who had held on to his Arian faith and was an old friend from her first tenure as queen. After her niece was installed as queen, the two intended to help the Arian Church, and the traditionalists that formed its base, regain some of their power. Their alliance was discovered. The bishop was condemned to exile, and the resourceful old queen was put in chains while Reccared decided what to do with her.

Early in 589, Brunhild learned two things. The first was that her mother was dead. The circumstances were murky. The only contemporary Visigothic source wrote in convoluted Latin that, shortly after her plot was discovered, Goiswintha "brought her life to an end." It's not clear if this statement means she died of natural causes (which might have been understood as divine punishment for her sin), or that the Visigothic queen, unwilling to spend her final years in a convent, had killed herself.

The second piece of news was that Reccared had hurriedly married. After all his bad luck with Frankish princesses, he had opted for an untitled Visigothic girl named Baddo.

King Guntram used the broken engagement as yet another pretext to campaign in Septimania. The invasion was to be his farewell performance. He had the backing of some Visigoths there who had been sympathetic to Goiswintha's plot, and he also had a more sophisticated strategy—he would send two separate armies to execute a pincer attack. But his dukes bungled the plan, showing up in the wrong spots, riding right into a Visigothic ambush. Guntram lost five thousand of his men and saw another two thousand captured. Sorely defeated yet again, he gave up his aspirations for Septimania for good.

Back in Neustria, Rigunth did not appear to be mollified at the news that her cousin's marriage to King Reccared had also fallen apart. The princess had not been terrified into submission by her mother's attack; if anything, she had grown bolder. The palace servants lived on edge, forced to intervene again and again in their "fisticuffs."

And Rigunth was not the only Merovingian princess in open rebellion that year.

CHAPTER 26

The Defiant Nuns

On March 1, 589, forty nuns showed up on Bishop Gregory's doorstep, announcing they were in revolt. They were led by two princesses.

When Radegund died, she left behind two hundred nuns at Holy Cross. Among them were Basina, daughter of King Chilperic and his first wife, Audovera, and Clotilde, daughter of King Charibert.

Clotilde had once, like her cousins, expected to make a good marriage and serve as a queen of a foreign kingdom, but after her father's sudden death, she had been shunted away to the convent by her uncles. Basina had joined her cousin at Holy Cross after Fredegund had the rest of her family murdered; she had refused her one opportunity to leave the convent to get married.

Agnes, the abbess that Radegund had appointed, had died shortly after the former queen. The princesses expected that one of them, as Radegund's nieces, would be chosen as her successor. Clotilde, the elder cousin, seemed the most likely choice. When another of the nuns, a relative unknown named Leubovera was selected instead, the princesses flew into an uproar.

"I am going to my royal relations to tell them about the insults which we have to suffer!" Clotilde was reported to have exclaimed. "We are humiliated here as if we were the offspring of low-born serving women, instead of being the daughters of kings!"

Clotilde, along with Basina and forty other nuns, walked out of the convent in protest, defying their vows of enclosure. They walked all the way from Poitiers to Tours, sixty-four miles in the cold, a journey that would have taken them around two weeks. The flooding that had become a hallmark of the 580s had forced them to trudge "ankle-deep in water." They arrived in Tours "quite exhausted and worn out" as well as very hungry.

They appealed to Bishop Gregory, complaining of harsh treatment and illicit goings-on at the abbey. Still, Gregory was hesitant to intervene. Clotilde then left the other nuns in his care while she traveled on, this time in a proper carriage, to plead her case to her uncle Guntram. King Guntram received his niece at court with full honors, and he reassured her that he would send bishops to investigate her complaints.

Clotilde returned to Tours to wait with the other nuns. When, after a few months, the promised investigators never materialized, the sisters returned to Poitiers, where Leubovera was still ensconced at Holy Cross with her supporters. The secessionist nuns couldn't enter the abbey's walled enclosure, so instead they commandeered a nearby church to use as their headquarters. For protection, the princesses pooled their resources to hire a band of armed ruffians, men that Bishop Gregory dismissed as "burglars, murderers, adulterers and criminals of all sorts."

This action finally seemed to get the Church's attention. Four bishops hurried to Poitiers, along with a handful of deacons and other clergy, to persuade the women to return to their convent. The nuns refused to do so unless their complaints were taken more seriously, but the bishops refused to negotiate. Finally, fed up with the nuns' defiance, the bishops declared them excommunicated.

At this threat of eternal damnation, Clotilde and Basina did not, as expected, weep and beg for forgiveness. Instead, they ordered their bodyguards to attack the bishops. The clergymen, finding themselves thrown to the ground and pummeled by ruffians, scrambled to flee the scene.

With nothing to lose, the princesses followed the playbook for early medieval sieges. The abbey sat on a promontory between two fertile valleys; they ordered their men to surround the convent and took charge of the farms below that provided its produce and milk. The nuns and their muscle then hunkered down in their annexed church, prepared to starve Leubovera out. Various Church officials tried to intervene and bring about a peaceful settlement. But the nuns refused to negotiate unless their excommunications were lifted first, and the Church refused to give in to any demand made by a band of female rebels. As winter set in at the end of 589, the bishops and the nuns were deadlocked.

. . .

The nuns' revolt was not a threat that the Church could afford to take lightly. Its grip on power, tentative to begin with, was now being openly challenged, and the nuns were only the latest and most visible example.

As the high floodwaters of the 580s persisted, crops suffered, and disease was rampant. There were grumbles that the bishops' prayers and the saints' relics did not seem to be warding off the dysentery, the rot on the vines. And the plague had returned.

The bubonic plague hovered over the early medieval world for over two hundred years, well into the 750s. In 588, it had flared again in the Frankish Empire in the port city of Marseilles. This outbreak was traced to a ship that had recently arrived from Spain. The people who purchased items from it died first. Bishop Gregory recorded that next, "like a corn-field set alight, the entire town was suddenly ablaze with pestilence." The plague marched north, from Marseilles to Avignon, then to Viviers, then Lyon, a distance of nearly two hundred miles, but a straight shot on the Roman roads.

The Franks had a rudimentary understanding of the basics of the plague's transmission, if not the specific vector. Although it is commonly believed that quarantines originated in the fourteenth century during the Black Death, in fact sixth-century Franks had already discovered some basics of public health; they knew to avoid others with the disease, and would block off roads to prevent travel—early medieval social distancing and travel restrictions.

Yet these were practical measures any civil administrator could take; they lacked the grand drama of divine intervention. Guntram imagined he had God's ear, and his pious intercessions could stop the disease altogether. He ordered his people to assemble in churches, putting them in close proximity to one another, and then commanded them to fast, taking nothing but bread and water, which taxed their immune systems further.

The plague, unsurprisingly, continued to spread. By early 590, it had reached as far south as Rome. Even the pope himself succumbed.

It was, clearly, the Apocalypse. There were portents everywhere, even in the sky—first comets, then a solar eclipse. Penitents roamed the streets in sackcloth and ashes, shrieking that the end was near. Terrified common people, especially women, flocked to itinerant preachers and faith healers; sometimes they were so taken by their claims that they would "rave and declare their leaders holy." The Church was accustomed to the nuisance of charlatan saints and prophets, but now they also had to deal with a growing number of Jesus Christs.

The most popular, and therefore dangerous, was the "Christ of Bourges." He called himself Jesus, accompanied by a woman calling herself Mary, and he roamed through the plague-stricken regions, laying hands on the sick and prophesizing about the future. The Christ of Bourges, like the biblical Christ, eschewed material possessions; when he was given gold, he promptly gave it to the poor. He might have been tolerated if his followers were all poor, but most terrifying for the Church, his followers were "not only the common ilk but bishops of the church." He amassed three thousand followers who followed him from town to town. Eventually, they began stealing from the rich and redistributing their wealth to the poor. When he openly challenged one bishop, the Church sent men to kill him; Mary was captured and tortured.

The Christ of Bourges's followers dispersed, but they did not lose faith. Bishop Gregory grumbled of their continued heresy: "They continued to profess that he was Christ and that Mary had a share in his divinity."

. . .

A year after the start of the nun's revolt, in the spring of 590, the sisters found themselves low on supplies. Their numbers were much diminished, as some nuns had decided to return home to their families, accept marriage proposals, or even enter another convent. Clotilde, who was rapidly emerging as the brains and backbone of the insurrection, decided they needed to take decisive action to regain momentum for their cause. She sent her hired muscle to breach the convent's walls and kidnap Abbess Leubovera.

It should have been an easy task. The men struck at night, and they had no trouble entering the abbey. Leubovera was suffering with gout and could not walk on her own. To evade the intruders, nuns carried the abbess into the tiny shrine that held the abbey's most treasured relic—the fragment of the True Cross.

Their hiding place was quickly discovered; the men drew their swords on the cornered nuns. One

An abbess wields her authority over the nuns of the convent

of them, though, had the presence of mind to blow out the candles. In the dark and confusion, the men accidentally grabbed the wrong nun. They carried her all the way back to their headquarters before they realized their mistake. They then returned to grab Leubovera and managed to drag her back and lock her in a home adjoining the commandeered church. Then, recalling all the riches they had seen in the crypt during their mission, the men returned a third time to loot the abbey, emptying it of all its valuables, including the True Cross.

The Count of Poitiers launched a mission to rescue Leubovera, leading to pitched battles in the streets and at the gates of the abbey. As the clash dragged on, the nun's forces became outnumbered. In a last desperate attempt, Clotilde fetched the relic of the True Cross and stood in front of her men, waving it around in the hopes of warding off the town's soldiers. She shouted, "Do not lay a finger on me! . . . I am the daughter of one king and the niece of another! If you touch me you can be quite sure that the day will come when I shall have my revenge!" The shrieking princess emerged from the battle unscathed, but her men were all wounded or captured.

Clotilde and Basina were dragged in front of a church tribunal put together by Guntram and Childebert to finally hear their complaints and decide upon appropriate punishments for the kidnapping, arson, and armed revolt they had engineered. The princesses' charges against Leubovera ran the gamut. They protested the "poor food, the lack of clothing, and . . . harsh treatment" at the convent, the exact sorts of complaints one might expect from princesses. But they also, more gravely, accused the abbess of introducing men into a cloistered environment. While Radegund was known for doing the most mundane chores in sackcloth and ashes while her charges slept, the new abbess, they claimed, partook in worldly pleasures instead.

Clotilde testified that Leubovera entertained a lover at Holy Cross who disguised himself by "wearing women's dress [and] who was treated as a woman, although he was unmistakably and most clearly a man, who gave constant attention to the abbess." Apparently, Leubovera had clumsily betrayed this visitor's gender by inadvertently using a masculine pronoun.

Bishop Gregory was serving on the tribunal, and although he was a noted prude, he was remarkably unfazed when the alleged lover appeared as a witness in court still dressed as a woman, which suggests that such a situation was not unheard of in the sixth century. The witness claimed, though, that he wore women's clothing all of the time, because "he could not perform a man's work." (This phrase is often interpreted to mean that he was impotent, and therefore, incapable of being the abbess's lover.) Furthermore, he claimed not to know Leubovera and to live a full forty miles away from the convent. The bishops accepted this explanation.

Clotilde next offered that, much like a Byzantine empress, Leubovera kept eunuchs at the convent. A castrated male servant was produced as evidence. A prominent doctor testified, though, that when the servant was young, he had suffered from a disease in his groin; Radegund had called him in to examine the boy and see if anything could be done. The doctor himself had removed the man's testicles, following "an operation I had once seen performed by a surgeon in the town of Constantinople."

Still, Basina and Clotilde complained about the presence of other men at the convent. They had to share a bathroom with male servants, they charged, who bathed there. The abbess was in the habit of entertaining relatives and friends, and worse, several nuns had recently become pregnant. The latter charge the bishops laid at the feet of the princesses—their insurrection had introduced all sorts of unsavory characters into the abbey. No wonder some of the nuns had been despoiled or seduced.

Leubovera ended up keeping her position, although she was chastised by the bishops for some of her behavior. The princesses' excommunications, though, would stand.

They complained again to their cousin King Childebert and to their aunt. Brunhild, who had a habit of looking after female relations, did not disappoint. The excommunication was lifted after just a few months. Basina agreed to return to Holy Cross, presumably certain that Leubovera would be careful not to cross her. Clotilde, on the other hand, still refused to accept Leubovera's authority. She was given a country estate, where she retired to live in great comfort.

CHAPTER 27

Allies and Assassins

After her mother's death and the collapse of Clodosinda's marriage plans, Brunhild rushed to find her daughter a suitable mate.

Back in 580, Brunhild had overseen the marriage of her niece Bertha to an Anglo-Saxon prince. The match seemed less than ideal originally—Britain was a backward, pagan place—but her niece now ruled in Canterbury as Queen of Kent. The marriage had even smoothed the path for an alliance between the Franks and the Anglo-Saxons of southeastern Britain, so much so that the pope now considered the people of Kent subjects of Francia.

A similar opportunity now presented itself for Clodosinda. One of the dukes Brunhild and Childebert had dined with during their triumphant royal tour in 588 was now on the hunt for a bride. Young Duke Chrodoald belonged to the ruling family of Bavaria, a Frankish vassal kingdom. He was a less prestigious prize than the King of Spain, but a marriage with him solved several problems. It saved Clodosinda from being shipped off to some yet-to-be-found spouse no one in her family had ever met, or worse, ending up like her cousin Rigunth, without any prospects at all. And given the recent rumblings of revolt in the area, the marriage would help guarantee the Bavarians' loyalty. Brunhild would have appreciated the efficiency of it all. Her daughter was apparently cherished by the Bavarians, and Chrodoald would prove to be a loyal son-in-law for many decades.

. . .

While the Austrasians secured one of their frontiers, Guntram struggled to do the same. He was facing difficulties on his westernmost border in Brittany, a peninsula jutting into the Atlantic. Its population of Bretons were pagan Celts and governed by a warlord named Waroch. As a vassal kingdom, the Bretons generally stayed within their territory and paid tribute to the Merovingians, but they had been emboldened by recent events in Burgundy. Guntram's failures in Septimania and a new plague outbreak had encouraged Waroch to send raiding parties into Frankish territories as far east as Nantes and Rennes.

Humiliated by his most recent defeat in Septimania, Guntram could not afford to allow the Bretons to test his borders. The old king knew his time left on earth was running out, and he was eager for a grand conquest, a great victory to be praised in the poems at his funeral. Guntram rallied his troops for one last campaign, sending two more dukes to subdue the Bretons.

Fredegund still held true to the adage that the enemy of her enemy was her friend, and she was on friendly terms with the Breton king, Waroch. They exchanged a flurry of letters, and Fredegund offered to send in troops to assist him in repelling Guntram's armies. As usual, the queen strove for maximum impact with minimal effort. She had long accomplished this with assassins; now she could wreak similar havoc with a few hundred soldiers.

Of course, she could not risk the combined wrath of Austrasia and Burgundy. But her early experiences as a servant, which taught her how to slip in and out of rooms, invisible, proved useful once again. Although no sketches or specific descriptions survive today, we know the Bretons had a distinctive ethnic hairstyle and costume. When Fredegund sent in a small contingent of Saxon troops to assist Waroch, she had them cut their longer locks and dress as Bretons. Guntram never discovered her subterfuge.

Guntram ultimately failed to subdue the Bretons. His dukes quarreled, as often happened with two egos on a joint campaign, certain that whoever was seen as the leader of the campaign would be due a big promotion upon return. They split up rather than remaining united, and each was ambushed. There were heavy casualties, and hundreds were taken prisoner.

Guntram's mood swings became ever more extreme. In a fit of rage, Guntram killed his trusted royal chamberlain, ordering him to be tied to a stake and stoned to death, all because he suspected the man had hunted in the royal forests without first getting permission. Later, Guntram bemoaned that he had behaved so "recklessly" and allowed his temper to best him. He could ill afford any more losses.

. . .

When the Burgundians taken prisoner by the Bretons were released, quite suddenly and without explanation, Guntram would have thought God had, finally, answered at least one of his prayers. The king never discovered that his bit of good fortune was thanks to a sick little prince.

Little Clothar had contracted dysentery.

Fredegund thought she was trapped in a dream world; events kept repeating themselves. First the rains, then the sweating and shivering little boy. The anxiety and grief she had lived through so many times before were intensified by the knowledge that if little Clothar died, she had no claim to power—she had no family, no husband, no other son. She clung to Clothar as her son clung to life.

Fredegund did not dare dabble with potions or salves. She had sought the intercession of certain saints before when her other sons had fallen sick; now she avoided those who had already disappointed her. She appealed straight to Saint Martin, patron saint of the Merovingian dynasty, making a staggering donation to his church in Tours. She also sent messengers to King Waroch, begging him to release all of his recently captured Burgundian prisoners of war.

Still, the fever would not break. The young king was so close to death that plans for a funeral in Paris were underway. Clothar was given the last rites while his wild-eyed mother moaned at his bedside. A report was sent to King Guntram that the young king had died; Guntram packed up to travel to Paris for his nephew's funeral. Guntram was a few days into his journey before word came that Clothar's fever had broken.

Even after Clothar had fully recovered, Fredegund was rattled. She, and Neustria itself, had come so close to total extinction. The queen vowed to never allow herself to be in such a vulnerable position again. Or, at least, if anything should happen to her son, she could make certain that it would not be her rival Brunhild who would triumph. Accordingly, in the fall of 590, Fredegund conceived of her boldest, and largest, assassination attempt yet.

Over the course of her life, Fredegund would be credibly linked to twelve political assassination attempts, six of them successful. And these are just the *documented* links where she is implicated by a formal accusation or an assassin's confession. There were many other assassinations attributed to her only through rumor and innuendo.

Kings certainly killed as much as Fredegund did, if not even more so, but they generally used their armies or personal guard to dispose of political rivals. Fredegund had her own personal guard, and she did use her soldiers to deal with some political opponents like the one-eared Count Leudast and her stepson Clovis. But she preferred to use poorer and more impressionable members of society, usually slaves, to carry out her missions.

She may have avoided dispatching soldiers so as not to leave an official trail back to her. An attack by a soldier could lead to a vengeful duke fielding an army and demanding justice through battle. But an attack by a servant could be credibly disavowed. Fredegund was also unsure of the loyalty of all her soldiers. She could not claim to be one of them, could not move about their camps; she could take no part in their easy camaraderie. She knew that their first loyalty would be to their commander, not to their queen.

On the other hand, Fredegund had a knack for connecting with the men of the lower classes, so much so that the rapport was attributed to a magic; they may have trusted her, in part, because of her own rags-to-riches story. Fredegund also understood how these men lived and worked, and how the upper classes were likely to react to servants, beggars, and commoners. She could position her assassins for best effect. But given that the slave-assassins who did not succeed were either publicly executed or brutally maimed—losing their hands and feet, for example—how did Fredegund manage to keep convincing men to continue to work for her?

Many, with a few coins in their pocket, could have simply crossed the border into Austrasia or Burgundy and found the biggest city, melting into the crowd and starting a new life as freemen. Others could have turned informant, and perhaps gained a greater reward from Brunhild's court.

There had to have been at least one successful assassin, a former Neustrian slave who had gone on to achieve status and riches—or, at least, the rumor of such a man. Slaves could become counts, could become queens; it was not difficult to imagine that a slave, in exchange for a quick jab with a dagger, could be transformed into a man of leisure, with a country estate and a giant jeweled ring.

These men would also have feared her not just as a queen but also as a witch. In most cases, Fredegund was said to have given the potential assassins wine beforehand; sometimes she claimed to add a special draught or potion to that wine. She would have had knowledge not just of fatal poisons, but traditional pagan herbal balms, salves, and potions. It is possible that Fredegund was able to add something to their wine to make them more relaxed and focused. It is more likely, however, that the placebo effect was at work—the would-be assassins, told that they were drinking a potion that would make them feel braver, did indeed start to feel more courageous.

The technique did not work for every assassin, however. One was found frozen in fear on the grounds of King Childebert's country villa.

While the king was striding to his private chapel, his servants spotted a man in the shadows. Upon questioning, he confessed he had been sent by Fredegund. He was supposed to strike Childebert as he prayed, but said he became paralyzed and unable to proceed. He also confessed that he was but one of twelve assassins. Six had been dispatched to kill Childebert, while the others had been sent to kill his elder son, four-year-old Theudebert.

Childebert ordered a search throughout the kingdom for the other eleven men. When they were caught, many did not survive the initial questioning. Some committed suicide, and some died while under interrogation. For those who survived, the punishments they were subjected to were as horrific as they might have feared: "some had their hands amputated and were afterwards released, some had their ears and noses cut off." They were not transformed into wealthy landlords, but rather "subjects of ridicule."

CHAPTER 28

Forlorn Little Boys

S pooked by the assassination plot, especially so close on the heels of the Dukes' Revolt, Brunhild was determined to root out any other disloyal nobles. One of the men picked up in such a sweep was a former official who had been on the periphery of an earlier plot against her. He had been exiled at the time, and then allowed to return (after his lands had been grabbed up by the crown). Now he was tortured, "flogged daily with sticks and leather thongs. His wounds festered. As fast as the pus oozed away and the places began to mend, they were opened once more." Under such persuasive treatment, the man confessed not only that he was indeed plotting to assassinate the king, but also that Bishop Egidius was, too.

Bishop Egidius had fallen far from his former position as a key player at court. After the alliance with Chilperic had collapsed, he had confined himself to his ecclesiastic duties. And after some of his old contingent engineered the failed Dukes' Revolt, Egidius had the sense to rush to beg for forgiveness from Childebert and to even, humbly, offer his longtime enemy Duke Wolf an olive branch.

There was no risk of the bishop leading a rebellion now; he was well past his prime and reported to be in ill health. But Brunhild and her son were not taking any chances. They had Egidius dragged off to prison while they ordered a church council to try him. Complaints from his fellow bishops about this unnecessarily rough treatment got Egidius released until his trial, but the bishops had less luck contesting the November date of the trial itself. That month "it rained continually and in torrents, and it was unbearably cold, [and] the roads were deep in mud," but they could not refuse the royal summons. And so the bishops trudged to Metz through the mire, grumbling the whole way.

When they arrived, Egidius was accused of accepting favors from King Chilperic, the "constant enemy" of the king and his mother.

"I cannot deny that I was King Chilperic's friend," the bishop admitted in court. But, he insisted, this association had not harmed the king and his mother.

The Nogent Accords, the alliance Egidius had engineered back in 582 with Chilperic, were entered into evidence against him. So, too, was private correspondence between Egidius and Chilperic "in which many insulting remarks were made about Brunhild." (Again, Gregory of Tours would not dare repeat what those remarks were.) Egidius's own servants testified that he had been rewarded for his treachery with land and gold.

Egidius, not surprisingly, was convicted of high treason.

His fellow bishops, while waiting to decide upon the sentence, expected Egidius to defend himself by justifying his reasoning or offering up some extenuating circumstances. They were surprised when he instead confessed and threw himself on their mercy: "I confess that I deserve death for the crime of high treason. I have repeatedly conspired against the interests of the King and his mother."

The bishops spared Egidius's life but ruled that he must be removed from the priesthood and sent into exile. Egidius was packed off to Strasbourg to live out his final days in disgrace.

When Brunhild arrived at court, there had been three distinct factions. Now two of those factions, the two that had opposed her efforts to avenge her sister's death and recover her sister's lands, had been completely wiped out. Punishing old enemies also gave Brunhild the opportunity to reward old friends, especially Duke Wolf, who had been a reliable ally for over two decades.

Wolf had a son named Romulf, who had not followed his father into the army but instead been ordained a priest. Egidius's post, the bishopric of Reims, now open, was filled by the son of his long-time enemy. For the first time in twenty years, with Wolf as duke and Romulf as bishop, church and state in the Champagne region were in complete agreement.

. . .

With domestic dissension squashed, Brunhild could turn her attentions once again to expanding her influence abroad. She had established stable and peaceful relationships with southern Britain and Bavaria, and with the Neustrian kingdom reduced to a strip along the coast of the English Channel, there was only one border left to worry about: the southern one, with the Lombards.

So far, none of the Frankish campaigns in Italy on the Byzantines' behalf had been successful enough to convince Emperor Maurice to return his valuable bargaining chip, little Athanagild. Still, Brunhild sent armies nearly every summer to harry the Lombards. While her primary motive was securing her grandson's release, Brunhild also realized the advantages of allowing her army to sate its desire to pillage outside of Frankish borders.

Yet the summer of 590 was the last time the Franks would invade the Italian peninsula. The plague kept the army home the following year, but even after the epidemic had waned, the Austrasian forces did not pick up where they had left off. The Lombards, for their part, starting in 590, paid the Austrasians twelve thousand solidi every year, providing a stable inflow of cash to the royal treasury that subsidized the building of roads and churches. And at some point after 590, Athanagild's name was added to a list of deceased family members for whom Brunhild prayed, right underneath that of his mother, Ingund.

A rumor would circulate that the little orphaned king had not, in fact, died. In the early seventh century, an exile named Ardabast made his way to Spain from the Byzantine court. He would marry the Visigothic king's niece, and his son would later become king. Genealogists at the Spanish court would record that this Ardabast was actually the son of Athanagild and a niece of Emperor Maurice.

It is a compelling narrative—the boy who had been held captive by the Byzantine imperial family eventually married into it; the boy who had been denied contact with his only kin was able to create a family of his own. Even better, these descendants reclaimed the Spanish crown Athanagild had been denied. But as romantic as this tale is, its truth is

An ivory tablet that belonged to Brunhild; the back is
inscribed with the names of her deceased family members

disputed by other genealogists. Most likely Athanagild never made it past age eight, and his entire life was spent as a Byzantine hostage.

Though Brunhild lost her grandson, the last living reminder of her dear daughter Ingund, his death also saved countless lives. There was no longer a reason for the Austrasians to do the bidding of the Byzantines and invade their southern neighbors. There was, however, an opportunity to reward another loyal ally. Dynamius, the governor of Provence, was awarded the task of overseeing a new friendship with the Lombards.

A strange hush fell over the kingdom—peace. For the first time in over a decade, Austrasia did not need to worry about a foreign invasion on any of its borders.

. . .

Fredegund knew the value of a good spectacle; eliminating her rivals with a public assassination would increase her prestige and serve as a warning to her own nobles. But with her latest attempt thwarted, Fredegund sought other means to consolidate her power. She decided, as Brunhild had, to decisively silence any opposition within her court. Even if Clothar remained perfectly healthy, he was only seven; it would be eight years until his majority. Eight years was a long time, long enough for her leading men to entertain the notion of pushing her aside in favor of a male regent. Maybe there *was* a hum around the court, some plan to oust her, or maybe the trauma of Clothar's illness had reactivated her paranoia.

Fredegund could not allow any slight to go unchallenged. Now she presided at the royal courts, as Brunhild did, administering its justice. Families were supposed to bring their complaints to her to be settled, but one blood feud between two clans in Tournai had so far resisted her attempts at a resolution.

The dispute was sparked when one man, angry at how his sister was being treated, accused his brother-in-law of frequenting prostitutes. During one confrontation, the man murdered his brother-in-law, and then was in turn murdered himself. A cycle of retributive violence consumed their immediate families, then flared up among their extended families and friends. Concerned, Fredegund issued several rulings that the families must "give up their feud and . . . make peace once more, for if the dispute continued it would become a public nuisance of considerable dimensions."

Salic law had been enacted by Clovis several generations ago for exactly this reason: to ward off the cycles of retribution that could spread through the court like wildfire, depriving a ruler of valuable administrators and commanders. But the families defied the law and defied Fredegund's attempts to negotiate acceptable wergelds.

When still the ambushes and killings persisted, Fredegund invited three members of the family, heads of the remaining branches of the kin groups, to attend a great banquet in her royal quarters. The three still-warring family members were seated on the same bench and forced to hand over their weapons and act civil for the duration of the banquet.

It was a long meal. They ate their fill, and they drank plenty. As the night wore on, they even seemed to develop some camaraderie as they clapped at the music, roared at the dancing, slapped one another's backs. As it grew even later, their servants dozed in the corners of the hall.

The men drank even more.

At a signal from the queen, "three men with three axes" lined up behind the three very tipsy guests. At another of her signals, the axes flews. Three heads rolled on the tiled floor. Fredegund, as she stepped onto the dais in the front of the hall, her guard lined up behind her, would not have needed to utter a word. The other guests, suddenly very sober and very much awake, gathered their things and hurried off, hushed.

. . .

Clothar's close brush with death, along with reports of Guntram's erratic mood swings and increasingly frequent bouts of gout, made Fredegund realize she could not delay her son's baptism any longer.

When Guntram had accused Fredegund of adultery, he cited her habit of continually postponing her son's baptism. He complained, "the boy is kept hidden, withheld from me." In this, at least, he was right. Clothar had been born in secret and raised in seclusion. His hypervigilant mother had not wanted to hand him over to anyone else, even his uncle. So many convenient accidents could befall a young king, even during a ceremony in a church.

But now she sent a letter to Guntram, pleading: "Will my lord the King please come to Paris? My son is his nephew. He should have the boy taken there and arrange for him to be baptized."

Guntram, pleased to be needed, quickly accepted her invitation. He sent three bishops, his household officers, and a handful of counts to Paris. He planned to follow, but he was delayed by another attack of gout in his feet.

The delay allowed Brunhild to get wind of the baptism plans. She did not want the event held in Paris. By the time Guntram had recovered and made the trip to one of his villas outside the city, Brunhild's envoys were waiting for him.

"This is not what you promised to your nephew Childebert," ran the messages, accusing Guntram of violating the Treaty of Andelot. "What you are doing is confirming this child in his right to the royal throne in the city of Paris. God will sit in judgement of you for having forgotten all your pledges."

Brunhild was right to be concerned. Paris was, again, a city shared among the three kingdoms. But Brunhild knew Fredegund's choice of venue was no accident—her rival wanted her son baptized in the old capital of Clovis.

Guntram protested he was not violating the treaty but rather doing his duty to God. Being asked to be a godfather, after all, was "a request which no Christian can refuse." In fact, he mused, "I tremble to think what divine anger I should incur if I did otherwise." He did, however, agree to a small change in venue. Clothar would not be baptized on the Île de la Cité but in the town of Nanterre, twelve miles north.

Fredegund would have carefully coached Clothar to appear friendly yet deferential to his uncle. She hoped that seeing his young nephew again might play upon Guntram's paternal feelings. The Church encouraged godparents to look after their godchildren as if they were their biological children, and Guntram was as prone to sentimentality as he was to rages. The boy appeared in his simple linen tunic, wide-eyed and solemn, and was led by his still-limping uncle to the baptismal font. Guntram, despite his promises to the contrary, did want to do something for his nephew. He had confided in Bishop Gregory his wish to leave Clothar at least a small part of his kingdom, "two or three cities . . . so that he may not feel that he is disinherited." Exactly as Fredegund had hoped, seeing his seven-year-old nephew in person had spurred Guntram to a kindly gesture. It would also be one of his last.

CHAPTER 29

The Fading of the Kings

Inside the shuttered chambers, incense hung in the air, thick and sweet. The king's breath rasped; the clergy droned their prayers. On March 28, 592, when Guntram finally gave up the ghost, he did so on linen sheets and anointed with oil. For once, there was no talk of poison. Guntram was, by Merovingian standards, a very old king. He was just past his sixtieth birthday. Guntram's own father had died around the same age, while his grandfather, great-grandfather, and great-great-grandfather hadn't made it past forty-five.

The aftermath of his death was also, by Merovingian standards, orderly. There was no chaos, no defections, no looting. Guntram was given the grand funeral he desired; he was buried in the church he had built for this very purpose in his capital city of Chalon-sur-Saône. The monastery adjoining the church ensured that the monks would perpetually pray for his soul.

Guntram's will was clear about what each of his nephews would inherit. He had made sure to reiterate, in public, his wishes that Fredegund and Clothar be allowed to keep their small kingdom, with the addition of a few cities Guntram had bequeathed his godson. Childebert, as promised, inherited Burgundy; his lands now dwarfed and encircled those of his aunt and cousin. The four Frankish kingdoms of 561 were now down to two.

Both Fredegund and Brunhild were now in their forties. The cusp of middle age is a liminal space for females in any era but even more so for a Merovingian woman. Her literal value declined daily, along with her fertility. Women may have commanded the highest wergelds in the empire, but "after she can have no more children" the average woman's price went down considerably, from six hundred solidi to two hundred.

Of course, the economic value of an aging queen was tallied a bit differently. Brunhild's mother, Goiswintha, for example, had remarried her second king while in her forties; he was not expecting her to provide children, but rather political expertise. Freed from the business of pregnancy and birthing, a queen's value might go up. She had acquired hands-on experience governing, accumulated a list of names in her head—allies and enemies and webs of extended families—and finely honed her sense of timing. She now knew how much pressure to apply to which duke, or which duke's mother, and exactly when.

These were the skills that proved invaluable as Brunhild oversaw the merger of two kingdoms. In order to effectively centralize power, she needed to reassure the Burgundians that their kingdom would not simply be absorbed into Austrasia. To assuage egos and quell future revolts, she allowed many Burgundian officials to keep their positions. But she also created new positions and staffed them with long-time loyalists. For example, she combined the cities of Marseilles and Arles and placed Dynamius, her old ally from Gogo's circle, in charge of both of them.

But she also made it clear that she and her son would not rule Burgundy under Guntram's shadow. Guntram's capital had been Chalon-sur-Saône, but Brunhild favored the town of Autun, thirty miles to the northeast. She relocated herself there to keep an eye on this new second kingdom, leaving her son and daughter-in-law up north in Metz.

She would not have felt comfortable leaving Metz if it were not for Faileuba. Whatever their personal feelings about the other may have been, the two women had a productive working alliance, presenting a united front when tackling issues and policies with Childebert.

Three years earlier, Faileuba had more than proved her loyalty by working with Brunhild to foil an attempted coup. The key figure in this plot was, surprisingly, not Fredegund but a nanny tasked with minding

Childebert's two toddler sons. Her coconspirators included her lover, the manager of the young princes' households, as well as two palace officials. The nanny, a pretty young widow, was on cordial enough terms with Childebert and concocted a plan: she would manipulate him into casting his wife aside, then assume the role herself. If she was not able to convince Childebert to dispose of Faileuba—and by extension, Brunhild—then she would take care of the king in the same way she had reportedly dispatched her first husband, with witchcraft. The two nobles would then step in, ruling as regents for the young princes.

Faileuba had just given birth; it had been a horrific ordeal, and the baby died soon after. She was bedridden for weeks afterward, and it was unclear whether she would survive. But as she drifted in and out of consciousness, she overheard her nanny whispering with her conspirators.

Faileuba crawled from her bed to report to her mother-in-law. The ambitious nanny's beautiful face was branded with irons, and she was sent far away from the bright life at court she so admired, sentenced to grind corn in a mill. More important, the palace officials involved were ousted and the coup averted. Once again, the female relationships Brunhild had cultivated worked in her favor. Brunhild would never have left Childebert to his own devices, but now she was reassured her son was in good hands.

Autun was a city that reminded her of her homeland. Over two hundred miles south of Metz, it was milder and sunnier, a much more Roman city that the Emperor Augustus had once declared "the sister and rival of Rome." Then called Augustodunum, it had been a noted center of learning, famous for its schools of Latin rhetoric well into the fourth century. Brunhild was setting the tone for her administration of the region by choosing an intellectual city over a more commercial river port. Once she was established, she embarked on a campaign to win over the city's bishop, Syagrius, a former favorite of Guntram's.

She also sought to centralize power by addressing the property tax system, which she felt needed to be "overhauled." She attempted to reform the system by conducting a census and sending out tax investigators to several cities. Many ordinary people listed on the rolls had died and their widows and elderly parents had been left to pay their share; by purging the rolls she could "grant relief to the poor and infirm." Her initiative was much more popular with the common people than it was with the wealthy; nobles resented paying higher taxes on their new lands and villas.

One thing that Brunhild did not do was organize any new military campaigns. She now commanded the largest military in Europe, and she could have immediately launched an invasion of Neustria. And yet she refrained, respecting the wishes laid out in Guntram's will.

. . .

The peace held for a year. Then, in 593, emboldened by the relatively weak status of Neustria, Brunhild approved an attack. It was to be a limited operation, launched from Austrasia, seeking only to take the city of Soissons and other towns in the vicinity. Soissons was the former capital of Neustria, and the subject of a years-long Merovingian tug-of-war. When Chilperic made Paris his capital, Soissons had lost some of its imporance, although the city still retained much of its wealth. Soissons then fell into Guntram's hands when he took control of Neustria on Fredegund's behalf. Soon after, as part of the Treaty of Andelot, Guntram had allowed the Austrasians to commandeer Soissons, but Brunhild had lost it in a skirmish. Since the city was right along her border, she wanted it back.

This area bordered the Champagne, but Wolf was no longer duke. It's unclear if he had died or merely retired, being too old to still ride out with the troops. This effort was headed up by his replacement, a man named Wintrio. Along with some of the nobles from both Austrasia and Burgundy, Wintrio and another duke used their combined forces to invade the villages and towns surrounding Soissons. The countryside was "devastated" by their attacks and all crops were burned to the ground.

Fredegund ordered her stalwart supporter Landeric to marshal what forces he could. And she decided to march out with the men.

Typically, men bonded while committing violence, and a queen—no matter how forceful a personality she had, no matter how ruthless her reputation for assassination or international machination—was excluded from this activity. Armies had their own culture, jokes, and shared history. Friendships were formed while marching, pitching camp, deciding strategy; fortunes were made while robbing and pillaging towns. A queen might occasionally be behind the front lines with her king or while being evacuated from one place to another, but she was decidedly not considered a warrior in her own right. Now Fredegund, whether by design or out of desperation, was about to change the script.

Fredegund, her general Landeric, and the troops they had been able to gather marched out to the royal villa of Berny-Rivière. There, Fredegund raided one of the treasury storerooms and, like a traditional barbarian king, distributed the valuables among the soldiers. Rather than allowing these riches to fall into the hands of the Austrasians, she had decided to give her men booty in advance of the battle to ensure their loyalty and steel their nerves once they realized how painfully outnumbered they would be.

Duke Wintrio's troops were camped out nine miles south of Soissons, in the fields outside the village of Droizy, preparing for their final offensive. Fredegund had no hope of defending the city of Soissons from a siege or beating the Austrasian-Burgundian forces in outright combat. She decided the battle to defend Soissons should occur at the enemy camp at Droizy; her only chance was a surprise attack. Fredegund followed the dictums of handbooks such as *De Re Militari*, as a Roman field commander might; she chose the battlefield and opted for trickery when confronted by a much larger army.

Fredegund ordered her army to march at night, not a typical maneuver. Further, she counseled her men to disguise themselves. A row of warriors led the march, each carrying a large tree branch to camouflage the horsemen riding behind him. Fredegund had the added inspiration of fastening bells to their horses. Bells were commonly used on horses that were let out to graze; the enemy had hung bells around their own mounts when they set up camp, so they could be more easily rounded up in the morning.

No contemporary accounts of the Battle of Droizy survive. The earliest surviving record of the battle dates from the eighth century, but the usually terse chronicler becomes so incredibly specific in this one instance that it seems they are drawing upon details immortalized by an account in a local monastery or an oral history. In this telling, Fredegund is unsure whether the ploy will work: "At first light, let's fall upon them, and who knows, maybe we'll beat them."

A sentry hearing the approach of tinkling bells is suspicious. He asks, "Weren't there fields in those places over there yesterday? Why do we see woods?"

Another sentry, though, laughs off this alarm: "But of course you have been drunk, that is how you blotted it out. Do you not hear the bells of our horses grazing next to that forest?"

With the warning disregarded, Brunhild's forces slept. At daybreak, the Austrasians found themselves surrounded, and then, slaughtered. Their leaders, including Duke Wintrio, were forced to flee. Landeric pursued Wintrio, who escaped only "with the aid of his very fast horse."

Fredegund's army saved Soissons, and then went on the offensive, riding east and penetrating nearly forty miles into Austrasian territory, making it all the way to Reims. In retribution for the damage done to the outskirts of Soissons, "she set fire to Champagne and devastated it." Her armies plundered the villages of the area and when Fredegund returned home, she did so like a true Frankish warrior—"with much booty and many spoils."

The reported dialogue in this account may be an embellishment, but the logistics of the battle itself appear accurate. One detail, though, seems wrong. Clothar is described as accompanying his mother into battle, but as a "small boy," so small that the queen rides while also "cradling the small king in her arms." While Clothar may have come along, since familiarity with battle was a necessary part of any Merovingian royal's education, the king was eight years old at the time, an age when most boys would know how to ride a horse. He may have sat in the saddle in front of his mother or another official, but he was certainly too big to be cradled. A later account states the boy was not carried but led in front of the troops, to remind them of who they were fighting to protect.

Fredegund's battle strategy, using a "walking forest" to disguise her men, was most famously adopted by Shakespeare in *Macbeth*, when Birnam Wood comes to Dunsinane. Scholars and folklorists find versions of this story throughout Western Europe. Mentions of this same strategy can be found in the eleventh century, used by the opponents of Bishop Conon of Trier, and again at the end of the twelfth century, employed by Danish King Hakon to defeat his adversaries. But the story of Fredegund predates even the earliest of these battles by over three centuries. There are, though, mentions of a walking forest in Celtic myths, which are difficult to date. These myths may themselves have been inspired by Fredegund—or perhaps she was raised in a Celtic community before her enslavement and picked up the strategy from an older pagan tale that was told to her as a child. It is impossible to say with more certainty because so few sources survive.

Around this time, two of the era's foremost chroniclers also set down their quills forever. In 594, the most prolific, if biased, historian of the age passed away. Gregory had served as bishop of Tours for twenty-one years, and throughout the period he had been Brunhild's unwavering ally. He may not have approved of women in power, but she had either earned his grudging admiration or he was too scared to speak against her. Gregory had observed both queens' political climbs, but he would be unable to record them at the summit of their power.

Portrait of Venantius Fortunatus as a priest in an Early Medieval edition of his work

Before he died, Gregory bestowed one last gift on his friend Venantius Fortunatus and ordained him as a priest.

Fortunatus had lost many of his oldest friends and acquaintances in quick succession. After Radegund and Agnes, he lost his dear Rucco, bishop of Paris, in 591. That same year, Fortunatus wrote his last poem. His verses provide an invaluable historical record and a glimpse into the personalities of nearly a quarter-century's worth of political and ecclesiastical players in Francia. But after his ordination and Gregory's death, Fortunatus bundled his still uncollected poems into one last book, his third. This book is marked by its nostalgia for his days in Poitiers and noticeable for its new religious bent; it includes an entire prose treatise on the Lord's Prayer, a more becoming subject for a priest.

In a few years, Fortunatus would be appointed by Brunhild as bishop of Poitiers. The stability of the convent where he had passed so many pleasurable afternoons had been rocked by the armed revolt of its nuns; he was tasked with restoring order to Radegund's beloved institution. Fortunatus would live to the ripe old age of seventy-nine, but for the last decade of his life, he would not publish another word.

It is a shame we cannot benefit from Fortunatus's insights into the following years, because on the heels of Gregory's death came another that was unexpected, destabilizing, and still unexplained.

In March 595, King Childebert, aged just twenty-five, suddenly died. Around the same time, his wife, Faileuba, disappeared from the historical record, too.

Childebert's passing must have been recorded in eulogies and poems of mourning, but they have not survived. Still, it is a testament to how forgettable a figure the young king was that his death hardly made a stir. A pro-Neustrian source written sixty years after the event expends only a sentence on the event: "In the fourth year after receiving the kingdom of Guntran, Childebert died." Other chronicles make no mention of the king's death at all. More than a century later, a Lombardian source would relay the salacious gossip that the young king "was murdered, as is said, together with his wife, by poison."

But who would have poisoned them? Given the pro-Neustrian bias of the first source, if Fredegund had managed to pull off such a coup, the chronicler would have praised her cleverness. One would also expect a planned assassination to be followed by a military assault or invasion, but it was not. And if Brunhild had been suspected at the time of doing away with her own son and daughter-in-law, the source would have roundly condemned her for such actions.

It is, of course, possible there was an attempted internal palace revolution, that the Austrasian nobles had grown tired of Brunhild and Childebert's rule. A similar attempt had been made years ago, spearheaded by the pretty nanny. But if so, this revolution failed spectacularly, as it only ended up concentrating power in Brunhild's hands. Most likely, the royal pair died of something much more banal—dysentery, perhaps, or food poisoning—and the sources written closest to the event made little mention of Childebert's death because, for all practical matters, it made little impact. Brunhild had been in charge before, and she continued to be.

Childebert left behind three children and, confusingly enough, all of their names started with *theude*: Theudebert, age nine; and Faileuba's children, Theuderic, age eight, and his younger sister, Theudelia. Childebert's kingdoms would now be split between his two sons. The Frankish Empire returned to its three-way division. But all of the empire was now, technically, ruled by children: Neustria was under the control of eleven-year-old Clothar, while Austrasia was ruled by ten-year-old Theudebert and Burgundy by nine-year-old Theuderic.

Of course, the real power lay with their mothers.

CHAPTER 30

The Dual Rule

In 595, as the sixth century lurched to a close, something was in the air. In Lombardian Italy, there was the queen who, once widowed, remained in power. The man she chose as her next husband got to rule with her as king. Halfway across the world, Japan was being ruled by its first reigning empress, Suiko having recently ascended to the crown.

And when Brunhild assumed the regency for her two grandsons, she ushered in one of the most unusual periods of European history—one of dual female rule. She and Fredegund reigned as regents at exactly the same time, and the empire they shared encompassed modern-day France, Belgium, the Netherlands, Luxembourg, western and southern Germany, and parts of Switzerland. Only Charlemagne would, briefly, control more territory than these two women.

It's difficult to overstate the significance of this moment and easy to bemoan how threadbare the historical record becomes; the lack of sources prevents their interactions from being better documented. We have lost the sorts of scenes that Bishop Gregory and Fortunatus were able to provide us—the dialogue and interplay at assemblies, trials, and treaty negotiations. Any snippets are relayed through the whisper network of distance and time.

We can assume the usual sort of contact between kingdoms, through envoys and bishops, continued. All trade and diplomacy did not suddenly grind to a halt. But in the letters exchanged between kingdoms, as they surely were, how did the monarchs address each other? Was it as one *domina regina* to another? We cannot be certain.

It's likely some foreign rulers addressed their missives to the underage boys who were only nominally in charge, who had not yet mastered their Latin, boys too young to shave. We can assume both queens wrote back as Brunhild once had to an earlier emperor, sharply reminding everyone where power really resided. The new pope, though, knew better than to make such a mistake. His letters to Fredegund have not survived, but those he wrote to Brunhild are addressed to *Brunigilda regina Francorum*—Brunhild, Queen of the Franks.

Later, this pope would be known as Gregory the Great; bequeath Gregorian chant and the Gregorian mass to Western civilization; and be canonized as a saint and acclaimed as the last pope of antiquity and the first of the medieval period. Now, though, he was simply a new pope, in an era when popes came and went. Gregory was the sixth holy father in the queens' lifetime; he had been elected to his post after his predecessor died in a resurgence of the bubonic plague. It was but one crisis of many in crumbling Rome—the Catholic Church was still recovering from not just the plague but also a series of natural disasters, and it was besieged by Arian Lombards on all sides. Gregory was constantly clashing with

A twelfth-century portrait of Pope Gregory I, also known as Gregory the Great

Emperor Maurice in Byzantium, who had just called him a traitor and a fool. The new pope had an ambitious platform of reforms and foreign missions, but he had few supporters.

Because of this, Gregory, unlike many of his contemporaries, was open to working with powerful women from all walks of life, from rich widows to royals. For the time period, he was downright progressive. Unlike many of his fellow clergy, for example, he saw no reason for women to be prohibited from entering churches or receiving communion during their periods; "the menstruous habit in women is no sin," he argued, "seeing that it occurs naturally."

Now this new pope dreamed of saving the souls of the Angles (or "Angels," as he was reported to have preferred calling them) in Britain. Their queen, the Frankish princess Bertha, had retained her Catholic faith after marriage, but her husband Aethelbert and many of his subjects were still pagans. Now her husband, after the recent death of his father, had become king and was considering converting. Bertha had requested the pope send missionaries to preach the Catholic faith. Gregory, convinced that the end of the world was imminent, was eager to convert tens of thousands of souls before Judgement Day.

It seems the Christians in Kent had first asked for help from the Franks closest to them, right across the North Sea in Neustria. Fredegund was either frantically busy with other domestic crises, or she did not see the usefulness in such a mission. She had plenty of support from her own bishops; perhaps she did not see the point in establishing better relations with Rome.

Naturally, the Anglo-Saxons and the pope next turned to Queen Bertha's other aunt, the one who had arranged her marriage, Brunhild. Pope Gregory had already sought out Brunhild, flattering her intellect and the education she had given her son. Then, in the summer of 596, less than a year after Childebert's death, Brunhild had looked to secure religious relics, as Radegund had done. That would be one way to set herself up as a spiritual leader of the two kingdoms. Pope Gregory had acceded to her request, sending her very valuable relics associated with the apostles Saint Peter and Saint Paul. But he asked for something in return—her assistance with his mission to Britain.

Such assistance would require considerable time and money. It was not just a matter of extending hospitality to the missionaries as they traveled through Francia. The holy men needed logistical support—transportation, food, lodging, and protection—as well as Frankish priests to join their numbers and Frankish translators who understood the Anglo-Saxons' language.

Brunhild threw herself into organizing and financing this mission. Why? She was likely still grieving her son, Childebert, and grateful for the distraction. The mission also gave her an opportunity to showcase her piety and gain a potentially valuable ally. What better stamp of approval could there be for her new regency than that of the pope himself? And while Brunhild would have been thrilled in expectation of a heavenly reward, there were practical benefits to this missionary work, too. Expanding her influence in Kent would put pressure on Fredegund, whose coastline looked out to southern Britain. If Brunhild wished to launch an attack against Fredegund in the future, as she surely did, it was wise to make sure her rival would not receive aid (or refuge) from her northerly neighbors.

In 596, the pope sent an Italian Benedictine named Augustine (who would become the very first Archbishop of Canterbury) to Kent, along with forty of his fellow monks. The mission was launched from a port southwest of Rome, then landed in Marseilles, and traveled through Aix, Arles, Vienne, Autun, and Tours, meeting with bishops and dignitaries along the way before setting sail for Britain. It is assumed that the monks met with Brunhild during this journey, probably in the city of Autun. Pope Gregory claimed Brunhild's efforts in this mission to the Anglo-Saxons surpassed all others and were second only to those of God Himself. Although no records of the meeting exist, it would have been very unusual for the queen to pour so many resources into this mission only to ignore it as it traveled right past her residence. Most likely, Augustine and his monks requested and were given an audience with their benefactor. The holy men were reported to be petrified of what awaited them in Britain. Aside from the usual (and very real) fears of wild beasts, and shipwrecks, they would have feared the Angles and the Saxons themselves—pagans were reported to torture and even kill those who came to save their souls. Brunhild would have offered the brave monks her kindly encouragement and asked for their blessing. She would have arranged the meeting so that all in attendance, from courtiers to clergy, would not question her piety, or her power.

. . .

Fredegund was less concerned with administrative matters, and with proving her piety. Instead, she conceived of a daring military campaign to restore Neustria to its former glory.

At this point, she did not need to worry about her rapport with her soldiers. Her success at Droizy had earned their respect. They would allow her to command them, in the vein of Iron Age barbarian queens like Boudica and Cartimandua. And so Fredegund rode into battle with her men. She did, however, follow the example of Brunhild, who had placed her son, Childebert, at the head of an army into Italy. Prince Clothar, now twelve or thirteen, was allowed to symbolically lead the troops for the first time. Together they seized territories along the Seine. They "took possession of Paris and other cities like barbarians," which suggests that the fighting was neither orderly nor conventional.

Brunhild put together a force from her two kingdoms, and her armies thundered toward Paris. Fredegund waited for them near a town called Laffaux. Fredegund again demonstrated her ingenuity in her choice of battlefield. She positioned her considerably smaller forces on a limestone ridge that runs between the valleys of the rivers Aisne and Ailette—a ridge of such strategic importance that over a millennium later it would continue to be selected as the site of major standoffs, including one battle between Napoleon and the Prussians and three more in World War I.

The ridge provided a vantage point from which to quickly spot the enemy's approach. They would be further hemmed in by two unfordable rivers; there was one way in and one way out. And the ridge contained natural limestone caves, quarries, and tunnels in the rock. It is highly likely that Fredegund's scouts availed themselves of these features to spy on the opposition. Her men charged down upon the combined forces of Austrasia and Burgundy and "cut their army up severely."

In the aftermath, Fredegund arranged a triumphal march for her son into Paris, where he was welcomed as a conquering hero. Since Chilperic's death, any time she had spent in the city had been as a runaway queen, hiding out in the cathedral, or as a guest of her protector Guntram. She had tried to have her son to be baptized there, only to be blocked by Brunhild. Now she was finally back in Paris on her own terms, as a queen regent, watching Clothar's head glint in the sunlight as their horses crossed the bridge over the Seine. They entered the city gates, and then processed down to the cathedral of Saint-Étienne and dismounted. Here, Fredegund had once begged for sanctuary for herself and her infant son. Now, they bowed their heads for the bishop, who blessed their victory in the former capital of King Clovis.

. . .

Neustria's prospects had come roaring back to life. Fredegund's mind for strategy led to a slew of military victories, all of which had earned her the

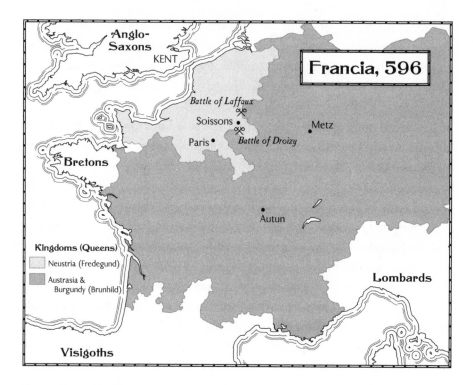

respect of her dukes, her soldiers, and even, begrudgingly, her rival. With her new conquests, Fredegund ramped up her ecclesiastical patronage, giving loyal bishops villas she'd seized, hoping to challenge Brunhild's seeming monopoly on the favor of Church.

The aristocracy was coming to realize, perhaps with some trepidation, that despite the reassurances Fredegund had given them years before, she might not be willing to step aside in a few years once Prince Clothar came of age. Power is, literally, intoxicating, corrupting the reward circuitry of a brain in much the same way as a drug. That rush of dopamine might have very well been interpreted by a sixth-century consciousness as divine right, might have felt like being chosen. And the prospect of its abrupt withdrawal would have felt unbearable.

After more than a decade of her regency, the Neustrian nobles intuited that Fredegund would wish to remain as an active queen mother, as the real power behind the throne, like Brunhild had done with Childebert. The usual ways to silence a female ruler were murder or a convent. That was how the powerful queens before her had been eliminated, and how those that dared to follow her example in subsequent generations would be erased.

Fredegund saved everyone the trouble.

The event was recorded with very little fanfare, just the year 597 and a terse statement: "Fredegund died." Later, that would be expanded to: "Queen Fredegund, old and full of days, died." But she was not exactly "old and full of days"—she was barely into her fifties.

Much was made of what a good death it was, how she died peacefully in her own bed, presumably of natural causes. There was no mention of some type of illness or of any epidemic raging at the time. Of course, there were plenty of things a woman around fifty could plausibly die from at the end of the sixth century. Still, Fredegund was very healthy right up until the end, and had participated in battle maneuvers that would have involved weeks of hard riding less than a year before. And it is curious that in the case of Childebert's sudden death there were suggestions of a poisoning, even with no other evidence to support that theory, but when Fredegund died, there was a conspicuous lack of such speculation. If nothing else, the timing of her death was incredibly convenient, following the positioning of young King Clothar II as an authentic warrior-king after his first victory march into Paris.

Fredegund's body was embalmed and wrapped in linen strips that had been soaked in oil and a mix of nettles, myrrh, thyme, and aloe. Then her body was dressed in her finest silks, draped with her most impressive jewels, and shelved away in a plain stone sarcophagus. The queen could not be buried near any of her five boys who had died young; their tombs were scattered in different church crypts throughout the realm. But she was laid to rest in Paris with great fanfare, as she had desired, and next to her husband in the church now called Saint-Germain-des-Prés.

Clothar was now nearly fourteen, on the cusp of fifteen, the usual age of majority. The Neustrian aristocrats no longer had to battle with Fredegund for influence over the young king; they stepped in, helped him grieve, and quietly assembled a board of advisers.

CHAPTER 31

Brunhild's Battles

B runhild could not help but be unmoored; her rival had been the one constant in the ever-shifting political waters. Fredegund's actions had informed her own for the past thirty years. She had grown so used to trying to anticipate Fredegund's next plot; it would have felt strange to drift to sleep without that worry. Brunhild also felt her age. Nearly every royal, bishop, and duke she had worked with or against was gone, replaced by their own children, or by a new family altogether.

Brunhild's political activities in the aftermath of Fredegund's death were strangely civil. She launched no attacks on Neustria, not even to take back the recently conquered territories. It is unclear whether that was due to bad advice by her military advisers or if Brunhild herself decided to allow Neustria to mourn its queen in peace.

But Brunhild could afford to be magnanimous.

Augustine's mission to Britain had been a huge success. King Aethelbert had converted to Catholicism along with thousands of his subjects in a mass baptism. The mission was such a triumph that the pope had thanked and praised Brunhild's "devout mind and pious zeal." Pope Gregory even solicited her help with a second mission, which would also work out favorably. Augustine would establish dioceses and a school to train clergy, placing Kent and its territories firmly under the authority of the Roman Pope.

Of course, deference has its time limits. Two years after Fredegund's sudden death, once Clothar had reached his majority, the combined Austrasian-Burgundian forces attacked Neustria. This battle took place thirty miles to the east of Paris, near a village called Dormelles. Brunhild concentrated her troops for a show of overwhelming force. Without Fredegund's eye for strategy, the Neustrian defense was clumsy. Clothar was forced to flee, and large numbers of his soldiers were taken prisoner. The cities Fredegund had seized just a few years earlier were sacked and plundered. Brunhild's dukes marched, triumphant, into Soissons, commandeering the old capital of Neustria. They also marched into Paris.

Humiliated, young Clothar was forced to sign a treaty, agreeing that he claimed possession of "twelve districts only, between the Oise, the Seine, and the shores of the Ocean sea," a triangle of territory in the northeast of Francia that would encompass just two regions of modern-day France, Normandy and Picardy. The small kingdom his father, Chilperic, had been so keen to enlarge was now even smaller than it had been back in 561. Neustria was on the verge of extinction.

Brunhild could have finished off her nephew, but again she hesitated. It seemed enough to leave him alive but hobbled, his lands so diminished they were scarcely a kingdom anymore. If she had wished, she could have reignited the rumors that her nephew was not legitimate, throwing doubt on his rights to even this sliver of the empire. If she had wished, she could have had Fredegund's tomb uprooted and placed somewhere less prestigious. But she did not desecrate her rival's grave. It's even possible that she stopped by the church where Fredegund lay while surveying her new lands, that she said a quiet little prayer.

With the Neustrian threat dispensed of, Brunhild embarked on a series of public works projects, in the vein of great Roman statesmen. She undertook repairs to the old Roman roads throughout both kingdoms with an eye for making trade easier. She also went on a building spree in Autun, aiming to restore it to its former Roman greatness. Chilperic may have built circuses and Guntram his own church; Brunhild seemed determined to have her own city. She erected a church dedicated to Saint Martin, complete with expensive marble and glittering mosaics, a convent for Benedictine nuns, and even a hospital for the poor.

. . .

In 601 Brunhild's eldest grandson, Theudebert, turned fifteen and formally took control of Austrasia. Around this time Brunhild moved permanently to Burgundy to oversee her projects in Autun and to continue serving as regent for her younger grandson, Theuderic.

Later chroniclers would circulate a story that King Theudebert had kicked his grandmother out of Austrasia back in 599 and she had been found wandering the countryside, alone and penniless. She was reportedly found by a poor man who took her to her younger grandson in Burgundy. To repay his kindness, she made the man the bishop of Auxerre.

The story is a fabrication, perhaps intended to show Brunhild committing the offense of simony, the buying and selling of church offices, whether for gold or for other favors. These events could not have happened in 599, as Pope Gregory's letters make it clear Brunhild was considered ruler of both kingdoms until 601. She was also already living in Autun for a portion of the year, overseeing her revitalization projects. And the supposedly poor man who found her, the future bishop of Auxerre, was actually a fabulously wealthy aristocrat.

The story does, however, convey a sense of what losing power, being pushed aside, might feel like—wandering alone through an unfamiliar countryside. The story also relays the fact that relations within Brunhild's family were growing strained. This might have been helped along by Theudebert's recent marriage. For his wife, he picked a girl named Bilichild, one of Brunhild's own slaves. Being so intimately acquainted with Fredegund's rise to power, Brunhild was immediately suspicious of the girl.

Brunhild had hoped for another Faileuba, a granddaughter-in-law who would be similarly deferential in exchange for legal and financial protections. This Bilichild was anything but deferential; she openly challenged and insulted the queen. Brunhild was incredulous at this lack of respect and "was always going on about Bilichild having been her slave." Brunhild took the marriage itself, and Bilichild's attitude, as a sign that her influence over Theudebert was waning; she assumed her grandson had fallen under the sway of others in his court.

But in Burgundy with her younger grandson Theuderic and granddaughter Theudelia, Brunhild was able to maintain the life to which she had become accustomed. Even after Theuderic turned fifteen, he was willing to allow his grandmother to operate as she had with his father. Ambassadors addressed "Queen Brunhild and King Theuderic."

Theuderic, who was reputed to be "handsome and energetic and very hot-headed," preferred to keep himself busy with the ladies. When he turned sixteen, he impregnated a concubine. She gave birth to a son in 602; he was named Sigibert, after his great-grandfather, Brunhild's assassinated husband. Another concubine would give birth in 603 to a second son, named Childebert, for Brunhild's son. A third son, Corbus, would follow, and eventually a fourth, Merovech.

It seems that Brunhild didn't just tolerate this state of affairs, she actively encouraged it. Burgundy now had its heirs, and she did not need to worry about being forced into retirement. As long as Theuderic remained unmarried, Brunhild could continue her reign as queen.

To this end, Brunhild even actively jettisoned a marriage alliance with the Visigoths. A Spanish princess had been selected for Theuderic, and she had even arrived in Autun with her dowry, as arranged, when Brunhild and Theudelia convinced Theuderic not to consummate the marriage and to send the princess back. This almost started a war with Spain.

Brunhild opposed the union because she discovered through her Visigothic sources that the girl's father was soon to be deposed; an alliance with a former king's daughter would be of no practical use to Burgundy. (These sources did turn out to be correct.) But sending the Spanish princess back was likely a personal calculation as well. The thought of being supplanted by a younger queen was intolerable.

. . .

While Pope Gregory praised the queen's piety, he also pushed her to do more for the Church. He was concerned that the queen treated the Jews in her kingdoms too liberally and also that she had not done enough to eliminate the buying and selling of ecclesiastical offices in her kingdoms. Along with missionary work, stamping out simony was one of Pope Gregory's pet projects—around the same time, he wrote to young Clothar II about the same issue.

The pope had pressed Brunhild for years to hold a Frankish council to address this issue. Finally, she did call a church council in 603, to be held at Chalon-sur-Saône. However, this council did not concentrate its efforts on eliminating simony, as Pope Gregory had hoped. Instead, the bishops were asked to consider the case of one Desiderius of Vienne, a wealthy and well-educated bishop from an old family in charge of one of the most powerful metropolitan dioceses in Burgundy. A metropolitan bishop from neighboring Lyons asked the council to hear a very serious allegation. A noblewoman named Justa then appeared and "made a complaint to the court that she had been ravished by the most blessed Desiderius."

In a shocking move, Desiderius was found guilty of rape; his fellow bishops stripped him of his rank and exiled him to a monastery on an island.

The contemporary reaction is predictable: the verdict could not possibly be true; it was "a most unjust sentence against the innocent man." The accuser is maligned. Even though she is of noble blood, she must be slow-witted and depraved, both "deformed in mind" and "lacking in virtues and . . . possessed by a huge number of vices." And so on. After three years of harassment by Desiderius's powerful family and followers, Justa recanted, said Brunhild encouraged her to bring the charges, and then promptly died.

The King of Spain, watching this unfold from afar, would write that the rape allegation must have been completely fabricated. He found it easier to believe in a vast conspiracy—whose actors included Satan, Queen Brunhild, and all the bishops at the church council—to frame Desiderius than to believe that a privileged man had committed rape. Rape was an unholy act, and Desiderius was a holy man; ergo, he could not have been a rapist.

Brunhild, of course, was certainly capable of the sort of calculation that might eliminate a metropolitan bishop on a trumped-up charge. Still, if she wanted to fabricate a case against Bishop Desiderius, it would have been much easier to claim he had slandered her or embezzled money; a rape case would be expected to be an uphill battle. Desiderius's rape charge may have been Brunhild's sincere attempt to address another of Pope Gregory's concerns. He had written to the queen a little over a year ago, scandalized by a rumor "that certain priests . . . live so immodestly and wickedly that it is a shame for us to hear of it." The pontiff called on her to "avenge these things" or risk being "smite[d]" herself. While Pope Gregory never describes these priests' sins, it is clear they are of a sexual nature, and his shocked tone seems to suggest they were more than the typical complaints about married priests sleeping with their wives. Curiously, in later chronicles this rape accusation is erased. Instead, it was commonly reported that Desiderius had challenged the queen's authority or had criticized teenage King Theuderic's morals.

After four years, Desiderius was allowed to return and resume his office. Yet from his pulpit, he continually condemned Brunhild and Theuderic for depravity, making it his life's mission to critique their reign; he "wholeheartedly took himself off to drive out all their sins." Not surprisingly, he was soon arrested at his cathedral in Vienne. A riot broke out, and the bishop was either bludgeoned by a frenzied man with a club or stoned to death by soldiers, depending upon which account one believes.

. . .

Desiderius was not the only man of the cloth Brunhild found herself battling. Just as Roman and Frankish missionaries flowed into the British Isles, Irish monks and missionaries flowed out, and along with them their brand of Celtic Christianity and their rigid asceticism. Desiderius represented the old guard of the Church; her other opponent, an Irish monk, the new guard.

The monk was Columbanus. He came from an Irish monastery known for its strict austerity and copious use of corporal punishment; now he wanted to found more monasteries based on this model in continental Europe. He also planned to forcefully convert any remaining pagans in the border regions, although he was not terribly persuasive as a missionary. In areas where the common folk still revered Woden and his oak trees, rather than trying to win them over with sermons, Columbanus simply cut down their sacred trees and set fire to their temples.

When Pope Gregory's monks first landed in Britain to convert the Anglo-Saxons, they behaved similarly. But relatively quickly, the pope decided upon a more moderate approach. Pagan temples could be rededicated to the Christian God and pagan traditional feasts and sacrifices associated with various saints and martyrs. But Columbanus did not bow to the authority of the Roman Pope, and he certainly didn't compromise. He stuck with his scorched-earth methods, and he was forced to move on more than once when his monks were murdered in retribution.

A Late Medieval fresco of the monk Columbanus

Brunhild and Columbanus were destined for some sort of conflict. Columbanus was an uncompromising fundamentalist; the queen had a more cosmopolitan worldview, as evidenced by the sort of missionary work she financed and her tolerance of the Jews in her kingdom. While traveling through Francia, Columbanus made it a point to condemn Theuderic for his lax sexual morals. He also publicly humiliated Brunhild by refusing to bless her young great-grandchildren because they were illegitimate. This position seems strange, given that he willingly gave his blessing to Brunhild's other grandson Theudebert, who was a bastard. Columbanus's followers, though, were slavishly devoted to him, and his quarrel with Brunhild meant that they, too, spoke out against the queen.

The struggle between Columbanus and Brunhild was linked to a larger struggle within the Church itself. Columbanus had fallen afoul of Frankish bishops for refusing to acknowledge their authority. Eventually, after clashes with local clergy and his fiery calls for Brunhild and Theuderic's downfall, the royals had him forcefully driven out of Burgundy; in turn, he sought refuge with King Clothar II of Neustria, and then with King Theudebert of Austrasia, before heading off to Italy.

Aside from the followers of Desiderius and Columbanus, other power players in Francia found reasons to be antagonized by Brunhild. To fund the Roman building spree, she attempted to fill the royal coffers through more direct taxation. The tax was unpopular with the Church, which fought for exemptions, and even less popular with the aristocracy.

A tax rebellion started brewing in the mountainous Jura region on the border between modern-day France and Switzerland. The people in this rugged district had come to enjoy peace with the Lombards, their southern neighbors; with no need for Merovingian royal protection, their leading families agitated for more independence. They had a regional aristocracy with little institutional memory of Rome; they lived in mostly rural areas and were contemptuous of the big cities. Why should they pay more taxes to fund road repairs hundreds of miles away? To bolster their calls for autonomy, these families created a nationalist movement with its own saints, even its own (mostly mythical) royal family. They did not owe their allegiance to the Merovingian royals, they claimed, because they descended from the old Burgundian kings from before Clovis's conquest.

There was a royal villa in the region located at Orbe. This town sat on the road over the Jougne Pass, at the crossroads of two trade routes—one connecting the Rhine and the Rhone and the other leading across the Alps to Geneva. The town had been the site of a palatial Roman manor; it's not clear if the Merovingians had commandeered this complex or built a new one. But to head off a potential rebellion, Brunhild made this villa a royal palace and installed her granddaughter Theudelia and her household there, so she might keep a close eye on the political situation.

Brunhild also appointed one of her favorites as governor of the region. In 603, while in her midfifties, she was rumored to have taken a liking to one Protadius, a charismatic and handsome official. He was described as "bright and energetic" but also as "too smart for his own good." One chronicler snidely notes that Protadius was given the position only because "Brunhild wanted to exalt him with honors in return for his sexual attentions." The locals were infuriated with the choice, as they wanted one of their own selected for the position rather than an outsider. But with a potential rebellion brewing, Brunhild needed a loyalist she could trust to support her granddaughter and report back to her.

. . .

Family tensions came to a head in 605 when Clothar, with Landeric serving as his general, launched an attack against Burgundy to take back Paris and Soissons. Theudebert had pledged to help his younger brother, but the promised reinforcements from Austrasia were slow to arrive. When they did, Theudebert then negotiated a separate peace with Clothar and his troops departed, leaving his brother behind to fight Clothar on his own. Theuderic handily defeated Clothar, but his Mayor of the Palace was killed during the battle.

As his replacement, Brunhild appointed the loyal but increasingly unpopular Protadius. One of Protadius's first moves was to organize an attack against Austrasia in retaliation for their desertion. The aristocracy were not in favor of this plan, and even less happy with Protadius's quick rise. While camped at Quierzy, "the whole army of Theuderic . . . rush[ed] upon Protadius," surrounding the tent where he was playing a board game with the camp physician.

King Theuderic, informed of the mutiny, sent an officer to tell his soldiers to stand down. Instead, this officer sided with the army and, disregarding the king's orders, told them to finish Protadius off. The soldiers then "cut through the tent everywhere with their swords and killed him." Brunhild had her revenge against two leaders who had agitated for Protadius's death—one had his foot chopped off and his property seized, and the other was killed. But she appeared to take the revolt against her favorite as a warning.

Brunhild toyed with the idea of at least a partial retirement, settling down in a villa in Autun with her four great-grandchildren, presumably overseeing their education. Sporadic battles continued between the brothers, though, while Clothar sat on the sidelines, egging his cousins on, allying himself first with one, then the other.

Preferring to negotiate with other women, Brunhild reached out to Theudebert's wife, Bilichild. The girl was strong-willed and independent, but she was also pragmatic and saw the impact of constant fighting on both kingdoms. A formal meeting was arranged "so that the two queens could meet to discuss making peace between Theuderic and Theudebert." At the last moment, Bilichild was blocked from attending by Austrasian nobles. Soon after, in 610 she was murdered by King Theudebert and quickly replaced by another queen. They had a son, whom they named Clothar, making it clear where their sympathies lay.

Whoever now had Theudebert's ear, they were not counseling peace. In 610, he ambushed his younger brother. Theuderic showed up to what he thought was a meeting to settle their territorial disputes, only to find himself surrounded by the entire Austrasian army. He was then forced to sign a treaty that ceded his rights to the Alsace and many other lands before he was released.

Fuming, Theuderic rode home, assembled as large an army as possible through a kingdom-wide levy, and turned back around to march against his brother. Theuderic defeated his older brother at Langres; Theudebert fled east to Cologne with his treasury. Theuderic pursued him, and the brothers had a final showdown in 612 at the Battle of Zülpich. It was said to be horrific: "The slaughter by both armies was such that in the thick of battle . . . the corpses of those killed had no room to fall, but the dead stood upright side by side with other corpses." Again, King Theuderic decisively defeated the Austrasian army, captured his brother, and took control of his royal treasury.

Theudebert's new baby was captured, too, and disposed of by Theuderic's men: "someone took the boy by the foot and smashed his brains out against a rock."

Theuderic was kinder to his brother; he let him live but stripped him of his royal robes, cut his long hair and tonsured him, and sent him off to a monastery, ending his brother's line for good.

. . .

In 612, Theuderic reunited Austrasia and Burgundy. Brunhild's position, as sole queen, was assured.

A few months later, while traveling through Metz on a military march, Theuderic collapsed. He had stopped to drink at a stream or a contaminated well. Days later, the young king—twenty-six-years-old, in prime physical condition, and at the height of his glory—was dead.

CHAPTER 32

The Fall

King Theuderic left behind four sons. Austrasia and Burgundy had been reunited for less than a year—it seemed incredible to split the kingdoms again, and this time into four parts, a sub-kingdom for each boy. And Brunhild's great-grandsons were all still minors. It also seemed unlikely that the aristocracy would allow her to serve as regent for all four sub-kingdoms.

Brunhild had another idea, borrowed from the old Roman, and now Byzantine, tradition of a single emperor. The oldest boy, Sigibert, was eleven. He might credibly be said to be twelve or thirteen, even. What if he were to rule the combined kingdoms by himself? Giving everything to the eldest son signified a break with the traditions of the Franks. But it would also keep the kingdoms united and the power centralized under one king, one regent, one palace. The other boys could potentially share in the kingdom once they came of age—she would have years to work out the details.

Brunhild informed the nobles and magnates of both realms that she would be assuming the regency yet again, just for a few more years. She appointed a Burgundian noble, Warnachar, as Prince Sigibert's new Mayor of the Palace. Warnachar hastily organized an assembly of the lords of both kingdoms; the prince was brought before them and crowned King Sigibert II.

. . .

King Clothar II had inherited his mother's wolfish instincts, if not her military prowess. He sniffed the wind. Fear.

Some of the nobles of the realm—especially those in Austrasia, Theudebert's former kingdom, and in the Jura region of Burgundy—were skeptical of Brunhild's third regency. A queen now nearing seventy, with an underage boy-king? Just across the border was a king in his twenties, now married and with a son. Some of these men, under the leadership of a bishop named Arnulf and a noble named Pippin, invited Clothar to come rule Austrasia instead.

Brunhild sent Sigibert east, to the vassal kingdom of Thuringia, either to protect him or to recruit soldiers to bring back to resist Clothar's advances. With him went his Mayor of the Palace, Warnachar, and a group of Burgundian nobles. One chronicler claims Brunhild handed one of these nobles an order for Warnachar to be killed once they reached their destination. She was concerned that Warnachar was friendly with Arnulf and Pippin, the men who supported Clothar. Brunhild no longer trusted Warnachar and wanted him removed and replaced. The order was read, torn up, and tossed away. One of Warnachar's servants then found the scraps and pieced them together.

Events could not have happened exactly in this manner, because Warnachar was allowed to remain in control of the army. Yet somehow Warnachar received information that his star had fallen. Seeing that he was doomed, he raced to make contact with King Clothar in Neustria.

· · ·

King Sigibert II, smooth-cheeked and skinny, was placed at the head of an army before his voice had cracked.

His younger brothers rode out with him. Childebert, the next eldest, could have been no older than ten at the time; Corbus was likely nine; and Merovech around six.

Warnachar traveled with them. The new king and the young princes had no way of knowing the Mayor of the Palace had been conspiring with Clothar himself, with Clothar's allies in Austrasia, and with the dissatisfied aristocrats from the Jura region who had been contemplating revolt.

When the four boys met Clothar's army, Warnachar and his men rode away before the signal to advance was given. The boys, along with a handful of loyal supporters, found themselves greatly outnumbered and were forced to flee.

Some say the boys were too disoriented by the scope of this betrayal to make it far; they were captured at the banks of Saône. Others say that they made it across the river and galloped south to the royal palace in Orbe, in the mountain pass. Then, reportedly, they fled from the palace and were found on the banks of Lake Neuchâtel, a glacial lake often shrouded in fog and ringed by the ridge of the Juras themselves and farther off, the snow-capped Alps.

Whether it was at the Saône or Lake Neuchâtel, the boys, on foot and hemmed in by the water, found themselves surrounded by men who loomed over them. In the confusion, one of the boys dodged the reach of his pursuers and swung himself up onto a horse. He kicked its side and took off, terrified, his heart thudding faster than his horse's hooves. It was Childebert, the ten-year-old prince, who somehow "mounted a horse and fled, never to return."

The others were not so lucky. Young King Sigibert II and his nine- and six-year-old brothers were roughly handled, chained up, and transported in carts as prisoners to their uncle. In the palace at Orbe, Brunhild and her granddaughter Theudelia were captured, too, at the point of their constable Herpo's sword.

The royal family had their last glimpses of the brooding landscape from behind the bars of their carts, jouncing through the winding, wooded Jougne Pass, part of the mountainous trade road to Geneva, which was barely passable. They were taken north, then east, the dark evergreens and precipitous drops gradually gentling into mounded hills and then mustard-colored fields, until they reached the small town of Renève. Just outside the town, on the banks of the Vingeanne, Clothar was camped out with his troops.

Here, the Vingeanne is shallow and runs clear—one can see straight through to the rocks and grasses in the riverbed, and it is easy to wade across. Past a few spindly poplars, as in Clothar's time, there is still a grassy field. What happened in this spot reverberated through Europe: in an era from which few documents survived, five different writers from different kingdoms made note of it.

Once the royal family was assembled at his camp, all except for runaway young Childebert, Clothar gave the order for Sigibert and Corbus to be executed. There is no record of the manner of their execution, but likely they were beheaded by ax.

Brunhild may not have witnessed the execution of her grandsons, but even from her tent she would have heard the clamoring, the long silence, and then the cheers.

The youngest, Merovech, though, was spared and sent to Neustria to be raised by a trusted noble. This was due less to Merovech's age and more to the fact that Clothar was the boy's godfather, a spiritual relationship he took very seriously. Also, given that Clothar had

A fourteenth-century illustration of Brunhild, captured by her own constable, being handed over to Clothar

only one son, it was useful to keep a nephew in reserve, just in case tragedy struck. If there proved to be no use for little Merovech, he could be sent to a monastery or quietly assassinated.

Princess Theodelia was also spared, destined to be shut away in a convent. Clothar now had to decide what to do with Brunhild. Since the usual punishment for an old queen was exile or the convent life, it was widely expected that Brunhild would follow her granddaughter.

But Clothar's decision was complicated by a few considerations. The first was young Childebert's escape.

Clothar had ordered an extensive manhunt. In the course of this search, Abbess Marcia of Arles would be accused of "secretly harboring a king." Clothar was so concerned he dispatched a duke to investigate, but by the time the duke arrived, there was no trace of the boy. Arles, though, was a very busy commercial port—there were at any time dozens of ships sailing for Egypt, Spain, and Byzantium, ships a ten-year-old boy might quietly slip aboard.

But the Gundovald affair had taught everyone that a disappeared prince could one day reappear, with calamitous results. If Childebert were to pop back up and Brunhild were still alive, she could verify his identity, legitimize his campaign. She was, however, an old woman, nearly seventy. She could not live forever, could she?

Clothar's father, King Chilperic, had once written that "the stalk which emerges from the soil will not wither until its root is severed." He had recognized that eliminating the opposition meant eliminating "the root" of the family, Brunhild. She was no ordinary queen.

· · ·

As the days dragged on, Brunhild grew increasingly confused. What was her nephew waiting for? She expected to be assassinated in her sleep, if she could manage to sleep without hearing the screams of her great-grandsons. That was the way queens were disposed of—quietly, in their chambers, as her sister had been.

A decade earlier, when a popular revolt broke out and Emperor Maurice was deposed by his general, he had been forced to watch his sons executed before he was beheaded himself, but Empress Constantina and her three daughters were spared and sent to a monastery. Public executions were reserved for kings and emperors, for powerful men.

And still, Clothar's allies clamored for her to be put to death. Warnachar did not want to take any chances. Brunhild, he pointed out, had proved exceedingly wily, maneuvering her way out of a convent once before. The other men Clothar had been forced to ally himself with, Bishop Arnulf and Duke Pippin, lobbied for the queen's death, too.

· · ·

The field was prepared for a trial. Brunhild was brought before them, straight-backed.

King Clothar II, from his makeshift dais, declared that the charge against Queen Brunhild was the death of ten kings.

She would have been incredulous.

Then, Fredegund's crimes were laid at Brunhild's feet—the assassination of her husband Sigibert, the suicide of her second husband, Merovech, and the staged jailhouse murder of Fredegund's other stepson, Prince Clovis. Brunhild was blamed for the death of Clothar's infant son, who had died from natural causes. Clothar's list of kings Brunhild had murdered also included her own great-grandsons, two of whom he himself had just executed. (The king listed three boys, either wanting to hide the fact that he had allowed young Prince Merovech to live or, more likely, wanting to hide news of Prince Childebert's escape.)

Only three of the deaths Brunhild was accused of could possibly be attributed to her—most understandably, Clothar blamed her for the death of his father, Chilperic, whose assassin had never been found. Blaming Brunhild was the only way to decisively clear his own mother of that charge. The deaths of Brunhild's grandson Theudebert and his baby son could also possibly be laid at her feet because she had supported Theuderic's feud against his brother.

Still, the assembled nobles and soldiers cried that Brunhild was guilty. Had not this wicked woman brought untold death and destruction to their realm?

Brunhild was then legally deposed, symbolically stripped of her royal finery as was the common practice. She stood motionless as her necklace, brooches, cape, and embroidered gown were ripped off her, and she stood before them in her linen shift, shivering.

Here was the part when she waited—exile, or a convent?

Clothar pronounced her sentence: death.

. . .

The clamor was disorienting, the sunlight too bright.

She had been "tortured in various ways for three days," likely whipped, beaten. Her face would have been bruised and dirt-streaked, her long gray hair bloody at the temples. She stumbled as she was yanked out of her tent.

She was led before a great hulking beast. When her eyes focused, she realized it was a camel. Clothar had somehow managed to secure one—all the sources agree on this specific point—and Brunhild was lifted upon it.

It may seem strange to expend the time and money to secure a camel when there were already numerous horses on hand. But this was a public ritual for humiliating deposed tyrants, a practice imported from Egypt to Byzantium. The victim would be whipped and then paraded around on a camel, facing backward, which was intended as the symbolic opposite of an emperor's triumphant entry into a city on horseback. (In Brunhild's native Spain, the Visigoths used a similar ritual but employed a donkey instead.) The symbolism of the camel would have been evident to Brunhild, of course, and not lost on Clothar's aristocrats. But even the common soldiers who had no knowledge of the origins of the practice would have understood that this foreign beast was meant to emphasize Brunhild's foreignness, her Visigothic roots or her intrigues with Byzantines—this was not how a good Frankish woman would have dared act.

Along with the Neustrian army, the aristocrats of Austrasia and Burgundy who had betrayed her lined up to watch. Many of these were the sons of the men who had craned their necks for a glimpse of her at her wedding.

Brunhild was "already broken by old age"; now she made "a most sorry spectacle." The crowd yelled insults or spat. This mockery went on "for some time," but when the men tired of shouting insults at a great-grandmother, they brought out the horses. In some reports there is just one horse, but regardless of number, they are always described as wild and unbroken, rearing as they are led forward.

Brunhild was dragged off the camel, and the men called for the rope. One source says she was bound to the horses' hooves, another that she was bound to their tails, and yet another specifies that she was bound to a single tail by "her hair, one arm and one leg."

At this point, she must have understood. Her nephew gave the signal, and the horses were let loose and given a smack, urged to gallop across this "pathless, rocky terrain."

The last thing Brunhild heard was hoofbeats.

. . .

Nothing remained of the queen. The King of Spain writes that "her nameless and bloody limbs, pulled apart, were spread out, widely scattered." A chronicler notes that she was "cut to shreds." Another notes the effort Clothar went to, even after her death, to destroy what remained: "Her final grave was the fire. Her bones were burnt."

Clothar could not take the chance that Brunhild would be regarded as a martyr, that her tomb would become a focal point for opposition to his rule. It seems, though, there may have been a tomb in the crypt at

Tombeau de Brunehaut à Saint-Martin d'Autun.

A sketch made of Brunhild's tomb before it was destroyed during the Revolution

Brunhild's church in Autun, complete with marble columns and mosaics. Although the church was destroyed during the French Revolution, illustrations and prints of this tomb survive. That suggests that someone present that day, whether a sympathetic noble or a priest from the local church, scooped up a few handfuls of ashes from the pyre, and carefully transported them seventy-four miles southwest to the good monks at Saint Martin's in Autun.

The overthrow and execution of Brunhild was not as unanimously supported as it might seem. Opposition to King Clothar II is recorded not just in Arles, where runaway Childebert was likely sheltered, but throughout Burgundy. In the town of Sens, the local bishop worked to frighten off the king's invading armies with his church bell; he was later exiled for this offense. Burgundian nobles and clergy also attempted to despose Clothar during the early years of his reign. The same chronicler who criticizes Clothar for having taken "too much notice of the views of women young and old" (a pointed reference to Fredegund) also unironically notes that this plot was foiled by the quick actions of Clothar's own queen.

. . .

Thanks to two women—his mother and her political rival—Clothar went from ruling twelve counties to an entire empire. For the first time in over fifty years, the kingdoms of the Franks were united under one ruler. But in destroying Brunhild, and accomplishing what his mother could not, Clothar set in motion the events that would doom the Merovingian dynasty.

Many who turned on Brunhild doomed themselves as well. Had they tolerated the queen for just a few more years, they would have avoided the much worse fate that awaited them. Clothar viewed them as opportunists rather than true allies, and at the earliest opportunity, he disposed of many of them. The aristocrats in the Jura region, who had supported Clothar in a bid for their own independence, found their revolt squashed and their leader executed. Others met their ends at the hands of the common people—Herpo, the constable who handed over Brunhild, was rewarded with a dukedom, and then promptly ripped apart by a mob.

When Clothar took the throne of a united Francia, one of his first acts was to hold the Council of Paris in October 614, which was attended by the bishops of Austrasia, Neustria, and Burgundy as well as bishops from newly Christianized Anglo-Saxon kingdoms. The resulting Edict of Paris is widely considered an early predecessor of the Magna Carta, Britain's landmark thirteenth-century legal document limiting the authority of the king. And rather than centralizing the Frankish Empire under one crown and one capital, as the great King Clovis had done, Clothar acquiesced to the aristocracy's demands to maintain three kingdoms, each with its own capital administered by its own Mayor of the Palace.

But these were not the only concessions Clothar had to make.

Before Clothar's forces had invaded Austrasia and Burgundy, a deal had been struck with Warnachar, the Burgundian Mayor of the Palace. Warnachar had been the one to give the signal to retreat, leaving young King Sigibert and his brothers undefended and able to be easily captured. Now Warnachar's position was made into a lifetime appointment. This was a significant change from having a Mayor who served at the pleasure of the king. First the position became a lifetime appointment; then it became hereditary. Fredegund's descendants came to be known as rois fainéants, or "do-nothing kings." They were transformed into mere figureheads—dominated, and then deposed, by their Mayors of the Palace.

The two nobles Warnachar had collaborated with, Bishop Arnulf and Duke Pippin, united their children in marriage to launch a new dynasty. Their descendants, the Carolingians, would secure the hereditary office of Mayor of the Palace and eventually replace the Merovingians as kings of the Franks. The men who betrayed Brunhild became the great-great-grandfathers of Charlemagne.

Backlash

T he summer I went in search of Brunhild and Fredegund, yet another Merovingian was found.

The grave of this elderly woman was at least the fifth such discovery in the early twenty-first century—and there were dozens more similar finds during the twentieth century, including the sumptuous grave of Fredegund's own mother-in-law, a queen named Aregund.

The Merovingians are everywhere, it turns out.

The grave goods of Fredegund's mother-in-law are under museum glass. The burial site of her father-in-law, Clothar I, and Sigibert, the king she assassinated, is now an active archaeological site; the abbey these crypts are a part of is in the process of being restored. The tomb of Brunhild's ally Radegund still lies in the crypt of a church that bears her name in Poitiers. One can still venerate the relic of the True Cross and listen to the hymn "Vexilla Regis," composed by Venantius Fortunatus to commemorate its arrival. Or watch how the world still comes to Radegund: people from all over make the pilgrimage to slip a letter under the lid of her sarcophagus, begging for her intercession.

And ordinary, unnamed Merovingians are turning up, too. In the lower level of a museum in Metz, their skulls grinned up at me with their perfect, perfect teeth (thanks to an early medieval recipe for toothpaste, my guide told me). I was surprised by how much else remains and is in the process of being resurrected—not just skeletons, but basilicas, abbeys, amphitheaters, crypts. Embroidered burial tunics, necklaces, earrings, and signet rings. Tucked away in the small towns of rural France and Germany, or under the cobblestones of its bustling cities, there is an entire lost dynasty.

The Merovingians have long been overshadowed by the bloodline that supplanted them—Charlemagne and his Carolingians, who had every incentive to portray themselves as triumphing over an uncivilized wasteland. But we have inherited this portrait of bumbling barbarians in part because the Carolingians worked hard to depose and then erase their predecessors, conspiring with a pope to do so. The Merovingians were further maligned by French Revolutionaries, who saw in the very first Louis (King Clovis) the origin story of their own reviled King Louis XVI.

Today, the Merovingians are receiving renewed attention from historians as the dynasty that oversaw the transition from the Roman to the medieval world and established the political borders of Europe that still exist, as well as many of the laws and social mores that do, too. Yet the Merovingian' two longest-reigning queens and regents have not yet received their due, and there's a very obvious reason for that.

. . .

Hardly any sources survive from the period immediately after Brunhild's execution, but those that do show King Clothar II quickly moved to obliterate the memory and legacy of his aunt and his own mother. At the beginning of his reign in his most public act, the 614 Edict of Paris, he erased Brunhild and her descendants entirely. The document lists tolls and taxes going back several decades to the reigns of his father, Chilperic, and even his uncles, but he makes no mention of Brunhild, her son, or her grandsons. The entire line was wiped from the public record.

More surprisingly, Clothar II makes no mention of his mother, either, even though Fredegund had issued her share of tolls and taxes. Clothar II was presumably a dutiful son who said the usual Masses for the repose of his mother's soul, but he did not allow her any legal recognition. Nor did he commission any poems or erect any churches in Fredegund's honor. He did not seek to have her made a saint—even though the bar was quite low at the time, and King Guntram had been quickly canonized. The chronicles, though, are scrubbed of reports of Fredegund's potential infidelities and the accusations that she killed King Chilperic to hide her affair with Landeric. This crime is laid solely at the feet of Brunhild, substantiation of the charge that she had killed many kings.

The language chroniclers used to document Brunhild's reign grew increasingly virulent. At first the execution is presented as a careful political calculation; within a generation, the disgust for Brunhild has become palpable, and the decision has become an emotional one. Clothar is full of hatred for his aunt (*odium contra ipsam nimium haberit*). The nobles fear Brunhild (*timentis*), yes, but they also hate her, and it is this hatred that motivates them to betray her (*odium in eam habentes*).

There were clearly nobles and church officials who had questioned whether Brunhild's method of execution had been overly violent, even bizarre, because these same chroniclers now scrambled to justify it as fated. They highlighted the battlefield standoff between Ursio and the queen nearly thirty years earlier: "Leave us or our horses' hooves will trample you to the earth!" the duke had threatened the queen then. Hadn't Brunhild been warned of what might happen if she did not rein in her ambition? For good measure, another prophecy was inserted. A Greek Sibyl was said to have predicted that "Bruna is coming from the regions of Spain, before whose eyes many peoples will perish. This woman will be broken by the heels of horses."

Clothar II not only erased political records and tacitly encouraged historical chroniclers to revise their accounts, but he also worked to erase Brunhild's influence on the Church. Instead of being lauded for her help Christianizing Britain, the queen was blamed for all of the simony in the empire, even though Clothar II himself had lately come under fire for the practice. There was no one left to counter his claims. Brunhild had been allied with a powerful pope, but Gregory the Great was not around to defend her piety, having died a handful of years before she did. During Clothar II's reign, there would be six different popes, none lasting long enough to consolidate power and develop as clear an agenda as Pope Gregory.

Without decisive opposition from the papacy, Clothar II moved to promote the clergy who had been Brunhild's most recent enemies. He first uplifted the cult of Desiderius of Vienne, lobbying for sainthood on behalf of a bishop who had preached against Brunhild and her grandson, and ignoring Desiderius's arrest for treason and exile for rape. The king also asked the brash Columbanus to come back to Francia. The monk refused, but when he died a few years later, Clothar II also promoted his cult. Another prophecy was fashioned and stuffed into the dead monk's mouth: Columbanus had condemned Brunhild as a "wretched woman," and predicted that Clothar II would rule all of Francia within three years. Clothar had only plotted her overthrow and death to fulfill the holy man's prophecy.

Another supposed prophecy by the fundamentalist monk was slid into a different work. Columbanus refuses to baptize Theuderic's sons because he realizes they are cursed: "They'll never take up the scepters of kings." The monk and Brunhild are also cast into a battle between good and evil: "The old serpent came to [Theuderic's] grandmother Brunhild, who was a second Jezebel, and aroused her pride against the holy man."

In the biblical story of Jezebel, men found a blueprint for how to destroy powerful queens and a shorthand for how to talk about them. Jezebel was the outspoken Phoenician queen who challenged the prophet Elijah. The Book of Kings casts her broad-minded liberalism in contrast to the prophet's inflexible fundamentalism. Jezebel was said to exercise undue influence over her husband, something both Brunhild and Fredegund were accused of doing; Jezebel was reported to be promiscuous, and both queens are accused of taking lovers. Jezebel met her end defiantly, dressing in her finery and applying kohl to her eyes while waiting for her murderers. She was thrown out a window, then trampled by horses. Her body was further obliterated, gnawed on by dogs; what remained of her was spread "like dung on the ground."

Brunhild's execution was clearly designed to eliminate her in the same way. But Fredegund, despite her prestigious burial, was obliterated as well. All traces of the bold and ruthless queen were scattered to the wind, replaced by those of a placid, devoted mother.

. . .

There were no Merovingian queen regents before them, but others followed in their wake, most notably Queen Nanthild (regent 639–42) and Queen Bathild (regent 657–64). The establishment had learned from its mistakes, though, and moved to quickly silence them—Nanthild was quietly murdered, and Bathild was packed off to a convent.

Things only got worse for Brunhild and Fredegund's reputations by the time the Carolingian dynasty took over in the eighth century. There were Carolingian women who attempted to rule as regents, too; the most notable of these was Plectrude, who managed to imprison Charlemagne's grandfather and stave off his attempts to grab the throne for four whole years before she, too, was forced into a convent, where she conveniently died. But chroniclers and clergy rushed to warn kings and the general populace of the dangers of females embroiling themselves in politics. Against this backdrop, the threat Brunhild's and Fredegund's reigns presented to the rapidly calcifying patriarchal order was so great that a systematic smear campaign was waged to discourage other women from following their examples.

Fredegund was recast as a femme fatale—"beautiful, very cunning, and an adulteress"—and Brunhild as a murderess lacking all maternal instinct. The civil wars between the Frankish kingdoms—the origins of which predated both queens' marriages into the dynasty—were blamed solely on Fredegund and Brunhild, who purportedly "incited [their husbands] on both sides." Brunhild is also blamed for the competition between her grandsons Theudebert and Theuderic; they war against one another because of her "evil counsel."

There is no question of the queens' transformation being accidental, the result of poor translations, sloppy transcriptions, or even a handful of scribes with personal axes to grind. It was a coordinated and methodical effort. The Carolingians systematically rewrote history, and as one scholar plainly notes, in order to do so their chroniclers "interfered deliberately with their material." Clearly, giving women power would lead only to chaos, war, and death.

It would be many centuries before the Frankish lands were graced by queens whose careers and accomplishments would parallel those of Brunhild and Fredegund, such as Blanche of Castille or Catherine de Medici. The next similar female political rivalry in Europe, between Elizabeth I and her cousin Mary, Queen of Scots, wouldn't occur until nearly one thousand years after their deaths.

. . .

Cut from the political landscape, the queens took root in legends and myths.

Fredegund's dogged elimination of her stepsons Merovech and Clovis was subsumed into existing lore of the evil stepmother. Stories of mothers eliminating inconvenient nonbiological offspring have existed throughout time and cultures, but it is clear the slave-turned-queen left her mark on the tradition. Her act of slamming a trunk lid down on rebellious Princess Rigunth's neck was preserved in a Norse fairy tale in *The Poetic Edda*, composed around 800, which makes mention of the use of a trunk lid to kill young girls. Another version of the Rigunth episode, albeit with the positions reversed, shows up in the early seventeenth century in an Italian version of Cinderella; the daughter kills her stepmother by slamming the lid of a trunk down on her head.

Perhaps the best-known example of Fredegund's resurrection in myth and literature is Shakespeare's use of her "walking forest" battle strategy in *Macbeth*. Two centuries before Shakespeare, though, Fredegund's tactic was highlighted in the poet Christine de Pizan's 1405 *Book of the City of Ladies*. Details of the sixth century Battle of Droizy may have only been preserved because of the efforts of women—the manuscript narrating Fredegund's leadership has been linked to a convent in Soissons. Christine de Pizan resuscitated this material to defend the female sex, praising Fredegund's military leadership during this battle: "the valiant queen kept out in front, exhorting the others on to battle with promises and cajoling words" and her men, not to be shown up by a woman, fought all the more bravely. The poet concedes that Fredegund "was unnaturally cruel for a woman," but she also praises the queen's "skillful handling of power." Fredegund was not just a clever general, she was a successful regent: "she ruled over the kingdom of France most wisely after her husband's death."

During the same time period, curiously enough, roads all over France were named after Queen Brunhild (or, as she was called in French, "Brunehaut"). Jean d'Outremeuse writes about one such road in 1398: the common people, puzzled by how straight this road is, concoct a story that Queen Brunhild was a witch who magically paved the road in a single night with the help of the devil.

These roads that bear Brunhild's name tangled up the facts of her life. Some said the roads were named after her because Brunhild repaired the old Roman roads; others that these roads were built over the paths the spooked wild horses made during her execution, tearing through the countryside as they dragged the old queen behind them. These multitudes of Chaussées de Brunehaut, most of which appear to be old Roman roads, persisted into the fifteenth, sixteenth, and seventeenth centuries, crisscrossing the lands of France, Belgium, and Germany. At least thirteen of them still exist: it's possible to ride a bike or take a Sunday drive down a Chaussée Brunehaut even today. A few of them converge in the French town of Bavay, where at the very center of the intersection they create is a nineteeth-century statue that commemorates Brunhild herself.

There are also two châteaus and several old towers named after Brunhild, along with a municipality in Belgium and a craft brewery. Other towns proudly claim to be the site of her execution. One legend situates her execution in Paris, at the corner where rue Saint-Honoré meets rue de l'Arbre Sec, close to the Louvre. The distinction is also claimed by the town of Bruniquel in southwestern France, which was too far south to have been the setting for the event but nevertheless claims the queen was dragged to her death along the Côte Rouge outside the village. The town's association with Brunhild, though, may have originally been due to its castle, which was built on the ruins of a sixth-century villa that adjoined the morgengabe Brunhild fought so hard to recover. It's plausible that the queen once stayed there during the height of her power.

There are dozens of references to Brunhild and Fredegund as individuals, but in death, as in life, the queens seem most potent in relation to one another. The queens resurfaced once again in the nineteenth century as Romanticism swept across Europe and along with it, an idealization of the past. In Britain there was an obsession with knights and King Arthur, and in France and Germany, with the barbarian tribes that swept through after the fall of Rome. In France, people wandered the halls of the 1819 Paris Exposition with long hair brushing their shoulders, dressed up as Merovingians. A flurry of works featured the queens—including an opera, an operetta, a pantomime, three plays, and a multitude of books and poems, prints, and portraits. In Germany, the twelfth-century epic poem *Nibelungenlied*, or *The Song of the Nibelungs,* was rediscovered and elevated as a national treasure. One of the main characters of this epic is Brunhild, the warrior-queen, and one of its main plotlines demonstrates how an argument between two royal sisters-in-law rips the realm apart. It was this medieval text that would serve as the inspiration for Wagner's opera cycle *Der Ring des Nibelungen.*

In the dominant version of Merovingian history that emerged in the nineteenth century and was passed down to us, the surviving pieces of the queens' stories were grafted onto a narrative that hinged entirely upon Galswintha's murder. It all comes down to the misogynistic tropes of the love triangle and the catfight: one woman is instrumental in the murder of another and steals her man, and a squabble with the murdered woman's sister ensues, touching off a terrible civil war between two royal houses. The civil war between Neustria and Austrasia raged for at least forty years, longer than the English Wars of the Roses. Yet this immensely consequential war of succession has been recast as a story of romance and revenge, a *Jerry Springer*–style brouhaha writ large.

Even so, the most impressive, and terrible, events of Brunhild's and Fredegund's lives have not been entirely overlooked. For example, Cersei from the *Game of Thrones* books and TV series undoubtedly alludes to the English War of the Roses and figures like Elizabeth Woodville, Margaret of Anjou, and Anne Boleyn, but historians claim she also draws from the lives of our two queens. Like Fredegund, Cersei is dogged by suspicions of infidelity, and when her adultery is discovered, she arranges for her king-husband to die while he is on a hunting trip, just as Fredegund's enemies claimed she did. Cersei also arranges the deaths of her husband's other children as Fredegund was said to, and in her we see Brunhild's paranoia about being replaced by a younger queen. Like both queens, while ostensibly serving as regent for underage boys, Cersei assumes the throne herself.

Their ghosts are everywhere; we just need to know where to look.

. . .

On August 25, 1632, in Autun a small audience attended a small ceremony to open a marble sarcophagus. Inside there was a lead coffin, and inside that, ash, coal, and a single spur, which were taken as proof that this, indeed, was the tomb of Queen Brunhild.

Brunhild's abbey in Autun was sacked during the French Revolution. Today only the lid of her supposed sarcophagus remains—two pieces of the smooth black marble slab are on display in a small museum in a small room alongside vases and statue fragments from antiquity. The ruins of the grand abbey now lie under a neighborhood park.

In contrast, Fredegund's remains slumber among kings, her sarcophagus dappled by purple and yellow light refracted through stained glass. In the twelfth century during renovations to Saint-Germain-des-Prés, she was unearthed and given a new and elaborate mosaic slab. Her likeness was rendered in stones and marble set into mortar and outlined by copper. The former slave holds a scepter and wears a crown. She is, however, faceless. It's likely that her face was once painted, but over the centuries this paint faded. A more sinister interpretation is that her face was purposefully left blank, designed to "imitate the veil" she should have retired behind in life.

Her tomb escaped the worst of the destruction wrought on Saint-Germain-des-Prés by the Revolution. In the early nineteenth century it was moved to the majestic Basilica of Saint-Denis and positioned right next to that of Clovis I, the king she so admired in life, as well as the tombs of her grandson and great-grandson. Yet for all the glory of the setting, her complicated legacy is reduced to the inscription FREDEGUNDIA REGINA, UXOR CHILPERICI RÉGIS—Queen Fredegund, wife of King Chilperic.

As a girl, I gobbled up biographies of female historical figures: activists, writers, and artists, but few political leaders, and even fewer from so deep in the past. I don't know what it would have meant for me, and for other little girls, to have found Queen Fredegund's and Queen Brunhild's stories collected in the books I read. To discover that even in the darkest and most tumultuous of times, women can, and did, lead.

The misogynistic logic of patriarchy is curiously circular: women cannot govern because they never have. But this big lie rests upon a bed of induced historical amnesia, the work of numberless erasures and omissions, collectively sending the message that the women who *have* ruled haven't earned the right to be remembered.

Even though the Dark Queens were absent from my books, they were in plain sight throughout my childhood as the women I was warned against becoming. The wicked stepmother in my fairy tales, the haughty Jezebel who was preached against in church, the fat lady singing at the

Remnants of the black marble lid of Brunhild's sarcophagus

Fredegund's tomb in the Basilica of Saint-Denis

opera: all were objects of hatred or ridicule. Between the silence of suppressed history and the oppressive blare of stereotypes, what space remains?

But the ghosts of Brunhild and Fredegund refuse to stay silent. They surface relentlessly, determined to be heard.

Is this because the queens have been robbed—of a voice? Of recognition? Of a connection with the living?

Or is this because *we* have been robbed—of foundational narratives about female power?

And if so, how do we begin to redress this injustice? Perhaps it's by imagining, and insisting upon, the sort of epitaphs Brunhild and Fredegund would have written for themselves. Not WIFE OF, MOTHER OF, but the title they demanded during their lives—PRAECELLENTISSIMAE ET GLORIOSISSIMAE FRANCORUM REGINAE—the most excellent and glorious Queens of the Franks.

A NOTE ON SOURCES AND METHODS

This book is not an academic history; it is a work of narrative nonfiction based on primary sources. These primary sources are, admittedly, fragmentary but enough survive to make it possible to assemble a narrative and to piece together the emotional lives and daily realities of these two queens.

Most of what we know of Brunhild and Fredegund comes from a history written by Gregory of Tours. The bishop began composing his rambling, ten-volume *History of the Franks* shortly after both queens entered public life, and he continued to work on it for the next two decades. During that time, Gregory was interacting with both queens and their emissaries. As a result, he provides us with real-time reportage and plenty of contemporary gossip.

Gregory's account, though, has its shortcomings. The bishop was (rightfully) insecure about his Latin, not well traveled, and by twenty-first-century standards, he was credulous and naive. Most important (but not at all surprising), he was a misogynist, suspicious of ambitious women, and particularly disapproving of politically active ones. Further, Gregory saw one queen as his adversary, the other as his patron, and was likely intimidated by both.

While Gregory does not appear to invent events outright, I have accepted the scholarly consensus that the bishop had his own agenda and manipulated his histories accordingly. Not only does Gregory genuinely misunderstand some events (for example, interpreting weather phenomena as divine signs), but he also purposefully omits certain details or events. The bishop is also prone to embellishments and exaggerations, usually to present himself in the best light.

I have supplemented the information we get from Gregory of Tours with other sources from the time period. Most prominent of these are the works of Gregory's friend and court poet Venantius Fortunatus, and letters, some written by Brunhild and her son, others by Pope Gregory the Great. Other contemporary sources include a terse chronicle by Bishop Marius of Avenches, as well as histories written in Spain by John of Biclaro and Isidore of Seville. I have also made use of church councils and secular laws and archaeological finds that suggest how Merovingians lived, ate, and dressed.

Other primary sources were written near the end of or shortly after the queens' lives, such as those written by King Sisebut of Spain or the monk Jonas of Bobbio. But the two other sources of which I make most use were written well after the queens' deaths: Fredegar's *Chronicle*, which seems to have been penned in the 660s, a half a century after Brunhild's execution, and the anonymous *Liber Historiae Francorum*, which came into wide circulation in the 720s. Both Fredegar's *Chronicle* and the *Liber Historiae Francorum* are based upon Gregory of Tours's work, but both add their own material—specific names of people and places, for example, or even dialogue—which suggests these authors had access to other, earlier sources.

Like Gregory, the authors of all of these other works also had their own loyalties and prejudices. I have tried to read skeptically, with an eye for how enmeshed an author was in the events they reported upon and whether they had a good reason to exaggerate or omit information. I've also consulted numerous scholars and historians' research into and interpretations of these primary sources. When confronted with competing narratives, I have tried to pick the version that seems most plausible and consistent with the character of the person in question. Frustratingly, sometimes interpreting a person's motives or the precise timing of an event hinges upon a verb tense or a vague phrase. There is often disagreement among scholars about chronology and causality; I have tried to be transparent about these ongoing debates in my notes.

In addition to multiple versions of events, there are also large gaps in the historical record. When these occur, I have tried to reconstruct events and speculate responsibly, and to indicate when I do so. As a result, there will be too many instances of "perhaps" for some readers and not nearly enough for most historians. I also fully expect that there is other evidence still waiting to be discovered. A gravesite, ruin, or parchment might cast an entirely new light on a motive or sequence of events in the future. In such cases, I will be delighted to be proved wrong.

I consider another primary source to be the landscape Brunhild and Fredegund interacted with. As part of my research process, I traveled to Metz, the former capital of the kingdom of Austrasia; Soissons, the former capital of the kingdom of Neustria; and the much-disputed city of Paris. In France, I also visited the sites of some of Fredegund's military victories, as well as Renève, the place of Brunhild's trial and execution. Additionally, I traveled to Trier, Germany, and Orbe and Lake Neuchâtel in Switzerland. Finally, I benefited greatly from visits to Brunhild's and Fredegund's final resting places in Autun and Paris; I hope readers benefit from them as well.

ACKNOWLEDGMENTS

It has been a privilege and a pleasure to work with Ben Hyman. This book is all the better for having such a dedicated editor. I am also grateful to Morgan Jones and Akshaya Iyer, as well as my Bloomsbury team: Marie Coolman, Nicole Jarvis, Jonathan Lee, and Rosie Mahorter.

I appreciate, too, the keen eyes of my copy editor, Gleni Bartels, and proofreader, Jasmine Kwityn.

I'm grateful to Mackenzie Brady Watson, loyal agent and tireless advocate. She and Aemilia Phillips shepherded both author and project along.

This book would not be possible without the scholarship, insight, and generosity of Erin Thomas Dailey.

For translations from the Latin, I am indebted to John de Boulton-Holland.

For the opportunity to tour many of the sites associated with the queens' lives, I'm grateful to Sophie Delange of Inspire Metz for the private tour of the Musée de La Cour d'Or; Thomas Wilwert for taking me underground to the Caves Sainte Marie; Monique Judas-Urschel and the Association Abbaye Royale Saint-Médard de Soissons for allowing me access to the abbey's crypt; the Office du Tourisme d'Orbe for allowing me to view the Roman mosaics of Boscéaz; and the kind staff at the Musée Rolin in Autun and the Basilica of Saint-Denis in Paris.

Special thanks to Henry Freedland, who first let me write about these queens for *Lapham's Quarterly*; Kate Bossert, for her research assistance and sympathetic ear; Joan Lattanzi of Interlibrary Loan for Baltimore County Public Library, who managed to secure many obscure texts for me, even in the middle of a pandemic; and Bonnie Effros, Shirin Fozi, Jeana DelRosso, Ray Bossert, and Bridget Quinn for answering my questions or pointing me to the right resource.

Thank you to my believers, especially Christy Brookhart and Jennifer Bedon.

Thank you to my family, who endured endless visits to museums and underground crypts and listened to endless bits of medieval trivia. Paul, your patience knows no bounds.

Lastly, this book is dedicated to Nate, history buff extraordinaire.

BIBLIOGRAPHY

PRIMARY SOURCES

In the list of primary sources that follows, I have given priority to the translations that I consulted. Often I consulted more than one translation of the same work. For those sources which I also found it necessary to consult in the original Latin, I have also included bibliographic details about the edition used. There are some instances in which I was not able to consult the most recent translation of a work due to library closures and restrictions related to the COVID-19 pandemic.

ABBREVIATIONS USED:

MGH—Monumenta Germaniae Historica
MGH AA—MGH Auctores antiquissimi
MGH SRM—MGH Scriptores rerum Merovingicarum

Aimon de Fleury. *Historia Francorum*. Edited by G. Waitz. MGH, Scriptores, Band xxvi. Hanover and Berlin, 1826–92.

Anthimus. *De Observatione Ciborum*. Translated by Mark Grant in *On the Observance of Foods*. London: Prospect Books, 1996.

Appollinaris, Sidonius. *Poems and Letters*. 2 vols. Translated by W.B. Anderson. Cambridge: Harvard University Press, 1963.

Baudonivia. *De vita sanctae Radegundis*, in *Sainted Women of the Dark Ages*. Translated by J. McNamara, E. Halborg, and J. Whatley. Durham, NC: Duke University Press Books, 1992, 86–105.

———. *De vitae sanctae Radegundis, Liber II*. MGH SRM. 2. Edited by Bruno Krusch. Hanover, 1888, 377-395.

Brunhild. "Letters 26–31." Translated by by Joan Ferrante. *Epistolae: Medieval Women's Latin Letters*.

——. "Letters 26–30." *Epistolae Austrasicae*. Edited by Wilhelm Gundlach. MGH, Epistolae 3: Epistolae Merowingici et Karolini aevi 1. Berlin: Widemann, 1892, 139–41.

Caesarius of Arles. *Regula ad virgines*, Sources Chrétiennes, vol. 345. Paris, 1988.

Childebert II. "Letters XXV, XXVIII." *Epistolae Austrasicae*. Edited by Wilhelm Gundlach. MGH, Epistolae 3: Epistolae Merowingici et Karolini aevi 1. Berlin: Widemann, 1892: 138–39, 140.

Chilperic. "IX, Chilpericus Rex," *Hymni latini antiqvissimi lxxv, psalmi iii*. Edited by Walther Bulst. Heidelberg, Germany: F. H. Kerle Verlag, 1956, 119.

Christine de Pizan. *The Book of the City of Ladies*. Translated by Rosalind Brown-Grant. Translated by Rosalind Brown-Grant. London: Penguin Books Limited, 1999.

Chronicon Moissiacense Maius, vol. 2. Edited by J.M.J.G Kats and D. Claszen. Leiden University, 2012.

Clothar II. "Constitution of Clothar." Translated by Alexander C. Murray in *From Roman to Merovingian Gaul: A Reader*. Ontario: Broadview Press, 2000, 564–65.

——. "The Edict of Paris of Clothar II, October 614." Translated by Alexander Murray in *From Roman to Merovingian Gaul: A Reader*. Ontario: Broadview Press, 2000, 565–68.

Concilia Aevi Merovingici. MGH: Leges, Sectio III, Tomus I. Edited by Friedrich Maassen. Hanover: Hahn, 1893.

Continuations of the Chronicle of Isidore. Edited by Thomas Mommsen. MGH AA XI: 489–90.

Earliest Life of Gregory the Great. Translated by Bertram Colgrave. Cambridge, UK: Cambridge University Press, 1968.

Edict of Paris, 614. Translated by by Alexander C. Murray in *From Roman to Merovingian Gaul: A Reader*. Ontario: Broadview Press, 2000, 565–68.

Epistolae Wisigothicae. Edited by Wilhelm Gundlach. MGH Epistolae 3. Berlin, 1892, 658–90.

Fredegar. *Chronicle: Book 3*. Translated by Jane Ellen Woodruff in "The 'Historia Epitomata' (third book) of the 'Chronicle' of Fredegar: An Annotated

Translation and Historical Analysis of Interpolated Material." PhD dissertation, the University of Nebraska–Lincoln, 1987.

——. *Chronicle: Book 4*. Translated by Alexander C. Murray in "The Sixth Chronicle of Fredegar, Book IV." *From Roman to Merovingian Gaul: A Reader.* Ontario: Broadview Press, 2000, 448–90.

——. *Chronicarum quae dicuntur Fredegarii scholastici libri N cum continuationibus.* Edited by Bruno Krusch, MGH SRM, 2. Hanover, 1888.

Fortunatus, Venantius. *De vitae sanctae Radegundis* in *Sainted Women of the Dark Ages.* Translated by J. McNamara, E. Halborg, and J. Whatley. Durham, NC: Duke University Press Books, 1992, 70–86.

——. *De vitae sanctae Radegundis, Liber I.* MGH SRM. 2. Edited by Bruno Krusch. Hanover, 1888, 364-377.

——. *Venantius Fortunatus: Personal and Political Poems.* Translated by Judith George. Liverpool, UK: Liverpool University Press, 1995.

——. *Poems to Friends.* Translated by Joseph Pucci. Indianapolis: Hackett Publishing, 2010.

——. *Poems.* Translated by Michael Roberts. Cambridge, MA: Harvard University Press, 2017.

——. *Vita Germani episcopi Parisiaci.* MGH SRM VII. Edited by W. Levison. Hanover, 1920, 337–428.

Germanus. "Letter to Brunhild." Translated by Joan Ferrante. *Epistolae: Medieval Women's Latin Letters.*

——. "Letter IX." *Epistolae Austrasicae.* Edited by Wilhelm Gundlach. MGH, Epistolae 3: Epistolae Merowingici et Karolini aevi 1. Berlin: Widemann, 1892, 122–24.

Grammaticus, Saxo. *Gesta Danorum.* Edited by Alfred Holder. Strasbourg: Karl J. Trübner, 1886.

Gregory the Great. *Epistles.* Edited by Philip Schaff in *A Select Library of the Nicene and Post-Nicene Fathers of the Christian Church.* Second Series. Buffalo, NY: The Christian Literature Co., 1886–90. vols. 12–13.

——. *Epistles.* MGH, *Gregorii Pape Registrum Epistolarum*, ep.6.55, 1.430.

Gregory of Tours. *Decem libri historiarum*. Translated by Lewis Thorpe in *Gregory of Tours: History of the Franks*. New York: Penguin, 1974.

——. *Decem libri historiarum*. Translated by Ernest Brehaut in *Gregory of Tours: History of the Franks*. New York: Columbia University Press, 1916.

——. *Decem libri historiarum*. Edited by Bruno Krusch and Wilhelm Levison. MGH SRM, 1.1. Hannover, 1951.

——. *De virtutibus et miraculis sancti Martini*. Translated by Raymond Van Dam, Translated *Saints and Their Miracles in Late Antique Gaul*. Princeton: Princeton University Press, 1993, 199–303.

——. *Liber Vitae Patrum*. Translated by Edward James. *Life of the Fathers* 2nd edition, Liverpool: Liverpool University Press, 1991.

Isidore of Seville. *Historia Gothorum*. ed. by Theodor Mommsen. *Isidori Iunioris episcopi Hispalensis historia Gothorum Wandalorum Sueborum*. MGH AA, 11. Berlin, 1894.

Jean d'Outremeuse. *Ly Mureur des Histors: Chronique de Jean des Preis dit d'Outremeuse*, vol. 2. Edited by Adolphe Borgnet and Stanislas Bormans. Brussels: Commission Royale d'Histoire de Belgique, 1869.

John of Biclaro. *Chronicle*. Translated by Kenneth Baxter Wolf in *Conquerors and Chroniclers of Early Medieval Spain*. Liverpool, UK: Liverpool University Press, 1990, 51–66.

John of Ephesus. *Ecclesiastical History*. Translated by R. Payne Smith in *The Third Part of the Ecclesiastical History of John Bishop of Ephesus*. Oxford University Press, 1860.

Jonas of Bobbio. *Vita Columbani*. Translated by Dana C. Munro in *Translations and Reprints from the Original Sources of European History*, vol. II, no. 7. Philadelphia: University of Pennsylvania Press, 1897.

——. *Vita Columbani*. Edited by Krusch. MGH SRM IV. Hanover, 1902, 1–156.

Les canons des conciles mérovingiens (VIe–VIIe siècles). Translated by Jean Gaudemet and Brigitte Basdevant. 2 vols. Paris: Éditions du Cerf, 1989.

Les Gestes des évêques d'Auxerre. Edited by Michel Sot. Vol. 1. Paris: Belles-Lettres, 2002, 8

Les Grandes Chroniques de France, selon que ells sont conserves en l'eglise de Saint-Denis en France. Paris: Paulin Press, 1836.

Liber Historiae Francorum. Translated by Bernard Bachrach. Coronado Press, 1973.

Marius of Avenches. *Chronica.* Translated by Alexander Murray in *From Roman to Merovingian Gaul: A Reader.* Ontario: Broadview Press, 2000, 100–108.

Pactus Legis Salicae [*The Laws of the Salian Franks*]. Translated by Katherine Drew. Philadelphia: University of Pennsylvania Press, 1991.

——. Translated by Alexander Murray. *From Roman to Merovingian Gaul: A Reader.* Ontario: Broadview, 2000, 533–56.

Passio Sigismundi regis. Edited by B. Krusch. MGH SRM II. Hanover, 1888, 333–40.

Paul the Deacon. *Historia Langobardorum* [*History of the Lombards*]. Translated by William Dudley Foulke. Philadelphia: University of Pennsylvania Press, 1907.

Pliny the Elder. *Natural History.* vol 8. Translated by W.H.S. Jones. Cambridge: Harvard University Press, 1963.

Procopius. *History of the Wars.* Translated by H. B. Dewing. 7 Vols., Loeb Library of the Greek and Roman Classics. Cambridge, MA: Harvard University Press, 1914, Vol. I.

Radegund. "De excidio Thoringiae." Translated by McNamara, Halborg, and Whatley in "The Thuringian War" in *Sainted Women of the Dark Ages.* Durham, NC: Duke University Press, 1992, 65–70.

——. "De excidio Thoringiae." Translated by Michael Roberts in *Poems: Venantius Fortunatus* Appendix 1. Cambridge, MA: Harvard University Press, 2017, 763–69.

Sisebut. *Vita vel passio sancti Desiderii.* Translated by A. T. Fear in *Lives of the Visigothic Fathers.* Liverpool, UK: Liverpool University Press, 1997, 1–14.

——. *Vita vel passio sancti Desiderii.* Ed. by Bruno Krusch, MGH SRM, 3. Hanover, 1896: 630–37.

Tacitus. *Annals.* Translated by John Jackson. vol 4. Cambridge: Harvard University Press, 1937.

Vita Desiderii episcopi Viennensis. Ed. by Bruno Krusch, MGH SRM, 3. Hanover, 1896: 620–48.

Vita Eligii. MGH SRM IV, Ed. B. Krusch. Hanover, 1902: 664–741.

Vita Hugonis monachi Aeduensis et priore Enziacensis. Acta Sanctorum II Apr. II. Eds. G. Henschenio and D. Papebrochio. Paris; Rome, 1866: 761–70.

Vita Lupi episcopi Senonici. MGH SRM IV, Ed. B. Krusch. Hanover, 1902: 176–87.

Vita Melanii. MGH SRM III, Ed. B. Krusch. Hanover, 1896: 372–76.

Vita Menelei. MGH SRM V, Ed. W. Levison. Hanover and Leipzig, 1910: 129–57.

Vita Rusticulae. Translated by McNamara, Halborg, and Whatley. "The Life of Rusticula"in *Sainted Women of the Dark Ages*. Durham, NC: Duke University Press, 1992: 122–36.

———. MGH SRM IV, Ed. Bruno Krusch, Hanover, 1902: 337–51.

SECONDARY SOURCES (ACADEMIC):

I would like to have consulted some of these materials more fully than I did, but the practicalities of conducting research during a pandemic inhibited that ambition.

Arnold, Ellen. "Rivers of Risk and Redemption in Gregory of Tours' Writing," *Speculum* 92/1 January 2017, 117–43.

Bacharach, Bernard. *The Anatomy of a Little War: A Diplomatic and Military History of the Gundovald Affair (568–586)*. Westview, 1995.

———. *Early Medieval Jewish Policy in Western Europe*. Minneapolis: University of Minnesota Press, 1977.

———. "The Imperial Roots of Merovingian Military Organization," in *Military Aspects of Scandinavian Society in a European Perspective*. Edited by Jorgenson and Clausen, Copenhagen, 1997.

———. *Merovingian Military Organization, 481–751*. Minneapolis: University of Minnesota Press, 1972.

Bischoff, Bernhard. "Sylloge Elgonensis. Grabenschriften aus merowingischer Zeit (um 600)" in *Anecdota novissima: Text of the vierten bis sechzehnten Jahrhunderts*. Stuttgart: Hiersemann, 1984, 145–46.

Bouchard, C. Brittain. *Rewriting Saints and Ancestors: Memory and Forgetting in France, 500–1200*. Philadelphia: University of Pennsylvania Press, 2015.

Bouillart, Jacques. *Histoire de l'abbaye royale de Saint-Germain des Prez*. Paris: G. Dupuis, 1724.

Bourgain, Pascale and Martin Heinzelmann. "L'oeuvre de Grégoire de Tours: la diffusion des manuscrits." *Supplément à la Revue archéologique du centre de la France* 13 (1997), 273–317.

Brennan, Brian. *Bishop and Community in the Poetry of Venantius Fortunatus*. PhD dissertation, Macquarie University, 1983.

———. "The Career of Venantius Fortunatus." *Traditio* vol. 41 (1985), 49–78.

———. "The Disputed Authorship of Fortunatus' Byzantine Poems." *Byzantion*, 66.2 (1996), 335–45.

Brundage, James. *Law, Sex, and Christian Society in Medieval Europe*. Chicago: University of Chicago Press, 1987.

Bothe, Lukas. "Mediterranean Homesick Blues" in *The Merovingian Kingdoms and the Mediterranean World: Revisiting the Sources*. Edited by Stefan Esders. New York: Bloomsbury, 2019.

Challamel, Augustin. *The History of Fashion in France: Or, the Dress of Women from the Gallo-Roman Period to the Present Time*. New York: Crown, 1882.

Chazan, Mireille. "Brunehaut, une femme d'etat" in *Chancels*. Societe des amis des arts et du Musée de la Cour d'Or, 2019, 3-10.

Cherewatuk, Karen. "Radegund and Epistolary Tradition" in *Dear Sister: Medieval Women and the Epistolary Genre*. Edited by Cherewatuk and Ulrike Wiethaus. Philadelphia: University of Philadelphia Press, 1993, 20–45.

Clark, Elizabeth Ann. *Women in the Early Church*. Collegeville, MN: Liturgical Press, 1990.

Clarke, Gillian. *"This Female Man of God": Women and Spiritual Power in the Patristic Age, AD 350–450*. London: Routledge, 1995.

Coates, Simon. "Regendering Radegund? Fortunatus, Baudonivia and the Problem of Female Sanctity in Merovingian Gaul." *Studies in Church History*, 34 (1998): 37–50.

Collins, Roger. "Gregory of Tours and Spain" in *A Companion to Gregory of Tours*. Boston: Brill, 2015. 498–515

——. "Merida and Toledo, 550-585" in *Visigothic Spain: New Approaches*. Edited by Edward James. Oxford, UK: Clarendon Press, 1980: 189–219.

Crisp, Ryan Patrick. "Marriage and Alliance in the Merovingian Kingdoms, 481–639." PhD dissertation, Ohio State University, 2003.

Dailey, E. T. "Gregory of Tours, Fredegund, and the Paternity of Chlothar II: Strategies of Legitimation in the Merovingian Kingdoms." *Journal of Late Antiquity* 7.1 (2014), 3–27.

——. "Gregory of Tours and the Women in His Works: Studies in Sixth-Century Gaul." PhD dissertation, University of Leeds, 2011.

——. *Queens, Consorts, Concubines: Gregory of Tours and Women of the Merovingian Elite*. London: Brill, 2015.

Day, Hendrik. *The Afterlife of the Roman City: Architecture and Ceremony in Late Antiquity and the Early Middle Ages*. Cambridge University Press, 2015.

de Jong, Mayke. "An Unsolved Riddle: Early Medieval Incest Legislation" in *Franks and Alamanni in the Merovingian Period: An Ethnographic Perspective*. Edited by Ian Wood. Woodbridge, 1998. 107-140.

Defente, Denis, Ed. *Saint-Medard: Tresors d'une Abbaye Royale*. Paris: Somogy, 1996.

Demoulin, Gustave. *Les Françaises Illustres*. Paris: Hachette, 1889.

Desrosiers, Sophie. "Luxurious Merovingian Textiles Excavated from Burials in the Saint-Denis Basilica, France in the 6th–7th Century." Textile Society of America Symposium Proceedings, September 2012.

Dolan, Autumn. "'You Would Do Better to Keep Your Mouth Shut:' The Significance of Talk in Sixth-Century Gaul." *Journal of the Western Society for French History*, vol. 40 (2012).

Dronke, Peter. *Women Writers of the Middle Ages*. Cambridge, UK: Cambridge University Press, 1984.

Dumézil, Bruno. "Gogo et ses amis: ecriture, echanges et ambitions dans un reseau aristocratique de la fin du VIe siècle." *Revue Historique* 3.643 (2007): 553–93.

——. *Le Reine Brunehaut*. France: Fayard, 2008.

Dundes, Alan. *Cinderella: A Casebook*. Madison, WI: University of Wisconsin Press, 1988.

Dunn, Marilyn. *The Emergence of Monasticism: From the Desert Fathers to the Early Middle Ages*. Oxford, UK: Wiley-Blackwell, 2008.

Eckhardt, Karl August. *Studia Merovingica*. Aalen: Scientia, 1975.

Effros, Bonnie. *Caring for Body and Soul: Burial and the Afterlife in the Merovingian World*. University Park, PA: Penn State University Press, 2002.

——. *Creating Community with Food and Drink in Merovingian Gaul*. New York: Palgrave Macmillan, 2003.

——. *Merovingian Mortuary Archeology and the Making of the Early Middle Ages*. University of California Press, 2003.

——. "Monuments and Memory: Repossessing Ancient Remains in Early Medieval Gaul" in *Topographies of Power in the Early Middle Ages*. Edited by Mayke de Jong and Frans Theuws. Leiden: Brill, 2001: 93–118.

Erlande-Brandenburg, Alain. *Le roi est mort: études sur les funérailles, les sépultures et les tombeaux des rois de France jusqu'à la fin du 13e siècle*. Geneva: Droz, 1975.

Esders, Stefan. "'Avenger of All Perjury' in Constantinople, Ravenna and Metz: St. Polyeuctus, Sigibert I and the Division of Charibert's Kingdom in 568" in *Western Perspectives on the Mediterranean: Cultural Transfer in Late Antiquity and the Early Middle Ages, 400–800 AD*. Edited by Andreas M. Fischer and Ian N. Wood. London: Bloomsbury, 2014. 17–40.

Evans, James Allan Stewart. *The Age of Justinian: The Circumstances of Imperial Power*. London: Routledge, 2000.

Ewig, Eugen. "Die Namengebung bei den ältesten Frankenkönigen und im merowingischen Königshaus." *Francia*, 18 (1991): 21–69

——. "Studien zur merowingischen Dynastie." *Frühmittelalterliche Studien* 8 (1974): 15–59.

Filerman, Robert. *Saxon Identities, AD 150–900*. New York: Bloomsbury, 2017.

Fossella, Jason. "Waiting Only for a Pretext: A New Chronology for the Sixth-Century Byzantine Invasion of Spain." *Estudios bizantinos* 1 (2013) 30-38.

Fox, Yaniv. "New *honores* for a Region Transformed: The Patriciate in Post-Roman Gaul." *Revue Belge de Philologie et d'Histoire.* 93.2 (2015): 249-286.

Fozi, Shirin. *Romanesque Tomb Effigies: Death and Redemption in Medieval Europe, 1000-1200.* Pennsylvania State Press, 2021.

Garver, Valerie L. "Childbearing and Infancy in the Carolingian World." *Journal of the History of Sexuality* (May 2012) 21.2: 208–44

Gillett, Andrew. "Love and Grief in Post-Imperial Diplomacy: The Letters of Brunhild" in *Power and Emotions in the Roman World and Late Antiquity.* Edited by B. Sidwell and D. Dzino. Piscataway, NJ: Gorgias Press, 2010. 127–65.

Gerberding, Richard. *The Rise of the Carolingians and the Liber Historiae Francorum.* London: Clarendon, 1987.

Goffart, Walter. "Byzantine Policy in the West under Tiberius II and Maurice: The Pretenders Hermenegild and Gundovald (579–585)." *Traditio* vol. 13 (1957): 73–118

———. "The Frankish Pretender Gundovald, 582–585." *Francia* 39 (2012): 1–27.

———. "Foreigners in the *Histories* of Gregory of Tours." *Florilgium* vol. 4 (1982): 80–99.

Goldewijk, K. Klein, A. Beusen and P. Janssen. "HYDE 3.1: Long-Term Dynamic Modeling of Global Population and Built-Up Area In A Spatially Explicit Way." History Database of the Global Environment. Netherlands Environmental Assessment Agency (MNP), Bilthoven.

Grant-Hoek, Heike. *Die Frankische Oberschicht im 6. Jahrhundert: Studien zu ihrer rechtlichen und politischen Stellung.* Sigmarin gen: Thorbecke, 1976.

Gradowicz-Pancer, Nira. "De-Gendering Female Violence: Merovingian Female Honour as an 'Exchange Of Violence.'" *Early Medieval Europe* 11.1 (2002): 1–18.

Halfond, Gregory I. *Bishops and the Politics of Patronage in Merovingian Gaul.* Ithaca: Cornell University Press, 2019.

———. "Sis Quoque Catholicis Religionis Apex: The Ecclesiastical Patronage of Chilperic I and Fredegund." *Church History* 81.1, 2012: 48–76.

———. "War and Peace in the *Acta* of the Merovingian Church Councils." *The Medieval Way of War.* Vermont: Ashgate, 2005, 29–46.

Halsall, Guy. "Awkward Identities in Merovingian Trier." *Historian on the Edge* (blog). 21 September 2015.

——. *Cemeteries and Society in Merovingian Gaul*. London: Brill, 2009.

——. "Nero and Herod? The Death of Chilperic and Gregory's Writing of History" in *The World of Gregory of Tours*. Edited by Kathleen Mitchell and Ian N. Wood. Leiden: Brill, 2002: 337–50.

Halsall, Guy. *Settlement and Social Organization: The Merovingian Region of Metz*. Cambridge, UK: Cambridge University Press, 1995.

Handley, Mark A. "Merovingian Epigraphy, Frankish Epigraphy, and the Epigraphy of the Merovingian World." *The Oxford Handbook of the Merovingian World*. Edited by Bonnie Effros and Isabel Moreira. Oxford University Press, 2020: 556–82.

Harbeck, M., Seifert, L., Hänsch, S., et al. "*Yersinia pestis* DNA from Skeletal Remains from the 6th Century AD Reveals Insights into Justinianic Plague." *PLoS Pathog* 9(5) (2013).

Hardison, Jr., O. B. *Christian Rite and Christian Drama in the Middle Ages: Essays in the Origin and Early History of Modern Drama*. Baltimore: Johns Hopkins University Press, 1965.

Hartmann, Martina. "Die Darstellung der Frauen im Liber Historiae Francorum und die Verfasserfrage." *Concilium medii aevi* 7 (2004): 209–37

Heather, Peter. *Rome Resurgent: War and Empire in the Age of Justinian*. Oxford, UK: Oxford University Press, 2018.

Heilig, Marc. "L'aqueduc de Gorze," *Archeographe*, 2011.

Hen, Yitzhak. "Gender and the Patronage of Culture in Merovingian Gaul" in *Gender in the Early Medieval World: East and West, 300–900*. Edited by Leslie Brubaker and Julia H. M. Smith. Cambridge, UK: Cambridge University Press, 2004. 217–33.

——. *Culture and Religion in Merovingian Gaul: A.D. 481–751*

Hereberti, Suvia. *The Arnegunde Project: Conjectural Merovingian Clothing construction of the Mid 6th Century*. February 15, 2013. Accessed April 20, 2021.

Heydemann, Gerda. "Zur Gestaltung der Rolle Brunhildes in Merowingischer Historiographie," in *Texts and Identities in the Early Middle Ages*. Edited by

Richard Conradini, Rob Means, Christina Pössel, and Philip Shaw. Vienna: Österreiche Akademie der Wissenschaften, 2006, 73–86.

Hillgarth, J. N., ed., *Christianity and Paganism, 350–750: The Conversion of Western Europe*. Philadelphia: University of Pennsylvania Press, 1986.

Hillner, Julia. "Empresses, Queens, and Letters: Finding a 'Female Voice' in Late Antiquity?'" *Gender & History* 31.2 July 2019. 353–382.

Horden, Peregrine. "Disease, Dragons, and Saints: The Management of Epidemics in the Dark Ages," in *Epidemics and Ideas: Essays on the Historical Perception of Pestilence*. Edited by Terence Ranger and Paul Slack. Cambridge, UK: Cambridge University Press, 1995. 45–76.

Hunt, Hannah. "Transvestite Women Saints: Performing Asceticism in Late Antiquity," in *RIHA Journal* 0225 (30 Sept 2019): 2-19.

Jones, Allen. *Social Mobility in Late Antique Gaul: Strategies and Opportunities for the Non-Elite*. Cambridge, UK: Cambridge University Press, 2009.

Kim, Hyun Jin. *The Huns*. London: Routledge, 2015.

Kirby, D. P. *The Earliest English Kings*. London: Routledge, 2000.

Klinkenberg, Emanuel. *Compressed Meanings: The Donor's Model in Medieval Art to around 1300*. Turnhout: Brepols, 2009.

Kroll, Jerome and Bernard S. Bachrach. *The Mystic Mind: The Psychology of Medieval Mystics and Ascetics*. New York: Routledge, 2005, 129–45.

Kurth, Godefroid. *Histoire Poetique des Merovingiens*. Paris: Picard, 1893.

——. *La Reine Brunehaut*. Paris: Bureaux de la Revue, 1891.

Kulikowski, Michael. "Plague in Spanish Late Antiquity" in *Plague and the End of Antiquity: The Pandemic of 541–750*. Edited Lester Little. Cambridge, UK: Cambridge University Press, 2007, 150–70.

Lasko, Peter. *The Kingdom of the Franks: Northwest Europe Before Charlemagne* New York: McGraw Hill, 1971.

Lenoir, Alexandre. *Museum of French Monuments*. Translated by J. Griffiths. Paris: The English Press, 1803.

Lestoquoy, Jacques. "L'étrange Histoire de la Chaussée Brunehaut." *Arras au temps jadis*. Vol. 3. Paris: Arras, 1946.

Lewis, A. R. "The Dukes of the Regnum Francorum, AD 550–751." *Speculum* 51 (1976) 381–410

Leglu, C. "The 'Vida'of Queen Fredegund in 'Tote Listoire de France': Vernacular Translation and Genre in Thirteenth-Century French and Occitan Literature." *Nottingham French Studies*, 56 (2017). p. 98–112.

Little, Lester, ed. "Life and Afterlife of the First Plague Pandemic," in *Plague and the End of Antiquity: The Pandemic of 541–750*. Cambridge, UK: Cambridge University Press, 2007. 3–32.

Longnon, Auguste. *Géographie de la Gaule au VIe siècle*. Paris: Hachette, 1878.

MacGeorge, Penny. *Late Roman Warlords*. Oxford, UK: Oxford University Press, 2002.

Martindale, J. R. *Prosopography of the Later Roman Empire Volume 3: AD 527–641*. Cambridge, UK: Cambridge University Press, 1992.

McClintock, John. *Cyclopædia of Biblical, Theological, and Ecclesiastical Literature,* Vol. 11. Harper, 1867.

McCormick, Michael, et al. "Climate Change during and after the Roman Empire: Reconstructing the Past from Scientific and Historical Evidence." *Journal of Interdisciplinary History*, 43:2 (Autumn, 2012), 196–97.

——. "Toward a Molecular History of the Justinianic Pandemic," *Plague and the End of Antiquity: The Pandemic of 541–750*. Edited by Lester Little. Cambridge, UK: Cambridge University Press, 2007, 290–312.

McKitterick, Rosamond. *History and Memory in the Carolingian World*. Cambridge, UK: Cambridge University Press, 2004.

McNamara, Jo Ann Kay. *Sisters in Arms: Catholic Nuns through Two Millennia*. Cambridge, MA: Harvard University Press, 1996.

McRobbie, J., "Gender and violence in Gregory of Tours' *Decem libri historiarum*," PhD dissertation, University of Saint Andrews, 2012.

Mezei, Monica. "Jewish Communities in the Merovingian Towns in the Second Half of the Sixth Century as Described by Gregory of Tours." *Chronica* vol. 5 (2005) 15–25.

Montfaucon, Bernard de. *A Collection of Regal and Ecclesiastical Antiquities of France, Volume 2*.

Morony, Michael. "'For Whom Does the Writer Write?': The First Bubonic Plague Pandemic According to Syriac Sources" in *Plague and the End of Antiquity: The Pandemic of 541–750*. Edited by Lester Little. Cambrdige, UK: Cambridge University Press, 2007, 59–86.

Mosse, George L., *The Culture of Western Europe: The Nineteenth and Twentieth Centuries: An Introduction*. London: Murray, 1963.

Murray, Alexander C., ed. *A Companion to Gregory of Tours*. Boston: Brill, 2015.

——. "Immunity, Nobility, and the Edict of Paris." *Speculum* 69.1 (Jan 1994): 18–39.

Muschiol, Gisela. *Famula Dei. Zur Liturgie im merowingischen Frauenklöstern*. Münster: Aschendorff, 1994.

Nelson, Janet. "Queens as Jezebels: The Careers of Brunhild and Balthild in Merovingian History," in *Medieval Women*. Edited by Derek Baker. Oxford, UK: Blackwell, 1978.

Norris, Herbert. *Costume & Fashion: The Evolution of European Dress through the Earlier Ages*. London: J. M. Dent & Sons, 1925.

Panofsky, Erwin. *Tomb Sculpture: Four Lectures on Its Changing Aspects from Ancient Egypt to Bernini*. New York: H. N. Abrams, 1964.

Périn, Patrick. "Saint-Germain-des-Pres, Rremiere Necropole des Rois de France." *Médiévales* 31, (1996): 29–36.

——. "Portrait Posthume d'une Reine Mérovingienne. Arégonde (c. 580), Épouse de Clotaire Ier (c. 561) et Mère de Chilpéric Ier († 584)." *Settimane di studio della Fondazione Centro italiano di studi sull'alto Medioevo* 62 (2015): 1001–1048.

Peterson, Leif Inge Ree. *Siege Warfare and Military Organization in the Successor States (400–800 AD): Byzantium, the West and Islam*. London: Brill, 2013, 206–23.

Pohl, Walter. *The Avars: A Steppe Empire in Central Europe, 567–822*. Ithaca: Cornell University Press, 2018

Prinz, Freidrich. *Frühes Mönchtum im Frankenreich. Kultur und Gesellschaft in Gallien, den Rheinlanden und Bayern am Beispiel der Monastischen Entwicklung*. Munich: Oldenbourg, 1965.

"The Queen's Royal Footwear." *Shoe Museum Lausanne.* 2014.

Rabben, Linda. *Sanctuary and Asylum: A Social and Political History.* Seattle: University of Washington Press, 2016.

Reimitz, Helmut. *History, Frankish Identity and the Framing of Western Ethnicity, 550–850.* Cambridge, UK: Cambridge University Press, 2015.

Riché, Pierre. *Education and Culture in the Barbarian West, Sixth through Eighth Centuries.* Columbia, SC: University of South Carolina Press, 1976, 210–46.

Roberts, Michael. *The Humblest Sparrow: The Poetry of Venantius Fortunatus.* Ann Arbor, MI: University of Michigan Press, 2009.

Rouche, Michel. "Brunehaut Romaine ou Wisigothe?" *Los Visigodos. Historia y Civilización* vol. 3. Universidad de Murcla, 1986: 103–115.

Samson, Ross. "The Residences of Potentiores in Gaul and Germania in the Fifth to Mid-Ninth Centuries." PhD dissertation, University of Glasgow, 1991.

Scheibelreiter, Georg. "Die fränkische Königin Brunhild. Eine biographische Annäherung," in *Scripturus vitam: Lateinische Biographie von der Antike bis in die Gegenwart.* Edited by Dorthea Walz. Heidelberg, Germany: Mattes, 2002, 295–308.

Schoenfeld, Moritz. *Wörterbuch der altgermanischen personen-und völkernamen; nach der überlieferung des klassischen altertums.* Heidelberg, Germany: C. Winter's University, 1911.

Southon, Emma. "Inventing Incest in Early Medieval Europe." *Notches.* 31 Oct 2017.

———. *Marriage, Sex and Death: The Family and the Fall of the Roman West.* Amsterdam: Amsterdam University Press, 2017.

Stafford, Pauline. *Queens, Concubines and Dowagers: The King's Wife in the Early Middle Ages.* London: Batsford, 1983.

———. "Powerful Women in the Early Middle Ages: Queens and Abbesses" in *The Medieval World.* Edited by P. Linehan and J. L. Nelson. London: Routledge, 2001, 398–415.

Stoclet, Alain. "*Consilia humana, ops divina, superstitio*: Seeking Succor and Solace in Times of Plague, with Particular Reference to Gaul in the Early Middle

Ages." *Plague and the End of Antiquity: The Pandemic of 541–750*. Edited by Lester Little. Cambridge, UK: Cambridge University Press, 2007, 135–49.

Thiebaux, Marcelle. *The Writings of Medieval Women: An Anthology*. London: Routledge, 1994.

Tillet, Jean du. *Recueil des rois de France*. Bibliothèque Nationale de France, 1566.

Thomas, E. J. "The 'Second Jezebel': Representations of the Sixth-Century Queen Brunhild." PhD dissertation, University of Glasgow, 2012.

Thompson, E. A. *The Goths in Spain*. Oxford, UK: Clarendon Press, 1969.

Trapp, Julien, and Sébastien Wagner. *Atlas Historique de Metz*, 2nd edition, Editions des Paraiges, 1992.

Ubl, Karl. *Inzestverbot und Gesetzgebung: Die Konstruktion eines Verbrechens (300–1100)*. De Gruyter, 2008.

Underwood, Douglas. *(Re)using Ruins: Public Building in the Cities of the Late Antique West, A.D. 300–600*. Boston: Brill, 2009.

Van Dam, Raymond. *Saints and Their Miracles in Late Antique Gaul*. Princeton, NJ: Princeton University Press, 1993.

Viard, Jules. *Les grandes chroniques de France*. Paris: Librairie Ancienne Honore Champion, 1789.

Verpeaux, Nathalie. "Saint-Andoche et Saint-Jean-le-Grand: Des Religieuses à Autun au Moyen Âge." PhD dissertation, Sorbonne, 2009, rtp in *Bulletin du centre d'études médiévales d'Auxerre* 14 (12 Oct 2010).

Wagner, Pierre-Édouard. "La 'Cour d'Or,' Palais Royale de Metz?" *Chancels*. Societe des Amis des Arts et du Musée de la Cour d'Or, 2019, 11–18.

Wagner, Richard. Translated by Stewart Robb. *The Ring of the Nibelung*. Dutton, 1960.

Wallace-Hadrill, J. M. "The Bloodfued of the Franks." *Bulletin of the John Rylands Library* 41.2 (1959): 459–87.

——. *The Long-Haired Kings and Other Studies in Frankish History*. Toronto: University of Toronto Press, 1982.

Wards-Perkins, Bryan. "Constantinople, Imperial Capital of the Fifth and Sixth Centuries." *Sedes regiae (ann. 400–800)*. Edited by Gisela Ripoli and Joseph Gurt. Barcelona, 2000. 63–81.

Wells, Peter S. *Barbarians to Angels: The Dark Ages Reconsidered*. New York: Norton, 2008.

Wemple, Suzanne Fonay. *Women in Frankish Society: Marriage and the Cloister, 500 to 900*. Philadelphia: University of Pennsylvania Press, 1981.

Wickham, Chris. *Framing the Early Middle Ages: Europe and the Meditarranean*. Oxford, UK: Oxford University Press, 2006.

Widdowson, Marc. "Gundovald, 'Ballomer' and the Problems of Identity." *Revue Belge de Philologie et d'Histoire Année 2008* 86.3–4: 607–622

Wijingaards, John. *No Women in Holy Orders?: The Women Deacons of the Early Church*. Norwich, UK: Canterbury Press, 2002.

Willard, Hope. "Friendship and Diplomacy in the *Histories* of Gregory of Tours" in *The Merovingian Kingdoms and the Mediterranean World: Revisiting the Sources*. Edited by Stefan Esders. New York: Bloomsbury, 2019.

Wilson, Stephen. *The Means of Naming: A Social and Cultural History of Personal Naming in Western Europe*. London: Routledge, 2000.

Wood, Ian N. *The Merovingian Kingdoms: 450–751*. London: Longman, 1994.

——. "The Secret Histories of Gregory of Tours." *Revue Belge de Philologie et d'Histoire* 71. 2 (1993): 253–70.

——. "Chains of Chronicles: The Example of London, British Library ms. add. 16974" in *Zwischen Niederschrift und Wiederschrift*. Edited by Richard Corradini, Maximilian Diesenberger, Meta Niederkorn-Bruck. Vienna, 2010, 67–75.

——. "The Mission of Augustine of Canterbury to the English." *Speculum* 69.1 (Jan 1994): 1–17.

Woolf, Henry B. *The Old Germanic Principles of Name-Giving*. Baltimore: Johns Hopkins University Press, 1939.

Wright, Craig. *Music and Ceremony at Notre Dame of Paris, 500–1550*. Cambridge, UK: Cambridge University Press, 2009.

SECONDARY SOURCES (OTHER):

Aggrawal, Anil. "Poisons in Myths, Legends, Folklore, Literature, and Movies." Guest Editorial. *Internet Journal of Forensic Med. & Toxicology.* 2009.

Åhlfeldt, Johan. "Tribonum: a Pleiades place resource." *Pleiades: A Gazetteer of Past Places.* 2012.

Al-Rodhan, Nayef. "The neurochemistry of power has implications for political change." *The Conversation.* 28 Feb 2014.

Antique Paris. Ministère de la Culture, France.

Brown, Katharine et al. *Guide to Provincial Roman and Barbarian Metalwork and Jewelry in the Metropolitan Museum of Art* (exhibition catalogue). The Met, 1981.

Castro, Luis de Salazar y, *Historia Genealógica de la Casa de Lara. Vol.1.* Madrid, 1696: 45.

Chevallier, Jim. "French Bread History: Gallo-Roman bread." *Les leftovers* (blog). 16 Feb 2016.

———. "Food in Frankish laws." *Les leftovers* (blog). 21 June 2014.

Clay, John Henry. "Brunhild: The Original Queen Cersei." *History behind Game of Thrones.* 16 Sept 2014.

Cochini, Christian. *Apostolic Origins of Priestly Celibacy.* Ignatius Press,1990.

Coote, Stephen, Ed. *Penguin Book of Homosexual Verse.* Harmondsworth: Allen Lane, Penguin, 1983. (Fortunatus poem "Written on an Island off the Breton Coast" on p. 112)

Edwards, Charlotte. "Eerie ancient sarcophagus cracked open to reveal 1,500 year old French skeleton from mystery 'Merovingian' period." *The Sun.* 19 August 2019.

"Fredegund, the 'Real Cersei Lannister.'" *Badasses Through History.* 25 Dec 2016.

Forbes, Charles. (Comte de Montalembert) *The Monks of the West.* Book 6: *The monks under the first Merovingians.* Edinburgh: W. Blackwood & Sons, 1861.

"Gender Ratio." *Our World in Data.* University of Oxford.

Gibbons, Ann. "Why 536 was 'the worst year to be alive.'" *Science.* 15 Nov 2018.

"La Reine Brunehaut." *Office de Tourisme du Cambrésis.* 2000.

Larrington, Carolyne. *Winter is Coming: The Medieval World of Game of Thrones.* London: Bloomsbury, 2015.

Macintosh, Robin. *Augustine of Canterbury.* Canterbury Press, 2014.

Marusek, James A. *A Chronological Listing of Early Weather Events.* SPPI Reprint Series, 2011.

"Merovingian Archeology." Rural Riches Project at Leiden University (the Netherlands).

Okey, Thomas. *The Story of Paris.* London: J. M. Dent, 1904.

Oman, Sir Charles William Chadwick. *The Dark Ages, 476-918.* Rivingtons, 1908

O'Neill, Dennis. *Passionate Holiness: Marginalized Christian Devotions for Distinctive Peoples.* Trafford Publishing, 2010.

ORBIS: The Stanford Geospatial Network Model of the Roman World. Stanford University.

Palmer, James. "The Lost Civilisation of the Merovingians." *Merovingian World* (blog). 23 Jan 2020.

Richter, Joannes. "King Chilperic I's Letters (ΔΘΖΨ) may be found at the beginning ("Futha") of the runic alphabet and at the end (WIJZÆ) of the Danish alphabet."

Sellner, Edward. *Finding the Monk Within.* New Jersey: The Paulist Press, 2008.

"Solving the Mystery of the Mummified Lung." *Archaiologia Online* 19 April 2016

Thierry, Augustin. *Tales of the Early Franks.* 1840. Translated by M. F. O. Jenkins. University of Alabama Press, 1977.

Wagner, Richard. *Der Ring des Nibelung.* Mainz: Schott, 1876.

Wexler, Philip, Ed. *Toxicology in Antiquity.* 2nd edition, London: Academic Press, 2019.

Wyman, Patrick. "The Decline and Fall of the Roman City." *Tides of History* podcast, 14 Nov 2017 (-13:44 point in audio).

Young, George, P. Frederick. *East and west through fifteen centuries.* Longmans, Green & Co, 1916.

NOTES

A note about abbreviations:

Throughout, I use the following abbreviations:

HF—Gregory of Tours's *Decem libri historiarum* (*History of the Franks*). Unless otherwise specified, this refers to the Lewis Thorpe translation.

LHF—*Liber historiae Francorum*

DvsR II—Baudonivia's *De vitae sanctae Radegundis, Liber II*

AUTHOR'S NOTE: SHADOW QUEENS

xii **a rare period of dual female rule that has no equivalent in the early medieval world:** A view expressed by the historians Janet Nelson (p. 287), Emma Jane Thomas (p. 185), and Ian Wood (*Merovingian Kingdom,* p. 120).

xiii **a hidden Messianic bloodline:** The theory is the Merovingian dynasty are descendants of Jesus Christ and Mary Magdalen, first widely publicized in the 1982 book *The Holy Blood and the Holy Grail.*

xiv **"Who am I if not your will?":** In German "wer—bin ich, / war' ich dein Wille nicht?" See Wagner, *Der Ring des Nibelungen*, p. 36.

DRAMATIS PERSONAE

5 **"Famous Warrior":** The meaning of Clovis's name is derived from the full Germanic *Chlodovech*. The meaning of his name, and all others in this section, are derived from Schoenfeld or from Wilson, p 71–73.

6 **Sigibert and Brunhild:** Spellings of all Frankish names vary widely, with different versions of the same name appearing even in the original sources. I have adopted the spellings that appear in Ian Wood's *The Merovingian Kingdoms,* hence "Sigibert" and "Brunhild." (Two exceptions are "Theudechild" and "Theudelia.") I have also opted to render names that begin with Chl- with the simpler Cl-.

7 **"Valiant Defender":** see Fortunatus, 9.1 (George p. 74)

CHAPTER I: A WEDDING IN METZ

10   **the spring of 567:** There is some disagreement about this date. Some scholars have argued the wedding was held a full year earlier, in spring 566. However, others (like Pohl, Heather, and Kim) show that Sigibert was busy fighting the Avars in the spring of 566 and thus not physically able to be in Metz for the wedding.

10   **the oaks were so thick that forty men could not drag a fallen one away:** Forbes, *The Monks of the West*, p. 500: "or oaks, the fallen trunks of which could scarcely be moved by forty men."

10   **wolves, some of whom could shapeshift into men:** See the Breton myth of sixth-century Saint Ronan, accused of being able to become a wolf.

10   **and child-eating dragons, too:** See the third-century Graoully dragon in Metz or the fifth-century Parisian dragon, both vanquished by bishops.

10   **altars in forest glens and . . . wooden idols:** See the 561 Council of Auxerre, which tried to outlaw pagan practices like celebrating "discharge[ing] vows among woods or at sacred trees or springs", and having the "feet or images of men out of wood" (quoted in Hillgarth, *Christianity*, p. 103).

11   **"with great treasures":** *HF,* 4.27: *cum magnis thesauris*

11   **the Golden Court:** A tenth-century charter refers to a *"mansus infra muros mettis qui dicitur aurea,"* or "a court within the walls of Metz which is called 'golden'." The origin of this nickname is unclear; it could have come from the golden cupolas on the roofs of the former Roman baths nearby (see Wagner, *Chancels*) or because of the Frank's love of booty and flashy gold decorations.

12   **a repurposed basilica:** There has been some debate about the location of the Merovingian palace; once believed to have been on the hill of Sainte Croix at the former *praetorium* (see, for example, Fisher and Wood, *Western Perspectives*, p. 30, 32), the palace has now been shown to have been the old basilica in the old Roman forum (next to which was built the current cathedral), thanks to the work of Pierre-Édouard Wagner; see also Halsall, *Settlement*, p. 233

12   **"of two old military roads":** Trier-Lyon and Reims-Strasbourg

12   **Sigibert also owned lands in the Auvergne and ruled over the Mediterranean ports:** See map in Murray, *A Companion*, p. 594

12   **"Caesar's marriage":** Fortunatus, 6.1 (George, p. 26)

12   **a tribal tattoo:** For evidence of tattoos' continued popularity in this time period, see Norris, *Costume and Fashion*, p. 228; for their earlier popularity, see Challamell, *History of Fashion*, p. 13.

13 **the old gymnasium had been transformed into a church:** This is a reference to the church of Saint-Pierre-aux-Nonnains. See Trapp and Wagner, *Atlas*, p. 78 for more details.

13 **no other way to expand but up:** See Samson, *Residences*, p. 47–48 for descriptions of Merovingian towns.

13 **A handful of the aqueducts in other cities did still serve:** Cities such as Senlis, Cahors, Arles and Nimes. See Underwood, *(Re)using Ruins*, p. 74–75.

13 **Metz's own aqueduct . . . repairs had stopped:** See Heilig, *Archeographe*.

13 *pulchra:* Fortunatus, 6.3 (Roberts, p. 360)

13 *venusta aspectu* and *elegans corpore:* HF, 4.27

14 **average height for a woman of the period, five feet, four inches tall:** Wells, *Barbarians*, p. 139

14 **around eighteen years old:** based on Ewig's estimate of a birthdate between 545-550 in "Die Namengebung" p. 58. Some sources do assign Brunhild a birthdate as early as 534, but it would be very odd for a king in this time period to wait to marry his daughter off until she was thirty-three. (It seems, too, that these other birthdates are calculated based on statements made about Brunhild's age at her death, but these statements were all estimates based on her appearance. It was also common in the era to round ages up or down or to exaggerate how old someone was.)

14 **hair loose . . . and wreathed in flowers:** Fortunatus, 6.1

14 **"glorious maiden":** Fortunatus, 6.1 (George, p. 31)

14 **"milk-white":** Fortunatus, 6.1 (Roberts, p. 357)

14 **"second Venus":** Fortunatus, 6.1 (Roberts, p. 355)

14 **"with every appearance of joy and happiness":** HF, 4.27, p. 221

14 **Sculptures made many centuries later . . . cheekbones are high:** from Sigibert's tomb in Saint Medard in Soissons, in Montfaucon Plate XII on p. 44 (link to image on p. 14)

14 **blond or redhead:** Sigibert's maternal aunt had blond hair (see Hereberti). So did many of his ancestors: see Sidonius Appollinaris's description of Frankish Prince Sigismer in "Letter 4.20" (vol 2 p. 35) and his mention that many Franks had greyish-blue eyes (vol 1 p. 81). The description of the Franks as blond and light-eyed can also be found in an account written a century earlier by Ausonius, and many centuries before that by Virgil and Tacitus, who noted that all of the Germanic tribes tended to be blond or red-haired.

15   **"Sigibert, in love, is consumed by passion for Brunhild.":** *Sigibert amans Brunhildae carpitur igne*, Fortunatus, 6.1 (George, p. 28)

15   **Chilperic . . . his statues portray a man with a slightly stockier build:** from Chilperic's tomb, Montfaucon Plate XI p. 42

15   **three hundred miles of border:** see Bachrach, *Anatomy*, p. 11, which states the shared border was five hundred kilometers.

15   **"had" her:** *HF,* 4.28: *quam prius habuerat*

15   **impulsive behavior:** even called "erratic" in Bachrach, *Early Medieval Jewish Policy*, p. 56

16   **life was worth less than that of a hunting dog, less than a cow:** See *Pactus Legis Salicae*, 10.6 and 25.9 for value of slave's life; 6.1–3 for the value of hunting dog; 3.1–6 for a cow.

16   **the coldest decade in the past two millennium:** See Ann Gibbon's *Science* article.

16   **Yersinia pestis:** Harbeck et al., in *PLoS Pathog* 9(5).

16   **slaves might seize the opportunity to run away:** See Little, *Plague*, p. 23 for evidence that more slaves were running away during this period.

CHAPTER 2: MEETING THE FRANKS

17   **"monsters":** According to Sidonius Apollinaris in his poem "Panegyric on Majorian" (translation in Norris, *Costume and Fashion*, p. 227)

17   **"from the top of their red skulls . . . nape" and "[nose]hair arranged with the comb":** Ibid.

17   **skimpiest of tunics:** See Apollinarius's descriptions in vol 1 p. 82-83 vol 2 p. 139

17   **"accustomed always to throw these axes . . . and kill the men":** Procopius, *History of the Wars*, 6.25.

18   **a five-horned sea creature called the Quinotaur:** Fredegar, 3.9.

18   **remnants of once-great Troy:** Fredegar, 2.4–6

21   **"taking wives who were completely unworthy . . . even marry their own servants":** *HF,* 4.27 p. 221

21   **extraordinarily messy love lives:** For evidence of the kings' various entanglements, see *HF,* 4.25, 26, and 28

21   **shrewd policy:** See Dailey Chap 5, *Queens, Consorts, Concubines*, especially p. 101 and 105.

22   **rumors that perhaps he was not that fond of women:** See Bachrach, *Anatomy,* p. 183 note 67 for this interpretation of mentions of Sigibert's chastity in the following: Fortunatus, 6.1 and *HF,* 4.27

CHAPTER 3: THE FALL OF CHARIBERT

23 **salt mines on its outskirts:** Trapp and Wagner, *Atlas*, p. 77

23 **barges and boats dotted the rivers:** The river Moselle, too, connected the waterways of the Rhone and the Rhine, bringing merchant ships and foreign goods into the city.

23 **"bright with flourishing fields":** Fortunatus, 3.13 (George, p. 1)

23 **upper windows of the Golden Court:** The palace was 52 feet tall, or 4 to 5 stories by contemporary standards, according to Trapp and Wagner, *Atlas*, p. 36

23 **Gladiator games . . . exotic animal hunts and bear baiting:** Gladiator combat had been outlawed in 404 by Honorius; evidence for the animal hunts can be found in *HF,* 8.36, which describes the king, from his window, watching some "wild beast" hunted by a pack of dogs in the amphitheater.

23 **something to be desired:** See Riché, *Education*, p. 256 for a description of how the Visigothic court that Brunhild grew up in followed the fashions of the more opulent Byzantine court.

23 **mimes and actors in residence, national epics:** See Riché, *Education*, p. 245–46; for additional information on the popularity of mimes and panto-mimes, see Hen, *Culture and Religion*, p. 228–31.

24 **her Latin was impeccable:** in addition to the evidence of Brunhild's own letters, see Chazan 3-4 and Dumezil, *Brunehaut*, p. 71

24 **"a very deformed kind of Latin":** Riché, *Education*, p. 221

24 **"no sooner born than buried":** *HF,* 4.26: *qui ut processit ex alvo, protinus delatus est ad sepelchrum*

25 **The Church prohibited marrying a former spouse's sibling . . . nuns:** see Provision 30 in the 561 Council of Auxerre and Provision 8 in 561 Precept, both in Hillgarth, *Christianity*, p. 104, 110; see also Southon, *Marriage, Sex and Death,* p. 42.

25 **wouldn't fill Fenway Park today:** The 2020 Boston Red Sox Media Guide lists the stadium's maximum seating capacity at 37,755; Paris's entire population is estimated to be, at most, 20,000–30,000 in this time period.

25 **Roman city:** called Lutetia

25 **the rue Saint-Jacques, crossed the bridge over the Seine:** Once one crosses the Seine, this route then corresponds to the rue de la Cité (see Day, *Afterlife*, p. 165). For maps see *Antique Paris*, "The Early Roman City: The grid layout."

25 **entered the city gates, and then proceeded down to the cathedral:** This procession is based on that of Clovis's entrance into Paris in *HF,* 2.38.

25 **"a man who wins acclaim . . . justice":** Fortunatus, 6.2 (Roberts, p. 363)

25   "Romans applaud him": Fortunatus, 6.2 (Roberts, p. 365)

25   "the great emperor Trajan": Fortunatus, 6.2 (George, p. 37)

25   "a disciplined mind [that] conducts itself with maturity": Ibid.

26   The Bible as we know it today . . . sixty of its books had been tossed out, declared apocryphal, and burned: See the *Decretum Gelasianum* (decree of Pope Gelasius I).

26   Arian Christians: Although Arianism was eventually squashed, it never completely died out. Its beliefs would crop up again during the Protestant Reformation (see, for example, the preaching of John Assheton or Michael Servetus) and lives on in the doctrine of today's Unitarians and Jehovah's Witnesses.

26   "it is no crime for one set of people to believe in one doctrine and another set of people to believe in another": stated by Aiglan, a legate sent from Spain to the court of King Chilperic, quoted in *HF,* 5.43, p. 310

26   "pagan abominations": response by Gregory of Tours in *HF,* 5.43, p. 310

26   tyrannize, and terrify, the most devout: Wood sees the Church emerging as "a power-house of psychological oppression" in *The Merovingian Kingdoms*, p. 72.

26   Charibert had annexed a piece of prime real estate that the Church thought of as its own: Halfond, "War and Peace," p. 29.

27   monks . . . must stop sharing beds: See 567 Council of Tours, Canon 15 (14) in *Concilia*, p. 125–26.

27   Married men had long been ordained: For a list of married sixth-century clerics, see Cochini, *Apostolic Origins*, p. 109–16 (earlier examples, p. 84–108)

27   "as brother and sister": See 535 Council of Clermont, Canon 13, and the 567 Council of Tours, Canon 13 (12) in *Concilia*, p. 68 and p. 125

27   find and excommunicate married clerics who were still sleeping with their wives: 567 Council of Tours, Canon 20 (19) in *Concilia*, p. 127–28

27   an epidemic that afflicted Paris in the fall of 567: See the bishops' letter to the people of Tours in *Les canons des conciles mérovingiens,* p. 395. For interpretation of this letter, see Dumezil, *Brunehaut*, p. 144 note 41 and Ubl, *Inzestverbot*, p. 163.

27   the bishops convened on November 18, 567: See 567 Council of Tours, *Concilia*, p. 121

27   the very first European king to be excommunicated: Note that Charibert's father had been excommunicated, but only by a single bishop (see Gregory's *Liber Vitae Patrum*, 17.2, p. 109). The action was not supported by the other bishops, and so it did not carry the same weight.

28 one of his villas close to Bordeaux: See Thierry, p. 17.

28 an old Roman fort: the *Blavia castellum*, LHF, 31.

29 some support for her bid: Dumézil, *Brunehaut*, p. 154

29 "She may come to me and bring her treasure with her. I will receive her and I will give her an honorable place among my people. She will hold a higher position at my side then she ever did with my brother.": *HF*, 4.26 p. 221

29 Chalon-sur-Saône: The location of their meeting as Guntram's capital is presumed in Thierry, *Tales*, p. 17.

29 "unworthy": the Latin *indigne*, *HF*, 4.26.

29 "packed her off to a nunnery at Arles": *HF*, 4.26, p. 221

29 one of his ex-wife's former slaves: Guntram's third wife was Austrechild; for more about her background *HF*, 5.17 and 5.20; Fredegar, 3.56.

29 Charibert's daughters were bundled off to convents: The king had three daughters: Bertheflede, Clotilde, and Bertha. Bertheflede was sent to Ingritrude's convent in Tours (*HF*, 9.33); Clotilde was sent to Radegund's convent in Poiters (*HF*, 9.39). Bertha also seems to have been sent to Radegund's convent before her later marriage (Dumezil, *Brunehaut*, p. 287-89). Note that Charibert's first wife was already in a convent, where she lived a long life (*HF*, 9.26).

30 "if he would carry her off to Spain and marry her there, she would escape the nunnery with what wealth remained to her": *HF*, 4.26, p. 221

30 "caught her red-handed" and "had her beaten mercilessly": Ibid.

30 "until her dying day, suffering awful anguish": Ibid.

CHAPTER 4: NEW ALLIANCES

31 his father publicly repudiated him: *HF*, 6.24: "This is no son of mine"

31 Charibert had been grooming his much younger half brother to be his heir: Bachrach, *Anatomy*, p. 6

31 to repeat the role of stand-in heir for his still-childless brother: Ibid.

32 a talented artist: Bachrach, *Anatomy*, p. 6

32 a painter of churches and chapels: *HF*, 7.36

32 "amiable and an easy person with whom to talk": Bachrach, *Anatomy*, p. 13

32 some have suggested there was a minor flirtation between the two: Bachrach, *Anatomy*, p. 13 and note 67 on p. 183.

32 Gundovald . . . shearing off his locks: *HF*, 6.24

33 Sigibert . . . the most bargaining power: Esders, "Avenger," p. 26

34   captured one of Chilperic's sons: *HF,* 4.23

35   Chilperic invaded . . . Tours and Poitiers: *HF,* 4.45 and 4.47

35   forcing his boy to break the solemn oath: *HF,* 4.47

36   "Whoever disobeys this order shall have his eyes put out": *HF,* 6.46

36   Sigibert . . . given Brunhild Tribonum: Thomas, "Second Jezebel," p. 37–41 and Åhlfeldt, "Tribonum." Note that Tribonum is now called Trébosc.

36   Galswintha . . . Bordeaux, Limoges, Cahors, Lescar, and Cieutat: See the Treaty of Andelot in *HF,* 9.20.

37   their code prohibited the keeping of concubines and mistresses: Wemple, *Women,* p. 39

37   a *sacramentum*: Wemple, *Women,* p. 39–40

CHAPTER 5: A MISSIVE TO BYZANTIUM

38   a building frenzy in Metz: Esders, "Avenger," p. 29–31

39   Justin II . . . lucky accident: Evans, *Age of Justinian,* p. 263–64

39   only a few of the royal children were spared: Kroll and Bachrach, *Mystic Mind,* p. 129

40   one of his brother's widows: Vuldetrada, a Lombardian princess (*HF,* 4.9) who it seems he planned to marry, but his "bishops complained" and he could not get his nobles on board.

40   the wife of a mill manager: *HF,* 7.14

40   her morgengabe: the villas of Péronne, Athies, and Saïx; see Dunn, *Emergence,* p. 108

40   was likely pure paranoia: Kroll and Bachrach, *Mystic Mind,* p. 130

41   "fear[ing] man more than God": Fortunatus, *Radegundis* 12 (McNamara, p. 75)

41   free daily meal and . . . baths: Fortunatus, *Radegundis* 17 (McNamara, p. 77)

41   bathing and cleaning . . . applying ointment to pus-filled wounds: Fortunatus, *Radegundis* 17 and 19 (McNamara, p. 77, 78)

41   more skilled medical practitioners who treated patients with herbs and salves: Fortunatus, *Radegundis* 20 (McNamara, p. 78–79)

41   "roughest of hair shirts": Baudonivia, *DvsR II,* 4 (p. 88)

41   "he had no wish to live unless he could get her back again": Ibid.

41   "was determined to end her life": Ibid.

42   the first . . . established in Francia: McNamara, *Sisters,* p. 98

43   the palace's vaulted ceiling . . . or the hair color of a slaughtered court attendant: Radegund, "De excidio" (Roberts, p. 761): "pale ashes have

overtaken the once bright ceilings that gleamed on high in a sheath of bright metal" and "the company whose hair outdoes in it brilliance flaming gold now lies stretched out on the ground white as milk"

43 **regularly wrote poems:** In his own poems, Fortunatus mentions that he is responding to Radegund's poems.

43 **the voice and tone are markedly different:** I'm relying on my academic background in literature to make this judgement. The emotional declarations in this poem seem much more nuanced and understated compared to those made when Fortunatus speaks as a woman in two other poems (6.5 and 8.3)

43 **attribute the poem to Radegund:** Scholars who acknowledge Radegund's authorship include Karen Cherewatuk, JoAnn McNamara, Charles Nisard, Jozef Szövérffy, and Marcelle Thiebaux.

43 **acknowledge that she must have had significant input in its composition:** Scholars who take this position include Peter Dronke, Jerzy Strzelczyk, and Anna Maria Wasyl.

43 **"torn":** Radegund, "De excidio" (Roberts, p. 761)

43 **"a wife's naked feet trod in her husband's blood":** Ibid.

43 **"I was tormented by anxiety, if we were not under the one roof; if you just went outdoors, I thought you had gone far away.":** Radegund, "De excidio" (Roberts, p. 765)

43 **"Fortune provided consolation to the men whom the enemy struck down; I alone was left surviving to weep for them all":** Radegund, "De excidio" (Roberts, p. 763)

43 **her brother's murder has opened old wounds:** Radegund, "De excidio" (Roberts, p. 769: "reawaken[ing] the tears I had laid to rest")

44 **"palace courts, where art once flourished" and "sad, glowing ashes":** Radegund, "De excidio" (McNamara, p. 65)

44 **"piously honor me as a mother":** Ibid., p. 70

44 **"her spirit blazing in a fighting mood":** Baudonivia, *DvsR II*, 16 (p. 98)

45 **Legates . . . were not the average deliverymen:** Bachrach, *Anatomy*, p. 23

45 **the alliance . . . was formalized:** *HF*, 4.40 and Bachrach, *Anatomy*, p. 24

45 **"loved" "with dear affection":** Baudonivia, *DvsR II*, 16 (p. 99)

45 **July of 568:** Fortunatus, 6.5

45 **"With motherly love . . . close exchanges":** Fortunatus, 6.5 (George, p. 46)

45 **"near the curved bed":** Ibid. Note that Fortunatus has Galswintha arriving in Poitiers in a silver-topped carriage, then going on to Tours, then crossing the Vienne "by an alder craft" (some sort of ferry). Then she is "received"

by the "slow-moving Loire," then the Seine, and ends her journey in Rouen. This language suggests Galswintha switched to boats for the latter portion of her journey. Additionally, Stanford's ORBIS records a traditional Roman route from Toledo to that closely mirrors the stops Fortunatus describes: Poitiers, Tours, then Orleans, then sailing past Paris north to Rouen.

45 **Chilperic's entire army on bended knee:** Ibid.

46 **"he showed no respect for her at all"; "the insults which she had to endure":** *HF,* 4.28, p. 222

CHAPTER 6: THE SLAVE QUEEN

47 **loaves of white bread:** See Chevallier, "French Bread History."

47 **beef . . . with salt and pepper:** For overview of the Frankish diet, see Wells, *Barbarians,* p. 134–35; for list of spices used, typical vegetables, and specific recipes, such as for beef with gravy, see Anthimus, *On the Observance of Foods;* see also Effros, *Creating Community with Food and Drink in Merovingian Gaul.*

47 **love of bacon:** Anthimus speaks of bacon as a "Frankish delicacy" (p. 55) and contains many mentions of how to best prepare it; *Pactus Legis Salicae* 9 and 27 on the fines for the theft of pigs attest to the value of this food.

47 **the beehives:** On how beehives were valued, see *Pactus Legis Salicae* 8.

47 **a garnet:** Derosiers, "Luxurious," p. 1 and 6; for more information on the importance of garnets and the garnet trade, see Birgit Arrhenius's *Merovingian Garnet Jewellery: Emergence and Social Implications* (Stockholm: Kungl, 1985)

47 **strawberry-blonde:** For this assumption about Fredegund's hair color see Jean Du Tillet's image of the queen in *Recueil des rois de France* F. 24–25v

48 **the captured were shackled up:** For more on the Merovingian slave trade, see Jones, *Social Mobility,* p. 171–72 and Bothe's entire chapter in *The Merovingian Kingdoms and the Mediterranean World.*

49 **Fredegund of Cambrai, or Fredegund of Montdidier:** as listed on Wikipedia and numerous ancestry sites

49 **"Chilperic ordered Galswintha to be strangled . . . and found her dead on the bed:** *HF,* 4.28: *Ad extremum enim suggillari iussit a puero, mortuamque repperit in strato*

49 **portrayed in art . . . the king of Neustria himself . . . his sleeping wife:** see *Grandes Chroniques de France,* Paris, BNF, Fr. 2813, fol. 31 recto. via GALLICA

49 **In some versions, Fredegund looks on.**

50 see *Grandes chroniques de France* MS M.536 fol. 26r via the Morgan Library

51 **One story in circulation more than a century later:** See *LHF,* 31 (Murray, p. 625–26). The *LHF* is widely assumed to have been written around 727.

51 **"Mistress, my lord king is returning as a victor. How can he receive his daughter joyfully if she is not baptized?":** *LHF,* 31 (Murray, p. 625)

51 **"No equal of yours can ever be found":** Ibid.

51 **"With whom will my lord sleep tonight . . . I'll sleep with you.":** Ibid.

51 **ban against the practice of "spiritual incest":** Issued by Gregory II in 721 at the Synod of Rome; see Southon, "Inventing Incest."

51 **evidence that Fredegund was literate:** See, for example, the letter written in Latin from King Leuvigild to Fredegund circa 584–85, quoted in *HF,* 8.28. Other evidence of her literacy can be presumed from her communications with her Saxon subjects and the Breton king Waroch in *HF,* 10.9 and 10.11, as well as other judicial rulings and messages to and from her generals.

52 **"Toledo has sent you two towers, Gaul . . . the first still stands":** Fortunatus, 6.5 (George, p. 40–50)

52 **went into shock:** Ibid.

52 **"fall on the brittle ice":** Ibid.

CHAPTER 7: ALL THE KING'S MEN

54 **The few tears Chilperic reportedly shed:** *HF,* 4.28

55 **toy animals made from clay and dolls made from ivory:** Riché, *Education,* p. 231

55 *comes,* **or count:** Halsall, *Settlement,* p. 37

55 **a** *dux,* **or duke:** Lewis, "The Dukes," p. 391

55 **serve as diplomats or judges:** Halsall, *Settlement,* p. 37

55 **two dozen counts . . . forty dukes:** see Lewis 386. Note that in Provence and southern Burgundy, the regions that had the longest tradition of Roman rule and were the most recently conquered, there were a handful of aristocrats with other titles—*rector* or *patrician*—that roughly corresponded to the position of duke. Lewis claims six patricians, three rectors. Also see Fox p. 249 for description of these positions.

56 **averaged just a few years in power:** Lewis, "The Dukes," p. 392

56 **these ranks became hereditary:** dukedoms, primarily; Ibid., p. 399

56 **average distance between towns was sixty-five miles:** see Patrick Wyman's *Tides of History* podcast.

56 **silver-tongued diplomat:** Fortunatus praised Gogo's gifts of persuasion: "with the nectar of your sweet eloquence you surpass the bees" (7.1). Given the importance of bees (and honey) in the Merovingian world, this was high praise indeed.

57 **just twenty-three years old:** Gogo was born in approximately 544; we know he was thirty-seven when he died in 581; see the *Epitaph Gogo* in Bischoff.

57 **became . . . Mayor of the Palace:** Fredegar, 3.59

57 **he had risen in life, thanks:** Dumézil, *Brunehaut*, p. 137

57 **Dynamius . . . prolific writer:** Some of his work still survives: two letters and two lives of saints, as well as one poem *"laeta sendes filomella fronde."* See Dumézil, "Gogo et ses amis," p. 571 and *Grammatici Latini*, vol 5, ed. Henri Keil, Leipzig: Teubner, 1857, p. 579, l. 13–14.

57 **"my love," "my source of light,"** and **"torn from my sight, you are with me, bound to my heart":** Fortunatus, 6.9 (George, p. 55)

57 **gone off to battle the Danes and the Saxons:** mentioned in Fortunatus, 7.7

59 **Duke Boso:** To make things easier on readers, I will often refer to Guntram Boso as Duke Boso. Know that there is another Duke Boso featured in the latter books of Gregory's chronicle. The Duke Boso that appears in 7.38 and 9.31 is a different man.

59 **the pro-Byzantine party:** Dumezil, *Brunehaut*, p. 140

60 **Galswintha shaking with fear:** Fortunatus, 6.5 (George, p. 41)

60 **"rivers of tears":** Ibid.

60 **"collapses in distress, her knees giving way":** Fortunatus, 6.5 (George, p. 49)

60 **a miracle that was reported:** mentioned by both Fortunatus, 6.5 (George, p.48) and Gregory, *HF,* 4.28

60 **a court was convened:** Dumezil, *Brunehaut*, p. 169

60 **born on Easter Day . . . baptized on Pentecost:** *HF,* 8.4

61 **a raised dais . . . benches . . . behind them were their vassals:** Thierry, *Tales*, p. 25.

61 **thirty-six on his left and thirty-six on his right, and take a solemn oath:** Ibid.

61 **fifty thousand solidi:** *HF,* 3.31, the wergeld for Queen Amalasuntha

CHAPTER 8: THE SIEGE

62 **Germanic pagans drawn from Sigibert's vassal kingdoms:** *HF,* 4.49

64 *praecellentissima . . . regin[a],* **"most excellent queen":** Germanus (Ferrante, *Epistolae*)

64 *unde magis pollens regina uocatur,* "growing more mighty, she is hailed as a queen": Fortunatus, 6.1 (George, p. 28)

64 "Show your prudence and the vigor and perfection of your faith towards this region . . . and let the people of [this] region live in quiet": Germanus (Ferrante, *Epistolae*)

64 a small section of the Right Bank: see Horden, "Disease, Dragons, and Saints," p. 68

64 a royal hunting preserve: This was the Forêt de Rouvray, which stretched all the way west to Rouen.

66 It was a towering, glittering basilica: *HF,* 2.14

66 his candidacy was met with some opposition: See Van Dam, *Saints,* p. 63–66 and Roberts, *The Humblest Sparrow,* p. 106–22

66 find out about Brunhild's role from Fortunatus's account: Fortunatus, 5.3; see also Roberts, *The Humblest Sparrow,* p. 106–22

66 "burned much of the district round Tours and, if the inhabitants had not quickly surrendered, he would have burnt it all": *HF,* 4.47 p. 244

66 "lightening was observed to flicker across the sky, just as we saw it before [his father] Clothar's death": *HF,* 4.51 p. 247

67 "not knowing whether he could escape alive or would be killed instead": *HF,* 4.51 p. 248

67 "cast aside" the baby and "desired to kill him": *HF,* 5.22: *a se abiecit et perdere voluit* (translation by J. Holland)

67 "wished he would die": *HF,* 5.22, p. 288

67 *ob metum mortis*: *HF,* 5.22

68 "rebuked": *HF,* 5.22: *obiurgata a rege* (J. Holland)

68 performed by Tournai's bishop: *HF,* 5.22

68 abandon Chilperic and declare Sigibert their king instead: *HF,* 4.51

68 Chilperic's nearby royal villas: Vitry-en-Artois; *HF,* 4.51

68 the fields . . . soldier's tents: See Thierry's recreation, *Tales,* p. 43

68 hoisted up on a shield: *HF,* 4.51

68 beat their shields with the flats of their swords: See Thierry's recreation, *Tales,* p. 43

69 Long live the king!: Evidence that this phrase was in use (as *Vivat rex!* in Latin) can be found in *HF,* 8.1

69 *duo pueri*: *HF,* 4.51

70 museums showcase cups: Some were on display at the Musee Cour d'Or in Metz (Aug 2019).

70 Poisoned arrows: *Pactus Legis Salicae,* 6.1, 17.2, 119.3

70 **nightshade and the sap of rhododendron . . . wolfsbane and snake venom:** For Roman knowledge of different poisons, see the work of Galen, Nicander, and Scribonius Largus. There was a long tradition of using snake venom on arrowheads among ancient peoples, including those in Gaul— see Wexler, *Toxicology*, p. 246–49. See Aggrawal, "Poisons," for more on wolfsbane. (Note that wolfsbane is also called monkshood or aconite).

70 **If this account . . . is to be believed:** The account in *HF,* 4.51

70 **"pretend[ed] they had something to discuss with him":** *HF,* 4.51, p. 248

70 **"they struck him on both sides":** Ibid.

70 **killed the two boys:** Fredegar 3.71 (Woodruff, p. 79)

CHAPTER 9: THE WITCH AND THE NUN

71 **"had already boxed [Chilperic] in" . . . "through deception":** Marius of Avenches, *Chronica*, p. 108

71 *Malificati:* *HF,* 4.51

72 *astrologi* to . . . *incantores:* A more extensive list of terms can be found in Jones, *Social Mobility*, p. 293.

72 **"evil spell"** (*maleficium*): *Pactus Legis Salicae*, 19.3 (a redaction, see Murray, *A Companion*, p. 551)

72 *strioportio:* *Pactus Legis Salicae*, 64.1

72 **"a witch eat[ing] a man"** (*granderba*): *Pactus Legis Salicae*, 64.3

73 **187 ½ solidi:** *Pactus Legis Salicae*, 64.2

73 **45 solidi if one falsely called her a whore:** *Pactus Legis Salicae*, 30.3

73 **higher than for forcible rape:** Falsely accusing a woman of witchcraft had a penalty of 187½ solidi (*Pactus Legis Salicae*, 64.2) versus 62 ½ solidi for forcible rape, or *uueruanathe* (15.2). Note that the Franks acknowledged many categories of rape—there was an even higher penalty for gang rape (200 solidi), and much lesser penalties for *firilasia*, what we would probably call statutory rape. There were also degrees of sexual assaults that distinguished between touching hair and grabbing a breast, for example.

73 **opportunistic Austrasians even joined them:** These included General Godin and Siggo, the Referendary; *HF,* 5.3.

74 **the boy was put in a bag and passed through a window:** Fredegar, 3.72

74 **the source closest to the event suggests that . . . alone:** Gregory, in *HF,* 5.1

75 **too distraught to think straight:** Ibid.

75 **five bundles of gold:** *HF,* 5.18. For calculations on how the worth and weight of such treasure, see Goffart, "Pretender," p. 16.

75 detain his nieces in Meaux: *HF,* 5.1: *filias vero eius Meledus urbe tenire prae-cipit.* Despite translations to the contrary, *tenire* (a form of *tenere*) means "to hold" or "to be detained" (versus "to be sent to").

75 his loyal chamberlain, whose family lived in this city: the chamberlain, Eberulf; *HF,* 7.29

76 Christmas Day 575: *HF,* 8.4

76 Gogo . . . the position of *nutritor* of the boy-king: Fredegar, 3.59

76 Les Andelys . . . established by Clovis's wife: Wemple, *Women*, p. 157

76 ordinary cloth or linen . . . only with simple white or black crosses: Caesarius of Arles, *Regula*, 45.

76 barred from having even a single lady's maid: Ibid., 7

76 completely cloistered, unable to ever visit the outside world: Ibid., 2

CHAPTER 10: BACK CHANNELS

78 their court in Italy: Ravenna was the seat of the Byzantines in Italy; *HF,* 7.36

78 Gundovald went on to marry and have two boys; his wife seems to have died in childbirth: *HF,* 7.36; for the assumption that Gundovald's wife died in childbirth see Goffart, "Byzantine Policy," note 104 on p. 97.

78 obvious choice for a new husband for Brunhild: Bachrach, *Anatomy*, 29–30

79 "barked like a dog . . . crow like a cock": John of Epheseus, III.2

79 "a little wagon, with a throne upon it": John of Epheus, III.3

79 didn't have the communication or transport networks in place to open marriage talks: see Bachrach, *Anatomy*, 30

80 ushered away with a baby in her arms: *LHF,* 31

80 rumors circulating: Gregory of Tours was one such person repeating them: *HF,* 5.14, 5.18.

81 Merovech was sent with the Neustrian army to conquer Poitiers: *HF,* 5.2

82 forbidden from doing sewing and cooking: Wemple, *Women*, p. 154

82 Radegund hung on to her dice: *HF,* 10.16

83 site where King Clovis had been crowned: *HF,* 2.38

83 Ingritude: She was either a sister or a cousin of Queen Ingund and so related to the Merovingian kings through marriage. She became a nun as a widow; one of her sons was the bishop of Bordeaux and the other had been an official at Sigibert's court; see Wemple, *Women*, p. 156 for details about her convent.

83 "did great damage": *HF,* 5.2 p. 255

83 **to visit his mother in Rouen:** *HF,* 5.2

83 **wreathed again with spring flowers:** The wedding took place at the end of April, right after Easter (which was April 18 according to *HF,* 5.17).

84 **Church law forbade a marriage to an uncle's widow:** Southon, *Marriage,* p. 45

CHAPTER II: UPRISING

85 **Some scholars:** See, for example, Ewig's "Studien," p. 33 and Nelson's "Queens," p. 40–41. For more background on the strategy of gaining power by marrying royal widows, see Stafford, *Queens,* p. 49–54.

85 **a widow for nearly half a year:** Sigibert had been assassinated in November and Childebert raised to the throne on Christmas. Brunhild's wedding took place at the end of March or very early April, around five months after she was widowed.

85 **"she brought *him* [Merovech] into matrimony":** . . . *ea quoque in matrimonio sociavit.* See E. T. Dailey, *Queens,* p. 146.

86 **the queen made use of . . . to engineer her escape:** This view is prominent in most nineteenth-century accounts. For another variation on this view see Goffart, "Pretender," p. 27. Kurth, *Histoire Poetique,* while puzzled by her motives, recognizes this as an act of "boldness" (*hardiesse*) p. 7.

86 **depose his father and rule Neustria:** see Grant-Hoek, *Die frankische,* p. 203–207 and also Dailey, "Women," p. 154–55.

86 **five bundles of gold and jewels:** *HF,* 5.18

87 **Rouen . . . declared Merovech its king:** Grant-Hoek, *Die frankische,* p. 203 and 206

87 **In the Champagne . . . many great warriors from illustrious families did the same:** *HF,* 5.3: *multus ex ea strenuos atque utilis viros,* "many strong and skillfull men"; and *LHF,* 33: *multosque ibi nobilissimos viros occidit,* "many of the highest born nobles."

87 **"burned, plundered, and slew":** *HF,* 6.31: *incendia, praedas et homicidia*

87 **an assassin:** Suggested by Dumézil, *Brunehaut.* p. 187

88 **threats and persuasion to lure them out:** *HF,* 5.2: *in multis ingeniis,* "by many dirty tricks"

88 **most likely, a siege:** Dailey, "Women," p. 153

88 **"built of wooden planks high on the city walls":** *HF,* 5.2, p. 255

88 **The right . . . to seek sanctuary on consecrated land:** See the 511 Council of Orange, quoted in Rabben, *Sanctuary and Asylum,* p. 40: "No one was

permitted of his own authority to remove by force from churches those who had fled to them, but they had to apply to the bishops."

89 "insofar as it was God's will he would not try to separate them": *HF,* 5.2, p. 255

89 treated Brunhild and Merovech as husband and wife: *HF,* 5.2

89 overcoming Wolf's forces and driving them away: *HF,* 5.3; also Bachrach, *Merovingian Military,* p. 47 and Dumézil, *Brunehaut,* p. 188

90 Austrasians who had defected . . . now fled: *HF,* 5.3

90 a sweep of his court: *HF,* 5.3; note he also gathered around him new advisers, like Duke Rauching and Ansoald, Bishop of Poitiers.

90 military command on . . . Chilperic's third son, Clovis: *HF,* 5.13

90 left five thousand of Chilperic's men dead: *HF,* 5.13

90 Chilperic added a peculiarly specific prohibition: See Ubl, *Inzestverbot,* p. 176–79.

91 Merovech . . . given the haircut of a monk: *HF,* 5.14

91 the monastery of Saint Calais in nearby Le Mans: *HF,* 5.14

91 "state prison": Prinz, *Frühes Mönchtum,* p. 155

92 return to Austrasia: Gregory refers to "when Queen Brunhild left the city of Rouen" (*HF,* 5.18) and not an escape; the *LHF,* refers to a delegation from Austrasia requesting her release; Dumézil in *Brunehaut* develops the theory of Chilperic making her an offer, which is supported by Goffart in "Pretender," who sees this offer as the entire point of Brunhild agreeing to the marriage.

92 "Let the woman have her goods back": *HF,* 5.18, p. 280

92 "a quarrel between me and Childebert my nephew" and *scandalum*: *HF,* 5.18, p. 280 and *HF,* 5.18.

CHAPTER 12: THE LAWS OF SANCTUARY

93 The message was from [Boso], urging Merovech to join him: *HF,* 5.14

93 Gailen . . . arranged an ambush: Ibid.

94 a political adviser: Dumézil, *Brunehaut,* p. 188

94 "They have come to learn what the king is doing, so they can report to Merovech!": *HF,* 5.14, p. 268

94 stripped of their possessions and sent off into exile: *HF,* 5.14

95 almost half a football field long: *HF,* 2.14: "It is 160 feet long and 60 wide and 45 high to the vault"

95 marble columns, and . . . towers: *HF,* 2.14

95 tin roof: *HF,* 4.20 and 10.31

95 "rebuilt . . . larger and higher": *HF,* 10.31, p. 601

95 a mutilated ear: *HF,* 5.48

95 "his cuirass [breastplate] and mailshirt, with his quiver hanging round him, his javelin in his hand and his helmet on his head": *HF,* 5.48, p. 315

95 against canon law: Halfond, "War and Peace," p. 43

96 Merovech's followers . . . raid Leudast's properties: *HF,* 5.48

96 royal physician attacked and robbed: *HF,* 5.14

96 "If you refuse, I will set your whole countryside alight": *HF,* 5.14, p. 268

96 praying beside the tomb of Saint Martin: *HF,* 5.14

96 get Merovech out of the church: *HF,* 5.14

96 "Boso was a good enough man, but he was much too given to breaking his word": *HF,* 5.14 p. 271; see also *HF,* 9.10.

97 "a ride through the open fields will do us good": *HF,* 5.14, p. 271

97 The woman foretold: *HF,* 5.14

98 At the end of April 577: Easter was always April 18, according to Gregory in *HF,* 17, and this event occurred right after Easter

98 Guntram . . . declared Childebert his heir: *HF,* 5.17

98 "Let one single shield protect us both and a single spear defend us.": *HF,* 5.17 p. 275

98 the fugitive prince could not stay at their court: *HF,* 5.14

CHAPTER 13: CRIME AND PUNISHMENT

100 "to ensure that the Queen has her way": *HF,* 5.18 p. 280

100 at least fourteen bishops: Halfond, "Sis Quoque," p. 57

100 at least three more: Ibid.

101 "You actually gave gifts and urged [Merovech] to kill me!" and "You have seduced the people with money so that no one of them would keep faith with me!": *HF,* 5.18. In this instance I have used the 1916 translation by Ernest Brehaut.

101 "they feared the fury of the queen, at whose instigation this was being done": *HF,* 5.18 in Latin: *timebant enim regine fururem, cuius instinctu haec agebantur;* note that some other versions substitute *regem* or *regem* (king) here.

101 mused aloud that Gregory was trying to hide his own collusion: *HF,* 5.18: Chilperic insinuated Praetextatus and Gregory were two of a kind, and "a crow does not tear out the eye of crow."

101 **Chilperic threatened to orchestrate an uprising:** *HF,* 5.18: Chilperic said he would get the citizens of Tours to shout about Gregory: "He is unjust and renders justice to no man!"

101 **"If the people cry aloud with false cries when you attack me, it is nothing, because all know that this comes from you. And therefore it is not I but rather you that shall be disgraced in the outcries.":** *HF,* 5.18 (Brehaut)

101 **"two hundred pounds of silver":** *HF,* 5.18, p. 279

101 **"I wanted to kill you and place your son on the throne":** Ibid., p. 281

102 **"a newly-copied [sixteen]-page insert" which declared "A bishop convicted of murder, adultery or perjury shall be expelled from his [office]":** Ibid.

102 **"grievously beaten":** Ibid., p. 282

103 **"I beg you not to allow me to fall into the hands of my enemies. Take my sword and kill me.":** Ibid.

103 **"There were some who said that [these] last words of Merovech . . . were invented by the Queen":** Ibid.; see, too, Marius of Avenches, *Chronica,* p. 108, who had heard the prince was "killed."

103 **"that Bishop Egidius and Guntram Boso had been the ringleaders in this ambush":** Ibid., p. 283

103 **"enjoyed the secret favor of Queen Fredegund":** Ibid.

103 **"one of her favorites" for quite some time:** *HF,* 5.18, Latin: *quod et iam longo tempore esset carus*

103 **Samson . . . fever and diarrhea:** *HF,* 5.22

104 **Arena of Lutetia:** Now known as Les Arènes de Lutèce.

104 **"to offer spectacles to the citizens":** *HF,* 5.17, p. 275

104 **theater performances and exotic animal hunts:** Gladiator combat had been outlawed more than a century before.

104 **"cruelly butchered":** *HF,* 5.18, (Brehaut)

104 **"on a mission to Spain to attend to [her] affairs":** *HF,* 5.40, p. 305

CHAPTER 14: "WISE IN COUNSEL"

105 **In a pattern that would continue throughout the new decade:** There were floods in 580, 583, 585, 587, 589. See McCormick et al., "Climate Change," p. 196, fn 21

105 **rained for twelve days straight:** *HF,* 5.33

105 **The bishop was a cousin of her husband:** *HF,* 8.2; he was one of Ingritude's sons

105 **the Basilica of Saint-Denis:** It sat on the same site as it is today

105 "spattered with human blood": *HF,* 5.32, p. 294

106 "were pierced with swords and javelins": Ibid

106 "witch," "man-eater," "whore": see *Pactus Lex Salica,* 64.2, 64.3, and 30.3

106 much of Italy was underwater, too: McCormick et al., "Climate Change," p. 196, fn 21

106 "dysentery spread throughout the whole of [Francia]": *HF,* 5.34 p. 296

106 boiled partridges and quinces, but barley gruel mixed with hot wine: see Anthimus, p. 61, 71-2, and 79

106 raw milk . . . bland foods like cooked rice: see Anthimus, p. 75

106 "had a high temperature, with vomiting and severe pains in the small of the back: their heads ached and so did their necks. The matter they vomited up was yellow or even green": *HF,* 5.34, p. 296

106 "a secret poison": Ibid.

106 purifying questionable water by boiling: See, for example, Pliny the Elder, Book 31, 23.40, p. 403.

107 "a greedy plunderer, a loudmouthed disputer and a foul adulterer": *HF,* 5.48 (Brehaut)

107 "fasted with all her household": *HF,* 5.49, p. 319

107 sandals, grafts of apple trees, as well as many books: Fortunatus, 8.21, 5.13, and 5.8b

107 gave Fortunatus a villa: Fortunatus, 8.19

108 "unusual literary ambience": Thiebaux, *Medieval Women,* p. 89

108 assisting in her efforts to broker a peace: See Judith George's introduction to Fortunatus's *Personal and Political Poems,* p. xx.

108 increasing repulsion for female bodies: See Fortunatus, 8, his two poems on virginity

108 longing for certain male friends: for more discussion of Fortunatus's sexual orientation, see Sellner, *Monk,* p. 285 and O'Neill, *Passionate Holiness,* p. 46–52.

108 "[your] body limp-lying on the bed": Fortunatus, 3.29 (Pucci, p. 22)

108 other poems . . . Rucco: Fortunatus, 3.26 and 9.10 (Roberts, p. 203 and 593). 3.26, retitled as "Written on an Island on the Breton Coast," would later be included in Coote's *The Penguin Book of Homosexual Verse.*

109 was kept the royal treasury: Thierry, *Tales,* p. 8

109 "valiant defender": Fortunatus, 9.1 (George, p. 74)

109 "in your honest speech are held the scales of just measure and the course of justice runs straight": Fortunatus, 9.1 (George, p. 77)

109 "the child he loved best": Fortunatus, 9.1 (George, p. 75)

109 **"feeble"**: *HF,* 6.46, p. 380

109 **"observed none of the accepted rules of prosody"**: *HF,* 5.44, p. 312

110 **"not [understand] what he was doing," "he put short syllables for long ones"**: *HF,* 6.46 p. 380

110 **smartest in the family**: Fortunatus, 9.1 (George, p. 77): "you surpass your whole family in your enthusiasm for learning"

110 **"exceptional"**: Fortunatus, 9.1 (George, p. 78)

110 **"a good mistress of [her] palace"** and **"of pleasing generosity"**: Fortunatus, 9.1 (George, p. 79)

110 **"rightful consort"** and **"greater honor"**: Ibid.

110 **"wise in counsel, clever, shrewd . . . [and] intelligent"**: Ibid.

110 **"shares the rule," "carries the oppressive weight of the cares of state,"** and **"guidance at [the king's] side"**: Ibid.

110 **"a great bar of iron was placed under his neck and they struck his throat with another'"**: *HF,* 6.32, (Brehaut)

CHAPTER 15: FREDEGUND'S GRIEF

111 **preferred to emigrate**: *HF,* 5.28

111 **pay one amphora of wine for each arpent**: *HF,* 5.28: *Statutum enim fuerat, ut possessor de propria terra unam anforam vini per aripennem redderit.*

111 **"five gallons of wine for every half-acre"**: *HF,* 5.28 p. 292

112 **tried to kill the tax collector**: *HF,* 5.28

112 **"It is the tears of the poor, the outcries of widows and the sighs of orphans that are destroying [my boys]!"**: *HF,* 5.34, (Brehaut)

113 **"was worn to a shadow and hardly drawing breath"**: *HF,* 5.34, p. 298

113 **"the men weeping and the women wearing widow's weeds"**: Ibid.

113 **prized hunting preserve . . . for all of the future kings of France**: A small portion survives today as the Forêt de Compiègne, site of the armistices of both WWI and WWII; *HF,* 4.21 for mention of Clothar I first hunting there; see Hincmar's *Annals of St.-Berton* for mention of Charlemagne hunting there in the 800s; other instances of later French kings and Napoleon hunting there are widely documented.

114 **"My enemies are now in my power and I can do to them whatever I choose"**: *HF,* 5.39, p. 303

114 *pavore nimio terrebatur:* *HF,* 5.39

115 **tied to a stake**: Ibid.; some translations claim Fredegund had the girl impaled but the Latin *defigere* ("to fasten") doesn't suggest that.

115 a few added details of her own: *HF,* 5.39

115 body was buried so quickly: Ibid.

116 **Some assumed Basina was raped:** See Dumézil, *Brunehaut,* p. 201 for this interpretation, repeated in popular sources. Based on *HF,* 5.39: *Soror ipsius in monasterio delusa a pueris reginae transmittitur, in quo nunc, veste mutata, consistit.* The word *delusa* can be translated as "tricked" or "deluded" but it can also be translated as "to make sport of" as a euphemism for rape, as it is used in *HF,* 4.47.

116 **"set alight while still alive":** *HF,* 5.39, p. 305

CHAPTER 16: BRUNHILD IN THE BREACH

117 **the heavy belt:** called a *cingulum militare;* Dumézil, *Brunehaut,* p. 204

117 **his candidate for young Childebert's regent:** a man named Wandalen; see *HF,* 6.1

118 **"armed herself like a man,"** *praecingens se viriliter:* *HF,* 6.4

118 **Frankish men who dressed . . . as women . . . in Radegund's abbey:** *HF,* 10.15

118 **a person biologically sexed as male was buried with all the trappings of an older woman:** called the Ennery grave 32, see Halsall, *Cemeteries,* p. 342–43

118 **accounts of women disguising themselves as men to enter monasteries:** see Hunt's *Transvestite Women Saints*

118 **"deprived of his arms":** *HF,* 5.3, p. 256

118 **"Warriors, I command you to stop this wicked behavior! Stop harassing this person who has done you no harm!":** *HF,* 6.4, p. 329

118 **"Stand back, woman! It should be enough that you held regal power when your husband was alive!":** *HF,* 6.4 p. 329

119 **he had vetoed one handpicked bishop:** *HF,* 5.46; see also Dumézil's interpretation of this event, *Brunehaut,* p. 196.

119 **"Stop fighting each other and bringing disaster upon our country, just because of this one man!":** *HF,* 6.4 p. 329

119 **"Now your son is on the throne, and his kingdom is under our control, not yours.":** *HF,* 6.4 p. 329

119 **"Leave us or our horses' hooves will trample you to the earth!":** *HF,* 6.4, (Brehaut)

119 **crying raggedly in public:** See Fortunatus, 9.2, written after the princes' deaths. It tells Chilperic to comfort the queen and get her to stop crying and notes that she is "desolate" (George, p. 84)

120 a decree abolishing the Trinity: *HF,* 5.44

120 "I will put these matters to men who are more wise than you and they will agree with me.": *HF,* 5.44, p. 311

120 "if he had been able to reach the paper on which [these decrees] were written he would have torn it into shreds": *HF,* 5.44, 311–12

120 "it was impossible to use them": *HF,* 6.46, p. 380

120 poor grasp of Latin and virtually none of poetic rhythm: For Chilperic's one surviving hymn, see "IX, Chilpericus Rex." Latin translator John de Boulton-Holland wrote to me, "Endings, genders, grammatical cases, verb tenses, in fact just about everything that goes to making Latin a precise language, are at times cheerfully ignored . . . There is no evidence of any stress pattern or rhyme either internally and at the ends of lines." Other scholars, such as Brian Brennan, also have a very low opinion of his abilities: "If [other poems] were of the standard of the one piece that has survived, were not very good at all" (*Bishop and Community,* p. 307).

120 "should be erased with pumice and rewritten": *HF,* 5.44, p. 312

120 these letters . . . live on: See Richter, "King Chilperic I's letters . . ."

121 blinded by an intense hatred: See, for example, Kurth, *Histoire Poetique,* p. 275–77 and Wallace-Hadrill, "Bloodfeud," p. 473–74.

121 "Childebert shall inherit everything that I manage to keep under my control. All that I ask is that for the term of my natural life I may be left to enjoy these things in peace and quiet.": *HF,* 6.3, p. 328

122 "if it is granted to me to live": *HF,* 6.2, p. 328

122 "For if my son Childebert would seek the path of reason, he would know at once that it was by my brother's connivance that his father was killed.": *HF,* 6.3, p. 328

122 Two thousand gold solidi: *HF,* 10.19

122 "The stalk which emerges from the soil will not wither until its root is severed": *HF,* 10.19, p. 578

122 not as his wife, but as his mother: See John of Ephesus, *Ecclesiastical History,* 3.7

123 three best-known Alpine passes: These are the Col de l'Argentière, the Col de Montgenèvre, and the set of Saint Bernard passes

123 his third wife: She was named Austrechild and, like Fredegund, had once been a servant to the prior queen.

123 581, the wily Duke Boso set sail for Constantinople: See Bachrach, *Anatomy,* p. 52 and Goffart, "Byzantine," p. 96.

123 a persuasive speaker and because he and Gundovald had been friendly as young men: Ibid.

124 swore an oath at each one: *HF,* 7.36

CHAPTER 17: THE REGENCY

125 Every prisoner . . . released; all fines . . . erased: *HF,* 6.23

125 Theuderic, was baptized on Easter morning, 583 [by] Bishop of Paris, Ragnemod: *HF,* 6.27

126 the most likely candidate was Brunhild: Dumézil, *Brunehaut,* p. 209 (Note that Bachrach claims it was Guntram in *Anatomy,* p. 81).

126 casualties . . . at least seven thousand on both sides: *HF,* 6.31

126 "Down with those who are handing [Childebert's] cities over to an enemy power! Down with those who are selling Childebert's subjects into foreign slavery!": *HF,* 6.31, p. 361

126 when one of his shoes fell off: *HF,* 6.31

127 Gundovald . . . had landed in Francia in September of 582: See Bachrach, *Anatomy,* p. 61

127 As a young man, Mummolus: *HF,* 4.42

128 the element of surprise: See description of battles in *HF,* 4.42 and Bachrach, "Imperial Roots," p. 29

128 the Lombards, and then the Saxons: *HF,* 4.42

128 a villa: of Saint-Saturnin, *HF,* 4.44

128 Mummolus . . . in the walled city of Avignon: See Marius of Avenches, *Chronica,* p. 108; *HF,* 6.1

129 Brunhild did not yet have the power to override him: *HF,* 6.40 and 6.42

CHAPTER 18: SET ABLAZE

130 Gregory . . . had no contacts in or special knowledge of Visigothic Spain: Gregory claimed Brunhild's mother, Queen Goiswintha, was an Arian fanatic and blamed Goiswintha for persecuting Catholics, even her own granddaughter. However, a Spanish source with close ties to Prince Hermenegild claimed it was her second husband, Leovigild, who instigated the persecution (see Isidore, *Historia,* 50; Isidore's brother Leander was Hermenegild's adviser). There is no evidence for Gregory's assertion: there was no similar persecutions under the reign of Athanagild and Goiswintha, and Goiswintha was not opposed to her daughters

converting to Catholicism. Hermenegild did convert from Arianism to Catholicism, but not until long after his revolt began, and likely to gain support from the Catholics in the south of Spain. On problems with *Gregory's* account, see Collins, "Merida," p. 215–17 and Bachrach, *Anatomy*, p. 201, note 75.

130 **a Visigothic source points to Brunhild's mother:** See John of Biclaro, *Chronicle*, anno 579: *Hermenegildus factione Gosuinthae reginae tyrannidem assumens in Hispali civitate rebellione facta recluditur, et alias civitates atque castella secum contra patrern rebellare facit.*

131 **Three generations of women . . . tangled up in succession politics:** See Thomas, "Second Jezebel," p. 127, who calls this an "axe feminine."

131 **In Goiswintha's vision, this second Visigothic kingdom:** Ibid., p. 122 for more details of this hypothesis.

131 **thirty thousand solidi to stay away . . . ignoring Hermenegild's cries for help:** Bachrach, *Anatomy*, p. 84; John of Biclaro, *Chronicle*, anno 584; and *HF,* 5.38, 6.40, 6.43

132 **he sent envoys to Paris bearing gifts for Chilperic:** *HF,* 6.40

132 **saying they intended to invade Spain:** *HF,* 6.42

132 **Chilperic left Paris to journey to Soissons, a two- to three-day ride:** calculated using the ORBIS database

132 **"May his father play with him, his mother feed him at her breast, and may he snuggle round his parents' necks":** Fortunatus, 9.2 (George, p. 86)

133 **"prostrate with grief":** *HF,* 6.34 p. 364

133 **"I can hardly think of celebrating my daughter's wedding when I am in mourning because I have just buried my son":** Ibid.

133 **likely that Fredegund had her soldiers rape Basina:** Dumézil, *Brunehaut*, p. 201 for this interpretation and prior note in Chapter 15.

133 **"It is not seemly . . . for a nun dedicated to Christ to turn back once more to the sensuous pleasures of this world":** *HF,* 6.34, p. 365

134 *maleficia et incantationes:* *HF,* 6.35

134 **did not require blaming herself:** See Jones, *Social Mobility*, p. 307, note 99

134 **"a certain herb," "if anyone who is attacked by dysentery drinks a concoction of it, he is immediately cured, however desperately ill he might be":** *HF,* 6.35, p. 365

134 **employed people who claimed to do this very thing:** *HF,* 7.44

135 **swallowing dust . . . had completely cured:** See Gregory, *De virtutibus et miraculis*, 2.1, p. 228 (also 1.37 and 3.60) in Van Dam's translation.

135 "roots of different herbs and . . . moles' teeth, the bones of mice, the claws and fat of bears": *HF,* 9.6 (Brehaut)

135 "loaded with jewelry": *HF,* 7.44, p. 427

135 "the prostitutes and women of the lower class": *HF,* 9.6 (Brehaut)

135 "hung to a beam with his hands tied behind his back," "stretched on the wheel and beaten with triple thongs," and "splinters under his finger and toe nails": *HF,* 6.35 (Brehaut)

135 *unctionis et potionis*: *HF,* 6.35

136 "Then the Queen used severer torture on the women and caused some to be drowned and delivered others over to fire, and tied others to wheels where their bones were broken": *HF,* 6.35 (Brehaut)

136 "filled four carts": *HF,* 6.35, p. 366

137 before Easter on April 18: Easter fell on April 18 (*HF,* 5.17) and occurs several chapters later in 6.40.

137 *ob metum mortis*: *HF,* 5.22

137 "sent messengers to his dukes and counts to tell them to repair the walls of their cities, and then shut themselves up inside these fortifications": *HF,* 6.41, p. 374

138 "in the manor of Vitry, for [Chilperic] was afraid that, if he appeared in public, some harm might befall him": *HF,* 6.41 p. 375

CHAPTER 19: *BRUNICHILDIS REGINA*

140 The letter would establish: See "Historical context" for Brunhild's Letter 26 by Joan Ferrante in *Epistolae.*

140 "The letter directed to our most distinguished son": Brunhild, Letter 26 (*Epistolae,* Ferrante)

140 an alliance would benefit everyone involved: *quod prosit rebus omnibus foederatis,* Brunhild Letter 26 (*MHG,* p. 168)

140 fifty thousand solidi: Paul the Deacon, *Historia,* 3.17, p. 117

140 the march into Italy would take at least eight weeks: see Bachrach, *Anatomy,* p. 85

141 first recorded instance: While there is no record of her doing so, it is possible that Queen Amulsuntha presided over court in Ostrogothic Italy in 530s.

141 "was summoned by Queen Brunhild and appeared before her": *HF,* 6.37, p. 370

142 "in a sack weighted with stones": Ibid.

142 "there suddenly appeared an eagle, which fished [a] sack out of the bottom of the river and placed it on the bank": Ibid.

142 an informal shrine: *HF,* 6.37

142 a turf war with the bishop of Cahors: *HF,* 6.38

143 "carted off in wagons": *HF,* 6.44, p. 377

143 "they wept bitterly and refused to go," "guarded closely": Ibid.

143 "hanged themselves in their distress": Ibid.

143 "vast weight of gold and silver, and many fine clothes": *HF,* 6.45, p. 378

143 "Everything you see belongs to me": Ibid.

144 "put aside quite a bit from my own resources, from the manors granted me, and from revenues and taxes": Ibid.

144 so extravagant: *HF,* 6.45: There was such concern about the size of the dowry he was sending with Rigunth that the Austrasians sent envoys demanding that Chilperic not seize any people or goods from the contested or recently conquered cities to send to Spain, too.

144 September 1, 584: *HF,* 6.45

144 three dukes, a count: Ibid.

144 gasps . . . unlucky sign: Ibid.

144 "a hundred of the best horses with golden bridles and two great chains": Ibid., p. 378

144 comparisons to swarms of locusts: Ibid., 6.45

145 armpit, then his belly: Ibid., 6.46

CHAPTER 20: THE KING IS DEAD

146 grabbed the meat and wine in the royal cellars: *HF,* 7.15

146 where he had fallen from his horse: Today in Chelles, a suburb of Paris on the Marne River, there is a large column called the *Pierre de Chilpéric,* commonly thought to be a marker of the assassination and listed by the Ministry of Culture as a historical monument. But a contemporary plaque notes that the column is not Merovingian; it was rather the base of a cross meant to mark the old town limits.

146 "singing hymns": *HF,* 6.46, p. 381

147 make her way to the cathedral: *HF,* 6.46

147 exotic black marble pillars . . . mosaics . . . large stained-glass windows: See Wright, *Music and Ceremony,* p. 4 and Fortunatus, 2.10 (Roberts, p. 97).

147 half an acre in area: Wright, *Music and Ceremony,* p. 4 lists the measurements as 70 meters long by 30 meters wide. That is 2,100 square meters, or over 22,000 square feet.

147 "Fredegund was in the bedroom": *LHF,* 35 (Bachrach, p. 88–89)

148 "drunk on her wine": Ibid., p. 88

148 "stabbed the king in the belly with two scramsaxes. Chilperic cried out and died": Ibid.

148 "Ambush, ambush, this is what King Childebert of Austrasia did to our lord.": Ibid.

148 written over a century after the assassination: *LHF* is widely agreed to have been composed in Neustria around 726.

148 Charlemagne's grandfather: Charles "the Hammer" Martel

148 Landreville, or "Landeric's villa": See Samson, *Residences*, p. 103

149 "to come live with her, but he had refused": *HF,* 7.21, p. 402

149 "the Nero and Herod of our time": *HF,* 6.46, p. 379

149 written in Burgundy half a century later: Fredegar's *Chronicle* is believed to have been written around 640–60.

149 "Chilperic was killed at the villa of Chelles, not far from Paris, by a man named Falco, who had been sent by Brunhild.": Fredegar, 3.93 (Murray *From Roman to Merovingian* p. 621)

149 perhaps the supposed name of the assassin: See Fredegar, Interpolation 23 (Woodruff, p. 170).

149 Brunhild's ambassadors . . . plant or hire an assassin: Dumézil, *Brunehaut,* p. 213

150 he and Brunhild were in Neustrian territory: Dumézil argues that the minor king would have been accompanied by his mother, *Brunehaut,* p. 218.

150 "lost no time in joining King Childebert": *HF,* 7.4, p. 390

151 marched north to try to take back the cities of Poitiers and Tours: *HF,* 7.13

151 one of the archipelagos off the coast of Marseilles or Cannes: Goffart, "Pretender," p. 19

151 a more distant spot like Corsica: Dumézil, *Brunehaut,* p. 263

151 a little over a week's journey: using ORBIS calculations for Toulouse to Osca on horse

151 "ridicule" "travel-stained": *HF,* 7.9, p. 394

152 *Furor: HF,* 7.15

152 "cooks and bakers" "beaten, plundered, and maimed": *HF,* 7.15 (Brehaut)

152 it seems Fredegund ordered a very specific inscription: Funerary monuments were arranged by living family members. The inscription speaks in two voices, and a wife would be the most likely one to pair her voice with that of her husband. Furthermore, other family members weren't available to commission this—Chilperic's son was an infant, his daughter was stuck in Toulouse, and his brother Guntram was quite far

away at the time of his funeral. See Handley, p. 558-559 for discussion of the inscription's authenticity.

152 "I, Chilperic, pray that my bones will not be removed from here": Handley, p. 558

152 "Tempore nullo volo hinc tolantur ossa Hilperici": ibid

153 "Let my lord come and take charge of his brother's kingdom. I have a tiny baby, whom I long to place in his arms. At the same time I shall declare myself his humble servant.": *HF,* 7.5 p. 390–91

154 "Hand over the murderess, the woman who garroted my aunt, the woman who killed first my father and then my uncle!": *HF,* 7.7, p. 392

154 "She has a king as her son and she therefore cannot be surrendered.": *HF,* 7.14, p. 397

CHAPTER 21: THE VEXATIONS OF KING GUNTRAM

155 **the middle of October of 584:** This date is calculated by a statement in Fredegar 4.2 that Gundovald's campaign began in November. For a more detailed chronology, see Bachrach, *Anatomy,* note 1 on p. 227.

156 **to the contested region of Limoges and was raised on a shield:** This occurred in the town of Brives-la-Gaillarde (HF, 7.10)

156 **always traveling with armed guards, even to church:** *HF,* 7.8, 7.18

156 **"three years at least" "full-grown man":** *HF,* 7.8, p. 393

156 **"hand over that witch Fredegund":** *HF,* 7.14, p. 397

157 **Boso helped himself to a portion of Gundovald's treasure:** Gundovald accuses Boso in *HF,* 7.36. Goffart, "Pretender," p. 12–17 claims that, rather than stealing, Boso was merely transporting money the Byzantine emperor had intended for an invasion of Italy. Most scholars disagree with Goffart's assertion; see Murray's *Companion* p. 488, note 103.

157 **introducing a Byzantine agent:** *HF,* 6.24, p. 352

158 **"It was your invitation which brought Gundovald to Francia! And it was to arrange this that you went to Constantinople!":** *HF,* 6.26, p. 354

158 **"There's nothing to be afraid of.":** Ibid., p. 355

159 **"You traitor, who have never been known to keep your word!":** *HF,* 7.14, p. 398

159 **"let him now step forward and speak out":** Ibid.

159 **ordeal by combat:** *HF,* 7.14

159 **"It becomes you ill, King, to talk so foolishly":** Ibid., p. 398

159 **an ax hanging over the king's head:** *HF,* 7.14

159 catapult garbage: Ibid.

160 "I am pregnant again.": *HF,* 7.7, p. 392

160 "astonished": Ibid.

160 shocked because Fredegund had so recently given birth: *HF,* 7.7

160 roughly two-month period: Chilperic seems to have been assassinated while hunting in October since the month of September was taken up with Rigunth's marriage preparations and farewell parties (*HF,* 6.45); it seems this dinner took place in December (*HF,* 7.11).

160 attempted abortions rather than face the public shame: See Fortunatus, *Vita Germani,* p. 372.

160 nurse their babies: Garver p. 235

160 "husband ought not to cohabit with her till that which is brought forth be weaned": Gregory the Great, *Epistles,* 11.64 (Schaff, vol. 13, p. 322)

160 avoid sex for . . . forty days after birth: Brundage, *Law, Sex, and Christian Society,* p. 156–57

161 another dinner guest . . . Bishop Praetextatus: *HF,* 7.16

162 *valde maesta*: *HF,* 7.20

162 "much of her power had been brought to an end": Ibid., p. 401

162 "by having his hands and feet cut off: Ibid., p. 402

162 "the ringleader": *HF,* 7.21, p. 402

163 "[I] will destroy not only Eberulf himself but also all his kinsmen to the ninth degree, in order that by their death the wicked custom of killing kings might be ended.": *HF,* 7.21 (Brehaut)

163 "cut[ting] him down in the vestibule of the church": *HF,* 7.29, p. 409

163 "brains scattered": Ibid., p. 412

163 "furious": Ibid.

CHAPTER 22: THE GUNDOVALD AFFAIR

164 Radegund . . . and Ingritude: *HF,* 7.36

164 Radegund . . . had kept her husband under surveillance: Bachrach, *Anatomy,* p. 7–8

165 rumors of an imminent marriage: Kurth, *Histoire Poetique,* p. 291, note 74, thinks these rumors came straight from Fredegund.

165 by the spring of 585, Gundovald controlled: Dumézil, *Brunehaut,* p. 226

166 "he demanded an oath of allegiance to King Childebert": *HF,* 7.26, p. 407

166 "When we meet on the battlefield, God will make it clear whether or not I am King Clothar's son.": *HF,* 7.32, p. 415

166 "all the more senior people": *HF,* 7.33, p. 416

167 "This is a sign that I have handed the whole of my realm over to you.": Ibid.

168 "a grown man": Ibid.

168 "I exclude all others from the succession. It is you who are my heir.": Ibid.

168 "not to give her any opportunity of writing to Gundovald or of receiving communication from him": Ibid., p. 417

169 "glorious in his eminence": Fortunatus, 10.14 (Roberts, p. 693)

169 Childebert's tutor died, Brunhild decided not to replace him: *HF,* 8.22

169 dispatched one of her dukes to Toulouse to collect Rigunth and . . . make contact with Gundovald: *HF,* 7.39

170 her hiding place in the little church of Saint Mary's: HF 7.10

170 Gundovald's first attempt . . . same existential threat: Goffart, "Pretender," p. 11

170 "great spring gush[ed] forth": *HF,* 7.34, p. 417

171 "last them many years": *HF,* 7.34, p. 418

171 private storehouses: *HF,* 7.37

171 "flaming barrels of pitch and fat" or "boxes of stones": *HF,* 7.37, p. 421

171 one of his men . . . casually tossing rocks off: Bishop Sagittarius, Ibid.

171 a missive Gundovald was sending to Brunhild: Bachrach, *Anatomy,* 126

171 come to Bordeaux: *HF,* 7.34

171 "Pretender! Puppet!": *HF,* 7.36

171 Guntram was holding his wife and young children hostage: *HF,* 7.38

172 "sobbing" "It was at your invitation that I came to Gaul!": Ibid., p. 422

172 "I am not such a fool that I cannot see through your words!": Ibid.

172 begged God to swiftly strike down: *HF,* 7.38

173 body was left to rot in the sun: Ibid.

173 run through by two lances: *HF,* 7.39

173 "were murdered where they stood at the church altars": *HF,* 7.38, p. 424

173 "bare earth": Ibid.

174 publicly accusing her of threatening to assassinate him: *HF,* 8.4; see Bachrach, *Anatomy,* p. 152–53 for an analysis of other circumstantial evidence that Guntram's accusation was not completely unfounded.

174 openly berated Fredegund's favorite, Bertram: *HF,* 8.2

174 "I am beginning to think he is the son of one of my *leudes*": *HF,* 8.9, p. 440

174 Landeric . . . called in favors: Wemple, *Women*, p. 65

175 three bishops and three *hundred* nobles: *HF,* 8.9

175 "with so many candles it was not possible to count them": *HF,* 8.10, p. 441

CHAPTER 23: THE DIPLOMATIC ARTS

176 Lombards had offered the Franks a bribe . . . the emperor . . . asked for his money back: *HF,* 6.42

176 summer of 585, Brunhild sent another army into Italy . . . Childebert . . . stayed at home: Ibid., 8.18

176 Ingund was buried there: Ibid., 8.26

177 "Renowned Lord, and with unutterable sighing and longing, Most Dear Grandson, King Athanagild, from Queen Brunhild": Brunhild, Letter 27 (Ferrante, *Epistolae*)

177 "sweetest" "great happiness": Ibid.

177 "my sweet daughter, whom wrong-doing has stolen from me": Brunhild, Letter 27 *MGH*, p. 139 (J. Holland)

177 "I do not lose [my] daughter completely if, with the Lord helping, her progeny is preserved for me.": Brunhild, Letter 27 (Ferrante, *Epistolae*)

178 "we recognize [you] as governing the Roman state with your spouse" "cause of common benefit": Brunhild, Letter 29 (Ferrante, *Epistolae*)

178 "mishap has brought it about that the infancy of my little grandson is consigned to be spent wandering in foreign parts": quoted by Gillett, p. 139

178 "would not see your most devout Theodosius carried off and so dear a son not separated from the embrace of his mother": Ibid.

178 "meet with the with the wretchedness of being orphaned, nor that you should pass your childhood without parents": Ibid., p. 146

178 Fortunes can quickly change: And they certainly did—Constantina would lose all five of her sons, as well as her husband, during a revolt in 602. The sixth son, Theodosius, the boy written about here, would be executed a few days after his father.

178 "that as I lost a daughter I may not lose the sweet pledge from her that remained to me, that as I am tortured by the death of the child, I may be comforted through you by the swift return of the captive grand-child": Brunhild, Letter 31 (Ferrante, *Epistolae*)

179 "may receive the mercy of glory from God who is the universal redeemer": Ibid.

179 "the charity between both peoples may be multiplied by this and the term of peace extended": Ibid.

179 "Quickly kill our enemies": *HF,* 8.28: *Inimicos nostros, id est Childeberthum et matrem eius, velociter interemite et cum rege Gunthchramno pacem inite, quod praemiis multis coemite. Et si vobis minus est fortassis paecunia, nos clam mittimus, tantum ut quae petimus impleatis* (J. Holland).

180 poisoned scramsaxes in their possession: *HF,* 8.29

180 "When you have prostrated yourselves at his feet, as though you are begging for a penny, stab him in both sides.": *HF,* 8.29: *Cumque pedibus eius fueritis strati, quasi stipem postulantes, latera eius utraque perfodite* (J. Holland).

180 "the boy . . . so heavily guarded" "Kill her as an enemy": *HF,* 8.29: *ut tandem Brunichildis, quae ab illo adrogantiam sumit, eo cadente conruat mihique subdatur. Quod si tanta est costodia circa puerum, ut accedere nequeatis, vel ipsam interemite inimicam* (J. Holland).

180 "so that at last Brunhild, who takes her arrogance from him, may fall as he collapses, and be subject to me": Ibid.

181 "stupid, malicious behavior" "boastful pride": *HF,* 8.31, p. 462

181 "In exile and out of exile I have always been a bishop, but you will not always enjoy royal power.": Ibid.

181 the vase at Soissons: anecdote relayed in *HF,* 2.27

181 On Easter morning: In 586, Easter fell on April 14, although Praetextatus's death is commonly attributed to February 25.

181 during Lent . . . single vegan meal every day: Hardison, *Christian Rite,* p. 87

182 antiphon—*Christus resurgens ex mortuis*: Ibid., p. 141–42

182 old bishop dripped blood over the altar: *HF,* 8.31

182 "lived to see the day when such a crime as this should be committed, and while you were performing the office too": Ibid., p. 463

182 "As long as you live you will be accursed, for God will avenge my blood upon your head": Ibid.

183 "You have never done anything worse than this!": Ibid., 463–64

183 absinthe, wine, and honey: *HF,* 8.31: *bibit absentium cum vino et melle mixtum*; this was probably not absinthe as we think of it today, but a wormwood flavored alcohol, what Goffart calls "a barbaric anticipation of Campari or vermouth" ("Foreigners," p. 83).

183 "lest you all perish with me!": *HF,* 8.31, p. 464

184 "We are quite capable of punishing local misdemeanors ourselves": Ibid., p. 465

185 put an ax in their skulls: *HF,* 8.30

185 lack of religion: Ibid.

185 One set . . . in a Neustrian diplomatic party . . . the other . . . in church: *HF,* 8.44 and 9.3

CHAPTER 24: THE DUKES' REVOLT

186 the plants bloomed again in September and the trees bore a second crop of fruit: *HF,* 8.42

186 Frankish words for *people* and *bright*: Wilson, *Naming,* p. 71–73

187 perhaps another bastard son: *HF,* 9.9

187 Rauching . . . sadistic treatment of his servants: *HF,* 5.3

188 "they were full of hostility" "humiliate her": *HF,* 9.9, p. 489

188 frantically signing orders to seize the duke's property: *HF,* 9.9

189 "until the whole of his brains were exposed": Ibid., p. 490

189 "bedecked with fine jewels and precious gems, bedizened with flashing gold": Ibid.

190 "loathed": *HF,* 9.8, p. 488

190 "heap[ed] abuse and insults upon Queen Brunhild and . . . encouraged her enemies, too": Ibid.

190 "I have sinned before you and your mother, I have refused to obey your commands, and I have acted against your will and against the public [good]": Ibid., p. 488–89

190 "I will take whatever action King Guntram ordains.": Ibid., p. 488

191 a collection of poems that honored Radgund: This collection included what is currently categorized as Books 8–9. See George's introduction to Fortunatus's poems, p. xxi–xxii, for more detail.

191 "that most serene lady, queen Brunhilda, whom she [had] loved with a deep affection": See Baudonivia, *DvsR II,* 16, p. 389: *Praecellentissimis enim dominis regibus et serenissimae dominae Bronichildi reginae, quos caro dilexti [dilexit] affectu* (J. Holland).

191 miracles—the curing of a blind man and of a possessed woman . . . drinking water from her tomb: Baudonivia, *DvrsR II,* 24, 27, 28, (p. 103–105)

191 summer flooding: *HF,* 9.17

192 "ran at full speed": *HF,* 9.10, p. 492

192 "Either obtain my pardon or we shall die together.": *HF,* 9.10 (Brehaut)

193 "sticking in his body and the shafts supporting him [that he] was unable to fall to the earth": Ibid.

193 "When the most excellent lords, kings Guntram and Childebert, and the most glorious lady queen Brunhild met lovingly in Christ's name at Andelot . . . it was affectionately settled, resolved upon and agreed between them": *HF,* 9.20 (Brehaut)

193 *domna regina: HF,* 9.20: *praecellentissimi domni Gunthchramnus et Childebertus regis vel gloriosissima domna Brunechildis regina*

193 placated by a provision: Murray, *A Companion,* p. 446

194 "while he lives, on condition that after his death they shall pass by God's favor with every security under the control of the lady Brunhild and her heirs": *HF,* 9.20 (Brehaut)

194 he chose to make his last stand at his friend's side: *HF,* 9.9

194 kill a great number of troops before he was overcome: *HF,* 9.12

194 "The main enemy of our master lies dead! Berthefred can have his life!": Ibid., p. 495

194 been the only truly independent ruling of his life: Dumézil, *Brunehaut,* p. 244

195 "polluted with human blood": *HF,* 9.12, p. 495

195 sunned themselves on the deck while harps and flutes played: Fortunatus, 10.9

195 "smoke-wreathed roofs": Ibid., p. 677

195 "couple" "royal pair": Fortunatus, 10.8 (Roberts, p. 673) and 10.9 (Roberts, p. 675)

195 "honey-sweet clusters," "level tracts of fertile farmland": Fortunatus, 10.9 (Roberts, p. 677, 679)

195 "enthroned in the banqueting hall," feasting on fresh salmon: Ibid. (Roberts, p. 679); Note that up until the 1950s, Atlantic salmon would spawn in the Rhine.

196 "cities, lands, revenues, and all rights, and every kind of property, both what they actually possess at the present time and what they are able justly to acquire in the future": *HF,* 9.20 (Brehaut)

196 "goods and men, both cities, lands, and revenues": Ibid.

196 "most excellent lords": Fortunatus, 10.3 (Roberts, p. 649)

196 Forgers learned to imitate her signature . . . nobles petitioned her: Dumézil, *Brunehaut,* p. 229

196 "mother radiant in glory": Fortunatus, 10.8 (Roberts, p. 673)

CHAPTER 25: A ROYAL ENGAGEMENT

197 Old King Leovigild had died in 586: John of Biclaro, *Chronicle*, anno 586 and *HF,* 8.46

197 "to acknowledge her as his own mother": *HF,* 9.1, p. 481

198 come to Guntram three times asking for peace: *HF,* 8.35, 8.38, 8.44

198 King Childebert proved more amenable: *HF,* 9.1

198 a wergeld of ten thousand solidi: *HF,* 9.16, p. 499

198 claimed he was still too distraught: *HF,* 9.16 and 9.20

199 "establish warm friendly relations": *HF,* 9.20, p. 507

199 "The 'friendly relations' which have bound them together": Ibid.

199 "Why do you hate me so?": *HF,* 9.34, p. 521

199 More boys were born every year but fewer of them survived: See "Gender Ratio" for detailed explanation of this phenomenon.

200 go back to being a palace slave, ought to start waiting on *her*!: *HF,* 9.34

200 "slaps and punches": Ibid., p. 521

200 "You can take all your father's things which are still in my possession and do what you like with them.": Ibid.

200 pulled the queen off of the trunk lid: *HF,* 9.34

201 "a great salver [tray] of incredible size made out of gold and precious gems . . . together with a pair of wooden dishes . . . which were also decorated with gold and jewels": *HF,* 9.28, p. 514

201 the soldiers even looking in his shoes: *HF,* 9.28

201 "You miserable wretch!": Ibid., p. 514

201 "Now you are carrying presents to Gundovald's sons and no doubt inviting them back to [Francia] to cut my throat!": Ibid.

201 "someone reported [these rumors] to him": Ibid.

201 One of Gundovald's staunchest supporters: Count Waddo; see *HF,* 7.39 and 7.43

201 "fled to Queen Brunhild, and she received him graciously [and] gave him presents": *HF,* 7.43, p. 426

201 Brunhild's envoy was reported to often visit Spain: *HF,* 9.28

202 renewed his accusations: *HF,* 9.32

202 a church council to convene on November 1, 588: Ibid.; likely to be held at the city of Andelot, according to McClintock, *Cyclopædia*, p. 156.

203 publicly swore an oath: *HF,* 9.32; this oath was likely made with the usual oath helpers required by law assisting her

203 bishop was condemned to exile: John of Biclaro, *Chronicle*, anno 589

203 "brought her life to an end": Ibid.: *Gosuintha . . . tunc terminum dedit* (J. Holland).

203 had killed herself: Dumézil argues that she was executed, *Brunehaut*, p. 286, note 136

203 Reccared had hurriedly married: At the Third Council of Toledo held in May 589, Baddo signed as queen.

203 lost five thousand of his men and saw another two thousand captured: *HF*, 9.31

204 "fisticuffs": *HF*, 9.34, p. 522

CHAPTER 26: THE DEFIANT NUNS

205 March 1, 589, forty nuns: *HF*, 9.39

205 "I am going to my royal relations to tell them about the insults which we have to suffer!" Clotilde was reported to have exclaimed. "We are humiliated here as if we were the offspring of low-born serving women, instead of being the daughters of kings!": Ibid., p. 526

206 walked all the way from Poitiers to Tours: This would have taken them around two weeks according to ORBIS calculations.

206 "ankle-deep in water": *HF*, 9.39, p. 529

206 "quite exhausted and worn out": Ibid.

206 plead her case to her uncle Guntram: *HF*, 9.40

206 "burglars, murderers, adulterers and criminals of all sorts": Ibid., p. 532

206 Four bishops: from Bordeaux, Angouleme, Perigeaux, and, of course, Poitiers

206 clergymen . . . scrambled to flee: *HF*, 9.41, p. 533

207 "like a cornfield set alight, the entire town was suddenly ablaze with pestilence": *HF*, 9.22, p. 511

207 early medieval social distancing and travel restrictions: McCormick, "Toward a Molecular History," p. 310–11

207 ordered his people to assemble in churches . . . then commanded them to fast: *HF*, 9.21

208 comets, then a solar eclipse: *HF*, 10.23

208 "rave and declare their leaders holy": *HF*, 10.25 (Brehaut)

208 "not only the common ilk but bishops of the church": Ibid.

208 "They continued to profess that he was Christ and that Mary had a share in his divinity": *HF*, 10.25, p. 586

209 To evade the intruders, nuns carried the abbess into the tiny shrine: *HF,* 10.15

209 men accidentally grabbed the wrong nun: Justina, who happened to be Bishop Gregory's niece

209 "Do not lay a finger on me! . . . I am the daughter of one king and the niece of another! If you touch me you can be quite sure that the day will come when I shall have my revenge!: *HF,* 10.15, p. 570

210 "poor food, the lack of clothing, and . . . harsh treatment": Ibid., p. 571

210 Radegund was known for . . . mundane chores in sackcloth and ashes: Fortunatus, *Radegundis,* 23 (McNamera, p. 80)

210 "wearing women's dress [and] who was treated as a woman, although he was unmistakably and most clearly a man, who gave constant attention to the abbess": *HF,* 10.15 (J. Holland)

210 "he could not perform a man's work": ibid

210 "an operation I had once seen performed by a surgeon in the town of Constantinople": *HF,* 10.15, p. 571; this seems to be an early, and successful, treatment for testicular cancer.

211 Clothilde . . . given a country estate: *HF,* 10.20

CHAPTER 27: ALLIES AND ASSASSINS

212 **Brunhild had overseen the marriage of her niece Bertha:** Bertha, sister of Clotilde, had spent some of her youth at Radegund's Holy Cross convent in Poitiers. For the argument that Poitiers was under Brunhild's control at the time of Bertha's marriage, and that Brunhild was the one to arrange the marriage, Dumézil, *Brunehaut,* p. 287–89

212 **an Anglo-Saxon prince:** named Aethelbert. For more on the timing of the marriage and his becoming king see Kirby, *Earliest English Kings,* p. 26–27 and Dumézil, *Brunehaut,* p. 286–87

212 **the pope now considered the people of Kent subjects of Francia:** Gregory the Great, *Epistles,* Letter 6.51

212 **Duke Chrodoald:** For evidence of this marriage, see Martindale's *Prosopography of the Later Roman Empire* vol. 3a p. 1231; and Dumézil, *Brunehaut,* p. 296, notes 23 and 25, which cite Bobbio's *Vita Columbani,* 1.22; Fredegar, 4.52

212 **recent rumblings of revolt in the area:** Paul Deacon, *Historia,* 3.30, p. 140 and 4.7, p. 154

213 loyal son-in-law for many decades: Jonas of Bobbio, *Vita Columbani*, 1.22

213 Bretons . . . governed by a warlord named Waroch: *HF,* 10.9

213 sending two more dukes: Beppolen and Ebracher; Beppolen was an old enemy of Fredegund (*HF,* 8.42).

213 on friendly terms with . . . Waroch: *HF,* 10.9 and 10.11

213 distinctive ethnic hairstyle and costume: Filerman, *Saxon Identities*, p. 67

213 cut their longer locks: *HF,* 10.9

214 "recklessly": *HF,* 10.10, p. 559

214 sent messengers to King Waroch: *HF,* 10.11

214 Guntram packed up to travel to Paris for his nephew's funeral: Ibid.

215 credibly linked to twelve political assassination attempts, six of them successful: Iin the following list, x = a successful assassination: Sigibert (x), Merovech, Clovis (x), Audovera (x), Praetextatus (x), Rouen civil leader (x), Childebert/Brunhild three attempts (*HF,* 7.20, 8.29, 10.18); Guntram two attempts (8.44, 9.3); three nobles (x) (*HF,* 10.27)

215 many other assassinations attributed to her only through rumor and innuendo: Such as some of the attempts against Guntram as well as the murders of Galswintha and her own husband.

216 Fredegund was said to have given the potential assassins wine . . . add a special draught or potion: *HF,* 8.29; Fredegar, 4.51; *LHF,* 35

216 said he became paralyzed: *HF,* 10.18

216 "some had their hands amputated and were afterwards released, some had their ears and noses cut off": *HF,* 10.18, p. 576

216 "subjects of ridicule": Ibid.

CHAPTER 28: FORLORN LITTLE BOYS

217 allowed to return (after his lands had been grabbed up): *HF,* 9.38

217 "flogged daily with sticks and leather thongs. His wounds festered. As fast as the pus oozed away and the places began to mend, they were opened once more": *HF,* 10.19, p. 576

217 beg for forgiveness . . . offer his longtime enemy Wolf an olive branch: *HF,* 9.13

217 reported to be in ill health: *HF,* 10.19

218 "it rained continually and in torrents, and it was unbearably cold, [and] the roads were deep in mud": *HF,* 10.19, p. 577

218 "constant enemy": Ibid.

218 "I cannot deny that I was King Chilperic's friend": Ibid.

218 "in which many insulting remarks were made about Brunhild": *HF,* 10.19, p. 578

218 "I confess that I deserve death for the crime of high treason. I have repeatedly conspired against the interests of the King and his mother.": Ibid.

218 a son named Romulf: See *HF,* 9.30 and 10.19

219 Brunhild sent armies nearly every summer to harry the Lombards: The years 584, 585, 587, 588, 589, and 590; the campaign of 587 had been most successful, allowing the Byzantines to recover some territory.

219 twelve thousand solidi every year: Fredegar, 4.45

219 Athanagild's name was added to a list: See and the discussion of its inscriptions on Dumézil, *Brunehaut,* p. 281.

219 Genealogists at the Spanish court . . . the son of Athanagild and a niece of Emperor Maurice: See Castro, *Historia Genealógica.*

220 disputed by other genealogists: especially Christian Settipani

220 Dynamius, the governor of Provence, was awarded: Dumézil, *Brunehaut,* p. 297, note 27: "Dynamius appears in September 593 in the papal correspondence about a diplomatic negotiation with the king of the Lombards Agilulf (Gregory the Great, *Epistles,* Letter 4.2), then again in July 594, still within the framework of the Lombard file (Letter 4.37)."

221 "give up their feud and . . . make peace once more, for if the dispute continued it would become a public nuisance of considerable dimensions": *HF,* 10.27, p. 586–87

222 "three men with three axes": Ibid.

222 "the boy is kept hidden, withheld from me": *HF,* 8.9 (translation in Dailey, *Queens,* p. 154)

222 "Will my lord the King please come to Paris? My son is his nephew. He should have the boy taken there and arrange for him to be baptized.": *HF,* 10.28 p. 587

222 "This is not what you promised to your nephew Childebert . . . What you are doing is confirming this child in his right to the royal throne in the city of Paris. God will sit in judgement of you for having forgotten all your pledges.": Ibid., p. 588

223 "a request which no Christian can refuse": Ibid.

223 "I tremble to think what divine anger I should incur if I did otherwise.": Ibid.

223 "two or three cities . . . so that he may not feel that he is disinherited": *HF,* 9.20, p. 509

CHAPTER 29: THE FADING OF THE KINGS

224 **March 28, 592:** Fredegar, 4.14 (Murray, p. 453)

224 **the church he had built for this very purpose in his capital city of Chalon-sur-Saône:** Saint Marcel, also the spot where Abelard (of Abelard and Heloise fame) later died.

225 **"after she can have no more children":** *Pactus Legis Salicae*, 24.9 (Drew, p. 86)

225 **a nanny:** named Septimima; the episode is recounted in *HF,* 9.38.

226 **two palace officials:** the palace constable and the Referendary; *HF,* 9.38

226 **with witchcraft:** *HF,* 9.38: *ipsum maleficiis interempto*

226 **"the sister and rival of Rome":** translation of the Latin phrase *"soror et aemula Romae,"* the motto that is now carved in the pediment of Autun's town hall. The phrase's origins are unclear but seem to be linked to the Roman historian Tacitus calling the city's inhabitants "the brothers of the Roman people"; see Tacitus, *Annals*, 11.25, p. 291

226 **"overhauled":** *HF,* 10.7, p. 553

226 **"grant relief to the poor and infirm":** *HF,* 9.30, p. 515; also referred to by Fortunatus, 10.11

227 **Wolf was no longer duke:** Wolf had been in power as late as 590 (*HF,* 10.19), but there is no mention of him after that date.

227 **"devastated":** *LHF,* 36, p. 90

228 **"At first light, let's fall upon them, and who knows, maybe we'll beat them.":** *LHF,* 36 (Murray, p. 627)

229 **"Weren't there fields in those places over there yesterday? Why do we see woods?"** Ibid.

229 **"But of course you have been drunk, that is how you blotted it out. Do you not hear the bells of our horses grazing next to that forest?":** *LHF,* 36, p. 91

229 **"with the aid of his very fast horse":** Ibid.

229 **"she set fire to Champagne and devastated it":** Ibid.

229 **"with much booty and many spoils":** Ibid.

229 **"small boy," "cradling the small king in her arms":** *LHF,* 36 (Murray, p. 627)

229 **a later account:** See that of Aimon de Fleury in *Historia Francorum.*

229 **eleventh century, used by the opponents of Bishop Conon . . . end of the twelfth century . . . Danish King Hakon:** See Kurth, *Histoire*, p. 398-9 and Grammaticus's *Gesta Danorum* 7, p. 237.

230 **ordained [Fortunatus] as a priest:** See George's introduction to Fortunatus's poems, p. xx

231 **wrote his last poem:** See Roberts's introduction to Fortunatus's poems, p. viii

231 **one last book, his third:** See George, p. xxii; it is possible that these were collected, instead, after his death by his friends.

231 **"In the fourth year after receiving the kingdom of Guntran, Childebert died.":** Fredegar, 4.16: *Quarto a anno, post quod Childebertus regnum Guntramni acciperat, defunctus est.*

231 **"was murdered, as is said, together with his wife, by poison.":** Paul the Deacon, *Historia*, 4.11, p. 159

CHAPTER 30: THE DUAL RULE

234 **traitor and a fool:** This letter has not survived, but we know of the emperor's insult due to Pope Gregory's response; see Gregory the Great, *Epistles*, 5.40 (Schaff, vol. 12, p. 175–77)

234 **working with powerful women from all walks of life:** Thomas, "Second Jezebel," p. 63, 79

234 **"the menstruous habit in women is no sin, seeing that it occurs naturally":** Gregory the Great, *Epistles*, 11.64 (Schaff, vol. 13, p. 322)

235 **"Angels," as he was reported to have preferred calling them:** Bertram, *Earliest Life of Gregory the Great*, p. 95

235 **first asked for help from the Franks:** Note that the one account usually relied on for the conversion of the Anglo-Saxons, that of Bede's *Ecclesiatical History*, has been shown to have serious flaws, or at least considerable embellishments (Wood, "Mission,"p. 3–4, 10–11) and almost completely eliminates the role of the Franks and of the queens.

235 **Fredegund was either frantically busy . . . or she did not see the usefulness:** Wood, "Mission," p. 8–9

235 **Pope Gregory . . . flattering her intellect and the education:** Gregory the Great, *Epistles*, 6.5 (Schaff, vol. 12 p. 189)

235 **asked for something in return—her assistance with his mission:** Gregory the Great, *Epistles*, 6.50 and 59 (Schaff, vol. 12 p. 202 and 205–6)

236 **wise to make sure her rival would not receive aid:** Wood, "Mission," p. 9

236 **The mission was launched from the port of Rome, then landed in Marseilles:** The probable route is mapped by Robin Macintosh in *Augustine*

of Canterbury, based on Gregory's letters bishops in these areas were asking for their hospitality and help in his *Register*, 6.50–53.

236 **claimed Brunhild's efforts ... were second only to those of God himself:** Gregory the Great, *Epistles*, 11.62 (Schaff, vol. 13, p. 317)

236 **reported to be petrified:** Wood, "Mission," p. 15: "Augustine and his companions ... who were clearly terrified at the prospect of their mission"

237 **"took possession of Paris and other cities like barbarians":** Fredegar, 4.17 (Murray, p. 453–54)

237 **one battle between Napoleon and the Prussians and three more in World War I:** Battle of Craone in 1814; and the three Battles of the Aisne

237 **"cut their army up severely":** Fredegar, 4.17 (Murray, p. 454)

237 **he was welcomed as a conquering hero:** Dumézil, *Brunehaut*, p. 307

238 **giving loyal bishops villas:** Bishop Bertram de la Mans, for example, was gifted a villa in Etampes; see Halfond, "Sis Quoque," p. 70.

238 **Power ... corrupting the reward circuitry of a brain in much the same way as a drug:** See, for example, Al-Rodhan, "Neurochemistry ...".

239 **how those that dared to follow her example ... would be erased:** For example: Nanthild, Bathild, and later, Plectrude.

239 **"Fredegund died.":** Fredegar, 4.17: *Anno secondo regni Teuderici Fredegundis moritur.*

239 **"Queen Fredegund, old and full of days, died.":** *LHF,* 37, p. 92

239 **wrapped in linen strips that had been soaked in oil and a mix of nettles, myrrh, thyme, and aloe:** We know this because of how Fredegund's own mother-in-law was embalmed. See "Solving the Mystery ..." in *Archaiologia Online*.

CHAPTER 31: BRUNHILD'S BATTLES

240 **"devout mind and pious zeal":** Gregory the Great, *Epistles*, 11.62 (Schaff, vol. 13, p. 317)

241 **a show of overwhelming force:** Fredegar, 4.20 (Murray, p. 454)

241 **"twelve districts only, between the Oise, the Seine, and the shores of the Ocean sea":** Ibid.

241 **a church dedicated to Saint Martin ... a convent ... a hospital for the poor:** Gregory the Great, *Epistles*, 13.6 (Schaff, vol. 13, p. 337)

242 **Later chroniclers ... King Theudebert had kicked his grandmother out:** Fredegar, 4.19

242 **Brunhild was considered ruler of both kingdoms until 601:** Dumézil, *Brunehaut*, p. 317–18

242 **the future bishop of Auxerre, was actually a fabulously wealthy aristocrat:** And, incidentally, he was from the city of Cahors, a city under Brunhild's control, from Galswintha's morgengabe.

242 **Bilichild . . . openly challenged and insulted the queen:** Stafford, *Queens,* p. 45 and Fredegar, 4.35 (Murray, p. 459)

242 **"was always going on about Bilichild having been her slave":** Fredegar, 4.35 (Murray, p. 459)

243 **"Queen Brunhild and King Theuderic":** *Epistolae Wisigothicae* 11, p. 677: *Brunigildem reginam et Theudericum regem*

243 **"handsome and energetic and very hot-headed":** *LHF,* 37, p. 92

243 **Spanish princess had been selected for Theuderic:** Princess Ermeneberga; see Fredegar, 4.30 (Murray, p. 458)

243 **the princess's father was soon to be deposed:** King Witteric had come to power by deposing the son of Reccared and was only in power for a handful of years (see Dumezil, p. 326-27); it has also been proposed that this entire episode never happened, and that the marriage was unconsummated simply because Ermenberga died on her way to Francia (see E. A. Thompson, *Goths in Spain*, p. 158).

243 **she had not done enough to eliminate the buying and selling of ecclesiastical offices:** Gregory the Great, *Epistles*, 9.11 and 9.109 (Schaff, vol. 13 p. 250–52, 272–73)

243 **wrote to young Clothar II about the same issue:** Gregory the Great 11.61 (Schaff, vol. 13, p. 317)

244 **"made a complaint to the court that she had been ravished by the most blessed Desiderius":** Sisebut, *passio Desiderii* 4, (Fear, p. 4)

244 **stripped him of his rank and exiled him to a monastery on an island:** Ibid.

244 **"a most unjust sentence against the innocent man":** Ibid.

244 **"deformed in mind" and "lacking in virtues and . . . possessed by a huge number of vices":** Sisebut, *passio Desiderii* 4, (Fear p. 3–4)

244 **"that certain priests . . . live so immodestly and wickedly that it is a shame for us to hear of it":** Gregory the Great, *Epistles*, 11.69 (Schaff, vol. 13, p. 328)

244 **"avenge these things" "smite[d]":** Ibid.

245 **commonly reported that Desiderius . . . or had criticized sixteen-year-old King Theuderic's morals:** See, for example, Fredegar, 4.24. There

are factual problems with both explanations, as they seem to conflate Desiderius' case with that of the monk Columbanus.

245 **"whole-heartedly took himself off to drive out all their sins":** Sisebut, *passio Desiderii* 15, (Fear p. 9)

245 **bludgeoned by a frenzied man with a club:** Sisebut, *passio Desiderii* 18

245 **or stoned to death by soldiers:** Fredegar, 4.32

245 **relatively quickly:** This change in Pope Gregory's thinking occurred in the summer of 601, over the period of less than a month; see Wood, "Mission," p. 12

245 **temples could be rededicated . . . and pagan traditional feasts and sacrifices associated with various saints:** Ibid.

246 **her tolerance of the Jews in her kingdom:** Bachrach, *Early Medieval Jewish Policy*, p. 59–60

246 **Columbanus made it a point to condemn Theuderic . . . also publicly humiliated Brunhild:** Fredegar, 4.36; Jonas of Bobbio, 31 and 32

247 **created a nationalist movement with its own saints, even its own (mostly mythical) royal family:** See *Passio Sigismundi regis* and Fredegar, 4.44's mention of one noble's claim to being "of the royal stock of the Burgundians" (Murray, p. 467).

247 **installed her granddaughter Theudelia [at Orbe]:** Dumézil, *Brunehaut*, p. 321

247 **"bright and energetic" "too smart for his own good":** Fredegar, 4.27 (Murray, p. 457–58)

247 **"Brunhild wanted to exalt him with honors in return for his sexual attentions":** Fredegar, 4.25 (Murray, p. 456)

248 **"the whole army of Theuderic . . . rush[ed] upon Protadius":** Fredegar, 4.27 (Murray, p. 457)

248 **"cut through the tent everywhere with their swords and killed him":** Ibid.

248 **a partial retirement . . . overseeing their education:** Dumézil, *Brunehaut*, p. 370–71

248 **"so that the two queens could meet to discuss making peace between Theuderic and Theudebert":** Fredegar, 4.35 (Murray, p. 459)

248 **[Bilichild] was murdered . . . replaced by another queen:** Fredegar, 4.37 (Murray, p. 464); See also Stafford, *Queens*, p. 87

249 **in 612 at the Battle of Zülpich:** See Fredegar, 4.38 (Murray, p. 464) and *LHF*, 38, p. 93

249 "The slaughter by both armies was such that in the thick of battle . . . the corpses of those killed had no room to fall, but the dead stood upright side by side with other corpses.": Fredegar, 4.38 (Murray, p. 464)

249 "someone took the boy by the foot and smashed his brains out against a rock": Fredegar, 4.38 (Murray, p. 465)

249 sent him off to a monastery: Fredegar, 4.38; Jonas of Bobbio, 57. Theudebert is commonly believed to have died at the monastery shortly afterward; likely he was murdered.

249 the young king . . . was dead: Fredegar, 4.39 (Murray, p. 465)

CHAPTER 32: THE FALL

251 a bishop named Arnulf and a noble named Pippin, invited Clothar: Fredegar, 4.40 (Murray, p. 465)

251 One chronicler claims . . . an order for Warnachar to be killed: Fredegar, 4.41

251 Warnachar and his men rode away: Fredegar, 4.42

252 captured at the banks of Saône: Ibid.

252 found on the banks of Lake Neuchâtel: See, for example, Oman, p. 174 and Young, p. 349.

252 "mounted a horse and fled, never to return": Fredegar, 4.42 (Murray, p. 466)

252 Brunhild and . . . Theudelia were captured: Fredegar, 4.42

252 five different writers from different kingdoms made note of it: Dumézil, *Brunhaut*, p. 381. These writers include: *Vita Desiderii episcopi Viennensis* (circa 613); Sisebut's *Vita Desiderii* (circa 613–21); *Continuations of the Chronicle of Isidore* (circa 624); Jonas of Bobbio's *Vita Columbani* (circa 640); and Fredegar's *Chronicle* (circa 660).

253 Princess Theudelia was also spared: Ibid., p. 382–83

253 "secretly harboring a king": See McNamara's translation of *Vita Rusticule*, 9: *Interim pia mater falso testimonio apud Chlotharium II regem delata est, quod "occulte regem nutrieret," rexque Faraulfum quendam ex optimatibus suis misit, qui eam adduceret. Falsis igitur testimoniis condemnata abbatissa ex urbe educta est.*

254 "the stalk which emerges from the soil will not wither until its root is severed": *HF,* 10.19, p. 578

254 Empress Constantina and her three daughters were spared and sent to a monastery: They were, however, later beheaded, too, once they were caught escaping.

254 the death of ten kings: Fredegar, 4.42

255 "tortured in various ways for three days": Fredegar, 4.42 (Murray, p. 467)

256 the Visigoths . . . made use of a donkey instead: See Rouche, "Brunehaut," p. 105

256 "already broken by old age" "a most sorry spectacle": Sisebut, 21, p. 14

256 "for some time": Ibid.

256 "her hair, one arm and one leg": Fredegar, 4.42 (Murray, p. 467)

256 "pathless, rocky terrain": Sisebut, 21, (Fear p. 14). This was a very creative means of execution; the only mention of this kind of death is of Thuringians killing two hundred Frankish female hostages: "They tied their arms around the necks of their horses," created a stampede, "so tore the girls to pieces" (*HF*, 3.7, p. 168).

256 "her nameless and bloody limbs, pulled apart, were spread out, widely scattered": Sisebut, 21, (Kursch, p. 637): *ac divaricate passim sine nominee membra cruentaque laxantur.*

256 "cut to shreds": Fredegar, 4.42 (Murray, p. 467)

256 "Her final grave was the fire. Her bones were burnt.": *LHF,* 40, p. 96

256 a tomb in the crypt at Brunhild's church in Autun: According to the thirteenth *Vita Hugonis monachi Aeduensis et priore Enziacensis,* p. 761: *Prae cunctis tamen istud extulerat coenobium, in quo suae sepuulturae mausoleum habere decreuerat; nam inter cerera donaria quae illi contulerat, columnis etiam marmorisa ac trabibus abietinis formosis illud decenter instituit: et musivo opera mirifice decorauit.*

257 illustrations and prints: Examples of such can be found in Erlande-Brandenburg, p. 192, fig. 30 and Demoulin, p. 53.

257 In the town of Sens, the local bishop: Saint Lupus of Sens's opposition to Clothar is recorded in the *Vita Lupi episcopi Senonici,* 9, p. 181–82

257 Burgundian nobles and clergy also attempted to despose Clothar during the early years of his reign: Fredegar, 4.44. This plot is dated to 614 or 615.

257 "too much notice of the views of women young and old": Fredegar, 4.42: *et posttremum mulierum et puellaram suggestionibus nimium annuens.*

258 their revolt squashed and their leader executed: Fredegar, 4.44

258 Herpo, the constable who handed over Brunhild . . . ripped apart by a mob: Fredegar, 4.43

258 Council of Paris in October 614, attended by . . . bishops from newly Christianized Britain: They were from the dioceses of Rochester and

Dover; see the Council of Paris subscriptions cited by Wood, *The Merovingian Kingdoms*, p. 141

258 **Warnachar's position was made into a lifetime appointment:** Fredegar, 4.42 (Murray, p. 467): "he received an oath that he would never be dismissed during his life."

258 **dominated, and then deposed, by their Mayors of the Palace:** McKitterick, *History and Memory*, p. 12

EPILOGUE: BACKLASH

259 **another Merovingian was found:** Edwards, "Eerie ancient sarcophagus."

259 **at least the fifth such discovery in the early twenty-first century:** Other discoveries include: in France, Savigny-sur-Ardres (2001), Saint-Aubin-des-Champs (2014), and Cahors (2019); in the Netherlands, Veldhoven (2017); and in Germany, Zeitz (2017)

260 **Hardly any sources survive from the period immediately after Brunhild's execution:** The years 613 to 622; see Wood, *Merovingian*, p. 142

260 **614 Edict of Paris:** See section 9, p. 567.

261 **the charge that she had killed many kings:** See Interpolation 23 in Fredegar, 3, p.168; also Fredegar, 4.42

261 *odium contra ipsam nimium haberit . . . timentius . . . odium in eam habentes*: Fredegar, 4.41 and 4.42

261 **"Leave us or our horses' hooves will trample you to the earth!":** *HF,* 6.4 (Brehaut)

261 **"Bruna is coming from the regions of Spain":** Interpolation 16 of Fredegar, 3, p. 146–49

261 **Clothar II himself had lately come under fire for the practice:** Gregory the Great 11.61 (Schaff, vol. 13 p. 317) and the *Vita Eligii* 2.1

262 **"wretched woman":** Jonas of Bobbio, 32 (Munro)

262 **"They'll never take up the scepters of kings.":** Fredegar, 4.36 (Murray. p. 460)

262 **"the old serpent came to [Theuderic's] grandmother Brunhild, who was a second Jezebel, and aroused her pride against the holy man":** Jonas of Bobbio, 31 (Munro)

262 **[Jezebel's] broad-minded liberalism in contrast to the prophet's inflexible fundamentalism:** See Lesley Hazelton's biography *Jezebel* (NY: Doubleday, 2007) for an account of this clash

262 **"like dung on the ground":** 2 Kings 9:37

263 "beautiful, very cunning, and an adulteress": *LHF,* 35, p. 87

263 "incited [their husbands] on both sides": Ibid.

263 "evil counsel": *LHF,* 38, p. 93

263 systematically rewrote history: McKitterick, *History and Memory,* p. 123: the Carolingian histories were "skillfully constructed and highly selective."

263 "interfered deliberately with their material": See Wood, "Chain," p. 67; We also know there are works that were lost or purposefully suppressed; there is, for example, a reference to a since lost work about Brunhild in a manuscript in the British Library (see Palmer, "The Lost Civilisation.")

263 Blanche of Castille: This queen ruled on her own as regent for twelve years from 1226–34 and 1248–52 (while her husband was away on Crusade).

264 Italian version of Cinderella . . . slamming the lid of a trunk: Dundes, *Cinderella,* p. 12–13

264 "walking forest" battle strategy: Kurth, *Histoire,* p. 39

264 the manuscript . . . linked to a convent in Soissons: Hartmann, "Die Darstellung," p. 213

264 "the valiant queen kept out in front, exhorting the others on to battle with promises and cajoling words": de Pizan, *City of Ladies,* p. 53

264 "was unnaturally cruel for a woman" "skillful handling of power": de Pizan, *City of Ladies,* p. 31

264 "she ruled over the kingdom of France most wisely after her husband's death": Ibid.

264 Queen Brunhild was a witch who magically paved the road: Jean d'Outremeuse, *Ly Mureur des Histors,* p. 225

264 situates her execution in Paris, at the corner where rue Saint-Honoré meets rue de l'Arbre Sec: Okey, *Story of Paris,* p. 29; also repeated in many guidebooks

265 distinction is also claimed by the town of Bruniquel: See the town's website: www.buniquel.fr

265 the 1819 Paris Exposition . . . dressed up as Merovingians: Mosse, *Culture of Western Europe,* p. 21–22

265 an opera, an operetta, a pantomime, three plays, and a multitude of books and poems, prints, and portraits: Opera by Louis Gallet; musicals include operetta by Emile Abraham and a pantomime by Henri Franconi; plays include those by M. Boucher de Perthes, Gardie, and Camille Saint-Saens; books like those by Augustin Thierry; and poems by Blandin and others.

266 for at least forty years, longer than the English War of the Roses: The War of the Roses lasted 1455–87 or thirty-two years.

266 **historians claim she also draws from the lives of our two queens:** See, for example, Clay's "Brunhild: The Original Queen Cersei"; "Fredegund, the 'Real Cersei Lannister'"; and Larrington, p. 3.

266 **August 25, 1632, in Autun . . . a small ceremony:** Kurth, *La Reine Brunehaut*, p. 352–53

267 **two pieces of the smooth black marble slab are on display:** in the Musée Rolin in Autun

267 **ruins of the grand abbey now lie under a neighborhood park:** Parc Robert Schulman, which, when I visited in the summer of 2019, was an active construction site.

267 **in the twelfth century during renovations to Saint-Germain-des-Prés . . . a new and elaborate mosaic slab:** For more on Fredegund's tomb slab and the circumstances surrounding its construction, see Fozi, p. 69–77. In the past, different dates for its construction were given: Montfaucon, p. 44–45 claims this mosaic is original, while Panofsky, *Tomb Sculpture*, p. 50 claims it was a replica made in the twelfth century (a claim repeated by the placard at Saint- Denis). There has been no carbon dating of the materials to determine conclusively. Also, for an account of how Fredegund's tomb was rediscovered in 1656, see Effros, *Merovingian Mortuary Archaeology*, p. 37—42; for a seventeenth-century account in French, see Bouillart, p. 251-254 and 303-308.

267 **"imitate the veil":** Lenoir, *Museum of French Monuments*, p. 174

267 **was moved to the majestic Basilica of Saint-Denis:** After St-Germain-des-Prés was commandeered and looted during the French Revolution, Fredegund's tomb was restored by Alexandre Lenoir, exhibited in the Museum of French Monuments in 1796, and then moved to the Basilica of Saint-Denis in 1816.

IMAGE CREDITS

p. 246 Wikimedia Commons

p. 253 British Library / Granger—All rights reserved.

p. 257 Bibliothèque nationale de France

p. 268 Courtesy of the author

p. 268 Courtesy of the author

PLATE SECTION

p. 1 Wikimedia Commons

p. 1 Petar Milošević / CC BY-SA, Wikipedia

p. 1 Courtesy of the author

p. 2 *Grandes chroniques de France* (15th century): Bibliothèque municipale de Lyon, manuscript Palais des Arts 030, f. 001, photo by the Institute for Research and History of Texts (IRHT/CNRS), France

p. 2 The British Library, Royal 16 G VI f. 64

p. 2 The British Library, Royal 16 G VI f. 69

p. 3 Bibliothèque nationale de France

p. 3 Bibliothèque nationale de France

p. 3 Bibliothèque nationale de France

p. 4 Sepia Times/Universal Images Group via Getty Images

p. 4 Sepia Times/Universal Images Group via Getty Images

p. 5 Bibliothèque nationale de France

p. 5 Bibliothèque nationale de France

p. 6 INTERFOTO / Sammlung Rauch / Granger, NYC—All rights reserved.

p. 6 Bibliothèque nationale de France

p. 7 Open Access Image from the Davison Art Center, Wesleyan University (photo: M. Johnston)

p. 7 Bibliothèque nationale de France

p. 8 © Lucien Metivet/Look and Learn

p. 8 Illustrated by Pierre Van Rompaey. Photo by Ville de Paris/Bibliothèque Forney.

INDEX

The letter *f* following a page locator denotes a figure, *m* denotes a map, and *p* denotes a photograph.

A NOTE ON THE AUTHOR

SHELLEY PUHAK is a critically acclaimed poet and writer whose work has appeared in the *Atlantic, Lapham's Quarterly, Teen Vogue, Virginia Quarterly Review*, and elsewhere. Her essays have been included in *The Best American Travel Writing* and selected as Notables in four consecutive editions of *The Best American Essays*. She is the author of three books of poetry, including *Guinevere in Baltimore*, winner of the Anthony Hecht Prize, and *Harbinger*, selected as a National Poetry Series honoree. *The Dark Queens* is her nonfiction debut. She lives in Maryland.